MYSTERY OF THE
LAST
OLYMPIAN

TITANIC'S TRAGIC SISTER
BRITANNIC

[handwritten inscription: "Lauren, Dive In [signature]"]

MYSTERY OF THE
LAST
OLYMPIAN

TITANIC'S TRAGIC SISTER
BRITANNIC

BY RICHIE KOHLER
WITH CHARLIE HUDSON

BEST
PUBLISHING
COMPANY

Best Publishing Company
631 US Highway 1, Suite 307
North Palm Beach, FL 33408

The opinions expressed in this work are those of the author and do not reflect the opinions of Best Publishing Company or its editors. Information contained in this work has been obtained by Best Publishing Company from sources believed to be reliable. However, neither Best Publishing Company nor its author guarantees the accuracy or completeness of any information published herein, and neither Best Publishing Company nor its author shall be responsible for any errors, omissions, or claims for damages, including exemplary damages, arising out of use, inability to use, or with regard to the accuracy or sufficiency of the information contained in this publication.

The editor, author, publisher, or any other party associated with the production of this book does not accept responsibility for any accident or injury resulting from the use of materials contained herein. Diving is an activity that has inherent risks. An individual may experience injury that can result in disability or death. All persons who wish to engage in diving activities must receive professional instruction. This book does not constitute legal, medical, or other professional advice. Information in this publication is current as of the date of the printing.

The typefaces used in this book mimic what the White Star Line used in the print shops on board its Olympic-class ocean liners.

Front Cover: Painting © Ken Marschall
Back Cover: Painting © Ken Marschall
Richie Kohler Author Photos: © Dave Moran, 2007
Charlie Hudson Author Photo: © Hugh Hudson, 2015
National Museums Northern Ireland Photographs © NMNI Collection Harland & Wolff, Ulster Folk & Transport Museum

Library of Congress Control Number: 2015960297

ISBN: 978-1-9305-3686-9
ISBN: 978-1-9305-3689-0 (ebook)

Printed in Canada

TABLE of CONTENTS

FOREWORD

FROM THE TIME I CAN REMEMBER, my life has been connected to the sea. Growing up in the South of France along the Mediterranean coast, I was never far from water's edge. When I was seven years old, my father, Jacques Cousteau, strapped his newly invented scuba gear on my back, which was originally called the "Aqualung." He gave my brother and I a nudge from our small boat and into the sea we went. When our faces hit the water, our eyes widened and gleaned with excitement for the fishes and colorful life we saw. We became instant divers, and I have never stopped since.

My father was an adventurous man with an unwavering drive and inquisitive spirit. To me, it came as no surprise that his fascination for the unfamiliar led him to explore the depths of the sea in search of sunken shipwrecks. One such expedition brought my father and his crew aboard *Calypso* to the Aegean Sea in search of the famed and mysterious shipwreck of *Britannic*. The sister ship of *Titanic*, *Britannic* too was dubbed "unsinkable," until it met its unexpected end in 1916.

As ideas circulated around what could have led to *Britannic*'s sunken fate, my father and his team became determined to find answers. He led an expedition in 1975, filming the adventure of his team's expedition. While they may not have found all the answers they were looking for, nevertheless, my father awakened intrigue and fascination for sunken shipwrecks and undersea exploration around the world.

In Richie Kohler's new book, *Mystery of the Last Olympian*, the same drive for adventure that captivated my father comes alive as Kohler rediscovers the mysteries surrounding the ship's fateful demise. Kohler's story is one of adventure and excitement as his team descends into the depths of the sea in search of the famed *Britannic*. Their journey spans across past and present, honoring the legacy of an unsinkable ship and the determination of those who risked or even lost their lives in the search to uncover its secrets.

In my seventy years of diving, I have never crossed paths with *Britannic*. But I have been ingrained with the same sense of drive and passion for the unknown that brought my father to the famed ship so many years ago. What my father began through his expeditions around the world, many people continue to carry on today. The more we explore our oceans, the more we realize how much our human actions have been changing the planet. As we continue to uncover truths of the past, we must remember to care for fate of our own futures.

Jean-Michel Cousteau
October 2015

PART I

TRAVELING THROUGH TIME
TO THE FATEFUL DAY

SECRETS OF THE SEA

T HE SEA IS HOSTILE BUT WITHOUT MALICE. For billions of years, she has spawned life and shaped this planet. Calm prevails, storms rage; there are sun-drenched expanses and fields choked with thick layers of ice. Walls of water can rise up to crash miles inland with astounding force, and harbors can rest in quiet stillness. When man decided to build along or close to her shores and set out in whatever the first crafts were, this was his choice. Humans have risked the sea's fury, a force that is not unleashed in any way other than according to the laws of nature. Our relationship with her has evolved, and to a degree we can control her with steadily advancing technology. There are moments when she reminds us with seemingly bestial ferocity that her power is greater than our engineering, and yet when she abates, we venture out again with new ideas.

She holds treasures of her own making and creatures we have never seen, much less understand. And from the moment we set out to float, paddle, and sail, maritime mysteries linked to human stories came to rest beneath her surface. To plunge into her depths and seek to coexist in her world has spurred our imagination for millennia, and we have capabilities today that grew from the wonderings of ancestors who refused to accept we could not accomplish this. There is adventure, challenge, science, and, yes, commerce. There are men and women who are drawn to explore underwater for the pure pleasure of sharing in these amazing sights. For others, it is the unraveling of puzzles, the discovery of unknowns, and overcoming limitations to be able to stay longer and go deeper. It is a realm we enter in search of answers and often find more questions to pursue. A desire to comprehend can become a challenge, a challenge can become a quest, and a quest can extend into a saga.

So it was for me with *Britannic*, a magnificent ocean liner overshadowed by her sister *Titanic*. When I was young and watched in awe as Jacques Cousteau and his aquanauts explored underwater, I dreamed about diving alongside them. Even though early diving experiences fired my imagination, they were not a premonition of the unexpected turn my life was to take. Whether by coincidence or fate, I was later caught by the lure of maritime mysteries. In "science and engineering meets history," diving as a teenager in warm waters changed dramatically with my adult discovery of deep shipwrecks.

I plunged into the realm of shadow diving made famous in Robert Kurson's book *Shadow Divers*, about our six-year saga to identify *U-869*, a World War II U-boat. The television series *Deep Sea Detectives* followed, and there was no turning back from my passion to seek answers hidden beneath the sea as I gained access to shipwrecks around the world. My desire to know each ship's history intensified, and I wanted to have a sense of the people whose lives were altered and sometimes tragically shattered. Of all the shipwrecks I have descended onto, *Britannic* is the most mysterious, her brief, doomed glory wrapped in irony.

Richie Kohler
October 2015

CHAPTER 1

RISE OF THE OLYMPIANS

A T 8:10 A.M. ON NOVEMBER 21, 1916, teenager Leonard George didn't have any idea his life would end within the hour. Why should he have thought so? It was a beautiful morning on the Aegean Sea, and HMHS *Britannic* had yet to pick up thousands of wounded and ill soldiers waiting in the port of Mudros to be transported home to England on the hospital ship. Captain Charles Bartlett had entered Kea Channel, aware there was always a level of danger when in a war zone and confident he, his crew, and the ship were prepared in the event of an emergency. This would not be the only mistake made in the chaos of that morning's tragedy, and nearly 100 years would pass before the truth of what happened became clearer. In actuality, this story began not in 1916, but in 1907, when a man revealed his dream to build a giant of a ship.

The need and desire for bigger and better ships was a constant through the centuries as design and technology brought changes with each new seaworthy idea. By the early 1900s, the world entered the Golden Age of Ocean Liners, a period lasting until the late 1940s. Hundreds of thousands of immigrants, business and leisure travelers, and cargo, including mail, all required passage, and as is the way of any industry, rivalries were commonplace.

The back-and-forth competition between the two English companies Cunard and White Star Line reached a new peak in 1904. Cunard stated it was building Royal Mail Ship (RMS) *Mauretania*, reported to be 790 feet long and 88 feet wide, and *Lusitania*, at 797 feet — the largest ships afloat. Cunard routinely boasted a faster Atlantic Ocean passage than White Star Line, and with the successful launch of RMS *Mauretania* in 1906, White Star Line President Joseph Bruce Ismay felt the pressure of falling behind. Lord William

Pirrie, chairman of Harland & Wolff shipbuilders in Belfast, Ireland, revealed a solution after dinner one evening. The unique relationship of trust between the shipping company and the shipbuilder reached back to 1869, when Thomas H. Ismay founded the company. In his book, *The White Star Line*, historian, author, and noted lecturer Paul Louden-Brown explained the two companies had established a compatible financial arrangement, and for fifty years there was virtually always a White Star Line ship under construction in the Harland & Wolff yard.

With this long-established history of performance and personal friendship of the two men, Pirrie confidently told Bruce Ismay he could build him a 1,000-foot-long ocean liner. More than a pride factor was involved in being able to bring about such a vision — this proposal was sound business. The clamor of immigrants wanting to seek new lives in America came with the willingness to pay, and the number of passengers they could accommodate in any given year was simple mathematics. In order to transport more, it required either multiple, faster, or larger ships. Each ship came with operating costs, and trying to match Cunard's speeds had proved to be problematic. That left size.

Pirrie's new ships could carry up to 3,000 passengers with the third class paying for the cost of operation. Based on those calculations, second- and first-class passengers as well as cargo services would generate all profit, and what better way to entice higher-paying passengers than to offer a greater level of luxury? To those who could afford it, the Olympic class of ship would provide such a degree of comfort, passengers would be willing to trade an extra day or two at sea. However, two to three ships would be required to guarantee weekly transatlantic service. Thus, in the library of Pirrie's home, the breathtaking idea of the Olympians — *Olympic, Titanic,* and *Britannic* — was forged.

The agreement to accomplish design and construction of the largest ship in the world in not quite three years was almost as stunning as the concept. Pirrie had to scale back his ambitious idea of 1,000 feet due to constraints of his Belfast shipyard dock that couldn't be expanded to handle anything larger than 900 feet. Even with the reduction, it was like nothing he or any of the men involved with design or build had ever seen. The height from keel to the top of the four funnels would be around 175 feet, and the gross tons would exceed 45,000. The triple-expansion steam engines would be fed by twenty-nine boilers installed in the cavernous interior of the ship away from the eyes of travelers. Neither would the public see the fifteen transverse bulkheads that created compartments isolated from each other when closing special watertight doors. This safety feature served to make the ships practically unsinkable — or so it seemed. Passengers, even down to third class, would enjoy more spacious accommodations than on previous vessels, and first-class passengers could book parlor suites outfitted with the finest of furnishings, a bedroom, a sitting room, a bathroom with a toilet, and a wardrobe room. Oil paintings would grace the walls, and the grand staircase would feature large glass domes, bronze cherubs, candelabra, and other intricately handcrafted details. Artistry would layer spectacular naval engineering.

Massive ships cannot be built without massive logistics and infrastructure, and it was not only Harland & Wolff who committed to modifying their shipyard to prepare for the enormous challenge. A special deepwater dock at Southampton, England, would be constructed, and the dock in New York City would likewise require extension.

It was July 1908 when approval was given to take the dream of the Olympians from paper to reality. On December 16, *Olympic's* keel was laid, with her sister *Titanic* slated to begin the following March. Twin 900-foot-long slips would allow simultaneous work on both ships, known by Hull 400 and Hull 401. Expansive scaffolding stretched the length of the ships and soared into the air in order for men to work without having to lose time repositioning their work platforms.

The workforce of almost 4,000 was a mix of seasoned veterans, new hires, and young boys engaged in various duties. Despite the definite celebrity status of the Olympians, there were multiple ships in various building stages to keep other workers busy. With each passing day, the pace to complete *Olympic* and maintain *Titanic* on schedule never slackened.

Engineers with the finest education of the day joined men with dirt and grease embedded under their fingernails, as the clang of metal rang continuously and smoke billowed from furnaces accompanied by the laying of the keels. Tens of thousands of hands-on steps had to be performed to make the 20,600-ton hull ready.

Well-known for hosting impressive launch ceremonies, the one Pirrie planned for *Olympic* was to surpass anything he'd done in the past. Pirrie could not order the weather of October 20, 1910, to be sunny and calm, and yet it was as if Mother Nature herself blessed the launch. Almost 100 reporters scrambled among dignitaries to gather the news they would blast around the world of the marvelous ship soon to slip into the Lagan River, where thousands of people lined the banks, waiting to cheer. The first noise arose from two rockets fired as warning in the unlikely event some vessel on the river was unaware of the launching. Ten minutes later, the third rocket was quickly followed by Pirrie's command to release *Olympic* from her restraints. The prolonged cacophony of whistles, applause, bells, and horns signaled the success. *Olympic* slid into the water, entrusted to the five tugboats it required to guide her to the outfitting wharf, where workers would spend seven months to complete the interior of the ship from the most mundane fitting in third-class berths to the elaborate Turkish baths. Wealthy passengers accustomed to fine hotels would find nothing lacking during their voyage.

The unrelenting pace to make the ship ready for her promised maiden voyage culminated in her sea trials May 2, 1911. Three thousand tons of coal and a crew of 250 men commanded by Captain Edward Smith made the two-day run to Liverpool and Southampton. Thomas Andrews, Pirrie's nephew and a naval architect, had taken on engineering responsibility for *Olympic* when Alexander Carlisle, Pirrie's brother-in-law and chief naval architect, resigned a year before. With the successful sea trials behind them, *Olympic* departed to be readied for her maiden voyage.

The majestic entry of *Olympic* into New York Harbor on June 21, 1911, was met with the fanfare the 882-foot-long and 45,324-gross-ton ship deserved. Headlines announced her arrival, and a special, colored postcard was drawn to commemorate her profile. The wealthy passengers who helped provide pure profit for Ismay had praised the splendid first-class lounges, smoke rooms, libraries, vast promenade, the gymnasium, and indoor swimming pool. Huge chandeliers had cast light, and they had dined sumptuously in gracious restaurants from specially commissioned china and crystal. The luxury promised had been delivered, and the opulence of *Olympic,* at least for the moment, had strong appeal among the highest-paying tier of travelers. The sister ship *Titanic* was on schedule for completion, and construction of the third ship, *Britannic,* was set to begin later in November.

Bruce Ismay, ever aware of the threat of his competition, knew his magnificent Olympic-class liners fulfilled the dream Pirrie had offered him. What he didn't know was the maiden voyage of *Titanic* was to be disastrously different from the glory of *Olympic.* Nor did he know there was a young woman serving as a stewardess among more than 900 crew members of *Olympic* whose destiny would seem oddly linked to tragedies the future held.

CHAPTER 2

ONE FATE INTERTWINED?

VIOLET CONSTANCE JESSOP was probably meant to be a world traveler. Her father, William Jessop, joined immigrants leaving Ireland, although not for North America as many did in the 1880s. His choice was the pampas of Argentina — commonly referred to as the Argentine — to seek a new life. It was October 2, 1887, when Violet was born to him and his wife, Katherine. The good that came to the family was sadly continuously pierced with tragedy as three of Violet's siblings died of illnesses, and she was diagnosed with consumption at a young age. Although she recovered, her ability to start and attend school was delayed. As the eldest of six children who did survive, Violet stepped into a caregiving role beyond her years, helping manage the household duties.

The greatest misfortune, however, was in 1903 when her father died unexpectedly. Since they couldn't remain in Argentina, they journeyed to London, where it was deemed more practical for the widow Katherine to live with the children. She didn't know how she was to live because few careers were available to pursue, and no relatives could provide much assistance. An arrangement for the boys to be taken into a Catholic orphanage for schooling brought some relief, and Katherine signed on as a stewardess to go to sea. Leaving her children for long stretches of time was hardly ideal, but choices were limited. Violet's role as substitute mother to her young sister, Eileen, was their only recourse, and struggles with finances were a reality they constantly coped with.

Life as a stewardess was never easy, and the woman who had borne nine children wept at the deaths of young ones, shouldered the loss of her husband, and leaned heavily on her oldest daughter, could not keep up the pace. Twenty-one-year-old Violet saw this and understood she would have to augment her mother's meager income. She had not been able to move up in her education and wasn't in a position to marry well, a common goal of the era. Taking her mother's place at sea was the obvious solution.

She knew of the demands and low pay, and despite more than one person trying to discourage her, she presented herself as an applicant, never imagining that an obstacle in her path would be her attractiveness. Violet's thick auburn hair, smooth skin, blue-gray eyes with alluring lashes, trim petite figure, and lingering Irish lilt were viewed as out of place among the older women considered more suited for such work. Despite Violet's mature nature, her mother understood the concerns, and when she and Violet discussed the problem, they decided a drab wardrobe for future interviews would be in order. The day did come when Violet was hired and assigned to the victualing staff. In this capacity, she provided routine cabin and passenger care to a certain section of the ship. Depending on the whim of the passengers, a stewardess's job was sometimes unpredictable. Work days were rarely less than sixteen hours, and cramped crew accommodations gave little comfort.

Despite the demanding duties, she did meet young Ned Tracy, fifth-class engineer, who brought her joy and heartache, unable to commit to her in the way she hoped. When she was later hired by the White Star Line, her voyages were across the Atlantic instead of the same routing as Ned.

The basics of Violet's role did not change with having a new employer, and she was keenly aware of the power of either passenger or superiors' complaints. Service in first class came with the value of tips to augment her paltry salary. The opportunity was balanced with a tacit understanding that if a passenger's wishes were not accommodated, there was a risk of being sent to serve a lower class or being fired at the end of the voyage.

When White Star was preparing the triumphant launch of *Olympic*, one of the considerations was to carefully select the crew. This was not an honor to be taken lightly, and Violet was among those chosen. *Olympic's* glorious entry into New York and glowing accolades bestowed on the magnificent liner were soon tainted by an incident on her fifth voyage. In departing the port of Southampton, the warship HMS *Hawke* collided with the ocean liner, creating two holes. The first was the impact of *Hawke's* bow to *Olympic's* stern above the starboard propeller. As a warship, *Hawke* was fitted with an underwater steel-and-concrete ram, and this damaged *Olympic* below the waterline, forming the second hole. Calm prevailed, and the ship was brought into Osborne Bay on the Isle of Wight, where the passengers were offloaded and the initial damage inspection occurred. Although the publicity of such an encounter so soon into the ship's life and the finger pointing of who was at fault made the wrong type of headlines, the White Star executives were quick to tout that even with two compartments of the ship flooded, the watertight doors performed as designed and the ship had never been in real danger. The term "practically unsinkable" was used and no doubt gave confidence to crew and passengers alike who admired the Olympians. It was therefore another honor bestowed on Violet when she was selected to serve on *Titanic*'s maiden voyage.

All was splendid and beautiful on the ship, and another crowd-filled greeting was anticipated in New York. Instead, in the terrible moments of April 15, 1912, when *Titanic* hit an iceberg, most passengers and crew did not comprehend the genuine danger that the senior officers masked in order to maintain an orderly evacuation. However, with an inadequate number of lifeboats, the mismanagement of filling the lifeboats, freezing conditions of the air and ocean, and no other ships nearby to assist, an "orderly evacuation" was horribly limited.

In the midst of Violet escaping in a lifeboat, a baby was thrust into her care with no idea of where the mother was. Many survivors later recounted watching the deck levels of the ship disappear into icy water and suddenly realizing there would be little chance for those who remained behind. Heart-rending stories were shared of how they alternated between hope and utter despair in the cold hours until they saw the shape of *Carpathia* on the horizon. During the rescue, some were reunited with family and friends, and there was the general assumption *Carpathia* had not been the only ship to assist. It was not until they docked in New York that they learned the extent of the loss of life. In the strange matter of the baby, a woman had rushed to the side of *Carpathia* as the passengers of the lifeboat were brought on board. She snatched the baby from Violet's arms, never exchanging names.

The following weeks were filled with sorrow, and with *Olympic* recalled to Harland & Wolff shipyards for design modifications and *Britannic* not yet fully constructed, there was no employment for Violet with White Star Line.

She gained a position with another shipping line as dangerous circumstances were building among Europe's great powers. The path to war was not understood by most, and the bubbling cauldron did not erupt until late summer 1914. Violet's brothers enlisted in the British Army, and Violet joined the newly established Voluntary Aid Detachment (VAD) to serve as a nurse. The VAD provided a means for ladies not medically trained to contribute to the war effort. For at least a while, Violet's time at sea was ended. (The rich details of Violet's life are revealed in her memoirs, not discovered until the 1970s and originally published as *Titanic Survivor* in 1997.)

CHAPTER 3

DEEP INSIDE THE THIRD SISTER

IN THE WAKE OF INVESTIGATIONS regarding the causes of the *Titanic* disaster, White Star Line and Harland & Wolff officials had few choices other than to strengthen both *Olympic* and *Britannic* and increase the number of lifeboats. Prior to his resignation from the shipbuilder, Alexander Carlisle had correctly calculated an increased lifeboat capacity for the largest ship ever built. He fully outlined the design of the new system to handle up to thirty-two lifeboats. This would allow for double the number of lifeboats the British Board of Trade regulations required for passenger liners. With his years of experience in ship design, he understood the official regulations had not yet taken into account the increased carrying capacity of the new ships. It had been folly to set aside Carlisle's recommendation and retain the usual number of lifeboats at only sixteen augmented by four collapsible boats. The enormity of the tragic decision stayed with everyone at White Star and Harland & Wolff who had been a part of the grave error.

The servicing passenger liner *Olympic*, which had been too far away to aid in rescue of *Titanic* passengers, returned to Southampton on April 21, 1912. For the next six months, White Star Line tried to soothe public relations and prove the worth of the Olympians. These months of intense work caused Violet Jessop to move to the P&O line.

As for *Britannic*, construction began on June 28, 1911, one week after *Olympic* triumphantly entered New York Harbor. On the day *Titanic* sank, the third sister's hull was being framed. Modifications could be incorporated with some unknown degree of delay, but not with nearly the difficulty in retrofitting *Olympic*.

For Harland & Wolff designers, a new gantry davits system to allow additional lifeboats and easier launching was something everyone could see. Strengthening the ship was less visible, yet vital. An inner skin was fitted, and all sixteen bulkheads were heightened. These measures were to allow *Britannic* to be able to stay afloat with six consecutive compartments flooded. The watertight doors between the compartments were now designed with a triple fail-safe means for closure. If the hull were breached and water flooded in, the doors could be closed to isolate the flooded compartment. The friction clutch holding the doors open could be released electronically from a control panel on the bridge or the wheelhouse. The second means was a switch at the door to be used for a manual closure. The third means was a float fitted to the mechanism to activate closure if the water level reached dangerous levels. If the watertight doors closed due to an emergency, alarm bells would ring to signal the men of the danger. By all standards, *Britannic* would be a ship of unquestionable safety.

The enhanced engineering solutions for the Olympians were publicized to restore confidence, even as deep inside *Britannic*, a fundamental function blended advanced technology (at the time) and the rawest of human effort. Steam, taken for granted by everyone on board who didn't engage in actually producing it, not only powered the massive engines, it also provided power for the electricity of the ship and heated the public rooms and parts of the cabins. None of this could be accomplished without the activities occurring within the belly of the ship, where not even the third-class passengers whose berths were in the lower deck would venture.

Like the rest of the ship, there was a strict hierarchy followed among the crew in this realm. Catwalks and engineer platforms were accessed by ladders and were the domain of engineers and their assistants. The "greasers" were allowed access to perform their critical duties. The array of gears and other moving parts required constant monitoring and adjustment of lubrication levels, whether it was direct lubrication or the filling of small reservoirs incrementally releasing oil as required.

A greaser might aspire to someday become an engineer through study and hard work. However, the greaser's messy and sweaty job was nothing compared to the firemen and trimmers of the rest of the "black gang." Despite other advances, in order for the boilers to function and deliver power to the engines, they required coal to be handled in a specific manner to feed the fires creating the all-important steam. Approximately 600 tons of coal per day was needed to achieve the desired crossing speed. Coal had to be physically shoveled from bunkers, loaded into wheelbarrows, pushed to the furnaces, and managed throughout each shift.

The trimmers and firemen worked in a rhythm in unrelenting 100-plus-degree heat as coal dust embedded itself into their skin. Firemen were in charge of the essential role of maintaining the fires in the furnaces — vital in order to keep the steam pressure constant. The coals had to be frequently raked and moved across the grates not only to keep a continuous blaze but also to burn at the proper rate. The firemen stood in front of or close by the immense boilers in order to reach in with their rakes. Aside from it being a skill learned through experience, the task required enough strength to adapt to the stifling conditions.

Trimmers worked with the firemen to bring the coal from the bunkers. The name relates to the part of their job to keep the vessel on an even trim by not taking too much coal from one or more of the bunkers and thereby upsetting the trim of the vessel. Trimmer relates to smaller vessels in use twenty to thirty years before the Olympic class, when maintaining trim was far more important than in a huge vessel like *Britannic.*

Since lumps of coal burn at different rates, another laborious task for the trimmer was to make a selection of coal and then break up larger pieces and remove any rocks from the coal. He would move the coal from the bunkers to the firemen using wheelbarrows in the dust-filled and dark spaces off the main boiler spaces.

As often happens, a subcommunity developed within the strata of men of the black gang, many either related or coming from the same neighborhoods in Liverpool. In general, they were tough, burly or wiry, as hard-drinking as they were hardworking, their griminess a point of special camaraderie few others understood. And with all the attention paid to the Olympians' luxury, who would want to see these sweaty and coal-stained workers moving back and forth? A 75-foot-long firemen's passage and pipe tunnel was designed and built to run between the crew's quarters and the boiler rooms. The main access out of the ship for them was a spiral staircase at the beginning of the tunnel. Each day at sea, they circulated in this pattern, their presence an absolute necessity as surely as it was screened from normal view.

When *Britannic* set forth on her maiden voyage, however, it was not to be for the purpose of carrying passengers across the Atlantic in luxury. The same unexpected events of war that altered *Britannic's* fate also brought change to millions of healthy and fit men who would be diverted from the paths they would have expected to take in their adult lives.

CHAPTER 4

THE UNFORESEEN ROLE
FOR *BRITANNIC*

W HEN ENGAGED IN WAR, there is only one certainty: People will be killed, injured, and fall to sickness if the conflict is prolonged. In one of the paradoxes of human existence, medical practices forged in combat often evolve into peacetime advances, and this was true of hospital ships. The recorded use of hospital ships dates into the 1600s, and Jack Edward McCallum's book *Military Medicine from Ancient Times to the Twenty-First Century* is an excellent reference.

In 1904, the great naval powers focused on retaining their supremacy of the seas where mighty battleships and battlecruisers displayed their strength. Support vessels such as hospital ships were important but took a lesser priority when determining the mix of a fleet. What became a naval arms race between Britain and Germany has long been considered a contributing reason to World War I. Although Britain's global naval reach was a hallmark of her might, France's and Russia's navies had gained prominence, and Britain was concerned about expansion of Kaiser Wilhelm's German war fleet.

In a feat intended to put the world on notice, Britain displayed HMS *Dreadnaught* in 1906 as a battleship with more big guns than any battleship afloat. She boasted steam turbine engines, which was cutting-edge technology for the day. No other navy had a ship like it. Germany took little time in setting their own designers and builders into motion, and by 1914 they too had newer ships with features they deemed superior with better armor and a greater emphasis on gunnery accuracy. While each country claimed they had no desire for war, it was a bristling environment at a time when dangerous, simmering currents rippled throughout Europe. In summer 1914, as shipbuilders turned out luxurious ocean liners, events came together to lead to a magnitude of death and destruction the world had never experienced before.

In a great simplification of history, the assassination of Archduke Franz Ferdinand and his wife in Sarajevo on June 28, 1914, caused Austria-Hungary to declare war against Serbia. Russia, allied with Serbia, announced a mobilization of their troops. Germany, allied with Austria-Hungary, interpreted this action as aggression and declared war on Russia on August 1, 1914. France, allied with Russia, was drawn into the conflict on August 3, when Germany declared war against it and invaded neutral Belgium as a means to attack France. Great Britain, with fragile hopes of remaining neutral, was allied with Belgium and somewhat with France, and therefore declared war against Germany on August 4. The declaration extended into the British colonies of Australia, Canada, India, New Zealand, and the Union of South Africa. Japan, allied with Britain, declared war against Germany on August 23, which also meant Japan was at war with Austria-Hungary.

Italy, navigating among multiple treaties, made no commitment, and the United States wanted to remain neutral. The U.S. population was split with strong feelings among many to side with Great Britain, while others supported Germany. Most preferred a policy of isolationism. Among the many foolhardy proclamations in the unfolding drama of Europe was the collective belief hostilities would end within only a few months. Instead, complicated alliances, colonial interests, and events entangled country after country in the Great War. The list of primary nations engaged after initial declarations in 1914 included Bulgaria, Turkey and the Ottoman Empire, Italy, Romania, Greece, and the United States. The clash between colonial powers had quickly spread throughout the continent of Africa. Among the lesser-known aspects of the war was England and France targeting the takeover of the four German colonies in Africa. German resistance led to the fierce East African Campaign as fighting extended into 1918 and encompassed more than two million people.

The actual number of countries engaged in the war ranged to 100, since involvement was not confined to large mobilization of troops and well-known battles. For some, participation was limited to merchant shipping or providing groups of volunteers who joined various forces.

Aside from the sheer magnitude of nations at war, fledgling and new technology invented during the course of the war added to the carnage that killed, wounded, and sickened tens of millions of military personnel and civilians. Airplanes, depth charges, flamethrowers, machine guns, poison gas, rapid fire artillery, and *Unterseeboot* (U-boats) all had direct devastating effects. Other items also facilitated the war effort. The use of aircraft brought about related functions of aircraft reconnaissance and aerial photography. On the noncombat side, blood transfusions became routine, although the practice of person-to-person transfusion led to the establishment of the first blood bank. Advancement with antiseptics and better infection control were additional measures promoted by medical personnel.

Widespread acquisition of hospital ships came to the forefront for the first time with the realization the maritime conflict was far deadlier than expected, and offensive campaigns were launched in multiple unanticipated territories. The small number of military hospital ships available could not manage this increased need, and for Britain, the only viable option to meet the demand was to commission civilian vessels. Massive *Britannic* was not immediately viewed for this purpose. It was 1915 when Great Britain decided to launch the Dardanelles Campaign, and the third Olympian was considered for her new role. The Dardanelles was the only waterway between the Black Sea in the east and the Mediterranean Sea in the west. If Britain could control the strait, it would have a direct line to the allied Russian Navy in the Black Sea and could facilitate munitions supplies to Russian forces in the east. The Allies were also competing against their enemies for support in the Balkans, and a British victory in Turkey could potentially persuade the neutral states of Greece, Bulgaria, and Romania to join the war on the Allied side. There was also the possibility that a massive Allied fleet appearing at Turkish shores could serve as an adequate threat and fuel underlying opposition within the Ottoman Empire, pushing Turkey to revert to a neutral state.

This mix of strategic and tactical plans unfolded as Britain had planned, but the end result couldn't have been worse for the British and their allies, and the disastrous campaign continued for months. Thousands of casualties from Gallipoli and other encounters had to be evacuated from crowded Mediterranean hospitals.

Olympic had already been designated for troop transport in September, and the executives of White Star Line and Harland & Wolff received official word on November 13, 1915, of the decision to commission conversion of *Britannic*. The ocean liner intended to be even more luxurious than her sisters was finally to be completed for a purpose everyone would have scoffed at when her keel was laid. Since the mooring trials of the powerful engines had been successful six months prior, outfitting was projected to be four weeks, an ambitious yet attainable goal. Many of the luxurious interior items had been ordered but not installed. They could remain in storage until she returned to the yard to take her rightful place as a passenger ship. This was the belief as work commenced.

In the words of White Star historian Paul Louden-Brown, *Britannic* was in some ways a "giant empty box" waiting to be transformed. Skilled craftsmen tasked with electrical and plumbing work did not find their jobs to be much different, but the carpenters who should have been creating beautiful cabins were securing more than 3,000 bunks instead. Not unlike the concept of "class" on the ocean liners, the officers' ward was located in the forward port promenade with drapes that could be drawn for privacy. The movement of cot patients and those on crutches or in wheelchairs would be easier to manage with elevators. Ambulatory patients would have promenade space to walk or more likely slowly shuffle, considering many would be suffering from pleurisy, an illness causing shortness of breath or coughing spasms with any exertion.

Surgical needs would depend on how quickly a soldier was evacuated from a field hospital. Most would have been treated and stabilized before coming aboard, but wounds could reopen, and with a large population, there was always the chance a new condition such as appendicitis would manifest on the voyage home. The men and women of the Royal Army Medical Corps (RAMC) couldn't claim the type of luxury *Britannic* would have had, although they were no doubt treated to better accommodations than staff assigned to smaller ships.

It fell to the painters to ensure the all-important exterior changes were made to clearly identify her as a hospital ship — white with a green band stretched around the hull and three large red crosses on both sides, one near the bow, one midship, and one toward the stern. With *Britannic's* electrical capability, a line of green lights was added beneath the promenade deck and an electric red cross was to be displayed at night. German U-boats prowling the seas under night cover could not mistake her for anything other than what she was.

War does not take holidays into account, and so a fully crewed, provisioned, and properly equipped *Britannic* set sail from Liverpool, England, late morning December 22 under command of Captain Charles A. Bartlett. She would make a stop in Naples, Italy, to take on coal and more water, then proceed to the Greek port of Mudros to accept a large number of patients. She would then reverse course, although destined to dock in Southampton at the special dock previously built for the Olympians.

The maiden voyage of *Britannic* was successful by all standards, although different from the celebratory reception to occur had she arrived in New York as a luxury ocean liner. Once disembarkation was completed and the long line of patients sent onward by hospital trains or other transport, the ship's crew reprovisioned. The continued use of *Britannic* as a hospital ship came into question after a few voyages. With the Allies retreating from Gallipoli, the Mediterranean theater of operations waned, and the massive liner sat idle during the delay in determining what to do with her. White Star could anticipate converting her back to her original role in conveying passengers on Atlantic crossings. This, the role she had been designed and built for, was never to be realized.

A new German offensive was launched in yet another territory. This time it was in the Balkans, and Britain and the Allies countered as the opposing forces clashed. The decision to release *Britannic* was reversed, and it was late

September when she was fully loaded, crewed, staffed with medical personnel, and departed from port to evacuate thousands more wounded and ill soldiers.

This was two months prior to Violet joining *Britannic*. When Violet was serving in the VAD, she contracted a serious infection in her hand. During her difficult recovery, an attending physician suggested a sea voyage might bring her back to health. In what seemed to be a continuing link of the young woman to the Olympians, she thought of the White Star Line for employment. Even though she could not resume nursing duties, the hospital ships required ordinary crew members as well as the additional medical personnel. She signed onto *Britannic* barely in time to make the November 12, 1916, departure.

No civilian on board, including Violet, was aware of German U-boat bases along the coast of the Adriatic Sea swelling with new vessels. The waters of the Mediterranean might be clearer than the Atlantic, yet the commanders were skilled in maneuvering at depths where they could remain hidden from sight until it was time to strike. Although attack U-boats were deadly, the development of mine-laying U-boats brought an additional dimension of danger to every ship entering the area.

CHAPTER 5

A DESTINY THAT SEEMED TO DEFY DEATH

VIOLET QUICKLY SETTLED INTO her stewardess duties on *Britannic*, and on a quiet Sunday morning she attended Mass as she always did. She had volunteered to prepare breakfast for one of the nurses who had taken ill. The sudden noise and then shudder of the ship took everyone by surprise. In the uncertainty among the nurses at breakfast, Major Harold Priestly, a member of the medical staff, told those who had leapt to their feet to sit down since the alarm had not yet been sounded. Priestly, who had suffered internment at the Wittenberg prisoner-of-war camp, was well-respected, and his calm courage would be of great value during the evacuation.

It took only a minute for the alarm to be given, and Violet quickly found herself alone when the large dining room emptied. Having been through this on *Titanic*, she later recorded she felt an odd absence of fear, and her thoughts went to the woman whose breakfast she'd been preparing. She went to her first and made sure a companion would see her to the lifeboats. Violet knew if the boat was sinking, she would need to protect a few items important to her. A new coat she had recently purchased was certainly not to be left behind, but despite knowing she would have to fasten her lifebelt under the coat, she failed to do so. Although she realized her error, she decided she should make her way to the boat deck rather than delay and adjust it.

Witness accounts differ as to the number of lifeboats deployed without permission, but for Violet and the other occupants, they suddenly faced an unexpected horror. The ship's massive propellers were turning, and two lifeboats had been drawn into them, slicing through wood and the boats' occupants. It was obvious they too were being pulled toward the propellers and would not be able to escape. One moment the lifeboat was filled to capacity, and then next, everyone jumped overboard, their temporary paralysis broken.

For Violet, there was a longer hesitation. She had never learned to swim. The choice was certain death or possible death. Taking a chance, she plunged into the water, her lifebelt loosened, and her beautiful coat absorbed water, adding weight to drag her downward. When she began to rise to the surface, rather than clear water above where she could gasp precious air, her head slammed into something that kept her underwater. She flailed and felt something to cling to — an arm. Despite her terrified state, she also understood she might easily drag someone under, so she released her grip. She managed to finally surface only to find herself in the midst of mutilated bodies. In closing her eyes once more, she felt how loose her lifebelt was, and in a sickening moment of wondering if this would be her death, an empty lifebelt came within reach. It was enough to support her, and she now floated with carnage all around, cries for help echoing, and the great *Britannic* sinking rapidly.

Many witnesses recalled greater calm of medical personnel and crew waiting patiently for lifeboats. Few individuals had been close to the point of impact below the waterline near the bulkhead between Holds 2 and 3 that also damaged the firemen's tunnel. Water gushed in, and reports that the watertight doors of Boiler Rooms 5 and 6 had not closed properly added to Captain Bartlett's concern for the ship. The firm belief in *Britannic's* ability to stay afloat with six compartments flooded was little comfort when faced with the reality of the wounded vessel.

Captain Bartlett, in considering his options, looked to temptingly close land. He reasoned he should be able to steer the ship and beach her, completely unaware of lifeboats in the water and the deadly consequences of the propellers in motion. He did order the engines stopped, but only because of the rapid rate at which water continued to fill the ship and his inability to move to shore as he had hoped. He was aware they would require assistance to gather and see to the survivors even if he could prevent them from sinking. Not certain of the cause of the severe damage, he had sent a distress call to declare they had hit a mine.

Officers worked to keep the evacuation as orderly as possible, the deployment of more lifeboats hampered by a set of inoperable gantries. As the speed of sinking became apparent to most, some of the men began to throw deck chairs and other items capable of floating overboard to people who were in the water. Then, in a faint pause as if the ship slowed in her sinking, Captain Bartlett ordered the engines started again. Despite the propellers being out of the water and water still rising in the ship, he attempted to move forward, striving to get *Britannic* to the stretch of land. It was not to be, and in acknowledgment of the inevitability facing him, he gave the blast of the horn to abandon ship. With the lower decks searched to ensure no one was left behind, he joined his countrymen swimming or floating, waiting to be rescued. In fifty-five minutes from the moment of explosion, *Britannic* had disappeared from sight. Any engineer who worked on the modifications to strengthen her against future disaster would have declared the ship sinking this quickly was impossible, but more than 1,000 witnesses knew otherwise. The largest ship in the world, the pride of Harland & Wolff, had joined her sister ship in a tragic ending.

Unlike the deadly cold and near isolation of the terrible night of *Titanic*, it was a bright, warm morning, and several ships were close to the busy Kea Channel, easily picking up on the distress call. Unsure of when help would arrive, the best the captain, crew, and medical staff could do was utilize *Britannic's* two motorized launches to pick up the most severely wounded and take them to Kea Island. The dead would have to be left until those who had a chance of survival could be rescued. The quayside of the harbor was crowded as doctors and nurses with no equipment attempted to staunch bleeding and manage with makeshift bandages.

Local fishermen from Port St. Nikolo brought their boats in to help as much as possible, and by what must have seemed to be a very long hour to those who had no boat to clamor into, the destroyer HMS *Scourge* arrived as did the cruiser HMS *Heroic*. The destroyer HMS *Foxhound* and cruisers HMS *Foresight* and *Chausseur* also made their way to the scene. With 1,066 personnel on board *Britannic* — some dead, some wounded — it was impossible to accommodate the living in any single place, and the survivors were subsequently shuttled among different ships and ports. As gruesomely as the day had unfolded, it would have been worse if the explosion had occurred after *Britannic* had received her full load of 3,000 patients from Mudros.

Kitchen scullion Leonard George did not live to see his eighteenth birthday. Violet, whom doctors had once believed would not survive through childhood, had now twice escaped a horrible death.

The men who died may not have agreed there was any fortune in the day, but later testimony and scattered memoirs that have been found often included comments about how beautiful the morning had been until the harshness of war struck. By late afternoon, a ship entering the calm Kea Channel would not have guessed at the morning's ghastly events. Word of the disaster spread, and watchmen on the lookout for deadly German U-boats and suspicious metal objects floating in the water were no doubt more vigilant than usual.

CHAPTER 6

WAS THE *U-73* COMMANDER CORRECT?

I N SOME WAYS, THE CONDUCT of submarine warfare during World War I
personifies the duality of the man of honor who fights for the sake of country and
the man who confuses personal glory with taking credit for as many "kills/hits"
as possible. Both types were wrapped within strategic decisions that intensified
the grimness of the war. The tragedy of *Britannic* is embroiled in this tangle, for
whether her end came due to torpedo or mine, the result was loss of the largest
ship sunk during the war and the men who perished. At the core of the debate
about hospital ships deliberately targeted were two important elements: the British
blockade of Germany and the movement of Germany between *restricted* and
unrestricted submarine warfare. Two excellent reference books about the scope
of U-boat operations are *Raiders of the Deep* by Lowell Thomas and *The U-Boat
War: 1914–1918* by Edwyn Gray.

While the image of U-boats is often associated with the German "wolfpacks"
of World War II, efforts at creating submarines as viable weapons had a fledgling
start in 1776. Other spurts occurred in the 1800s with the American Civil War
submarine *H.L. Hunley*. The practical ability was not fully achieved until 1885,
when Thorsten Nordenfelt of Sweden impressed the Greek and Turkish navies
with his vessel. Other countries showed interest, and Wilhelm Bauer of Bavaria
had invented a submarine five years prior with brief success before it sank in
Kiel Harbour. Germany's early experience sparked supporters as pro and con
arguments mounted within the highest levels of naval command. Men who
initially dismissed it learned of their error in judgment at a steep price.

In the ironies that punctuate history, the British Royal Navy had a
powerful presence of warships at the Kiel Week celebrations in June 1914,

where the German Navy displayed their U-boats and attracted the attention of Kaiser Wilhelm. The German emperor's admiration was not lost on the navy faction promoting this advanced technology. When word came of the June 28 assassination of Archduke Ferdinand in Sarajevo, the festivities ceased immediately. Speculation about war permeated every conversation. Neutral at the time, British ships left for home, not knowing barely two months would pass before they had a bitter taste of what a U-boat could accomplish. Britain entered the expanding war August 4, 1914, her Grand Fleet unaware German U-boats had already departed westward.

Rather than thundering gunfire between opposing battleships, Britain's initial hostile naval act against Germany was an immediate blockade of her northern ports and harbors. Few countries in Europe had sustainable levels of food, medicine, fuel, industrial supplies, and other necessities, so ocean transport was vital. Germany's open-water access was limited, and its vulnerability to a well-orchestrated blockade was an indisputable geographical fact. Although blockades had been a traditional tactic for millennia, international law was established to govern the conduct of blockades and transport of goods as dependency on seaborne trade grew with the Industrial Revolution.

The Royal British Navy was permitted to stop vessels in the North Sea suspected of carrying contraband. They could board the vessel and demand to see cargo papers. If the boarding party determined contraband was or could be aboard, a prize crew of designated men would escort the vessel into a harbor, and a prize court declared if the cargo contained contraband to be confiscated. Usually, the transport ship was released with some compensation. The supplies, however, were denied to the intended destination. There was *absolute contraband, conditional contraband,* and *free goods.* Obvious war materials were absolute, fuel and foodstuffs were conditional, and other items were free goods, which were not subject to seizure. Conditional contraband had certain protections from seizure if they were on a neutral vessel and not directly bound for the enemy.

Another aspect of the blockade was to lay naval mines leading to the enemies' ports, intending to deter would-be blockade runners. Britain maintained what was dubbed the "hunger blockade" for the duration of the war. Many historians agree nearly 763,000 deaths by starvation were attributed to how severely the lack of fertilizer supplies hampered German agriculture. Despite Germany's belief the war would last no more than six months, they wanted to send the U-boats into action at the outset. Proponents pushed to demonstrate the deadly potential this weapon could have against the might of the British Fleet. Gray's book expertly addresses the impact of Germany's decision.

Although the initial foray of nine U-boats made it to the British Orkney Islands, three were destroyed, and they counted no significant damage to the

British. The military reality, however, was U-boats were operating almost 500 miles from the nearest German base — a feat traditionalists had declared would not be possible. A second attempt in mid-August was also unsuccessful, and the German high command shifted to a new tactic to allow U-boat commanders to launch their patrols in different directions in smaller groups. The almost immediate effect came on September 3, 1914, when the commander and crew of *U-21* fired a single torpedo to sink the British cruiser *Pathfinder*. It was a "David against Goliath" moment and changed the course of naval warfare forever. Less than three weeks later, the *U-9* commander and crew accomplished the unthinkable. They found, torpedoed, and sank three armored cruisers off the coast of the Netherlands within minutes of each other. No one could any longer doubt submarines as an offensive weapon.

It was October 20 when the commander of *U-17* took another unprecedented action. The British merchant ship *Glitra* was fourteen miles off Norway's coast, loaded with fuel, coal, and other items, although not munitions or weapons. The *U-17* commander stopped the ship, and in accordance with international law, he ordered the sailors into their lifeboats. There was no friendly harbor in range, no prize court available to make a determination of contraband, and no ability to transfer seized cargo into the limited space of the submarine. The prize crew scuttled the ship, becoming the first U-boat to sink a merchant ship. The commander's action drew some criticism for behaving in an uncivilized manner, but more influential German admirals praised the initiative. Their approval of this interpretation of the law set into motion permission to target shipping vessels as well as military targets.

Commanders had orders to adhere to *restricted submarine warfare* — firing only a warning shot to signal a ship to stop. If the captain determined contraband was aboard, the ship was to be sunk after passengers and crew were permitted to safely evacuate. It didn't take long for U-boat commanders to demonstrate different views of these orders. Soon after the *Glitra* sinking, the *U-24* commander fired a torpedo with no warning into a French steamer carrying more than 2,000 Belgian refugees. Everyone was rescued by another nearby ship, but this was by fortune rather than design. The U-boat commander officially explained he thought it was a troopship.

Successes of the U-boats empowered them to venture further, taking on more targets. By the end of 1914, fifteen ships had been lost and more than 40,000 tons of merchant supplies sunk. Ships quickly adopted the pattern of following a zigzag course because this disrupted a U-boat commander's ability to estimate a target's course and speed and increased the odds of a torpedo missing the mark. Greater defense measures were needed, and as destroyers began to accompany battleships, a proliferation of anti-submarine nets and additional undersea mines were deployed along British coastlines. Aircraft, also adapted for the first time for warfare, made bombing raids against Germany's submarine pens.

The advent of Q-ships in late 1914 stirred another controversy as the enemies hurled accusations of violations of international laws. Q-ships were otherwise harmless-looking vessels such as cargo ships with guns hidden from view. The intent was to tempt a U-boat into surfacing for an attack. Rather than targeting a perceived defenseless craft, the now vulnerable U-boat could be shot. Germany, in feeling the strain of the blockade, seeing the impact of U-boats, and being threatened with Q-ships, escalated to *unrestricted submarine warfare*. A proclamation signed February 5, 1915, to take effect February 18, declared all English seas as war zones, and merchant ships could be destroyed without regard to passengers and crew safety.

Protests from the United States regarding ships flying under neutral flags caused the kaiser to delay the campaign start date. The kaiser did not want to draw the United States into the war, and the proposed ferocity of unrestricted submarine warfare risked swaying the powerful nation from its official neutral status. Those urging escalation claimed a mere six weeks of unrestricted warfare would strangle Britain's supplies and bring them to the bargaining table. They calculated the United States would not shift its political position in such a short time.

Britain did not yield, as predicted, and they encouraged merchant ship captains to fly false neutral colors, which was permitted in wartime. Aside from Britain's resilience, on May 7, 1915, the passenger ship *Lusitania* was sunk with a loss of 1,195 lives, including 128 Americans. The outrage was immediate, and those in the German high command who opposed unrestricted warfare pressed their case with the kaiser.

The subsequent August sinking of the ocean liner *Arabic* brought a directive once again requiring U-boat commanders to allow crew and passengers of nonmilitary ships access to lifeboats before the ship could be sunk. Unfortunately, the directive was violated as early as September, and Germany declared a temporary pause in the intense campaign. This was not to lessen offensive action but to slightly shift focus. Germany had designed and produced the UC type of U-boat to serve as a dedicated minelayer. They carried a dozen mines, and with their smaller profile, they could slip into more waters than before, sowing minefields with little chance of being seen. Attack by torpedo was a deliberate offensive maneuver in which a commander could make a decision about his target. The laying of mines was another matter. Once mines were in place, there was no means of differentiating between a true enemy vessel, a neutral vessel, or a hospital ship.

Germany had utilized mines in the Austria-German War of 1866 and in the Franco-German War of 1870. They had improved their mines and developed a large store, enabling them to outmatch their enemies in the early part of the war. The high-quality mines were equipped with automatic anchors that used hydrostats to set mine depth and lock the mooring cables. Their mines were of such quality, the British reverse-engineered a captured German Hertz horned mine in order to produce their first reliable contact mine. In the never-ending development of defensive measures, minesweepers then came into existence. Britain's minesweeping force was too small to cope with Germany's superior threat, and in August 1914, the Royal Navy began to requisition trawlers and adapt them for minesweeping duties. The procedure was to "sweep" areas suspected of being mined using wires to bring the mines to the surface and detonate them by firing on them. This was a successful, if hazardous, process, as handling explosives always brings a level of danger.

As military campaigns expanded into the Mediterranean, minelaying UC-boats were included in the German fleets. On November 14, 1916, the French troopship *Burdigala* was sunk, and her survivors were picked up by the British destroyer HMS *Rattlesnake*. The crew of *Burdigala* was convinced they had been torpedoed. Historians later concluded the ship was sunk by a mine.

According to information contained on the website *uboat.net*, Gustav Siess is credited with a total of nineteen ships hit while in command of *U-73*, and two of the nineteen are *Burdigala* and *Britannic*.

In the aftermath of *Britannic's* sinking, the brief report submitted to the British Admiralty could not definitely conclude if she had been torpedoed or hit a mine, although a mine was deemed to be more likely. The willingness of the British press to claim a torpedo instead is understandable considering the times. Unrestricted submarine warfare was reinstated in late 1916, and Edwyn Gray's book contains a chilling passage about the deliberate torpedoing of the clearly marked hospital ship *Asturias* soon after *Britannic* sank. *British Official History* lists sixteen hospitals ships destroyed during the war, nine by torpedo. It shows *Britannic* as destroyed by a mine, but it isn't difficult to understand how some *Britannic* survivors remembered their own tragedy caused by a torpedo.

The subject of U-boats contains three closing ironies. First, White Star Line had more than *Britannic* called into service. A number of its ships, including massive *Olympic*, were used for troop transport. By all rules, troop transports were subject to attack, and six White Star ships were sunk with two more damaged by U-boats. On May 12, 1918, the commander of *U-103* prepared to torpedo *Olympic* despite it being protected by four destroyers. German commanders and crews took pride in their willingness to stalk the convoys, select a target, maneuver to attack, then immediately submerge and escape. Well-understood, however, was the risk of being spotted during the vulnerable window of surfacing for attack. *Olympic*, made aware of the threat, swung into the U-boat, damaging the hull and catching it against the ship until one of the huge propellers cut it open. The

U-boat commander and approximately half the crew were rescued by another ship, and the venerable *Olympic* had avenged her sister.

In continuing the threads of historical connectivity, *Carpathia*, the only ship able to respond to the *Titanic* disaster, had also been called into service as a troopship. Almost precisely two months after *Olympic's* U-boat encounter, the Cunard liner was attacked as she was steaming to Boston to receive thousands of troops. In the same way *Britannic* had not yet picked up her load of wounded and ill soldiers, less than 300 crew and passengers were aboard *Carpathia*. She was damaged as two torpedoes slammed into her, killing five crew members. Still afloat, despite the damage, the third torpedo was more than she could withstand. She sank to lie silently on the ocean floor until she was discovered eighty-two years later.

By the war's end, more than 300 U-boats had been lost in action or surrendered (mostly due to the armistice). Their toll had been great, however, in being credited with destroying more than 5,700 ships of various sizes. The human loss neared 20,000, and some historians believe the actual number could have been greater.

And the final irony of this subject? On October 30, 1918, the Ottoman Empire surrendered, ending the Mediterranean campaigns. Gray's book recounts that not knowing how quickly Germany's entire military was collapsing, the commander of the remaining Mediterranean U-boat fleet appointed a temporary commander to lead thirteen U-boats to make their way to Kiel in Germany, where they would receive new orders. If they could not make it safely, they would seek internment in Spain. The temporary commander maintained the formation through the treacherous journey, unaware that when they had arrived in November with battle flags fluttering, Germany was admitting defeat.

Who was the man arriving at port in his home country to prepare for a new mission? Gustav Siess, the U-boat commander who had laid the minefield credited with sinking *Britannic*.

CHAPTER 7

STIRRING THE SLEEPING SHIP

THE SINKING OF *BRITANNIC* was not a loss of life on the scale of *Titanic* — the 1,000-plus survivors were stranded and scattered in Greece. Captain Hugh Heard and his chief engineering officer, George Staer, of HMS *Duncan* conducted an immediate inquiry with Captain Bartlett and his senior officers. A limited number of witnesses were available who claimed to have noticed something unusual before the explosion. The November 24, 1916, typewritten report submitted to the British Admiralty contained fewer than 800 words and addressed nine major points.

They recorded witness testimony of a single explosion on the starboard side low near the bulkhead between Hold 2 and Hold 3, with the probability of damage to the bulkhead breaking Hold 1 and Hold 2. Water filled Hold 1, although they agree it might have been due to water flooding in through the firemen's tunnel. They cite the issue of several watertight doors not being fully closed, and acknowledge only one to two minutes lapsed when action could have been taken to close the doors. They offer no definitive conclusion as to why the doors were not fully closed. They also cite a lapse of approximately fifteen minutes before the scuttles on Deck E, normally twenty-five feet above the water line, were flooded.

What caused the explosion? The depth of Kea Channel argued against the idea of a mine, and three witnesses expressed belief they had been torpedoed. Other witness testimony did not support the idea, and no one reported seeing a column of water shooting up outside the ship, a normal signature of a torpedo attack. The inquiry's conclusion: It could have been a torpedo but was probably a mine.

Some British headlines didn't express doubt in their proclamation and trumpeted charges of Germans once again deliberately attacking a hospital ship. In the battle of propaganda, Germany countered with accusations of Britain abusing the status of hospital ships to secret military supplies or personnel aboard. They asserted perhaps the explosion had been caused by clandestinely transported munitions. Paul Louden-Brown provided an interesting insight into the possibility.

"I am certain, other than a few troops armed in order to maintain order on board, no munitions or other prohibited cargos were carried," he said. "The risk of detection was simply too great. That, however, should not be misunderstood to think that the British would attempt such things if the chances of detection were deemed to be low. *Lusitania* casts a shadow over this particular subject as that vessel was carrying a quantity of munitions — but many passenger vessels did, and you know my involvement with *Arabic* — she was nicknamed 'Queen of the Munitions Fleet' but never served as an HMS or HMHS — nevertheless she carried war cargos on many of her scheduled passenger voyages. Of course all of this seems bizarre to us now, that a country would put passengers of all nations at risk by loading war supplies in a vessel, but the rules of war have developed over time and through bitter experience."

These types of allegations were always vehemently denied by Britain, but there were people willing to believe the ship was used for covert purposes, whether illegal troop movement or munitions transport.

With no means of definitively proving fault and the war raging, the matter of *Britannic* was quietly closed as another unfortunate tragedy. The British government fully compensated White Star Line for its loss according to the standard formula used to calculate fair payment. (The huge number of ships destroyed during the war led the British government to agree to be the primary insurer for war risks.)

It was not until well into the twentieth century that technology fundamentally changed the ability to perform underwater exploration. The famous Jacques Cousteau, an innovator in many aspects of diving, and his ship, *Calypso*, became household names. Still on the leading edge of introducing the world to self-contained underwater breathing apparatus (SCUBA), Cousteau had captured the attention of viewers with documentaries such as the award-winning *Le Monde Du Silence* (*The Silent World*). The Cousteau team was to be in the Aegean Sea on an archeological expedition, and in 1975, when William Tantum IV, vice president of the Titanic Historical Society (THS), learned of the Cousteau team's plans, he asked the Cousteau group to undertake the task of locating *Britannic*. Cousteau's well-known research vessel was equipped with not only the vertical sounding system he routinely used but also with the new invention of side-scan sonar. Dr. Harold Edgerton, the inventor of the side scan, agreed to be part of the expedition to help with the search. What greater credentials in underwater exploration could be desired, and who better to engage in the search?

The location given to Cousteau from the British Hydrographic Office was not helpful. Was this a simple error, or had the German accusations of British duplicity been true, and the government did not want the ship found? Cousteau expanded his sweep outside official coordinates and was rewarded December 3, 1975, with finding a very large object on the seabed in an area away from where he had been searching. Cousteau and engineer Jean Mollard were ready with the SP-350 diving saucer *Denise*. Designed as the first underwater vessel specifically for scientific explorations, the two-person mini-submersible could be lowered by a crane into the water and lifted up to the rear deck of the ship after roaming underwater. The saucer could function as deep as 1,000 feet for as long as four to five hours. It homed in on the target indicated by the sonar, and mighty *Britannic*, lying on her starboard side, came into view. With this major accomplishment achieved, consideration could now be given to launching an expedition of magnitude.

Cousteau and his team had never dived at the depth of nearly 400 feet, and the saucer shape of the SP-350 could not penetrate inside the ship to find answers. The diving saucer would provide powerful lights during the operation and film overhead views of the wreck, yet willing men had to physically enter *Britannic* if they wanted more than exterior access. In thinking through the process, the plan would involve a number of "firsts" to enable the expedition to succeed. Like so many of Cousteau's endeavors, these activities would also advance the science of diving.

It's important to take a quick detour into the physiology of diving to explain that aside from running out of air, one of the greatest dangers a diver faces is decompression sickness (DCS), more commonly known as "the bends." This condition occurs when a diver spends time underwater and the air breathed is absorbed or saturated into the diver's body, flesh, organs, and bones. This is an exponential process — the longer and deeper a diver goes, the more gas is absorbed. If a diver ascends rapidly, these gases will expand and severely injure or kill a diver. The longer a diver stays down, or the deeper he goes, the slower he must ascend to let the absorbed gas come out through normal respiration, i.e., *just breathe*.

Through trial and error, scientists created tables to dictate how slowly one must ascend, depending on a set rule of time and depth. These decompression tables minimize the chances of suffering from DCS, but other variables, such as water temperature and the diver's health or physiology also play into whether a diver suffers from DCS, even when these tables are followed to the letter. Additionally, the deeper a diver goes, the more rapidly the diver consumes "air," and depth time duration is reduced. For every thirty-three feet a diver descends, the usable gas volume is reduced by a third due to pressure. A diver's time at a depth of 400 feet is severely limited, but as the diver ascends and the pressure is reduced, there is more air available to breathe. The gases most often used in the 1970s, in addition to compressed air, were helium and nitrogen. Trimix, new at the time, blended in oxygen as well. The exact blend was experimental, with no established types of tanks for this mix. New triple diving tanks specifically assembled for this project were developed.

Even with the gas mixture problem solved, two hours and forty-five minutes of decompression would be required. The process involved stopping for a designated number of minutes at a designated depth before ascending to the next decompression stop. (Think of it as ascending stairs and having to pause periodically.) This was prior to the invention of the drysuit, and other equipment later followed to allow divers to perform lengthy underwater decompression stops without the risk of hypothermia.

Even though the waters of Greece are far warmer than the Atlantic, when you descend, the temperature drops. In a typical scenario, the water temperature can be 70°F/21°C on the surface and 60°F/15°C on the bottom. Cold water (less than 70°F) can lower your body temperature, and if your body temperature drops too low, you may pass out and drown. The human body cools twenty-five times faster in cold water than it does in air. The rule of thumb at 60°F would be for exhaustion or unconsciousness to set in between two to seven hours. Therefore, the divers could not remain at the depth needed for decompression without this simultaneous risk.

An interesting solution for the significant problem of managing decompression stops was on board *Calypso*. Because of the remote locations in which the research vessel operated, Cousteau had equipped the vessel with a portable decompression chamber, and they decided to dual-purpose it. They would lower it into the water at approximately half the depth to the shipwreck. The divers would physically enter the water, descend to the sunken ship as rapidly as they could, spend a scant total of fifteen minutes underwater, and then ascend to the decompression chamber. Service divers would assist the explorers in removing their bulky tanks and strap the tanks to the exterior of the chamber, while the chilled divers entered the chamber. The chamber would be lifted back onto *Calypso*, where the divers would complete their decompression time in the cramped, but safe, space before they could emerge. The new tanks with trimix, the plan to submerge the portable decompression chamber, and the team of divers willing to take these risks came together for the 1976 *Britannic* Expedition.

William Tantum IV and other officers of THS had celebrated *Britannic's* discovery. To receive a telephone call inviting him to participate in the expedition was an offer he hadn't expected, and in early October he was on his way to

Greece. He wrote subsequent articles about the experience for *The Titanic Commutator*, the official journal for THS.

In the same manner Cousteau was a pioneer in underwater exploration, he was also a master of publicity. Cousteau interviewed *Britannic* survivors, where the question of the rapid sinking came into focus. Eight individuals, including eighty-six-year-old Sheila Macbeth Mitchell, who had been a nurse within the Royal Army Medical Corps, gathered with Cousteau to provide their memories. One of the eight was absolutely certain the ship had hit a mine, others were equally certain *Britannic* had been torpedoed, and two were convinced there had been two explosions probably caused by two torpedoes.

In light of these firsthand observations, Germany's old counteraccusations of *Britannic* carrying munitions became a central mystery for the expedition. Although dozens of dives were needed, the amount of time to search the ship would be extremely limited. Careful planning required a tight focus. Looking into the potential areas where munitions may have been stored was one of the priorities.

Calypso left port crowded with extra equipment and special passengers, including Mitchell for a short while. She had spryly agreed to be flown in by helicopter to be a part of the adventure. Everything would be recorded as footage for an episode of the television series *Jacques Cousteau Odyssey*. *Calypso's* search for the *Britannic* was eagerly awaited. Intrigued audiences watched safely as Cousteau and his team entered into the Aegean Sea past the blue water to the dark realm where it was often more like twilight. The 882-foot *Britannic* rested on her starboard side as home for soft and hard corals, sponges, and thousands of marine creatures who inhabited her as an artificial reef.

Torn pieces of metal, dangling ropes, cables, and wires can ensnare a diver's gear, and the inherent instability of heavy items dislodged inside a ship poses the hazard of breaking free to pin a diver against a wall. In addition to potential equipment malfunction, these were all risks to the divers who could see no farther than the radius of the lights they carried. The disorientation of the ship on her side was another factor because floors were "walls," and even though they had a model of *Britannic* on board as well as detailed plans, it was not the same as actually trying to maneuver through the darkened wreck. The experienced Cousteau and his team were intellectually prepared, yet as they approached the massive ship, there was a sensation of insignificance.

The gaping hole ripped open during the explosion and the holds they could access were the main search targets. While the team made a total of sixty-eight dives, descent to the depths ranging from 320 to 390 feet took approximately six minutes, leaving only nine minutes to explore before the divers were required to head to the decompression chamber or otherwise risk death or injury. Additionally, one diver had to carry as much light as possible and another, the camera for filming. These restrictions meant they would have a maximum of approximately ten hours during the entire expedition to be inside the ship.

The amount of exploration time was reduced because not every attempt went as planned. The sections of the ship they searched yielded no sign of munitions. There had also been speculation that the portholes the nurses had opened to take advantage of the beautiful day had contributed to the rapid sinking, though Cousteau's analysis did not support this. By the time *Britannic* had listed far enough to starboard, allowing water to flow in through her open portholes, her fate had been sealed by the thousands of tons of water already flooding the ship through the wound caused by the explosion.

What they did find were pieces of coal blown almost 100 feet from the hull. If observations from the witnesses who reported two explosions were correct, then rather than two torpedoes as had been thought possible, what if coal dust had somehow ignited to cause an almost simultaneous second explosion? This was a logical deduction. A second explosion could have accounted for why this other "unsinkable" ship had plunged to her doom within less than an hour of the initial tragedy. Without the technological means to explore more deeply inside the ship, the coal dust factor provided a viable answer.

On the more personal note of Mitchell's arrival on board *Calypso*, she was thrilled with such an opportunity and happily provided the researchers with descriptions of the ordinary items she'd had in her cabin. Her treasured alarm clock that folded up like a cigarette case, sheet music she carried for nights of music, and other possessions were all lost. She had hoped the clock could be located and cheerfully accepted it hadn't been likely. As a final treat, Mitchell was allowed to be one of the few nonresearcher passengers to descend in the diving saucer. She enthusiastically submerged in the vessel to see the shipwreck for herself, a remarkable experience she had never dreamed would come her way.

Cousteau stirred the immense ship in her grave and brought her back to the world's attention. His exoneration of the British government from accusations of illegally transporting munitions was settled for those who dealt in facts. Barring people who were convinced the White Star Line operated under some type of curse, Cousteau's discoveries planted the seed that more of *Britannic*'s secrets were waiting to be discovered. No one knew who would follow him or when, nor would they foresee the mighty Olympian would claim yet another life in pursuit of her elusive truths.

In a strange twist of fate, Violet Jessop would serve on all three Olympians and survive the sinking of both *Titanic* and *Britannic*.

Men wait for one of the 24 double-ended boilers to be fitted into *Britannic*.

Above: This excellent view shows one of the many changes made that were influenced by the loss of *Britannic*'s sister *Titanic*: rows of lifeboats and the newly designed gantries for launching them.

Left: A cutaway shows *Britannic* as intended: an opulent passenger liner. Note the firemen's tunnel leading into the boiler rooms and the Turkish bath above Boiler Room 4.

Brightly painted and lit by 500 light bulbs, *Britannic* was clearly
marked as a noncombatant.

Britannic sank twice as fast as *Titanic* and
under mysterious circumstances.

U-73 drops mines in the Kea Channel in October 1916.

An aft view shows a watertight door in the closed position. At lower left is the float designed to automatically close the door if the electrical system were to fail. *Right:* An open watertight door in sister ship *Olympic*

PART II

THE LURE OF THE QUEST

LAYERS OF SECRETS

T ELEVISION VIEWERS WERE THRILLED to see Cousteau and his team's documentary of the *Britannic* expedition, but in reality, significant advances in underwater exploration did not quickly follow their innovative solutions. Only those tantalizing glimpses of *Britannic* were possible for another twenty years.

As small groups of undersea adventurers consistently broke more barriers, information about the achievements were somewhat isolated without today's ease of Internet exchanges and online postings. Largely due to *Deep Sea Detectives*, my circle of pioneering shipwreck explorers in the United Kingdom expanded. The number of amazing vessels we highlighted on the shows fueled my appetite for mysteries, and enticing wrecks previously considered out of reach became challenges divers were determined to overcome. In hindsight, there was a period of time when I moved in and around people engaged with *Britannic* while my attention was elsewhere.

Once you commit to a quest, you discover new questions along the way, and *Britannic* is no exception. I entered this new circle and have been privileged to work with two categories of individuals who have pursued *Titanic's* equally tragic sister's secrets. The historians, artists, authors, engineers, enthusiasts, and scientists who are not inclined to "get wet" can leave you spellbound with their knowledge of the ship during her brief glory and in the knowledge they have gleaned from archives and data delivered from exploration. The men and women who descend from the azure surface of the Aegean Sea to watch the immense wreck materialize in her ghostly magnificence all have stories to share as they have slowly extracted clues since Cousteau located the ship. These people are not the only ones who have sought answers, but they are the ones I have been personally involved with.

CHAPTER 8

THE URGE TO KNOW

A NY COMPETENT MATHEMATICIAN will tell you thirty deaths compared to the millions killed during World War I are statistically insignificant. Yet the people who died on *Britannic* mattered to loved ones, and every person on board was forever affected by the tragedy. Some lost limbs, some bore physical scars, and all had watched in disbelief as the massive ship disappeared from sight — not the sort of image forgotten with the passage of time.

Britannic, in her majesty and mystery, captivates individuals for different reasons. Her casualties symbolize abrupt, unnecessary loss of life, and her history is a part of our drive to create and produce. While the breathtaking ocean liner has never captivated the attention of millions like her infamous sister, *Titanic*, *Britannic* was the last of only three Olympic-class ocean liners built. Had she not been converted for hospital use, her opulence would have exceeded that of her sisters. There are records of a number of the changes required, but in the rushed schedule to complete her for service, making a detailed list of interior alterations wasn't a priority. And unlike *Olympic* and *Titanic*, there were no colorful publicity brochures or newspaper advertisements to showcase her. In addition to the pressing questions about why she sank in such an improbable manner, there is historical curiosity about which artistic and decorative features were set aside for future use and which were installed.

It was Paul Louden-Brown, FSRA (Fellow of the Royal Society of Arts), historian for the White Star Line, author, and former vice president of THS, who greatly expanded my understanding of the Olympic class of ships.

I met Paul after our 2005 *Titanic* Expedition. We were working to have documentaries made about the expedition and went to England and Northern

Ireland to shoot the backstory and add more historical interest. Paul kindly invited me to his home outside a small village, complete with gently rolling hills, a country lane, cows grazing, and wild pheasants. He and his family graciously welcomed me, and I found myself almost hypnotized during the interview. It isn't just that he speaks eloquently. The best thing about listening to him is not only does he have fantastic recall of events, people, and things, but he has such great ability to turn a phrase and deliver a line with timing and a smile. I think he could probably read the ingredients off a cereal box, and I would clap.

His initial interest in *Titanic* came from watching the 1958 movie *A Night to Remember*, a film adaptation of Walter Lord's 1955 book of the same title. His inclination toward history, especially maritime history, dated to before then since he grew up in Northern Ireland. One of his family's companies wove the carpets and rugs for *Olympic* and *Titanic*, and his family was large shareholders in a shipping line with several vessels built by Harland & Wolff. Another influence was his mother, who took an unusual step considering her gender and the time when women of her social standing rarely pursued a career. She became a Marconi wireless operator with CIE, a travel company that was the Irish national authority for public transport. Although the shipping world embraced the Marconi wireless in the early 1900s, the general public recognized it as the device used to send *Titanic*'s distress call. Paul's mother, one of the few women operators ever certified, was so proficient she taught her younger brother Morse code as he thought about a career. He was immediately hired as a Marconi operator, and Paul remembered his uncle's visits when he would return to tell stories of far-flung ports of call.

"His uniform was grand and had these magnificent buttons," he recalled.

Young Paul didn't have an inkling of how his professional path would intertwine with the White Star Line, although this was the shipping line he was most intrigued with. His mother also dealt part-time in antiques, and she let it be known her son was in the market specifically for a White Star Line artifact. When Paul acquired a small silver bowl at around age fourteen, it did not occur to him he would ultimately own the largest collection in the world of White Star artifacts, photographs, and documents.

Schooled in England, he became a shipwright at the Exeter Maritime Museum, and among ancient skills of carpentry, canvas, and seamanship, he learned the mechanics of ships, including how to operate a triple-expansion steam engine. Immersing himself into the history of ships and especially of Harland & Wolff shipbuilders, White Star was a natural extension. Studies in commercial design and exhibitions and interiors then brought him to the attention of other museums. His list of consulting and lecturing accomplishments is lengthy, and aside from authoring books, he has played an integral role in building Titanic Belfast, the world's largest *Titanic* visitor attraction. Walking with him across the ground where thousands of workers passed each day and standing at the edge of the water from which hundreds of Harland & Wolff ships were launched, it's easy to envision crowds gazing in amazement at the Olympians towering above their heads.

On the other hand, Paul is hardly some dry historian who spends all his time burrowing through stacks of files. Even though he doesn't dive, he has actively worked with multiple salvage companies. Modern salvage operators look at each wreck they have the legal rights for or access to if in international waters. From their perspective, historical and academic study isn't where profit lies unless there was something such as a shipment of precious antique porcelain or a cash payroll in coin. Who better to turn to than a maritime historian who is familiar with searching through handwritten shipping manifests and documentation in order to answer questions about a shipwreck's potential cargo?

Paul expertly provides this service, and a telephone call one day from a client brought *Britannic* into an entirely new perspective. Of all the people connected to *Britannic*, Mr. Simon Mills is the only one who can lay claim to owning the ship. How did this come about? The telephone call to Paul setting everything into motion was from an industrialist who wanted to sell the title rights of almost two dozen ships he had purchased from the British government. When he mentioned *Britannic*, Paul immediately thought of Simon, whom he knew through their mutual research. He didn't really consider Simon would actually want to buy the ship, but the fact an individual held the legal title to her was an interesting topic for discussion.

Unlike Paul's broad knowledge of the entire White Star Line, Simon's focus was *Britannic*, a ship he learned about somewhat accidentally. His father, Alec Mills, had spent more than fifty years working as a cinematographer in the British film industry and worked on seven James Bond movies during his extensive career. Following in the family footsteps, Simon has worked behind the camera on several Bond movies himself as well as with such notable names as director Steven Spielberg. Always keenly interested in maritime history, while carrying out some research for one of the many *Titanic* documentaries following the discovery of the wreck in September 1985, his curiosity was roused not just by the story of *Titanic* but also of her two sister ships, about which there seemed to be little information.

Seeking to know more about these incredible feats of nautical engineering, he began to concentrate on *Britannic*. His personal archive steadily grew, and in 1992 he published *HMHS Britannic: The Last Titan*.

"It was never about the sensationalism for me," he explained once. "The truth is sensational enough. I don't need the embellishments and conspiracy theories."

Despite all his research, owning the ship was never something Simon expected to do. When the call came from Paul, he was filming a two-part television production of Jules Verne's *Twenty Thousand Leagues Under the Sea*, which he always thought was mildly ironic timing. Simon was intrigued when told the British government's legal title to the wreck was actually controlled by a man whose family owned a major British company, equivalent to the Caterpillar Corporation, among his various holdings.

Simon placed his telephone call to the industrialist during a break in filming to talk about *Britannic's* status. He remembered the conversation well. "Mark confirmed he did own the wreck (actually when he heard I was working in Pinewood Studios, he spent much of the call talking about Norman Wisdom films)," Simon recalled, "and the issue of purchasing the wreck came up kind of by accident. It was never planned — it just happened."

Simon declined any interest in the other nineteen wrecks, which collectively cost less than the *Britannic* on its own, but understandably wanted to check into a few aspects about ownership before committing to the deal, although he didn't want to risk losing the opportunity.

It didn't take long to decide, and Simon smiled as he recalled, "That was without a doubt the most expensive lunch break of my life."

Owning *Britannic* comes with complex relationships. The woman from the Greek Foreign Ministry who spoke of his legal rights and obligations explained that despite Greece honoring the ship as a British government warship, the wreck rested in Greek waters.

This basically means that although Simon has certain unique rights insofar as *Britannic* is concerned, he still accepts the need to work within the Greek administrative system. The Greek Ephorate of Marine Antiquities also strictly enforces what can and cannot be done when diving on any shipwreck more than fifty years old, so obtaining the proper permit for an expedition is rarely, if ever, a speedy process. Even so, Simon has been involved in each expedition to some degree.

His participation in the first trip to the Kea Channel was in August 1995, when he was contacted by Kirk Wolfinger, who was producing the documentary to be aired after completion of Robert Ballard's *Britannic* Expedition. As the only published *Britannic* author, Kirk came to Simon for help with background research in the vaults of the British Film Institute, during which they even located the previously lost newsreel footage of *Olympic*, the first of the "Three Olympians" being built and launched.

The initial exchanges led to an invitation from Kirk, on behalf of *NOVA*, to go along on the trip as one of the expedition's resident experts. This was Simon's first direct contact with *Britannic*, which was to have more of an effect on him than he originally expected. The following year he obtained the British government's legal title to the wreck, possibly making him the only person ever to buy a shipwreck "as seen." Having now authored or contributed to four different books about *Britannic* and having been on multiple expeditions himself, he might be persuaded someday to chronicle his experiences as her owner. I'm sure there are some interesting stories to be told.

When I met Simon, I didn't know much about his background. We were in England in 2004 shooting *Deep Sea Detectives* episodes, and Simon was an associate producer in addition to serving as a fixer to help out with the inevitable issues encountered when working in an unfamiliar area. Not surprisingly, we discovered some mutual acquaintances, and during those conversations, neither of us expected to someday be together on a *Titanic* visit and two *Britannic* expeditions.

Following this common thread of nondivers who knew *Britannic* before I did and were connected to each other, Parks Stephenson has also always loved a good mystery. He discovered early on how written history is subject to interpretation or can be manipulated to serve an agenda in either a positive or negative way. For Parks, stripping away popular myths and misconceptions fit nicely with his engineering mindset. When he graduated from the U.S. Naval Academy and earned his Naval Flight Officer wings in the E-2C Hawkeye airborne early warning aircraft, he spent a varied career aboard submarines, aircraft carriers, and amphibious ships. In those odd coincidences that occur in life, in the latter part of his military career, he adopted the call sign of Sparks, which for him was a logical play on his name. Others, however, immediately homed in on it as the historical nickname for Marconi wireless operators, and they often assumed it was the basis for his call sign. Parks, never reluctant to delve deeply into new subjects, decided to learn everything he could about the Marconi.

He had not yet heard of Paul and didn't have the faintest notion they would someday be linked through *Titanic/Britannic* and have ties to the Marconi system. Neither did he imagine he would receive a call from film director James Cameron, who had been told about his expertise. The director, well-known as an undersea explorer, wanted to discuss the Marconi system with him as it related to *Titanic*. Cameron not only subsequently included Parks on his *Titanic* expedition team, he then paved the way for him into documentary filmmaking. Parks pioneered the use of 3-D models in his forensic analysis to accomplish things such as illustrating *Titanic*'s Marconi telegraph room. His amazingly realistic work has been seen on the series of documentaries in National Geographic's *Titanic: The Final Word with James Cameron*, Discovery Channel's *Titanic's Last Mysteries*, and History Channel's *Titanic 100: Mystery Solved*.

With this kind of experience, Parks was highly recommended to work with us on the post-*Titanic* expedition analysis in late 2005 and early 2006, and I was impressed as hell with him.

Looking at the most famous of the Olympians broken into pieces, his words — "If you want to know *Titanic*, look at *Britannic*" — struck us as we worked together. The sisters aren't identical twins, but as we were to learn, hundreds of aspects are identical. Parks is not a man who likes to say, "Oh, that's close enough." He strives for precision and understanding of what an object is rather than accepting a hasty, inaccurate description. For him, *Britannic* is a window into history, frozen in place, her secrets waiting to be revealed.

Insistence on historical accuracy is shared by a man who originally introduced Parks to director James Cameron. Ken Marschall has brought *Titanic, Britannic,* and other famous ships to life on canvas and in book illustrations, but his incredible artistry doesn't come from only sitting in a studio. In 1995, he sat in the American research submarine *NR-1* as part of an expedition with a name as famous as Cousteau — Dr. Robert D. Ballard, the man who showed *Titanic* to the world. This expedition heralded a new era in the ongoing quest to pry secrets from the mighty ship.

CHAPTER 9

LOOKING FROM THE OUTSIDE

ORD OF DR. BALLARD and his team locating RMS *Titanic* grabbed
headlines in September 1985, and I was not immune to the thrilling
news. (I also had no idea I would someday experience visiting
Titanic.) And when the tenth anniversary of finding *Titanic* came around, why
not mount an expedition to her sister ship *Britannic* to also coincide with the
twentieth year since Cousteau found her? Granted, the undersea exploration
technology leaps aboard the *NR-1* submarine were not the type most individuals
had access to. The research vessel completed in 1969 included an array of
distinctive features of three viewing ports, exterior lighting and television, and
still cameras for photographic studies, sophisticated computers, and electronics.
The ability to remain at one site and completely map or search an area with a
high degree of accuracy was another feature not available to Cousteau's team.

NR-1 could explore independently, but at her size and designed for slow
speed, she was most often towed by a larger surface boat also equipped to
conduct simultaneous research. Ken dug into his old journals to recount his
unexpected experience.

> "I was invited by Dr. Robert Ballard to participate in his 1995
> exploration of *Britannic*. As a student of the Olympic-class
> liners for almost thirty years at that time and the illustrator
> of Ballard's anticipated book *Lost Liners*, he wanted me
> to see firsthand what the wreck looked like as well as lend
> my expertise. I had accompanied him during his *Lusitania*
> exploration in 1993, in the same capacity then, diving on that
> storied wreck twice in the mini-sub *Delta*.

"MV *Carolyn Chouest* served as our research and support vessel from which two ROVs would be piloted — *Phantom S2* and *Voyager*, one of them using a stereo camera. But the most impressive piece of equipment on the trip was undoubtedly the 146-foot nuclear-powered submarine *NR-1*, employing multiple cameras, side-scan sonar, and a small observation space with three viewports. Both *Chouest* and *NR-1* were operated by the U.S. Navy.

"After the wreck was relocated, no time was wasted getting to work. Ballard was the first to dive and returned with enthusiastic reports of how beautifully intact *Britannic* looked, seemingly unchanged from when Cousteau had last left her nearly two decades before. The sub accommodated a maximum of thirteen people, almost all of whom were necessary crew, with very little spare room for outside researchers or observers. I was accompanied by only one other specialist from Ballard's team — a camera/video technician who would make sure the various equipment operated in sync with the sub's system.

"Ballard wanted me to go for two days to help guide the sub pilots to specific points using a grid profile navigation map of the wreck that I had created. This was far longer than I'd anticipated and came as quite a surprise. Not yet a seasoned submariner, I thought, 'How could anyone stand to be in such a small sub with a dozen other guys for *two days*?' But I got the sense from a few crew that, not to worry, they would probably resurface after a day, at most. I was further encouraged by fellow historians aboard *Chouest* who reminded me that I would be the first person so intimately familiar with *Britannic* to see the wreck. It was a humbling realization.

"After traversing by Zodiac to the submarine, I climbed into the confined space in the sub's 'sail' and then down through two rather constricting hatches. It was these narrow hatches, of course, that gave me pause and my only sudden rush of claustrophobia. I continued down, reassured by the knowledge that countless others had traveled the world in this sub and dived to much, much greater depths, and no one had drowned yet.

"At about 4 p.m., August 30, *NR-1* began its descent. This was done in stages, and after several minutes I could see that we were finally completely submerged, and the sub began to dip downward at the bow. The pitch increased to an angle that I thought surely could not get steeper, and then it increased more. It was quite an unsettling sensation, and I looked around for something to hold on to so that I wouldn't slide along the blue linoleum. Not long after this the sub leveled out again.

"The observation area, right below the bridge, was a small space into which one maneuvered down through a hatch in the floor. The three five-inch viewports were about three feet apart, and each port looked in a direction that was about 35 to 40 degrees different from each other. This tiny 'crawlspace' had a very low ceiling, and since it was at the bottom of the rounded pressure hull, had a concave floor, curving up on the sides. In the beginning, one or two navy personnel were down there with me, monitoring the situation and speaking with the bridge above via a headset. Later, I would often find myself alone in there, freely able to move from one port to another to get the best view.

"My first impression was of the vivid aqua-blue of the water outside. At *Lusitania* two years earlier, where the gravelly bottom is at about 300 feet, it was dark, the water a rich, deep green, and visibility not great. Here at *Britannic* it was markedly different. The deep aqua-blue was much brighter than the ambient light at *Lusitania*. I remember at one point, when we were at a high altitude, being amazed to be able to make out the fuzzy, diffused silhouette of the wreck far below us, darker than the reflected 'glow' of the seabed much farther down. The water clarity can be so amazing here in the Aegean, I had heard, that under the best conditions the wreck can be faintly detected visually almost from the surface or not too far below, and I got this distinct impression myself after a while.

"After years of analyzing *Titanic* wreck imagery and doing multiple paintings for books by Ballard about her discovery, I was used to that ship's 'rusticle'-covered appearance, completely devoid of plant life because of her great depth and nearly so of animals. Here, on *Britannic*, with the highest part of her hull at the relatively shallow depth of less than 300 feet in this sunny, warm, and very clear water, her upturned port side was covered with marine growth. Yet, upon closer inspection, many areas were oddly almost clear of encrustations. I could sometimes see the edges of hull plates and rows of rivets.

"From a great height, the wreck has a monochromatic appearance, the intense ambient aquas and blues canceling out any warm colors that may exist. Approaching nearer, one can see the blotchy surface of the hull, carpeted with marine life, but still no warm colors are visible. Seemingly white or light-gray growths festoon the sides of the superstructure. Only as we grow still closer do the true colors of these various plants and animals begin to materialize. You'd never know it from a distance, but those 'whitish' things are actually bright yellow sponges, while other growths range from beige to orange to a purplish magenta.

"The sub ran a grid pattern back and forth over the wreck, shooting video and still photographs. I shot my own stills and video, took notes, and made small sketches from the little observation area. The crew had standing orders not to get closer than twenty to twenty-five feet from any part of the wreck, which made for less than optimal study of details and handicapped my photography.

"I was amazed by the structural integrity of the ship after nearly eighty years in this warm Mediterranean water. Witnesses had watched *Britannic's* funnels fall away as she rolled over to starboard, but it appeared to me that except for the missing funnels, hardly another thing was misplaced. Her cargo cranes and deck equipment were still firmly fitted despite the hull resting on the bottom at an almost eighty-degree angle to starboard. Even more surprising was the fact that all her steel deckhouses were still attached as was most ventilation equipment atop them. That these heavy structures, intended to be vertical, were still holding on, suspended out in space nearly horizontally despite eight decades in this warm, corrosive sea water, was astounding. I'm not aware of another early twentieth-century wreck, on its side, with anything like this integrity.

"I was struck by the immense scale of the huge gantry davits angling up and almost *above* my viewport, so far were they extended beyond the side of the ship. Like the heads and necks of some huge undersea reptiles, the tops of these davits drifted silently past, surprising me by their nearness.

"While most promenade windows had been lowered during *Britannic*'s last few days, I noticed some that were partway up, unbroken. I thought of that fateful voyage seventy-nine years before, when someone either didn't lower that window all the way or raised it back up a bit, intentionally. Somebody *did* that. These rare glimpses of mundane human activity on board so long ago, frozen in time, were wonderful and moving.

"I had mixed feelings, though, when *Britannic*'s massive three-bladed wing propeller loomed into view below me. At twenty-three feet nine inches diameter, her two outboard propellers are three inches bigger than her earlier two sisters' and are said to be the largest fitted to any twentieth-century liner. But this enormous port propeller that I was beholding has a tragic history. Still rotating quickly and rising above the water as the ship was sinking, two lifeboats drifted helplessly aft and were dashed to pieces by it, resulting in thirty deaths, the only casualties of the sinking.

"I watched the distinctive groupings of portholes and windows move past, so familiar to me after decades of studying archival photographs and construction drawings. I noticed many open portholes, something that survivors had reported. As we slowly moved along, I knew exactly what was coming next — here's the condenser discharge, there's that coal door, there's the first-class dining saloon.... It was hard to grasp that after so much research and study spanning more than half my lifetime, I was actually looking at one of these great Harland & Wolff leviathans with my own eyes, the largest passenger vessel on the world's seabed.

"All these years *Britannic* had been little more to me than a few rare old photographs, deck plans, and historical accounts. I always spoke of her in the past tense — *Britannic was* — lost, obscure, forgotten ... in fact, the finest vessel ever built for the White Star Line sunk before she ever carried a paying passenger. Yet now, as her huge, unmistakable hulk slowly passed below me, objective and subjective realities clashed, and my mind could hardly accept it. Far from being lost to history, I was *looking* at her. She had always been right here, waiting, just out of sight.

"The experience was unreal, otherworldly, so out of the realm of my experience. Unlike the murky darkness at *Lusitania*, here I was peering off sixty feet or more. With every passing minute, I grew more incredulous at the ship's amazingly intact condition. Two decades after Cousteau's photography, I expected some new deterioration, surely, or at least a thicker blanket of growth, obscuring all but the largest portholes and windows. But the level of encrustation had not increased at all, that I could see. I could find no corrosion of the hull itself and virtually no rust, in fact. *Britannic* was a Walt Disney shipwreck, I thought, a huge movie-prop ocean liner looking way too good to be anything but a Hollywood creation.

"Moving forward beyond the bridge, the horrific damage wrought by *Britannic's* collision with the seafloor came into view. The bow was not at all aligned with the hull but angled considerably clockwise to it. And while the rest of the hull was over on its starboard side, the bow forward of the well deck was far less canted, more upright, at something like forty-five degrees.

"As we traversed the hull and I studied the monstrous, slumbering liner, I shook my head with pity. Such a feat of human ingenuity and naval engineering, such an imposing architectural wonder she once was. And *still is*. Just look at her, I thought. She seemed like a gigantic horse that had somehow stumbled and fallen, lying on her side to rest for a while, awaiting a time to rise up and run again. I was overwhelmed with the feeling that this beautiful creation was never meant to be down here. The whole scene looked unfairly and cruelly out of place, this masterpiece of shipbuilding now resting grotesquely sideways in the sand, hidden from view, a time capsule mummified and entombed forever in this silent, ghostly, blue netherworld, only feet below the busy shipping lanes where she was intended to be.

"While I busily occupied myself at a viewport, the daylight faded and the sub's thalium iodide lights took over. The ambiance outside transformed dramatically from a rich turquoise-blue to an even more eerie, and frankly spooky, green color. In daylight,

I could see much farther, but now, with only the lights from the sub, the visibility was much reduced. With night fallen and photography less effective, the crewman on watch next to me, hooked up to the bridge with the headset, turned and said that the guys above wanted to know where I wanted to go. He told me I had the run of the ship. 'The sub's all yours.'

"Among my hoped-for goals was a search for the missing funnels. Likely candidates were detected on *NR-1*'s sonar, so off we went to an area northwest from the wreck. I was glued to a port and peering down at the sand below in the eerie green light. Finally, several hundred feet from *Britannic*, the collapsed end of a funnel drifted into view. It was unmistakable. The identification was complete when I noticed a large telltale pipe emerging from inside. It was the Number 4 funnel, the only one with such a pipe, which carried away smoke and gases from the galley.

"Unlike *Britannic*'s hull, the funnel was remarkably unencumbered by marine growth. Although I could see a few small corrosion holes in the thin steel and the funnel was somewhat collapsed, I was thrilled to see that it still retained much of its original elliptical shape. Of the six stays, or guy wires, that secured the funnel to the deck on each side, several were right there, still attached, their shackles looking as functional as ever. I was breathless. This was a major highlight of my dive.

"As it was the middle of the night and photography was far from optimum, it was decided to try some side scanning. There was virtually no current, and we could get some very steady runs. So we ran numerous ruler-straight courses back and forth over and beside the wreck from various directions while the side-scan printing machine clicked away. As the crew learned what worked best and at what altitude, each run got better results. Some were just breathtaking in their detail. When the printouts were later reversed so that the light areas were dark and vice versa, they were almost like photographs. The side scans proved to be one of the most valuable harvests of the entire weeklong expedition.

"At some point, news came that the weather was deteriorating up top, and although I learned that we were indeed to have surfaced that day, it was decided to stay down, hovering over the wreck or doing more side scanning. It looked like I would remain below for two days, after all. I got myself some food, and the crew showed me a rack where I caught some sleep.

"As Day Two progressed, the wind and waves were still bad, so our underwater stay extended further, through a second night. By the time we finally surfaced, on the afternoon of September 1, I had been aboard just under forty-eight hours. Later that night, showered and snug in my bunk aboard *Chouest,* I wrote, 'I'm exhausted but content, fulfilled, satisfied completely.... The experience was just surreal. Another world. I feel like I've returned from exploring another planet.'

"I learned so much from the dive, from a much better idea of the wreck's condition and attitude to new details about her architecture, where her funnels ended up, and so on. *Britannic* is the prettiest wreck I think I've ever known of. With the clear Mediterranean water, the bright sand, and the remarkably intact condition of the ship, she makes for the dream dive. Who can believe that, even today, all her deckhouses are still attached, still hanging on at about a seventy-eight-and-a-half-degree angle off the vertical, after a century! Compare that to the shocking condition of *Andrea Doria,* for example, also on her starboard side, a wreck that is four decades younger, although admittedly there are swifter currents where she lies. Then there's *Empress of Ireland,* another liner on her starboard side. Sunk in 1914 in the Saint Lawrence River, her entire superstructure — riveted steel, just like *Britannic* — fell away long ago.

"In the forty years since Cousteau explored *Britannic,* she appears to have changed little. There is scant evidence of new corrosion beyond the few examples where the steel was very thin, all the more remarkable considering the warm water in which she rests. The great liner seems to be in a state of suspended animation, a virtual time capsule from 1916."

Ken Marschall, September 2015

CHAPTER 10

RISK ISN'T THE SAME AS RECKLESS

THE VIDEO FOOTAGE, PHOTOGRAPHS, AND Ken's artistic renderings from the 1995 Expedition showed *Britannic* in a new light, but for all the technology used to look from the outside, the information provided couldn't resolve the questions of what happened on the fateful day. There was no way to determine exactly what damage had been inflicted, the source of the explosion, or why the ship had gone down in less than an hour.

To best share the fascinating saga surrounding *Britannic*, we will mix science into the narrative to bring the story to life and light. The developments in scuba technology in the ensuing two decades since Cousteau and his team penetrated *Britannic* have made our adventures possible and also spawned a long-standing argument about deep shipwreck exploration.

As ROVs and submersibles have improved, there are absolutely people who take the position it's foolish to risk divers' lives in what are unquestionably dangerous situations. In other cases, deep-sea explorers get tired of dealing with the equipment-intensive, physically draining, mentally tiring effort of diving in hazardous conditions and prefer the confines of a submersible or watching images sent from an ROV. Being in a submersible isn't without risk, and it definitely isn't always comfortable, but generally speaking, the odds of being severely injured or dying while on scuba are greater than if in a submersible.

Beyond 2,300 feet deep in the ocean, humans cannot visit as free-swimming divers due to the intense pressure of the seawater pushing down on them. Water has weight, and the deeper we go into the sea, the more weight a body must bear. The air (or gas) a diver breathes must be at the same pressure as the surrounding water in order for the lungs to move back and forth. At 2,300 feet, humans have hit a wall in their ability to neurologically handle the density of the breathing gas. Our bodies are mostly water, and we can equalize the air spaces in our body to the surrounding water pressure (lungs, sinuses, etc.) so a diver's body is totally unaware of this weight or pressure. The problem is as we exceed the pressures of 2,300 feet, the gas we breathe becomes so thick our pulmonary system cannot correctly manage its normal functions, and our neurological system fails in what is referred to as high-pressure nervous syndrome (HPNS).

To explore deeper, humans must now use either a submersible or a remotely operated vehicle to "see" what lies deep in the crushing pressures. Smaller and less expensive to build and operate than submersibles, ROVs are fast becoming the tool of choice for many explorers because they remove all the danger of deep ocean exploration for human beings, who now sit safely in a control room aboard a ship and, much like a video game, use onboard cameras to see and joysticks to remotely control what is essentially an underwater robot, thousands of feet below. ROVs not only can film, but they also can collect specimens and conduct experiments with the use of robotic arms and tools.

And now for the "human" side. If we can use ROVs and submersibles to explore the bottom of the ocean depths, why take chances and risk one's life as a free-swimming scuba diver to explore in the shallower waters of less than 2,300 feet? The answer is simple: No video monitor can tell us what something "feels" like or what the experience means to the explorer. The best lens in the world cannot capture the sense of awe, trepidation, and victory endemic in the human spirit of exploration, that which drives us to climb mountains simply "because they are there." Our desire to see, touch, feel, and smell for ourselves leads us to explore despite the risk of life and limb; some would say the closer to the edge we get, the more alive we feel. In shipwreck exploration, an ROV can take hours of video and reams of photographs and is a wonderful tool for the researcher, but it cannot surpass the ability and dexterity of a human explorer. As a free-swimming diver, we can explore deep inside the maze of the interior of a 100-year-old ship and move like church mice, leaving the smallest of footprints of our visit. An ROV requires a long cable leading back to the ship above, and a cable can easily become entangled inside the wreck. Cables limit how far an ROV can peer inside and also risk getting the ROV caught up or worse, damaging the shipwreck. It is here the diver excels and is the better tool to use. In the case of our work on *Britannic*, we have traveled a few hundred feet into the wreck, navigating around numerous obstacles that would have assuredly snagged the ROV umbilical. The diver in this case can go where no ROV can.

This is a similar argument to the debate about manned and unmanned space exploration. If you watched the movie *The Right Stuff*, about the birth of the astronaut program, you might remember the astronauts' resistance when there were plans to continue sending chimpanzees into space instead of men. It is the same spirit of knowing machines and primates have their places, but it isn't the same as what a person can feel and comprehend.

When Cousteau's team broke a number of barriers in their abbreviated dives on *Britannic*, other divers watched the footage of what they accomplished, and they too wanted to take diving to this new, exciting level. As a member of the Atlantic Wreck Divers group, back in the days before "shadow diving" became synonymous with Robert Kurson's book *Shadow Divers*, I was making dives to the edge of our abilities. This was not the simple act of strapping a single tank onto your back like I had done in the warm, shallow waters of Florida, where I spent most of my teen years. In taking my first deep, dark dive into the cold waters of the Atlantic, I moved into the world where shipwreck artifacts beckoned and needed to be properly equipped to continue. From the mid-1970s and through the 1980s, my deep-diving rig was double steel tanks, and when filled to the working pressure, each tank held seventy-two cubic feet of air. The next improvement came in the way of aluminum tanks, and these held eighty cubic feet of air each, allowing me to stay underwater longer. Unlike the steel tanks, the aluminum ones became buoyant when empty, so I had to wear more lead on my weight belt.

A quick discussion about buoyancy will explain what might seem to be a contradiction about floating and sinking. Yes, the intent of diving is to go underwater and weight pulls you under. It's like taking off and landing in an airplane. You generally have to taxi out to the runway. In diving, it's common to enter the water and stay afloat for about a minute to make sure you have everything you need and everything is working before you start your descent. You hit a button of the control to the "vest" that you wear to pump little bursts of air in it to provide enough "lift" to hold your head out of water while you perform the last check. Then you release the air in your vest so all that weight now tugs you down.

While diving, maintaining your buoyancy is important. The weight you're wearing wants to take you to the bottom, and that usually isn't where you want to go, particularly if you're on a wreck and you want to explore very specific parts of the ship. You add a few bursts of air to your vest, and that allows you to maneuver through the water at your desired depth in what is called "neutral buoyancy." Once perfected, this is as close to weightlessness you can ever feel without going into space. Once you've finished the dive, maintaining buoyancy and control is part of a safe ascent plan, especially when you've been deeper than 130 feet and need those multiple decompression stops to avoid the risk of the bends. If you've become too buoyant, you rise too quickly. You release some of the air you added to your vest during the dive so you can control the ascent until it's time to put your head above water. At that point, it's like the airplane taxiing to the gate. Unless you pop up right at the boat, you'll need to be buoyant enough to swim over without expending the energy to "fight" the weight you're carrying that wants to drag you back below.

Mastering buoyancy control is a key element of penetrating into wrecks (or caves) because you have narrow spaces in which to maneuver, and you don't want to bounce into all those dangling items that can snag you or crash down into the bottom, disturbing the mud and ruining your visibility with clouds of dirty water.

By 1985, one of the seasoned veterans of our group thought I was ready for my first dive on *Andrea Doria*, the infamous Italian luxury ocean liner that sank in July 1956. We refer to her as the "Mount Everest of Diving" because of extremely difficult conditions. She sits at 240 feet in current ranging from noticeable to so strong you can't even attempt the dive. I wasn't about to go in with anything less than the right equipment. That meant I was wearing twin aluminum tanks with the regulators, valves, and harness at a weight of 100 pounds, and the drysuit came in around fifteen pounds. The lights, knifes, fins, gloves, and mask tallied up another twenty pounds, and then I added the weight belt with forty pounds of lead, so I had 175 pounds of equipment on me. Carrying a camera added to the weight, making any kind of movement before plunging into the water slow and awkward.

The magnitude of my first *Doria* dive will stay with me forever, and I didn't know at the time how the experience would prepare me for a new direction in my life.

In the early 1990s, technology brought quantum leaps in scuba, and the term *technical diving* came into common use. Dive computers became available. New steel 120 tanks containing 50% more air than aluminum 80s were a huge jump for duration and safety. Because these tanks were heavier, back-mounted buoyancy compensators or "wings" were needed to offset the weight in the water. At depth, you depend on what light you carry, and while better underwater lights came out with larger batteries housed in canisters, they were also heavier. The biggest advantage was the use of other-than-air gases for making longer and deeper dives. Both trimix and nitrox had been used in the commercial dive world for years, but the recipes for the right mix and the decompression tables to go with them were a closely guarded trade and, in some cases, military secrets. This was one of the things Cousteau's team experimented with, and once "the genie was out of the bottle," there was no turning back. Expanding the edge of underwater exploration was too alluring.

Trimix is air with the addition of helium that lowers both the oxygen and nitrogen content. Decompression sickness is the most well-publicized diving danger, but at depth, too much nitrogen has a narcotic effect, and too much oxygen can induce seizures. As an inert gas, helium is the perfect way to lower both the oxygen and nitrogen in your tanks to help prevent these conditions. But when you are underwater, you're carrying your life support system on your back. The trimix is in the double tanks on your back, and now you carry two additional tanks called stage bottles — one under each arm — filled with nitrox for decompressing.

The way this works is relatively straightforward. The larger capacity of tanks on my back and the benefits of trimix was what I would use on the deep part of the dive, breathing almost all of the gas in those tanks. Then I would swap over to breathe from the stage bottles under my arms as I made my ascent with the multiple stops that added up to different times depending on how deep I had been. Being able to extend my time underwater was great, but the new and better lights I carried came at an increase of another ten pounds. When you added the weight of the higher-capacity tanks and two extra tanks under my arms, the total weight of the equipment was almost 240 pounds. I was as self-sufficient as I could be and about as awkward as a beached seal when I was getting on and off a boat.

For me, these advancements in diving and being willing to take the risks of deep-shipwreck exploration forever changed my world. Aside from facing the enjoyable phrase of "so many shipwrecks and so little time," I didn't know how closely I would eventually work with divers across the pond in the United Kingdom.

CHAPTER 11

FOUR GIVENS YOU CAN'T IGNORE

A S I WAS TO LEARN, mounting any manned *Britannic* expedition comes with four givens. First, it will be expensive. Second, it will be a significant and intricate logistical effort. Third, problems ranging from minor irritation to a full-blown crisis will occur. Fourth, diving to a depth of 400 feet whether by submersible or on scuba comes with recognizing the risk of potential injury or death.

To orient the geography, the body of land closest to the shipwreck is Kea Island, sometimes called Kéa, Zea, or Tzia. If you've never had the opportunity to visit the Mediterranean area, its beauty is matched only by its history. It was an important route for merchants and travelers thousands of years ago, as it allowed for trade and cultural exchange between several ancient civilizations located around its shores. In the way humans have done since the dawn of mankind, it also enabled colonization and war.

The Mediterranean is an inland sea bordered on the north by Europe, the east by Asia, and the south by Africa. You enter from the vast Atlantic Ocean, and the approximately 2,300 miles in length takes you to the Black Sea through the Dardanelles Straits, where so many lives were lost during World War I. The 969,100-square-mile body of water is subdivided into the Adriatic Sea, Aegean Sea, Balearic Sea, Tyrrhenian Sea, Ionian Sea, and Ligurian Sea. Kea Island is in the Aegean Sea, approximately thirty-seven miles southeast of Athens. The island, with an arid climate and hilly terrain, is only twelve miles long and six miles wide. It's popular for sailing, but due to different winds that blow from multiple directions, passage around the island is considered to be some of the most difficult in the Mediterranean. There is a small heliport on Kea Island but no airplane landing strip. The island is serviced a few times a day in peak season by large roll-on/roll-off ferries coming from either Lavrion or Piraeus. The route from the "new" Athens airport is on a major highway for a short while, and then you take secondary roads to whichever port city you depart from. The roads are scenic, with small olive and fig farms along the way. The ferry trips take about two hours, and on the beautiful days that are so common to the region, aquamarine water meets azure sky. If you've ever watched the movie version of *Mamma Mia!*, it was filmed on location on a similar island in another part of the Aegean Sea.

On Kea Island, the port of Korissia, also known as Livadi, is the first place you see when you arrive since that is where the ferry docks. The one harbor is the island's only major seaport capable of landing and loading large ferries, and a small marina on the opposite side of the bay handles smaller vessels. There is a long, sandy beach, and above the port on the hill of Agia Triada are the ruins of the ancient acropolis and an archaic temple believed to be dedicated to Apollo.

Despite the attributes of Kea Island, it is not well-known as a tourist destination and even less so for diving. You can find replacement masks and fins and not much else in the way of scuba equipment. Whatever you need for diving, you bring with you or make arrangements well in advance with the limited number of suppliers on the mainland for the limited items they handle.

It is a plus there have now been more than a dozen *Britannic* expeditions, and Simon Mills talks to each team about what has been done and learned from previous expeditions. This information helps avoid going over old ground. After you've managed the complicated logistics, completed the multilayered permitting process, and brought highly qualified team members who have a lot of deep-shipwreck diving experience, you still face the issues of variable wind and current. High wind equates to rough seas — the more wind, the rougher the sea. There are days where the wind is blowing, and it's a wonderful sunny sailing day, but it is not a good diving day.

The problem isn't the boats being able to handle rough weather; they are built for that. The real problem with rough seas is not getting in the water, it's getting back out. We can easily jump into the water from a pitching boat with all our gear and then make a dive — that's gravity at work. But with all our equipment (drysuit, back-mounted and extra tanks, cameras, and lights), on the surface we move through the water with all the grace of a beached seal, expending lots of energy with little actual movement for our effort. Compound the fact you're already tired after a dive and long decompression stops, the bulk of the boat rising and falling with the waves is a recipe ripe for a cracked skull, broken arm, or even worse when trying to climb back up on the wildly moving ladder.

To add insult to this, after making a long and very deep dive, we must try *not* to exert ourselves at all. Strenuous exercise has been proven to facilitate the formation of those bubbles in our muscles and joints that can give a diver the bends, even when proper decompression has been completed. Dives to 400 feet is an extreme exposure of decompression, so we are already at the greatest possible risk and must mitigate any additional factors that can cause stress or exercise. Even if the dive conditions are great in the morning but the forecast is getting worse, the dive will be aborted because after the long decompression time underwater, you'll be coming out of the water when the winds are higher.

Current by itself is not a real problem for divers. Many divers make what is called a drift dive, where they swim down and let the current move them along while they take in all the sights. They tow a diver-down flag that floats on the surface. The boat above will always know where the diver is. This is a wonderful and stress-free way to dive. Even on deep-wreck dives, we can jump in the water up-current of the wreck and rapidly swim down, letting the current push us to the wreck. Once there, we make the dive by hiding in the lee, out of the current on the wreck. When we're done, we send up a submersible marker buoy (SMB), which is a long tubular balloon on a line, to let the boat up top know where we are. This works great and is common practice among experienced divers.

Our problem on *Britannic* is you are diving in the middle of an active shipping channel. There simply isn't enough room in the Kea Channel for large ships to maneuver around a drifting dive vessel trying to prevent its divers from getting chopped to pieces from the huge propellers of ships or ferries.

The Greek Coast Guard rule is that all diving operations on *Britannic* must be done while anchored. If the current is up to 2 knots, from top to bottom in 400 feet of water, the divers will be physically exhausted from trying to hold onto the line during the long 5-hour ascent. If divers lose their grip, they could never swim against the current and regain the line. In a 2-knot current (which equals 2.3 mph), they will drift 11.5 miles away from the wreck during a 5-hour decompression stop. Although we can have underwater decompression stations set up in a way to ease the need for divers to physically cling to the line, things can still go wrong. An emergency situation of a diver who has come loose and adrift would wreak havoc in the crowded shipping lanes, while the mothership would be anchored out of sight and over the horizon when the diver surfaces. These high-risk scenarios are why we try not to dive in anything over one knot on a moored dive.

Without getting into all the details involved in securing a permit for an expedition, you have to understand going in you *will* lose diving days. There's nothing wrong with having an ambitious plan of how many dives you hope to make and goals you hope to accomplish while diving, but you have to prioritize those goals and probably let some of them go if you run short of days, unless you are able to extend your time on the island. The groups of 1997 and 1998 laid the initial building blocks for later expeditions, and we've had the advantage of listening to them and reading their reports. Simon Mills always incorporates the lessons learned when he works with the new expedition leader to develop a dive plan. This not only adds to the safety of the expedition, but it also helps avoid duplicating previous work.

As Simon once explained, "I always give the divers as much information as possible about what to look for and where, and as each dive plan is based not only on the original Harland & Wolff technical drawings but also the *Britannic*'s own specification book, it probably makes the dive plan about as complete as it is possible to be. Keep in mind that although they are sister ships, *Britannic* is not the same as *Titanic*; if a dive team ever decides to work from a set of plans of *Titanic*, then they could miss something very important."

These aren't the only expeditions to have taken place. The great website Hospital Ship Britannic (*http://hmhsBritannic.weebly.com/*) by Michail Michailakis maintains a wealth of information he's gathered over the years and lists all known *Britannic* expeditions to date. In carrying on the theme of coming to *Britannic* through her sister ship, Michail "was captivated" by the story of *Titanic* when he watched the film *A Night to Remember* on television around 1984. He became interested in the subject but didn't extend the interest into research. In 1996, while studying pharmacy in Italy, he enjoyed spending time in bookstores and spotted the book *Titanic: An Illustrated History* by Don Lynch and Ken Marschall. One of Ken's paintings of the wreck of *Britannic* was in the last pages along with a brief note about her career and fate. That was the first time he became aware of *Britannic*'s story.

Soon after he "was quite shocked when I found that the wreck was located in my country and it was in such a good shape, when compared to *Titanic*." He began to actively look for more information about her and created the website in 2000 when he had collected a large amount of material to display.

CHAPTER 12

SETTING A NEW STANDARD

I T IS FITTING A MAN WHO was greatly inspired by Jacques Cousteau led the first team from the United Kingdom to physically dive on *Britannic* after the twenty-one-year gap from the 1976 Expedition. Kevin Gurr is not merely in a small tier of divers who push the known technological boundaries to enable deeper and longer dives, he is an innovator and adventurer as well.

Kevin didn't set out to be a pioneer. Instructions for his initial dives during a Mediterranean vacation essentially consisted of "Don't hold your breath," and "Be sure to clear your ears." It was an experience like no other, and Kevin spent the week in the newfound wonder of underwater. He soon joined the Andover Sub-Aqua Club (BSCS 942) to be officially certified. Diving all around the United Kingdom is similar to the New York/New Jersey area where I learned to dive on deep wrecks. The water is cold and dark often with strong currents and tricky tides. Underwater in the United Kingdom, however, are thousands of shipwrecks, many of them "virgin" as in having not been recorded as being dived and many more not being positively identified. There's an incredible thrill in going to a location where your only information is "something's down there," plunging into water where you lose all visibility within a few feet, and shining your underwater light through the murky gloom to see the wreckage of an unknown ship. It might be a hapless modern vessel overcome in a storm. Or it might be an impressive bronzed gunned man-of-war eighteenth-century French Napoleonic frigate.

Kevin is more than passionate about diving. He possesses a mind constantly thinking and creating, and as he states, "Scuba was somewhat 'frozen' in the 1970s and 1980s. We weren't trying to be the first in order to be the first, but we were able to make some quantum leaps in the 1990s."

This is a classic understatement. New gases and equipment used by military and commercial divers didn't exist outside of those closed communities. Kevin helped create today's "technical diving" for sport divers, and many of us have turned to him for instruction in either new equipment or techniques. There were plenty of skeptics about the use of mixed gases, and yes, there were injuries and fatalities when the envelope was stretched too far or people were careless. By Kevin's own admission, he's "not very insurable." Inventor, test diver, Spanish galleon hunter, cave diver, he has explored underwater around the globe to include the Arctic Circle. He heard about *Britannic* while diving and teaching in Greece with young Alexander Sotiriou. When he returned to England to discuss mounting an expedition, everyone understood they were about to embark on something historic. It would be the first expedition to *Britannic* to use diver propulsion vehicles (DPV), also called scooters. (Think of the scene in the James Bond movie *Thunderball*, when the bad guys came after Bond underwater.)

Although DPVs are commonplace now, they weren't widely available in 1997. The scooter carries a diver and camera/video equipment, and combined with the increased time they could remain underwater because of advanced mixed-gas technology, divers wouldn't be as limited as the Cousteau team in trying to cover the massive Olympian.

Another technological advantage over Cousteau's team was drysuits, which to a nondiver might seem inconsequential. It is, however, one of those crucial developments for allowing longer and deeper dives. While a drysuit rarely keeps a diver genuinely dry, it does block all but trickles of water from getting past the neck, wrist, and ankle seals during the series of in-water decompression stops of approximately six hours after a dive as deep as *Britannic*. (Yes, adult diapers are often a part of the ensemble, and there is a "relief valve" as part of the design.)

When added up, hundreds of details had to be planned in the almost two years it took to obtain the proper permits for the expedition. While narrowing the team to fourteen members, preparation accelerated for the 1997 International Association of Nitrox and Technical Divers (IANTD) *Britannic* Expedition. Aside from Kea Island's logistical limitations, equally critical is that medical care on the island is not robust. A physician team member was important. (*See Appendix B: Members of Selected Expeditions.*)

Kevin's book provides a detailed account of the technical workings of the expedition, even though he didn't get into all of their problems, such as the Greek official initially not allowing their loaded cargo truck to leave the main port or having a piece of equipment explode in the area they used to fill tanks. (Remember Given #3 about expeditions to Kea Island: Problems ranging from minor irritation to a full-blown crisis will occur.)

The initial mission statement, "To video and survey HMHS *Britannic*, lost in 120 metres of water off Greece in World War I," was refined into a mission plan that partly stated, "We want to explore as much as possible and especially the blast area." Since this expedition was to use in-water decompression stops and there were several unknowns as to how the divers' bodies would respond to the actual dive conditions, as much as everyone wanted to achieve specific goals, safety was foremost. The diving philosophy reflected part of that plan.

"We have ten bottom divers and two permanent standby divers," Kevin wrote. "When you are not diving on the wreck, you are surface cover only. We could have seven to ten days of diving. I currently propose we have a shift system of 'one day on' and 'one day off' in two teams of five. This is a decision based around safety and the need to film/explore. The team format will be: scooter camera, scooter tender, main diver camera, diver camera tender, free-swimming diver. Obviously the scooters will stay together, and the three non-scooter divers will also act as a team. Aside from the two standby divers, there will be a midwater cameraman who can assist as required. I suggest we leave this for now as it will probably change from day to day for a variety of reasons and can be amended within these safe parameters on-site."

As the expedition developed, they discovered the decompression times and system setup were effective, and some divers were able to dive consecutive days. Everyone meticulously logged their dive data and recorded exactly how long and at what depths they dived. They used Doppler after the dives, which is a technique similar to the way a sonogram sees a baby in the womb. For this purpose, Doppler is used to specifically quantify the amount of bubbles in your heart and see if there are bubbles in your blood as potential signs for decompression sickness. Yes, the physician on the team would have responded to a problem, but the idea was to prevent dive-related accidents, not treat them.

One special aspect of the 1997 Expedition was devoted as a tribute to Cousteau and his team. Kevin had contacted the Cousteau family and offered to take something commemorative down to the wreck. Everyone admired the bronze plaque custom-made for the purpose, and no one gave much thought to the weight of around fifty-six pounds. Or at least no one did until it came time to work out where and how to affix the plaque. With divers' gear weighing in at approximately 200 pounds when they went into water, the addition of an extra 56 pounds became an issue. The scooters were not designed for this either, and you can't simply drop a plaque in the vicinity of the ship and hope to find it later in 400 feet of water.

Kevin's solution was not what most people should attempt. After he was geared up, they literally strapped the plaque to him. The plan was for his dive partner to "splash in" immediately behind him, although Kevin would be descending at a faster rate. There wouldn't be too much of a lapse between them, then his buddy would cut the plaque away, and they would proceed to mount it.

The first part of the plan went smoothly. However, when Kevin was on the bottom alone, unable to free himself without assistance, the idea seemed less brilliant. For some reason, his partner had not heard the "go signal" and was slightly delayed with his entrance into the water. Kevin wasn't getting nervous, but he was relieved when his partner settled next to him to cut the plaque loose. That, though, wasn't the only glitch. They naturally took video of the tribute in its new place and had taken video and still shots at different spots on the island — holding the plaque up to catch the light, include a nice backdrop behind it, etc. Having successfully secured the plaque in its underwater home, they were stunned to be approached by the local police the next day. In carrying the plaque around, someone took it to mean the divers had *removed* an artifact from the wreck — an act prohibited by the Greek authorities.

They managed to communicate they had taken the plaque down to the wreck and had video to prove it. This seemed to be a reasonable response until a suspicious policeman inquired, "How do we know this? Perhaps you are playing the video in reverse to trick us?"

The question took some time to resolve between the misconception and language barrier, and it was not to be the last time police questioned events of a *Britannic* expedition.

Two uncontrollable factors of weather and water conditions hampered the expedition divers, but despite losing a number of days for operations, they completed twenty-six manned dives and logged new underwater video. One of their significant discoveries was to pinpoint the precise impact site on the wreck. The military had agreed to supply side-scan sonar and sub-bottom profiling equipment. In conducting an extensive exterior survey, they found a chunk of wreckage and indications of mine emplacement a little north of the ship. Neither Cousteau nor Ballard had been able to capture this data, and it strengthened the view *Britannic* did strike an undersea mine.

Even though the primary purpose was exploration of *Britannic*, the team also logged important physiological data for future analysis in the field of dive medicine. Mathematical calculations and computer modeling about the effects of deep diving are important, but measurable human reaction is a component for which there is no real substitute. To the diving world, however, it was a momentous event because it clearly demonstrated a group of "regular" guys could mount a successful expedition without the level of financial backing of someone like Cousteau or the heavy technological edge of the Ballard Expedition. As a quick note, the term "regular guys" refers only to the fact they weren't military or commercial divers. Every single member of the team was highly experienced and skilled, many working in the dive profession. You did not then and do not ever take "beginners" to *Britannic*.

Some of the video footage was later used in the documentary *Inside the Britannic,* and several articles were published.

Kevin, in his quiet manner, once said, "We were surprised with the interest afterward. We didn't intend for it to be a big deal — I just wanted to see it."

As amazing as it had been for Kevin when he first saw the shape of *Britannic* below him, the later opportunity to descend onto *Titanic* in a submersible placed him in the category of only four men in the world who, as of the writing of this book, have been on *Titanic* in a submersible and physically diving on *Britannic.*

Although I knew Kevin by reputation, I didn't meet him until 2005 while we were shooting an episode for *Deep Sea Detectives* on the wreck of *Flying Enterprise.* The connection to Kevin partly came about through my friendship and business relationship with Leigh Bishop, who had told me about their 1998 Expedition.

CHAPTER 13

THE FIRST TRY WITH A REBREATHER

I T ISN'T OFTEN THE FIRST TIME you dive with someone, he's wearing a cast, and that alone says something about Leigh Bishop. It was 1999 on a U-boat search expedition in the English Channel organized for fun by a guy named Innes McCartney. Leigh showed up with a broken arm (in a wrist cast) and wore a string of lifting bags across his chest like a Mexican bandit's bandolier. One of the companies he worked with manufactured drysuits and created this unusual get-up to allow him to dive without ruining the cast.

I liked him immediately, and he reminded me of an English version of my friends in the Atlantic Wreck Divers group. He loved to talk about artifacts and virgin shipwrecks, even though I don't think he was as big a fan of diving U-boat wrecks as I was. We stayed in touch by email as we had common friends and plans. He urged me in 2002 to get on with what was then the still early stage of closed-circuit rebreather (CCR) technology, which was an adaptation of something the military had been using for a while. I wasn't ready for it, and he warned me that if I didn't make the transition, wreck diving would leave me behind. At the time, I didn't realize how right he was or how radically things were going to change for me.

Divers always talk about special dives, and Leigh had been with the Starfish Enterprise team on the 1998 *Britannic* Expedition when fellow shadow diver John Chatterton broke the barrier of using a rebreather on the wreck. Starfish was the diving group Leigh joined after he fulfilled two of three of his life's ambitions early on. He'd become a fireman in 1989, and even though he can't pinpoint the exact time in the 1970s when he set underwater exploration as one of his goals, he always knew it was something he wanted to do. Casual recreational diving while vacationing in warm waters wasn't what he had in mind — not with tens of thousands of shipwrecks surrounding the United Kingdom and people using mixed gases to extend dive depth and duration. Kevin had taught most of the Starfish Enterprise dive group about technical diving, and Leigh echoed similar thoughts as Kevin.

"We weren't doing what we did to make headlines — we just wanted to dive all these amazing wrecks."

And dive they did. Seeking out virgin shipwrecks in the English Channel was a favorite past time, and as Starfish Enterprise divers pushed a number of envelopes with mixed-gas diving and later CCRs, they looked to a significant challenge. The mighty *Lusitania*, the Cunard luxury liner that had spurred creation of White Star's Olympic liners, had been located in 1935 in the Celtic Sea at a depth of approximately 305 feet. The diving world was intrigued to see how "amateur" divers would fare, and their successful expedition demonstrated another clear advancement in technical diving for those willing to devote the time and money to be properly equipped and trained.

And in diving famous World War I shipwrecks, what could be more enticing than the largest ship sunk — HMHS *Britannic* — with the mysteries surrounding her? During the process of finding out how to get a permit for the dive, Starfish members discovered they were on the same quest as Kevin's group. In discussing the complexities of putting together an expedition, the Starfish divers decided to use 1997 for preparation and take the opportunity to learn from the experiences of Kevin and his team.

As assignments to team members were reviewed and handed out, Leigh would take photographs, a task involving an intriguing issue. Underwater camera technology tried to keep up with what new depths divers achieved. The increased pressure at increased depth was the essential problem.

There's no real difference in what camera is used; it's the housing the camera fits into. The housing is specially designed to protect the camera against the worst and most common problem of flooding. This is when the integrity of the housing or its sealing system is compromised and water enters. The best case is a small slow leak detected before the camera is a total loss. The accepted procedure is to turn the housing face down, return to the surface, remove the camera and batteries, and pray. If you're much below sixty feet deep, you can't return quickly to the surface because of the safety issue. The other common problem involves an operational camera failure. Mechanical controls on the housing must be properly designed to function at extreme depths. If springs are not strong enough, buttons will not return or may even "press themselves." Housings may actually deform or warp under extreme pressure, causing controls to jam or not function properly. Electronic controls can have similar spring problems as well as certain normal problems associated with designing electronics for a saltwater environment. You can have corrosion, shorting out, and poor connectivity. The human element also comes into play if the batteries haven't been fully charged or installed properly. As if those weren't enough things to consider, even if everything is perfect with the housing and camera, your video lights might fail for many of the same reasons.

As a total novice when it came to underwater photography, Leigh spoke with enough experts to realize the best they could come up with was a camera and housing designed to shoot safely at around 180 feet. It was less than half the distance they would be diving to, but why not give it a try? After all, the 1997 team had captured plenty of video.

Two major lessons were taken from the 1997 team: The weather was likely to be better in September, and to use a popular phrase, they really did "need a bigger boat." The thirty-three-footer accompanied by a smaller rigid inflatable boat (RIB) had been barely big enough to fit the requirements of the 1997 group. Team leader Nick Hope assembled a team of sixteen men and four women, having more of an international flair this time with the addition of four Americans and a Canadian. (*See Appendix B: Members of Selected Expeditions.*) They engaged a caïque with an RIB as had the 1997 team, but the main vessel was *Atlas*, a tugboat provided by Tsavliris Maritime. (A caïque is a small boat used throughout the islands for fishing, carrying goods, and tourist or family transportation.)

Logistics for staying on and working from Kea Island hadn't improved though, and Leigh and one other team member accepted the task of driving a truck crammed with equipment from England. Leigh remembers it as "a sporty four-day drive with a few wrong turns along the way."

As with the 1997 Expedition, DPVs, their scooters, would allow them to cover much more of the wreck than by swimming. They had the advantage of an ROV as well. If the divers weren't able to be in the water for some of the days, conditions may allow at least use of the ROV. With only two weeks allocated, they wanted to minimize lost time.

In the years Starfish Enterprise group had been making dives other people viewed as too risky, they experimented with different ways to improve the ability to manage long decompression stops underwater on a floating station rigged with short lines to allow divers to "rest" while decompressing. They modified their usual arrangement for this expedition, and it fit nicely into the RIB. They were able to easily place the station into the water and recover it each day after the last divers surfaced.

The excitement of diving *Britannic* had been pricked a bit when they were told no interior penetration would be allowed. What? A ship with all these questions still to be answered and they weren't going to be able to venture inside where they might be able to solve the mystery of her rapid sinking? Shipwreck owner Simon had taken the concern to heart about bubbles created by divers potentially damaging the anaerobic condition of certain areas and accelerating deterioration of the wreck. Newly developed closed-circuit rebreathers that resembled a large backpack produced few bubbles. This feature reduced the likelihood of bubbles stirring up the silt or dislodging any debris from overhead and seemed to be a good solution.

Rebreathers were definitely leading-edge technology. John Chatterton, equipped with one, wasn't about to give up on the goal of trying to locate a way into Boiler Room 6 to see if the watertight door between Boiler Rooms 6 and 5 was open or closed. On the morning of the attack on *Britannic*, it had been reported as not properly closed, but the team looked for verification.

Despite the thrilling adventures they had all experienced on other explorations, *Britannic* was an extraordinary wreck.

"The sheer size struck us all," Leigh recalled. "It's hard to describe, but it's like looking at a block of flats. Even without the story about her, the size would do it."

When you picture a ship almost the length of three football fields laid end-to-end, you can appreciate the sensation. He didn't know the first day's great visibility would be the best he would ever have, but he absorbed all he could see as he landed on the bridge.

The day they used the scooters to circumnavigate the ship topped his list of great dives and helped build the store of valuable video footage.

The weather wasn't perfect every day, and equipment failures were inevitable. The team worked well together, finding solutions when problems arose. If you weren't in the water, you filled tanks and took care of other important topside tasks to be ready for the next excursion into the deep. Collectively, they were able to complete seventy-eight dives, most for at least twenty-five minutes. There were major finds and smaller ones, all adding pieces to the puzzle of *Britannic*. Simon had asked them to check on the color of the tiles covering the floor of the bridge. How had they held up over the years under those conditions? Whatever luxury custom tiles had been ordered had apparently either not been received or not installed because when the team looked closely at what was left, they found red-and-white linoleum.

The search to find the letters *Britannic* on the side of the ship was to no avail with the thick layer of encrustation along the bow. Marine creatures and underwater plants had been spreading out for six decades and obscured large segments of the surfaces.

One of the major finds came with John and his Aura CCR 2000 rebreather. The CCR was a prototype but also the only model he could get.

As he recalls, "I made a total of six dives with the CCR 2000 on *Britannic*. The CCR 2000 worked surface-to-surface on three of those dives and had catastrophic failures [on] the other three. The electronics caught fire in my hotel room while recharging one night. Rebreathers were an adventure in those days.

I was dedicated to the rebreather and did not make any OC [open-circuit] dives on *Britannic*. Going back to OC would have been admitting defeat.

"My first dive was tying the shot into the wreck after the first mooring pulled out, before we even started the expedition diving. The mooring coming loose was unexpected, and no one else on the boat had all their gear. It was my first *Britannic* dive, it was a working dive, the rebreather worked fine, and I had the wreck all to myself. They put Rob Royal in the water as a safety diver, and everyone, including me, was somewhat unsure how well it was going to work."

With the initial dive successful, John remembers one of the big events. "The Fireman's Tunnel [sic] was one of the things on our group's list to locate or explore. I located the entrance to the tunnel in the break and thought it was tight. The CCR 2000 was physically a big rebreather and not very well suited for the tunnel, so I left my open-circuit bailout outside. I got to the end of the tunnel and the entrance to Boiler Room 6. It had taken a while to navigate the tunnel, and it was tight, but I stopped to check everything before venturing further.

"I looked at my controller screen, and it was completely blank. Dead. The CCR 2000 ran everything from the computer controller. Not a bad concept, but at that time reliability was in short supply. When it failed, you had no information on PPO$_2$, gas supply, depth, bottom time, or decompression. In addition, there was no O$_2$ being automatically added to the counterlung. I was in the dark, both figuratively and literally. So I turned around and exited about as fast as possible and eventually bailed to open circuit. I did not have the opportunity to go back. After *Britannic*, I never dived the CCR 2000 again. For me, the diving I did with the Starfish Enterprise group was an amazing experience. They were very well organized and had a real sense of accomplishing things as a group. It was that environment that allowed experiments like rebreather diving."

The disappointment of not being able to do much penetration was offset by locating the firemen's tunnel leading deep into the ship to the boiler room watertight doors. The danger of John's CCR malfunction had kept him from proceeding, but now between Simon's research and the team's exploration, they knew the access location. More important, CCR technology had been used, and it would be the key to future expeditions. New and better CCR models were being produced, and proponents confidently knew they were the way of the future. Another major milestone for the 1998 Expedition was not only including the first woman to dive *Britannic*, but she also set a new record for depth for women in the process.

Once again, the diving world clamored for information about how this amateur group had been so successful with such a complex venture. While most of the team members were amateur only because they weren't in the dive profession, their pioneering experiences in the technical diving realm qualified them to be selected for the expedition. They were unquestionably in the top tier of what was still a small percentage of divers. Publicity followed them, to include a documentary film, *Titanic's Sister: HMHS Britannic*, produced by Periscope Publishing, Ltd.

Leigh was invited by several dive clubs to talk about his experience and the leading role he was playing in technical diving. Inspired with his initial attempts at underwater photography, he became highly skilled. His impressive body of work has been published in numerous magazines and books since then, as have many of his articles.

Going back to those early lectures, a young man approached him one evening from among the lingering crowd after the initial question-and-answer period. Carl Spencer was eager to know more and wanted to understand the level of preparation needed to face the challenges of *Britannic*.

CHAPTER 14

TECHNOLOGY AND PASSION EDGES TOWARD THE TRUTH

A LL OF US WHO HEARD CARL SPENCER introduce himself as "just a plumber from Staffordshire" would at least chuckle inwardly or exchange comical glances with each other if we could get away with it. Not that he wasn't a plumber, and no doubt a good one. Finding yourself on an expedition to *Britannic* with Carl was just one of many adventures a person could count. Before getting to *Britannic*, it's time for a science detour to explain the important technological leap of closed-circuit rebreathers (CCR).

When the edict was issued to permit only CCR divers to penetrate *Britannic*, I hadn't made the conversion from the elaborate and weighty rigging of my technical diving setup allowing me to carry all the gas I needed to make a dive, leaving nothing to chance. Yes, extra tanks were waiting on the anchor line, under the boat, or even on the dive boat itself, but as the saying goes, "shit happens," and those may not be there when I needed it. I couldn't count on it when planning my dive. That 200-plus pounds I had attached to my body was what I depended on.

Eventually my open-circuit trimix dives hit a wall, as I was limited by how much gas I could carry and the risk I was willing to assume. On deep open-circuit dives, some believed a buddy could be more of a liability than a benefit when the gas you're carrying is already in the margins. Back then, most of the time I chose to dive alone, and if someone did have a gas problem, we simply didn't carry enough gas for two. Comfortable in my gas management, it's a risk I was willing to assume. But by pushing that line, something really bad was going to happen.

I was jumped twice by out-of-air divers on *Andrea Doria* expeditions. The first time it happened, I was blindsided and nearly drowned, never seeing it coming. The second instance, I saw the diver coming at me, hand slashing across his throat to indicate he was out of air and needed some from me. Despite my offer of a backup regulator, I was bowled over, and he yanked the one out of my mouth. In both cases, emergency gas was dropped over the side of the dive boat and both out-of-air divers only suffered bruised egos and some pissed-off people who had to respond to their near panic. Both incidents occurred at twenty feet under the boat during the decompression phase of the dive. If absolutely necessary, I could have risked early surfacing in those cases, but I was beginning to see it was only a matter of time before someone had a major gas issue at depth. If either of those situations had occurred at eighty feet or lower, the odds are one or both of us would have died.

That cold reality finally hit on a 280-foot dive after having just located the German U-boat *U-215* on the Georges Banks 150 miles off Shelburne, Nova Scotia. It was a fantastic dive, everything had gone well during the bottom phase of the dive, and I was elated; then I noticed the other two members of my team were buddy breathing on the ascent (passing a single regulator back and forth between them to share gas). The tide had turned, roaring, and it was everything we could do to hold on to the down/ascent line. A pea soup fog had come in, and our planned drift deco had been flagged off without our knowing. Our *one* support/safety diver had a problem (with his then new-fangled CCR), and he was unable to even get in the water at all. (Note to self: All future support divers are *to use only OC scuba tanks,* never CCR.) The drama unfolding with the gas management issue below was completely unknown to anyone topside.

The boat captain was more concerned with the fog and possibility of losing his divers at sea, so no one was sent in the water to break the line free for our drift decompression or even check on us. When it rains it pours. Splitting one cylinder of deep decompression gas, the pair having problems barely eked out a marginal profile and surfaced a little pale, but no lasting harm was done. When I surfaced, every gauge I had was in the red, and had I been asked for gas, I had none to give. The ripping current had forced me to work harder than planned and exacted a toll on my gas supply, taking my safety margin of gas to the red line. That's as close to the line as I ever want to be. Something had to change in my planning and execution for these types of deep dives. Was a closed-circuit rebreather the way to go?

Rebreathers were not actually new technology because they'd been used by the military and science researchers for decades. They appeared complex and cost thousands of dollars, which was the downside. The upside is the one box on your back replaced multiple tanks and regulators (literally hundreds of pounds and thousands of dollars in additional equipment) and would keep you alive underwater for up to twelve hours with just two little tanks. As an added bonus, the gas filling costs for oxygen and helium would significantly decrease. What's the magic in the box?

With each breath we take in, our lungs only use a small portion of the oxygen, exhaling most of it back out with each exhausted breath; those are an OC scuba diver's bubbles in the water. With a rebreather, we capture that exhaled breath (no bubbles), bring it around in a loop, removing or scrubbing out the carbon dioxide, and then rebreathe it again. As the oxygen is used up, we add a tiny bit more oxygen to replace it. Three small sensors or cells measure the amount of oxygen in the loop to ensure we have the right amount, which is called the set point. By doing this, the diver can have the best possible mixture of oxygen with every breath and at every depth, making dives longer and decompression time shorter.

Bringing down the cost of CCR was a goal of manufacturers in addition to demonstrating to the scuba world you didn't have to be a Navy SEAL to master one. In 1996, my dive partner, John Chatterton, was willing to test emerging equipment. He used various experimental and homemade rebreathers, and the outcomes were not always good. For me, at that time, the technology had not yet arrived. My disturbing experience in Nova Scotia was closely followed by dozens of deep and exciting dives while working on the television program *Deep Sea Detectives*, and I began to rethink my attitude about CCR. As a member of a four-man team, I was the only OC cog in the machine as the others were all diving the Inspiration model of rebreathers. Over a period of three years, we dived in a variety of conditions, some remote. There were absolutely no failures of the rebreathers. The advantages of diving CCR became evident to me, especially when on some of the deeper dives. With motivation to reexamine CCRs and the advent of Ambient Pressure Diving's Evolution rebreather, I became a convert. In time, I was so impressed with the new technology and all its advantages, I felt compelled to work to become an instructor. I love the ability this technology gives me, but this ability comes with a cost.

I often use a parallel with my students between flying a plane and diving a rebreather. The reality is both activities are dependent on machinery, and the outcome is almost totally in your hands. Our life support is dependent on the rebreather being properly maintained, but rebreathers do not have the regulatory control established for aircraft. Planes cannot fly unless they have at least minimum regular maintenance and inspections. The final preflight inspection is done by the person who will fly the aircraft, and this is guided by specific checklists, as are other phases of flight. The diver strapping on a rebreather is in a similar position. Human beings will make mistakes and have memory lapses. Complacency can settle in over time because the technology does work. On a rebreather, you are the pilot and ground crew, taking your life literally into your own hands. The CCR checklist is our primary defense against something going wrong and if something does, being prepared for it. Even if you always follow the checklist, you cannot guarantee the unit won't fail. Any machine or system can break.

There is a very specific order to follow on the checklist. You need to assemble your CCR in a particular fashion. You need to analyze and correctly label gases so there is no mistake, and you need to confirm your scrubber material (which absorbs the carbon dioxide) is adequate and good for the planned dive. Give yourself plenty of time during assembly, and check everything. Accept zero failure.

After powering up the assembled unit, you need to confirm the oxygen cells are working, the electronics are within parameters, and everything is ready for diving. Only after full satisfaction of the checklist are you ready to do the predive sequence and dive the unit on the surface. You should prebreathe a rig for a minimum of five minutes. You make sure your scrubber material and cells are reacting, the gases are flowing, and appropriate levels are being held. Your primary defense is the right checklist completed correctly.

Failure to do everything right makes failure inevitable; it is simply a matter of when it happens. You have to be willing to commit this level of attention and responsibility if you want the added benefit of diving a rebreather. We prepare and train for equipment failure. We have a great advantage over pilots who cannot jump into another airplane mid-flight. We can carry bailout systems and use them to swap from the rebreather back to the OC tanks we carry under our arms.

Getting back to that parallel between diving and flying an aircraft, the first time I sat in the cockpit of a helicopter, it occurred to me there were many similarities to rebreather diving. As a helicopter pilot, I have the cyclic in one hand, the collective in the other, and both feet on the pedals. A lot of input is required for controlled flight in three-dimensional space. Rebreathers have a much higher level of complexity in contrast with OC scuba systems. A very smart person once said the most dangerous thing you will ever do is manipulate your own breathing medium, and this is what you are doing on a rebreather. It is your obligation to ensure you are constantly on the stick because, as in flying a helicopter, there is no autopilot. You need to constantly monitor the rig. Let it get away from you, and it will kill you.

Over the past few years, I have lost friends, each of whom planned to have a good dive but in the end they didn't come home, and each died while diving a rebreather. Some died very shallow, some died very deep. They were not fools, but they made foolish mistakes. Each experienced one or more events that can be described as a failure: incomplete use of a checklist, failure to turn on oxygen, jumping back into the water and never realizing the oxygen was turned off, failure to properly analyze and label gases, failure to change scrubber, or failure to monitor the oxygen levels. These divers were just like a pilot flying a working aircraft directly into the ground. It's important to remember these divers were smart, but they made mistakes. As heartbreaking as it is to lose friends, we should not fail to learn from their mistakes. It isn't so much failure is not an option — it's failure in these situations can kill you.

When I met Carl Spencer in September 2005, I found out he, like Leigh Bishop and Kevin Gurr, was an expert in the CCR technology world. We were on a shoot in Brighton, England, for the *Deep Sea Detectives* episode about *Duke of Buccleauch* that sank in 1889 while en route to India. She was transporting china and glassware. Her sinking was a result of a tragic collision with *Vandalia* striking her amidships. All forty-seven of her crew perished, and the captain of *Vandalia* had gone on record as blaming *Duke* for the accident. This segment for the show was after the reunion with Leigh where we'd been on *Flying Enterprise* a few days earlier, and I'd met Kevin who had given me some mentoring with my first deep CCR dive. It was a long drive from Salcombe to Brighton for the next shoot and round of diving.

After the drive, we met at our hotel on the beach in Brighton. It was a typical English rundown seaside resort area for working-class folks. The elevator (or lift as they say in England) was too small for two people plus luggage (physically and by weight limit). We had traveled all day and didn't realize trying to move all the gear and luggage to our rooms would cause the elevator to jam, or maybe we actually broke it. In either case, hauling everything up narrow flights of stairs was not fun. We also discovered the hotel had communal showers and bathrooms down the hall, which goes to show being involved with television production doesn't always equate to traveling first class.

After finally dropping our bags, my wife, Carrie, and I were in the pub adjacent to the hotel with most of the crew before going to dinner. Leigh, who had not traveled with us, walked in with two guys, one very thin and rawboned but with piercing eyes (Mark Bullen) and another with a softer face but with Boy Scout good looks (Carl Spencer). He was very enthusiastic, and after Leigh made the introductions, I went to the bar to order another round. When Carl said "Diet Coke," I recall saying something I regretted later on. (I found out he wasn't a drinker for a reason.) We all drank and chatted. Mark had brought some of the crockery he had recovered from the wreck on a previous dive to show the team what type of cargo had been on the vessel, and as we ogled it, Mark graciously gave a few pieces to my wife.

I noticed Carl didn't really care for the "bits." He wasn't an artifact guy like Leigh or me, but he loved the big picture and loved to shoot video. He was happy to be doing some of the underwater camera work the next day. I recall how excited he was about our dives/work on *Titanic*, and in the self-effacing way I was to come to know him for, he spoke a little about his work with James Cameron and his passion for the Olympians. (None of us knew almost exactly a year later we would all be diving *Britannic* together.) We were one of a small club right there — Carl, Leigh, and me. Carl didn't make a super impression on me that night (either way) or even on the dive the next day, which was another typical working shoot where things went wrong, as often happens, and there was a level of frustration we all worked through. Despite the aggravation, the first day of diving and shooting went well. Mark was familiar with *Duke of Buccleauch*, and of the hundreds of wrecks Leigh has been on, *Duke* is his favorite.

We followed them and filmed the piles of crockery that were part of the story. The people who originally found the wreck thought they'd hit it big by finding a ship filled with 1800s "Flow Blue" China, but it was actually all seconds going to Australia! The name of the china comes from the blue glaze that was blurred or "flowed" during the firing process, and it's prized by collectors. The seconds have no significant monetary value.

The next day brought us trouble. First, Kevin's suit flooded during the dive, and he had to bail out on John, so John took the camera to film with Leigh and Carl. Evan Kovacs, part of our crew, filmed me, with Mark doing the lighting for him, and then Evan had a major malfunction with his CCR. All three oxygen cells gave a different reading, one good or normal, one way too high, and one way too low. Evan had no choice but to bail out to OC diving, and since we were all on full-face masks with built-in communications to the support ship, I called topside and said, "We have a diver in trouble doing an emergency ascent on open circuit."

I shot a marker buoy to let them know where he would be when he surfaced, and then handed the line attached to the marker to Mark asking him to go with Evan and "take care of my friend."

I swam to find Carl, Leigh, and John, and we worked together to film the break in the hull where amazingly the wooden sailing ship had hit and sank the steel steamship. It was my first dive with Carl, and even though it was uneventful from there, I was anxious about Evan. Fortunately, everything was fine, and after the dive, we had to do some interviews with the locals, and Carl volunteered to take my wife sightseeing while we worked. She liked him immediately, and they became good buddies. We all parted as friends, and it wasn't until later I learned about the successes of the 2003 dive team Carl had led to *Britannic*.

CHAPTER 15

ENTERING THE FIREMEN'S TUNNEL

As MUCH AS WE HAD ENJOYED our time in England, I didn't give much thought to Carl Spencer right away. I learned about some of his unusual dives and explorations after our initial meeting, since he wasn't a guy who bragged about his adventures, such as being 400 miles above the Arctic Circle, accompanied by two British Navy minesweepers, looking for the lost World War II midget submarine *X5*. I also learned a truly unique fact about him as it related to the Olympians.

In our discussion about the thrill of seeing *Titanic* in a submersible and briefly discussing *Britannic*, he mentioned visiting the White Swan Hotel in Alnwick, Northumberland. Of the three Olympic-class ocean liners, only *Olympic* was in use for the full life of the ship. She was finally retired from passenger service in 1935 and scrapped in 1937, ending the chapter of White Star's greatest ocean liners. However, the luxury of the fittings and artwork had not diminished, and many of them were auctioned before the ship was dismantled. The owner of the White Swan bought numerous elements, such as the revolving door to *Olympic*'s restaurant, and incorporated the items into the hotel in all their grandeur.

In 2007, Carl was on the wreck of *Carpathia*, the only ship that had taken survivors from *Titanic*. All these experiences mean, at the time of writing this book, the exact number of divers who have been on *Titanic* in a submersible, physically dived on *Carpathia* and *Britannic*, and dined in the Olympic Suite at the White Swan is exactly one — Carl Spencer.

It was 2003 when National Geographic and Channel 5 jointly financed a new expedition where Carlton International (a UK company) would produce a documentary for television. Carl put together the dive team and had spent a lot of time talking with Kevin and, of course, Leigh. This would be Carl's first time on *Britannic* and Leigh's second, and they worked out an ambitious dive plan with Simon. Of the other 2003 team members I was to later dive or work with, Richie Stevenson, Edoardo Pavia, and Canadian scientist Lori Johnston were included. Richie taught Carl about rebreathers, and the instructor/student relationship quickly became friendship.

Aside from his credentials such as diving *Carpathia*, Richie Stevenson owned *The Loyal Watcher*, a vessel large enough to accommodate their needs as a support boat. Carl was aware of the effort it took to get equipment by truck to Kea, and he came up with one of the significant "firsts" of the expedition when he asked Richie to bring *The Loyal Watcher* from Plymouth, England, fully loaded. By doing so, they avoided the need for international truck transportation or a local large boat. Unlike in 1997 and 1998, every member of the dive team was equipped with closed-circuit rebreathers. Since all the members would be allowed to penetrate into the ship, the different assignments could be spread among the entire dive team.

Another first was planning to have divers deploy selected science experiments. Narration of film footage of *Titanic* often discusses the growth of rusticles that seem to be eating away at the mighty ship. Scientists have been observing these and other deterioration factors since the early 1990s. Even though the rusticles bring to mind small stalactites, they are actually fragile and crush easily in a fog of powdery, reddish material. In limited scientific terms, the complex chemistry involves the growth of various microbes. The rusticles "mine" the ship's steel for its iron content and are advancing biodeterioration of the wreck. Four specially designed test platforms with different types of marine steel were placed onto the ship in 1998, and as theorized, rusticles are forming on the platforms. The platforms can be recovered in order to study this phenomenon.

Carl thought there would be a special interest in what scientists would find on sister ships sunk only four years apart, in completely opposite underwater environments — *Titanic* at 12,500 feet in the North Atlantic Ocean, more than thirty-one times the depth of *Britannic* in the warmer water of the Aegean Sea. He contacted Droycon Bioconcepts, Inc. (DBI) as they had extensive experience with corrosion and biological material. DBI scientist Lori Johnston explained that although there hadn't been much time to build test platforms, DBI pulled together equipment to conduct short- and long-term experiments on-site on the wreck.

Since this would be the first time anyone examined the biological aspect of *Britannic*, the information would be critical for comparative study. Most experiments were to be deployed at the beginning of the expedition, since this would give enough time for the short-term experiments to be brought back up during the final dives (seven to fourteen days). Long-term experiments would

U.S. Navy submarine *NR-1* on the surface during Bob Ballard's 1995 *Britannic* Expedition

Jacques-Yves Cousteau, father of modern scuba diving, found *Britannic* in 1975.

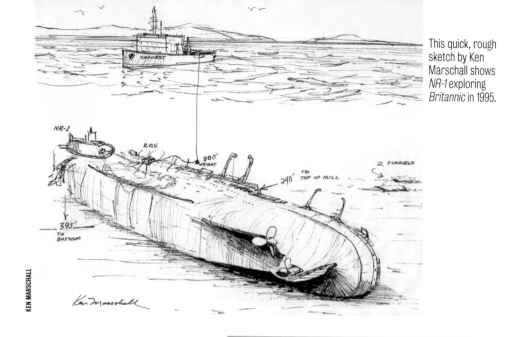

This quick, rough sketch by Ken Marschall shows *NR-1* exploring *Britannic* in 1995.

The 1998 Expedition, led by Kevin Gurr (*far left*), used this Greek caïque (*below*), which was nearly overloaded with equipment (*left*).

When *Britannic* sank, the forward section cracked open upon striking the seafloor. Otherwise the ship is incredibly intact.

Below, left: The 2006 team converted a large fishing boat into a dive and camera platform for the History Channel film project.

Below: Evan Kovacs prepares to dive *Britannic* in 2006. Note the full-face mask, bailout tanks, and the 3-D Bumblebee camera in the background.

Carl Spencer, 2009 project leader, displays the experiment and collection devices that were to be deployed on *Britannic*.

Opposite: Carl Spencer prepares his rebreather for the dive to *Britannic*.

Below: Spencer gathered his dream team for the 2009 *Britannic* Expedition and based it aboard the Belgian salvage vessel *Cdt Fourcault*.

RICHIE KOHLER

This aerial view shows the 2009 dive operations in the Kea Channel. You can see the divers on the deco station and the island of Kea on the horizon.

LEIGH BISHOP

Evan Kovacs films Carl Spencer with the Bumblebee as Spencer is about to enter the wreck. Within the hour, Spencer would be struggling for his life.

be left in place to be retrieved on future expeditions. Rusticle samples retrieved would be examined and tested onshore and/or sent back to the laboratory. The samples deteriorate very quickly when removed from their natural environment, so examination had to occur within the first twenty-four to forty-eight hours to capitalize on all available information. Onshore examination would include microscopy work and determination of types of bacteria and populations from specific areas and specific sample types. Samples shipped back to the lab would provide different, although still valuable information. Lori, not trained to dive CCR, was in charge of telling team members where to place the test platforms and handling the experiments as well as sending samples to the lab.

Despite everyone's intense and thorough preparation in putting together the expedition, Given #3 applied: Problems ranging from minor irritation to a full-blown crisis will occur. With the two weeks allotted in their permit, Mother Nature whipped up some stormy weather, and a few other unanticipated problems caused them to lose more precious dive days.

Dives did commence, and Leigh chronicled many of the details in a 2004 article for *DIVER Magazine*. As amazed as the divers were with the colossal wreck, the sonar team was equipped with high-quality sonar equipment. They had been given the objective to look for proof of the underwater minefield Gustav Siess claimed had been the demise of *Britannic*. Part of Simon Mills's extensive research included finding contemporary German plans of the mine barriers, and he provided information to the sonar team to carry out their search. They homed in on the correct area where they did find mines — mines located in the direction *Britannic* would have passed through. These findings were more specific than the initial 1998 data. (Additional video imagery in the area carried out in August 2008 with the Hellenic Centre for Marine Research would later confirm some of the objects first detected in the 2003 scans were indeed mine fragments.)

Getting to the boiler rooms was a high priority, and years later Richie Stevenson good-naturedly said he'd been given the assignment to enter through the firemen's tunnel either because he was the only one with cave-diving experience or because he wasn't present at the meeting when tasks were discussed.

"The tunnel was close to the break where Leigh told me it would be," Richie said.

Darkness, silt that rained down with his movement, and broken pipes waiting to snag his gear awaited him in the same area where John Chatterton had encountered his CCR failure in 1998. Richie took a reel in and ran it as far forward as he could. He went through three doorways, including the one into the first boiler room (Boiler Room 6), and tied off the line, providing a guide for him coming back out and a point of reference for future divers to follow. He filmed as he made his exit and did not encounter closed doors located in the bulkheads.

The doors were open? Witness testimony in 1916 had indicated the doors hadn't "properly closed," but did it mean they hadn't closed at all? If true, the dive team felt certain they now had the answer to *Britannic's* rapid sinking. For analysts like Parks Stephenson, it wasn't quite as clear-cut. He respected what the team found but concluded they weren't taking into account what the Harland & Wolff chief naval architect had said about *Britannic*. Following safety modifications made after *Titanic's* disaster, *Britannic* should have been able to stay afloat with any group of six adjacent compartments flooded.

In the bow area, *Britannic* could lose the forepeak, Cargo Holds 1, 2 and 3, and Boiler Rooms 5 and 6. Losing Boiler Room 6 was well within the margin of error. That was different than *Titanic*, which could stay afloat only if no more than five adjacent compartments flooded. Parks's assessment when he heard about the 2003 Expedition was divers would have to penetrate deeper into the ship in another expedition for a longer look.

The team had plenty to show the world though, and the documentary *Mysteries of the Deep: Titanic's Doomed Sister* aired in March 2004. Among previously unseen underwater footage was the spiral staircase in the forecastle leading from the firemen's quarters to the forward pipe tunnel and the Marconi room where the multiple tuner was located. The Marconi tuner was identical to the one used on *Titanic*, a rare historical piece of equipment.

Simon remembers an ironic twist. "The Marconi is a bit of a funny story actually — they filmed it not realizing what it was (one of the divers thought it was a fuse box of some description), and it was only identified for what it was when I was analyzing the footage back in London after the expedition had wrapped."

The resounding successes of 2003 answered some of the elusive questions. Carl was determined to return again. He too was hooked on *Britannic*, wanting to discover her secrets one by one.

CHAPTER 16

TOUCHING HISTORY ON EVERY DIVE

B RAD MATSEN'S BOOK *Titanic's Last Secrets* chronicles how the incredible opportunity to visit *Titanic* came about and also contains a section about our *Britannic* expedition. In the thrilling descent onto *Titanic* in the submersible *Mir II* in 2005, it didn't occur to me I would then make my way to her equally tragic sister. We didn't feel our research into *Titanic* was complete, and we wanted a second go at her to look for the expansion joints designed and installed by the Harland & Wolff engineers in order to strengthen the ship's infrastructure. We were disappointed to learn no trips could be scheduled for the foreseeable future, but with the designs of the Olympians so similar, an expedition to *Britannic* could serve our purpose. Questions had been raised about a third joint included in the newer ship, and, if so, had the engineers detected a problem they were trying to quietly correct?

We'd been working with a number of experts — naval architects, forensics analysts, artists, and imaging technicians. They thought if we found the joints on the wreck of *Britannic* were different from those of *Titanic*, it would indicate the engineers had made a deliberate modification. Our specific target was to look for and film the location, number, and shape of the expansion joints. There is no argument now, since most experts agree the break of *Titanic* did occur at the exact point of an expansion joint, but the experts disagree about the strength of the ship and how much force an expansion joint should be able to take without breaking.

An example of this is when you're trying to tear open a bag of potato chips. When the bag is prenotched, it will easily tear along from that point — a weakness in the plastic. Some argue the crude design of the joints on *Titanic* was the same as that notch. Since no mention of changes to the expansion joints on *Britannic* were ever found in any of the surviving construction details, any change to the joints could indicate the White Star/Harland & Wolff partnership were covering up what they may have felt was a design flaw. Or, as another analyst explained, it could have been an evolution of the original design. In either case, the first step was to find the answer of *what* before trying to figure out the *why*.

Never one to let a show idea go to waste, I thought of the conversations I'd had with my contacts in England about *Britannic*'s unanswered questions, especially when it came to those watertight doors. Her mysterious story could be a totally separate show idea and project unto itself — it would be double-dipping at its best. History Channel was intrigued enough to agree *Britannic* was a great follow-up.

I was no stranger to the complexities of shooting on location or arranging for dive trips, but arranging an expedition to Kea was in a category beyond what I was accustomed to. Simon Mills, as the owner of *Britannic*, had provided enough information for me to understand this would take a hell of a lot of planning. In dividing up the project, I agreed to take on the extensive logistics list, and there was no reason for me to "reinvent the wheel," as the expression goes. Not when I was friends with Carl. I would rely heavily on his help in the months it took to put the trip together. We swapped dozens of emails and phone calls to get the 2006 Standard Operating Procedure (SOP) and project firmed up. (*See Appendix A: HMHS* Britannic *2006 SOP.*) It's no exaggeration to say I couldn't have done it without him mentoring me on this level of diving and providing physical support.

When you're putting together the kind of team you want on an expedition of this magnitude, there are some hard choices to make. Technical divers of the caliber qualified to dive *Britannic* come with pretty big egos, too, and juggling those can be a fact of life. Just as real, however, is skill may win out over personal preference. You might think a diver is a total ass, but you won't necessarily exclude him from your team. You may also think a guy is great, and you're happy to dive with him under a lot of circumstances, but maybe not on a wreck like *Britannic*. In some situations, an individual you'd like to have isn't available. It is ideal, of course, to find the talent, mindset, and personalities that mix smoothly, and in this case, the men I'd met in England when working on *Deep Sea Detectives* episodes came with the added bonus of Carl and Leigh's experience on *Britannic*.

Every member rounding out the fourteen divers was carefully selected. Martin Parker is the owner of Ambient Pressure Diving and inventor of the Inspiration and Evolution CCRs most of the team was using. He supplied a lot of the equipment (loaners) and brought with him his test diver and top technician, Mike Etheredge, as a dive buddy and to repair any CCRs if needed. Mike Fowler was my CCR instructor and a decent cameraman; Mark Bullen, Mike Pizzio, and Frankie Pellegrino were all excellent deep divers, but Frankie and Mark also had construction experience and brought tools with them. Mike Barnette (Barney) was a solid deep diver and also a good friend.

Evan was there because he was on the *Deep Sea Detectives* team and worked with Lone Wolf Media as their underwater director of photography/ cameraman, plus he was now working on and off with Woods Hole Oceanographic Institution (WHOI). Evan is a great example of how an initial encounter can lead in a completely unexpected direction. I first met Evan around 2001–02, when he was crewing on a Long Island, New York, dive boat, *Eagle's Nest*, on a charter to *U-869*, the submarine made famous in the book *Shadow Divers*. I was aboard as a paying customer, just going back out to the wreck for a visit. As a member of the crew, Evan went in to tie the line to the wreck, and when he was decompressing, the boat came adrift. Evan was flustered as he was sure his tie-in didn't come loose. Captain Howard wasn't happy, and as we tried to lift the line back aboard the boat, we saw a huge piece of wreckage still wrapped around the chain; Evan had done a good job, but the wreck (or part of it) tore apart under the weight and tug of *Eagle's Nest*. I liked the kid; he had moxie. I found out this was his first dive on my wreck and his first deep trimix dive to boot, in crappy seas and late (dark) afternoon conditions.

In speaking with him, I found out he did a little carpentry work with his dad, but his real job was working off-Broadway as a lighting grip, and he'd done a little acting here and there, too. We stayed in touch, me giving him pointers on how to get stuff from wrecks and he finagling with CCRs. When I started work on *Deep Sea Detectives* for History Channel and we planned to do a program on *Andrea Doria*, the underwater cameraman assigned to the project asked if I knew a diver who could help with underwater lighting. Evan came immediately to mind. He hadn't been to *Andrea Doria* yet, but he was rock solid, and I vouched for him. This was the initial spark that set Evan onto a new career path. He continued to work on almost every episode of *DSD*, rising first to second camera, shooting both above and below the water, and then ultimately became the underwater director of photography (DP). Evan was working with me and Lone Wolf Pictures (now Lone Wolf Media) when we went first to *Titanic* in 2005, and he didn't want to miss the chance to dive her sister.

Heeth Grantham was the second topside camera for Lone Wolf who also was certified to dive. We enlisted him as a support diver. Joe Porter was the editor and owner of *Wreck Diving Magazine* and had been with us on *Titanic*. He became our second support diver. Jonathon Wickham was the writer for Lone Wolf, and Kirk Wolfinger was the director and producer along with another topside cameraman, Joe Brunette, and soundman Tom Eichler.

As much as I acknowledged the value of Carl, Leigh, and John's previous experience diving the wreck, with it being my first time, I wanted to understand as much about the ship as possible before plunging 400 feet and penetrating into the darkness of the interior. Simon was the man who had been over the plans more times than he could count, and Parks had come up with an interactive computer simulation of the bow as well as his other magic. Having both of them on the island meant we could pour over the plans and graphics to have as much of a "feel" of the ship as possible before diving. Simon brought Rosemary Lunn (Roz) with him as his assistant. She was a great sport about getting into the act, playing Violet Jessop for the show, jumping in the water, and then cracking her head on a boat. We gave her a lot of credit for dealing with the awful heat during the shoots while she wore heavy period clothing and the coat Violet hadn't been willing to abandon when she headed for the lifeboat.

William Lange headed up the WHOI team and brought Evan Kovacs and Maryann as technical assistants. For those who haven't read the Matsen book, Bill Lange is a man that you might not know, but you owe him a huge *thank you* if you've ever watched underwater footage. He was always interested in photography and imaging, and when he settled in at WHOI more than thirty years ago, it was to apply his incredible ability to an amazing number of projects. His official position is the director of the Advanced Imaging and Visualization Laboratory (AIVL) that specializes in the development of new imaging sensors and imaging techniques to collect, process, assess, and interpret scientific imagery for scientific, educational, and entertainment purposes. The technology to probe our oceans and go deeper is only half of the equation — capturing the images moves the science and education forward and brings it to our televisions.

Bill Lange is one of the men who invents or improves the cameras and auxiliary equipment that can withstand the pressures of deep diving. These are the complex cameras mounted in ROVs and submersibles or carried by divers. Included was the innovative 3D "Bumblebee" camera. It would provide great images and physically resembled the namesake insect. AIVL also maps and creates graphic models for science and use in documentaries. Without men like Bill, we wouldn't have these amazing "eyes" underwater. If you're not impressed yet, he monitored the video screen around 1:00 a.m. on September 1, 1985, when they located *Titanic*. That's the type of expeditions Bill Lange has been a part of.

In continuing with team members not directly involved in diving, Dr. Petar Denoble of Divers Alert Network (DAN) was there to observe and collect data from the divers. DAN, headquartered in North Carolina, has the most extensive research database in the world when it comes to scuba diving. We also had Bob Blumberg from the U.S. Department of State, Bureau of Oceans, Environment and Science with us. He too had been on the 2005 *Titanic* trip, and he was trying to enact legislation to protect the ship. Brad Matsen, writing *Titanic's Last Secrets* at the time, came as an observer for a portion of the expedition.

Our boat was *Apollon* with the captain and his three men, and you can't run an operation on Kea without the local talent of a fixer. We would usually have someone on almost all of our overseas filming in countries where English was not spoken widely.

The best individuals are actually recommended from producer to producer, and they work hard for their money. As the name implies, they fix things: translating; schmoozing and meeting with local bureaucracy; making sure all local permits are covered; and finding batteries, a bottle of Pepto-Bismol, scotch, or a specific camera or lens to rent. Fixers are always fluent in not only the local language and English (many are polyglots) but also wise in the needs and ways of film crews, doubling as gaffers, boom handlers, or sometimes as a stand-in. They arrange local travel, know all the scenic places for an exterior shoot, and can smooth over an irate farmer when you jump his fence and scare his goats just to film a nice vista. (Yes, that happened!)

Tina Tavridou was hired by Lone Wolf, and we couldn't have been more impressed. She can get you a 60-person crew bus or a moped, an 80-foot fishing boat or a small inflatable. She has an amazing memory for faces and names, and it seems there is nothing she can't do, find, or get. We had also been assigned a man by the Greek Ministry of Antiquities who unfortunately wasn't an English speaker.

We had around thirty people, and despite our best efforts, not everyone could always fit onto the boat. The original plan for the expedition was to have the support vessel moored to the wreck. Unfortunately, we ran into issues because of the size of the vessel and available mooring lines. This affected the operation of the high-quality imaging systems that were fiber-optically tethered as well as the ROV. Bill had to operate the fiber-optic tethered cameras from *Apollon's* RIB. It was not an ideal setup, but being the guy he is, he made it all work. The fuse box on the main boat burned up at one point, and then there was the day when *Apollon's* captain ran over our transducer, and we lost communication to the divers when he severed the line.

The majority of the first week was basically hard, hot, sweaty work, unloading the gear from the ferry and sorting out and moving dozens of cylinders, luggage for twenty-five people, lumber to use as building material, and huge packing crates filled with WHOI gear. We had to accomplish two goals upfront: turn a commercial fishing boat into a diving vessel and create a dive shop/gas-mixing facility on the island.

The first part involved taking plywood and studs to make benches to seat up to six fully geared divers at a time (in the shade), build a series of steps and a platform complete with handrails for the divers to climb up and over the 3.5-foot gunwale, and build a 16-foot steel ladder to climb back on the boat and recover divers. The carpentry work was done by Frankie and Mark, with me overseeing them. The steel ladder was welded together on-site by the captain.

The fill/mixing station was down the street, 100 yards from our hotel, in an open-air museum for old mining equipment. It was far enough from the hotel and other homes so we could run the noisy compressors late at night without being obnoxious. We needed power, and the existing system was hodgepodge and "Rube Goldberg" at best, so Carl fixed the power so we could run the electric booster pump and lights at night, going so far as to have Tina go to the mainland to get a new breaker box capable of handling the demand. Dozens of various sized scuba tanks and large K-bottles of gases had to be physically loaded into our one tiny pickup truck and brought from the ferry to the mixing station.

Getting ready to set up the mixing station was when we ran into the first of what would be a number of major problems. The absolutely vital tanks and compressors were pretty close to worthless. Setting aside the frustration of the excellent money we'd paid, the bottom line was we weren't going to be able to dive without these items. I can't begin to print the kind of profanity streaming out of my mouth. When I'd finished the first blast of cursing, Carl said something like, "I have an Italian mate who might be able to help."

Help? No, Edoardo Pavia (Edo) didn't *help* — he saved the entire project. I don't know how in the hell he pulled it off, but Edo showed up within a few days with everything we needed, a cheerful *ciao*, and his prior experience from the 2003 Expedition. He became our fifteenth diver and the fourth *Britannic* veteran.

One of the most gratifying things to see was the project as a true team effort. Everyone helped carry the tons of equipment to and from, both on and off the boats on dive days, from the hotel to the mixing station and back to the boat every dive day. I'm talking about cameras, rebreathers, and basically all of the dive gear. The only kit left on the boat at night was the emergency bailout tanks. We only used the single small pickup truck for the heaviest gear. It was quite the schlep every dive day, and even with wagon/carts to help, it was exhausting. By the time John stepped off the ferry and joined us on Kea, we had everything sorted out (thanks to Edo) and were ready to dive.

The next day, we did a full dress checkout dive in the harbor, a precaution any team is wise to follow. No matter how often you check your equipment, getting wet is the only way to know for certain you don't have leaks or instrument failures.

Unfortunately, but not surprisingly, we lost a few days to bad weather and used those days shooting background footage and doing interviews. When we got to dive, Leigh and Mark went down to tie a downline from the support boat to the wreck in what we call "setting the hook." That allows divers to use the line as a guide and descend to a specific point on the wreck. We didn't realize Leigh and Mark were going to spend almost an hour filming at depth. The long bottom time meant they had about six hours of underwater decompression to perform, and the sun was low on the horizon when they surfaced. We attached a white plastic marker buoy to the line so we could tie right into it the next morning. Not the most glorious marker for this magnificent ship, but anything nicer would be stolen by a local fisherman. You could also lose a marker if it was run over and destroyed by a passing ship.

We arrived at the site the next day ready to penetrate the firemen's tunnel to look at the door to Boiler Room 5, past the point where Richie Stevenson had been in 2003 when he tied off the reel. John and I planned to go through the lower boilers between Boilers 4 and 3 on the way in and come up and out through Boilers 2 and 1, where the reel was. The route seemed like a good idea because we knew silt was a serious issue. The deep interior of the ship has little to no moving water, so almost 100 years' worth of silt accumulates on every surface, even something as thin as the line Richie had laid. Our movements could shake the silt loose, but the physical presence of our bodies caused a certain amount of disturbance. By entering one way and exiting another, we would have a better chance of not swimming through our own mess and hopefully having clear water the whole way. Clear in the belly of the ship was not the clear of the exterior, but clear enough with our lights to be able to see ahead as far as our lights could reach.

I was comfortable with the plan, but I was nervous. Not throw-up, dry-mouth, shaky nervous, but rather the high, almost giddy type of nerves. This was my first dive to the wreck, and it would be the deepest wreck dive of my career at that point. Besides, you should always be a little excited and anxious, otherwise what the heck are you doing it for? My wife, Carrie, was on deck and hugged me before we jumped. Her tone in telling me to be careful made me a little nervous in a way I wasn't used to. Generally, I'm always careful, but there is truth to the "out of sight, out of mind" aspect to risky behavior. With Carrie on the deck, it's hard to be flip or cocky or use any other tool we testosterone-driven males use to stifle fear and project confidence. I was also working here with the film crew sticking cameras in my face, asking questions. It's very different from a "fun" dive, although to me it's all fun. There's a sense of obligation, of expectation, that all these faces needed us — me — to perform, to make it happen. It was a slight tug of weight on my shoulders, the need to get inside the wreck and get the shot — to get to the answer deep inside the wreck, a wreck I'd never seen before. I had experienced this sensation before, and when I stand up to dive, I have to put the feeling of extra responsibility somewhere else mentally. . . . I dive for me and me alone, and that must guide my choices.

Leaving the deck, it was god-awful hot, and despite sitting in the shade and having buckets of water spilled over our heads, my undergarments were soon bathed in sweat inside my drysuit. *Apollon* could not anchor or moor into the wreck, so the captain was live boating. He had to motor to the downline and drive close to it, where we would stand and then climb up the steps to jump over the high gunwale and drop twelve feet down to the water.

There was no current for this dive or on the 2006 trip either. (I didn't know every other dive I would make on *Britannic* would be in current.) The drop was good, and the swim to the downline was easy. I was using a loaner CCR. My lid (or electronics) was mine, but the actual harness and backpack was a loaner from Martin. I'd made a test dive with it the day before, and all was good. Maybe it was the big (twelve-foot) jump to the water or maybe it was just bad luck, but as I descended, I had a small low-pressure diluent leak, a tiny stream of gas bleeding from the ADV valve next to my left ear. I was also carrying a little extra weight, maybe four pounds. That doesn't sound like much compared to all of our equipment, but it is when every variable volume space on you starts to crush in at 250 feet. It was around that depth I started to realize I was heavy and added more gas to my wings and suit to offset the negativity. I had dived too shallow for our test dive, and not all the air had vented from my suit wings, etc., nor had all the neoprene I wore been crushed by water pressure. The difference between the thirty-foot checkout dive was now apparent.

I touched down on the side of *Britannic*'s hull at 300 feet. Maybe because of the leak or my weight issue, I don't recall actually seeing the wreck until I landed on it. I was focused on the lights below, pointing up to film our descent, so I'm sure that blinded me a little. It was darker and colder than I expected. Clear, but dark, and the colder water actually gave me a bone-deep chill. I was damp with sweat under the drysuit. John uncharacteristically landed on top of me with a clunk. He also was too heavy and didn't have the degree of control that he normally had. Mike Fowler saw the leak in my suit, came over, and tightened down on the loosed fitting, which solved the problem. We dropped a few pounds out of our weight belts and trimmed up a little better before John led the way to the edge of the break in the ship's hull. We descended to the rectangular entranceway, ready to penetrate into the firemen's tunnel.

The tunnel was a little confining and claustrophobic, but not more than the inside of a submarine. When you're not the lead dog, the view never changes, and all I looked at was John's fins frog kicking into the blackness ahead. The moment we broke out through the watertight door into Boiler Room 6 is fixed in my memory. I was amazed at how intact and still it all was — a deafening silence experience. I stared and took in how perfect everything was despite a thick layer of silt and rusticles like you see on *Titanic* dripping from the iron. The catwalks the engineering crews had used, the pipes, gauge faces, and lights still with the glass intact gave us a direct look into the past.

It was time to get to work, and my job was to light the strobes. I then followed John down to the deep side of the compartment, ready to slip between Boilers 1 and 2, head aft, film the door leading to Boiler Room 5, then ascend and exit through Boilers 3 and 4. The problem started as John got halfway through the tight space between the boilers and came across an obstacle. A wheelbarrow probably used to move coal from the bunkers had become wedged in the opening we wanted to pass through. John huffed and worked harder, creating clouds of silt as he tried to free and move it, but it was stuck fast. Behind him, I listened to him bump against the boilers and in short heavy breaths explained (on our communication system) what I couldn't see ahead of him.

After a minute or so I called, "Abort, abort!"

Between my diluent leak, which I couldn't tell if it had begun again and was cautiously monitoring my gas pressure, and now this, I felt it prudent to call off the dive. John did not argue. We reversed order, and I exited the wreck first. It wasn't a great first dive by any means, but still no mean feat either. On the ascent, I was finally able to really see the wreck. The visibility was much better without camera lights in my eyes, and I found myself staring straight down during my deeper decompression stops. I could just make out the wreck's shape against the white sand as I ascended to 200 feet, and then it disappeared into the dark blue of deep water. The ascent was the best part of the dive. It wasn't for the camera or for John, it wasn't to solve a mystery. It was simply a beautiful wreck, and it was mine. The score for that was day was Wreck 1, Divers 0, but "tomorrow was another day."

The next day was another weather blowout, and a problem popped up that no one had anticipated. About half the entire team came down with an extremely nasty case of dysentery. If you've never suffered from this, be glad of it. We guessed it was from locally grown produce at one of the restaurants but couldn't be sure. The debilitating illness causes you to stay no more than a few feet from a bathroom and leaves you so weak you can barely crawl into bed for almost a day after the effects are over.

With John seriously afflicted and staying locked in his hotel room, I teamed up with Barney and the rest of the unaffected the following day to pursue answering the question that pertained directly to *Titanic*. Working with Mike Fowler and Mike Etheredge, we were tasked to locate and film the interior and exterior of the expansion joint to see if it was different than on *Titanic*. My second dive (described very well in Matsen's book) was much more enjoyable. It was another penetration dive but into the promenade deck, which was light and airy compared to the stifling blackness and silt of the boiler room. Above our heads were large picture windows letting in light. (Almost every window and porthole had been left open the day *Britannic* sank.) Our teammates swam along above us, tracing our path and filming us.

The workload was light as well, with having only to locate the expansion joints. They were easy to find by counting windows until we came to the brass floor plate. On the way in, we saw the remains of wheelchairs and gurneys strewn in the passage, and it was obvious to see this was a hospital ship. Peering down into doorways, the darkness within beckoned. We both wanted to drop in and do what we love, to explore for exploration's sake, but we had a job to do, and this dive was not ours. After we reached and filmed our goal, it was time to turn the dive and head back out the way we came. The visibility was good, and there was much to see — all eye candy for the wreck diver. Once out in the blue water, we stole a few minutes for ourselves and swam to the bridge to enjoy the view and imagine, as we always do, what it was like almost a century before on the day the ship was lost. I could envision Captain Bartlett in his pajamas giving orders, crewmen leaping into the blue sea, and Violet being lowered in a lifeboat as the ship leaned heavily over. Having accomplished the major task of filming the expansion joints, we returned to Kea confident and happy we would again try the boiler room the next day to check on the watertight door.

Unfortunately, John was still sick and didn't want me making that particular dive without him, so we scrubbed it until he was 100 percent better. He came out on the boat, not up yet for diving, but none of us anticipated it would be our last day to dive.

We put some of the other divers in to get more beauty shots of the wreck. Frankie, Mike, and Martin dived with Evan to light and pull fiber-optic cable for great wide shots, and I think Edo was filming them film. We then had one of those situations you are often faced with by people who don't comprehend the dangerous nature of these expeditions. A reporter from Athens had come out to do a story on the History Channel Expedition, and he wanted to dive and film the decompressing divers. We didn't want him or anyone in the water on our permit who wasn't a member of our team, as they jeopardized the safety of our people. If they got hurt, it took away resources and assets for the team. We were told by the Greek lawyer who worked on matters with Simon this was not a choice because the Ministry wanted pictures in the paper promoting the expedition.

The guy agreed he would take photographs at only thirty feet deep, which was all he was equipped for in a short wetsuit and single aluminum tank. Leigh served as dive marshal, and I was in the RIB with Carl doing topside support for most of the day. The reporter snapped a few pictures like he was supposed to, and then handing his camera to one of the decompressing divers, he started to pull himself down the line, hand-over-hand disappearing out of sight! A few minutes later, he ascended rapidly up the line like a ballistic missile, waving to the stunned decompressing divers as he passed them, breaking the surface in a froth, clearly out of control.

He yells in Greek to the boat, later translated loosely as, "*Britannic, Britannic, I did it, I don't need a rebreather!*"

He had done what we call a bounce dive to 300 feet, touched the wreck, and then realized he wasn't equipped with the buoyancy vest he should have been wearing. He dropped his weight belt and shot to the surface like a cork coming out of a champagne bottle. A lot of people have died from an embolism (expanding air in the lungs) when rocketing uncontrollably to the surface from nowhere near that deep.

To make matters worse (well, at least he wasn't dead), the guy couldn't seem to grasp what a risk he'd taken. They pulled him onto *Apollon*, and Dr. Denoble checked him. The guy continued on about "how great the wreck is" and how "he didn't need a CCR."

Dr. Denoble, who after each dive would do Doppler and neurological tests on every diver and accumulate all the dive and decompression data, put the Doppler on this guy. He listened to the bubbles clicking around in this guy's veins, and it sounded like "glasses in a dishwasher." He told the man in his heavy Croatian accent, "You should sit down." Petar sounds a little like Count Dracula when he's being serious, and this was a serious situation.

I'm thinking (in a cleaned-up version), "Great, what if we've killed a member of the media?" They put him on oxygen and had him lie down, but he kept ranting and raving about the dive, taking the regulator out of his mouth, with Petar pushing it back in, giving him water, and hoping for the best. As furious as we were with what he'd done, we were about to face a far greater problem.

On the way back in, our Greek representative from the Ministry of Antiquities had become upset with us. Unfortunately, Tina was on the mainland running an errand, so no one understood what he said. We assumed it was about the media guy, but he stormed off the boat once we hit the dock, and we still had no idea what he was pissed about. The media guy seemed OK, so we sent him packing and began the conga line of getting cameras and gear to the hotel and the mixing station. We were all ready for the day to be over, expecting a less drama-filled tomorrow.

The next morning after breakfast, we went to the boat to load up. Since John was feeling better, the two of us would try to get back into the boiler room. Accompanied by port police, the Greek representative was waiting at the boat, and a Hellenic Coast Guard vessel was tied up against *Apollon*. Tina was back and translated. The representative said we violated our permit by going inside the wreck and also filming the seabed around the wreck.

Yes, we did go in and showed him and the officials our English translation/version of the permit allowing us to go inside the wreck, but the Greek version of the same contract said we couldn't. We had no idea how the hell this happened, since our Greek lawyer should have made sure our versions were in sync. On Kea or in Greece, Greek versions of contracts trump English, and we were told to hand over all our footage to the port police. Things went rapidly downhill from there with a lot of excitement and shouting that landed us in the police station.

Bob Blumberg, the State Department representative with us, gave it his diplomatic best, but we stayed in the sweaty block building all day, confined to a bench. Pal and FBI agent Mike Pizzio showed up and stayed with us, trying to smooth things over, while emphatically telling us to say and sign nothing. Evan, Maryann, and Bill didn't know what the hell was going on, but they made copies of all our film for the police and the minder and stashed the originals for safekeeping.

We stayed on the island for a few days, trying to get the ban lifted, but our time limit for the permit was running out. Months of careful preparation, and this was how we had to end the expedition. Talk about something we hadn't planned on.

In breaking out of the frustration at the abrupt ending, we focused on the multiple goals we did achieve. Although primarily a film expedition, other objectives included the launch and recovery of numerous science experiments (both on the exterior and interior of *Britannic*), and we encountered many firsts. Areas of the wreck were explored where divers had not ventured in previous visits, and stereo high-definition footage of the wreck like never before was obtained thanks to the high-definition cameras custom-made specifically for this expedition. The high-definition footage of the expansion joints answered our questions about how *Britannic*'s design differed from her more famous sister, *Titanic*.

DAN had been able to conduct its first ever "deep technical rebreather field study" and collected data about gas mixes, switching of gases, and decompression algorithms as well as the actual black box information of every second of the dives. Paired with the ultrasonic device Doppler for measuring postdive bubbles in our divers, the combined data was going to be critical in the overall observations and findings. This precise information would further our understanding of the effects of long decompression profiles on free-swimming technical divers.

By safely pushing the limits and putting together our abilities as a team, the expedition was a success, even without getting the number of dives we wanted. A documentary film, *Titanic's Tragic Sister Britannic*, aired on the History Channel in April 2007, and Matsen's book *Titanic's Last Secrets* was released in 2008.

There was no question *Britannic* had captured my interest, and I wanted a chance for more exploration.

CHAPTER 17

DETERMINED TO SUCCEED IN 2009

C ARL'S PHONE CALL IS THE KIND wreck divers like me *love* to get. "Hey, mate. I'm heading up a dive team back to *Britannic* in 2009. You in?" He had to be smiling like the Cheshire Cat on the other end because he knew there was no way I was going to let this pass. This is what I do, and after my first experience on her, I agreed *Britannic* is the simply the best wreck dive in the world. There was more to it because Carl knew I had to get back to the wreck after our 2006 Expedition had ended the way it did.

As Carl laid out the details of the plan he and Simon had developed, I realized this project was larger and even more ambitious than the one he and his pal Leigh had been with us on. For starters, the dive vessel we would be using was like something out of a wreck diver's dream: a 200-foot-long ship from Belgium called *Commandant Fourcault* (also referred to as *Cdt. Fourcault* or *Fourcault*). The vessel was totally geared for technical diving, with multiple compressors, inflatable chase boats, tenders, and even an onboard decompression chamber. It operated regularly as a diving and salvage vessel and would also provide all the support staff we would need, both topside and in water. The *Fourcault* would even pick up all the dive equipment, CO_2 absorbent, dozens of large helium/oxygen cylinders, and camera equipment in the United Kingdom prior to steaming to the Aegean Sea. Using a boat in this way was the same technique Carl introduced in 2003, and it removed all the complicated logistics issues from our 2006 Expedition. And as if to add a cherry to the top, the *Fourcault* included an onboard Bell Jet Ranger helicopter for aerial filming!

The misunderstandings we had with the Greek Ministry had been resolved, and the resources of National Geographic were once again behind this expedition.

If that wasn't enough to make any explorer happy, in typical Carl fashion, he hadn't stopped there. He had submitted the form "Application for the Privilege of Carrying the Explorers Club Flag."

Carrying a numbered flag on the expedition would be another first for *Britannic*. The full background of this historic organization and a wonderful archive can be found on their website, *explorers.org/*. The organization, founded in 1904, is headquartered in New York City. Members of the Explorers Club have been the first to the places where history is made — the North and South Poles, Mount Everest, the deepest part of the ocean, and the moon. Their research collections contain amazing information, maps, and history, and they encourage public interest in exploration and the sciences through public lecture programs, publications, travel programs, and other events. To be allowed to carry a numbered flag means you have demonstrated that your expedition will further not just exploration, but science as well.

As of the writing of this book, there have been 202 numbered flags awarded — flags that have been around the globe, above it, and below to the ocean. Being awarded a numbered flag is indeed a privilege, and Carl understood the significance.

The preparation for this expedition was as good as it gets. Not only was *Fourcault* the best dive boat support platform you could ask for, but the team Carl assembled included some of the best technical divers and underwater cameramen in the world. Carl planned to field up to four dive teams per day, each team operating on various missions throughout the wreck at the same time, so the team would be equally split between veteran *Britannic* divers and the new guys. The roster included Carl Spencer, Leigh Bishop, and Richie Stevenson (UK); Evan Kovacs, Jarrod Jablonski, Casey McKinlay, and me (USA); Edoardo Pavia (Italy); Danny Huyge (BE); and Pete Mesley (NZ).

Just like the 2006 Expedition, the Lone Wolf Documentary Group would be aboard for topside filming along with technicians from WHOI, who would be providing not only high-definition fiber-optic-controlled *and* 3-D camera systems, but also two ROVs that would be in the water with the divers and performing around-the-clock for unmanned filming and exploration of the wreck.

I had shared the stage with Jarrod Jablonski and Casey McKinlay at a few diving events/symposiums through the years, and their reputation as incredible cave and technical divers was legend. In 2007, they completed an extraordinary cave jump, basically going in one underwater cave system, making the connection to and exiting out of a totally different cave. In the process, they traversed 36,000 feet underwater and spent a total of 21 hours in the water at depths in excess of 300 feet. It was a huge accomplishment in the technical diving world, and they really were the "hats off" belles of the ball on this project for that endeavor.

Richie Stevenson and I had been at the Euro-Tek advanced diving conference the previous year and stayed up late drinking and telling diver stories. Carl had told me I would be teamed up with Richie and tasked to finish the goal of seeing if we could make it through Boiler Room 6 and film the doorway into Boiler Room 5. Richie was stoked to get another crack at it, as was I. We were both tasked with the gas-filling requirements aboard *Fourcault*. We would spend hours together at the compressor filling, analyzing, labeling, and documenting the tanks. We would work hard and late into the night to get it done before each dive day, but it was all part of being a team.

I hadn't heard of Pete Mesley prior to this project. It was his first time on *Britannic*, and it didn't take long to find out that he was a good diver and still photographer. I'm not sure how he and Carl connected or how he came to be on the team, but Carl would have thoroughly vetted him. I liked his swagger.

I first met Danny Huyge in 2005 at a dive show called Extreme Duiken in Antwerp, Belgium. Both John and I did a presentation on the book *Shadow Divers*. Danny was one of the many Belgian divers who came to listen to us and other presenters, and we connected on that trip. My fifteen-year-old son, Richie III, had come with me. With the laws about drinking being different in Europe, he enjoyed the Belgian beers at the show. Danny warned me to look out for my son because "the Belgian beer was very strong, not like American beer." As this was my son's first trip to Europe, it was a blast for him to have a beer or two, and I appreciated Danny looking out for us both.

Two years later, John and I were invited to present again at Extreme Duiken on our 2005–06 work on *Titanic* and *Britannic*. We both brought our wives to enjoy Belgium, and Danny arranged a wonderful rooftop private dinner event in the heart of Antwerp. In 2008, I would again see Danny and met his Belgian dive buddy Danny Moens on an *Andrea Doria* trip I put together for Carl, Edo, and me.

Due to his work, Carl couldn't make it and canceled at the last minute, but Edo came and stayed with me at my home in New Jersey, excited to finally dive the Mount Everest of wreck diving. The first day of exploration went great on the famous Italian passenger liner, when suddenly tragedy struck on the second day. One of the divers failed to surface from his morning dive. We immediately called the Coast Guard and did a surface search, but after talking to the divers on board, it became apparent he'd had some kind of event near the surface. He never even made it to a dive buddy that waited for him on the anchor line.

On a hunch, Edo and I went down to look for him, not on the wreck but far away from it, out in the desolate sand. After nearly 40 minutes of searching, we found his body 250 feet down on the seafloor and almost 300 feet away from the wreck. As agreed with the boat captain prior to diving, Edo and I only marked the body with a line and blinking strobe light, leaving the body for recovery by a second team. Then we began our long and sad decompression.

The dive boat crew went down after us to send up the body, but because they were on open circuit and not CCR, they only got part of the way out into the black water before turning around, low on air and unable to make the far swim. I now had to either wait until morning to get the body or ask a paying customer. Edo and I couldn't dive again that day because our bodies had become saturated with nitrogen from our long dives. Besides me, only Danny Moens had experience with body recovery, so I asked the Belgian team if they would do it. We couldn't just leave the man out there all night knowing where he was. What if the line broke, a shark ate him, or the weather turned and we had to go back into shore? The two Dannys, talking quietly, slowly and methodically tripled checked all their gear and then with dusk falling, made the dive and sent up the body. I will forever think the world of both of them for doing this. (It was later ascertained the diver had died of a heart condition.)

I was happy to hear Danny was on the 2009 team and that I could give him some pointers about the wreck and the operations, much as Carl had done for me on my first *Britannic* dive.

Also aboard were three DAN hyperbaric technicians and doctors, including Dr. Petar Denoble from the 2006 Expedition. He would oversee all the testing of the team, both pre- and postdives. The Olympic-class historical and design expert Parks Stephenson was also back, as was *Britannic*'s owner Simon Mills. Rounding out the research team, World War I historian Marty Morgan joined the group. Carl had contacted DBI to participate in the expedition, but due to scheduling conflicts they couldn't send personnel. They provided long-term experiments to be deployed and requested the previous ones be recovered. Having worked with Carl before, they felt confident he would be able to handle the task with their instructions.

One of the most daunting penetrations planned would be to reach the famed Turkish baths, an opulent steam room located deep in the bowels of the ship. There was no verification this room was even completed before *Britannic* was turned into a hospital ship, and it was a mystery Carl intended to solve. To get to this area of the wreck was confusing even on blueprints, so Carl tasked legendary cave explorers Jarrod Jablonski and Casey McKinlay with finding the way in.

Richie Stevenson and I would go back to the firemen's tunnel and figure out a way to get past the obstruction in Boiler Room 6 that John and I had encountered in 2006. Our mission was to get to the back of the compartment and see if the door to Boiler Room 5 was open or closed. This was by no means an easy penetration, but both of us had been in the compartment before. We needed photographic evidence for analysis to be able to solve the mystery surrounding how and why the ship sank even faster than *Titanic*.

Carl would be diving with Evan to deploy a new science experiment on the boat deck and recover the one we left in 2006. They intended to then drop into the radio room to see if the rare Marconi telegraph sat precariously on a steel beam as it had been in 2003 when they filmed it. This was one of the only examples of this equipment known to still exist. Negotiations were ongoing to obtain permission from the Greek government to recover the priceless artifact before it fell from its perch and was destroyed or lost forever. If we could locate it early in the expedition, maybe the Antiquities Minister would allow it to be removed. Other missions were to gain access into the engine room via the skylights and also document the first-class dining areas. Neither area on *Britannic* had been explored before, so every piece of film shot would shed new light on the ghostly spaces. The WHOI imaging experts were tasked with creating the first photomosaic of this 882-foot-long ship. It was an aggressive agenda, but Carl had put together the team to pull it off.

Before we could even start, we needed to establish a downline to the wreck, and that was where I was going to earn my salt. Carl asked me to "set the hook" on *Britannic*. I was a logical choice for the water work. With my previous dives on the wreck, I knew the lay of the land, and I had done deep tie ins on other wrecks too many times to count. Still, it's an honor and a great obligation to set the hook; it means the entire team trusts you. If you don't tie in correctly, then hours will go by, possibly the day lost, and another team has to do the work. If you do a bad job and the line severs or parts at the wreck, the team can be separated and set adrift in the shipping channel.

I would be setting the hook with veteran Richie Stevenson (who was carrying a camera and couldn't be of much help) and Danny Huyge, who was making his first dive to the wreck. As the three of us pulled our way down to the wreck, it became obvious the *Fourcault* crew had put too much line in the water. Instead of being nearly straight up and down, the line was at a near forty-five-degree angle, and it seemed we moved laterally through the water at times, not down. The weighted end of the shot had landed high on the hull at 300 feet, but with the long descent in a stiff blowing current, all three of us were exhausted when we hit the wreck. Thankfully, there was about seventy-five pounds of weight on the shot line, and it didn't move at all as we pulled down the rope.

Once we caught our breath, we tied in on the mooring bollards, which was the only place Simon wanted the line tied on his wreck. (A bollard is a short post used on a ship principally for mooring when it comes in to dock.) Once I wrapped the heavy chain around the bollard and used a shackle and pin to secure it, I took a short piece of wire and secured it through the pin on the shackle so it couldn't back out. Richie was able to get a video shot of the bridge area, but we had burned so much time descending and working that we had to start our ascent. We were into our decompression stages when it became apparent Richie had a minor issue and was low on O_2, but there was a bottle of gas that had been placed on a line in case a diver was running low. We weren't sure why he'd "lost" gas, and he didn't need to use the waiting bottle after all, but it was good to know it was there if he needed it.

Danny was also having an issue with the readings on one of his two dive computers. It was telling him to stay in decompression for two hours longer than us. This didn't make sense because we'd all been diving essentially at the same depth for the same amount of time, but you don't want to second guess what your computer shows. It's safer to spend the extra two hours at a decompression stop than to take the risk.

As we were hanging at the underwater decompression station and the other teams were on the bottom, the current was still strong on the line. And as can happen, *Fourcault* started to swing on her anchor line when the wind shifted. The stern of the ship snagged the top float attached to the downline, severing the line near the surface. Fortunately, almost all of the divers had already transferred to the floating decompression station moored to the wreck, and Jarrod and Casey shot a marker buoy to the surface when they found the severed downline laying on the seafloor. These possibilities had been planned for, and with the proper support teams and equipment, everything was handled quickly. The RIB slowly towed Jarrod and Casey over to the decompression station, and all divers were recovered safely just before dusk.

The next day I was tasked with setting the hook again with Danny, but this time Edoardo would join our trio with the camera. (This was, after all, a film expedition.) Given the problems with the current the previous day, we shortened the line from 600 feet to 500 feet, but this time the weighted shot line didn't land on top of the hull; it was down in the sand about 30 yards away. In the fantastic visibility, we could see the awesome sight of *Britannic* in the distance rising 100 feet above us. No matter how often you see it, you have to pause and take it in.

There was a long chain clipped to the heavy sacrificial weight. I unfastened it, draped the chain across my shoulders, and started to walk across the sand toward the wreck, while Danny pulled 500 feet of half-inch line behind me. I think Edo just shot video, or he may have been helping. I couldn't tell because I was too focused on my breathing, slowly and evenly, making sure I didn't work too hard. (If you work too hard underwater, you can overwhelm your rebreather's ability to "scrub" out the exhaled CO_2. Too much CO_2 in the loop can be debilitating to a diver, at first inducing confusion, headache, and double vision, ultimately leading to unconsciousness and death.)

When we got to the wreck, I paused and looked up at a net hanging down the deck of the wreck like a curtain. With the chain around my neck, I slowly climbed hand-over-hand up the net while Danny pulled up the line and bore the weight from above me, each of us trying to make sure neither I nor the chain fouled in the net. It was almost 100 feet straight up, and I was exhausted when done. Even though I moved slowly and deliberately, the work had taken a toll. I sat on the hull for a few minutes catching my breath and enjoying the view, but there was no time for any exploration since this dive took almost forty minutes for us to tie in. The other teams fared much better, achieving some of their goals on Day 2, but the surface current was still strong and made the decompression phase of everyone's dive taxing.

On Day 3, we awoke to find the large orange float marking my downline was gone! Everyone looked at Danny and me at breakfast, and there was that pause as you're trying to decide what to do or say. We knew we did a solid tie in, so where the hell was the line? Did a ship run it over in the night?

Carl looked at me and said, "I can't ask you to tie in three days in a row, but if you are up to another dive today, do you think you can help them with locating the right spot?"

Under the best of circumstances, I shouldn't have made three dives in a row, but I felt good and rested and agreed to dive. As Carl and I talked, the captain of *Fourcault* put the tender in the water, and the boat driver went over the top of wreck. He reported he could see the large orange float underwater with the line still attached. The strong current had pulled it down to seventy feet, collapsing most, but not all, of its buoyancy. I was relieved I wouldn't be needed to tie in again.

The captain sent down a support diver, who affixed lifting bags and sent the limp float back to the surface, where additional floats were attached. I was one step away from pondering if I would dive at all when word came that Richie Stevenson was going back to the firemen's tunnel to try a new route to the next boiler room. I decided to join him. This is what I was here for, and I wasn't going to skip a dive if I didn't have to.

The plan was simple. Richie Stevenson would lead the way through the firemen's tunnel and lay a new penetration line inside the wreck, and I would film and light him from behind with the two huge HID lights on the one-of-a-kind 3-D WHOI camera I used. Once we navigated the long narrow corridor of the firemen's tunnel, I watched Richie's fins disappear in the tiny crack separating the first set of huge boilers we needed to pass through. I took a few private moments to look around and film the pristine condition of this compartment. Glass-faced gauges and brass plaques were mounted on the bulkhead, light fixtures contained the bulbs still inside, shovels and wheelbarrows had their wood handles intact, and everything was blanketed in silt, mummified in the still water.

I secured, then activated, a two-foot-long stainless-steel cylinder on a rusted pipe over my head. This was the pressure-tight body of a science experiment for a sampling device, which would record temperature, oxygen content, and salinity at different times over the next few days deep inside the wreck. According to Leigh, this device was worth $25,000, and I had carried it carefully until I secured it in place. Following Richie, I pushed through the tiny space between the huge double-ended boilers in Boiler Room 6 and then dropped down nearly thirty feet to the next corridor that led to Boiler Room 5. Surprisingly, the water going into Boiler Room 5 was gin clear, and as Richie swam in, I stopped at the edge of the corridor and filmed as he continued on through the next hallway through the open door into Boiler Room 5.

We were 360 feet down and nearly 200 feet into the wreck, farther than anyone else had ever been, and we could see the door was wide open! Richie tied off the line on the far side of Boiler Room 5 and swam back. He gave me a quick OK hand signal, followed by thumbs up, indicating it was time to turn the dive and head out. I let him pass me since we now had to go back through the turbid water we had disturbed on our way past the boilers. Our lights were useless in the milky brown water. The thin white line Richie had laid was our only clear sense of direction in the swirling storm of silt. I felt rather than saw myself pushing through the restriction between the boilers, my stomach pushed down in the century of soft silt, the top of my rebreather bumping along the huge boiler above me.

Pushing the camera in front of me, I could hear the clank and bump of Richie ahead but couldn't see anything at all. I moved painfully slow in what was a true braille dive, feeling an innate sense of location working with memory to create a visual in my mind of where I was. This helped when I sensed more than saw that my head and camera had passed through the boiler and was in free water. The visibility improved only slightly as Richie exited ahead of me. It appeared as if the compartment was on fire with thick silt mimicking billows of smoke rolling through the water around me.

As I made my way across the compartment, I was suddenly stopped in my tracks — something caught behind me. Sensing it was on my right side, I kept the guideline in my left hand and steadied myself by grabbing out to the vague pipe shape it was looped around. This area of the compartment was a lattice work of piping and walkways, everything topsy-turvy as the wreck lay on her side. I needed to stay on a path in this maze, and in the near-zero visibility the line was my only clear direction out. I needed to hold the line at all costs, but I also wanted to steady myself to free whatever knit me to the wreck. As I grabbed it, the frail pipe collapsed, and I started to descend deeper into the silt-choked water, the broken pipe causing my lifeline to sink down. Still maintaining my loose grip on the lifeline, I pumped a little air into my drysuit, caught my buoyancy, and just floated there, blind in the coffee-colored water.

The large camera dangled between my legs on a lanyard, threatening to get further entangled on objects I couldn't see in this mud soup. I found something solid to hold onto in the murk and focused on the only thing I could see — the two green lights of my heads-up display (HUD). Those beautiful little lights told me at least everything was going well with my rebreather, which put me at ease, because when things go sideways while diving, my mantra is, "If you're breathing, everything is OK, so just focus on the problem at hand, fix it completely, and move on." Reaching back, I felt a thin wire or line wedged against the oxygen valve on my rebreather. It had looped around the emergency bailout tank I carried under my arm when I had descended.

My fingers methodically traced the wire's path around my equipment; visualizing this in my mind's eye, I gently worked it around the tank and off the valve. Now able to move, I picked up the camera, thankful that it hadn't gotten caught on anything else. I swam out of the huge silt cloud and into the long tunnel, escaping this labyrinth of pipes and cables, back into the open water. Swimming out of the wreck and into the blue water, I looked for Richie and saw him about seventy-five feet above me. He held onto the ascent line and looked straight down at me as if he willed me to make my appearance. Making eye contact, he raised his arm in a fist pump of victory and elation to see me. The entanglement had delayed my exit by only two minutes, but for Richie waiting for me to exit, it must have seemed like hours.

As I slowly ascended and began the long decompression ahead, I looked back down at this huge and magnificent wreck. It occurred to me then, and I still believe, it was one of the best dives of my career.

After the long seven hours of decompression, I surfaced, was towed back to *Fourcault* by the diving tender, and quickly taken up onto the deck by the crane-operated stage lift. I was immediately aware something was very wrong. Ordinarily, there would be a throng of people and cameras. The film crew would be asking questions about the dive, and the DAN techs would be wanting to poke and prod while asking, "How do you feel?" But aside from two of *Fourcault's* Belgian deck crew who helped me out of my gear, the deck was empty.

As I secured my gear, Bill Lange finally walked over to me. Bill normally has a no-nonsense, tough-as-nails disposition, but his face was etched with such sadness and pain, it startled me.

Putting a hand on my shoulder, he quietly said, "He didn't make it."

The words were almost inaudible as his head tilted down to the deck. A mixture of fear and confusion rose inside me. I asked, "What . . . who . . . what are you talking about, Bill?"

It dawned on him I had no idea what had happened. He grabbed me by both shoulders, looked me in the face, and said, "Carl . . . Richie, it's Carl. He didn't make it. . . . Carl is dead."

I couldn't register this information. I felt as if I had been struck hard in the gut. I couldn't grasp Carl was dead. We had spoken just eight hours ago, a smile and a backslap wishing me luck in the boiler room. Now he was gone?

My mind struggled with this, and my heart felt stabbed as I thought of his wife, Vicky, who would soon get this terrible news. I slouched down and sat there on the deck, stunned and shattered. After a while, one of the DAN technicians grabbed me to go to his cabin for my postdive examination. It was all a fog, and everything seemed far away and slow.

How could this have happened? How could Carl be dead?

CHAPTER 18

TRAGEDY ECLIPSES THE VICTORY

O F COURSE I WAS OK FROM MY DIVE, just as I had been on every other dive, just as we all had been. The physical data DAN collected was removed from the searing emotional pain we felt. Petar and his team had done everything possible, knowing how hopeless it was even as they worked on Carl before he was evacuated by helicopter. For me, and others who had been underwater, the story came in fragments, pieces strung together in somber voices.

Carl, with all of his responsibilities as expedition leader, had not been diving until that day. He was with Evan Kovacs and successfully deployed a new science experiment on the wreck before going inside to check on the Marconi radio. For reasons that weren't clear, Carl exited the wreck swimming quickly to the ascent line and then bailed off his rebreather at 300 feet. He began a controlled open-circuit ascent up the line, fully supported by Evan, who followed procedure and signaled topside with his submersible marker buoy to alert them to an emergency below. Support divers with even more gas were provided to Carl within minutes, and he continued to ascend under open-circuit decompression protocol to 120 feet. We had included a bailout plan from CCR as part of our safety measures as we always did, and the plan worked; every aspect from gas management to signaling topside went like clockwork despite the adrenalin surge when people realized this was a total open-circuit bailout on a *Britannic* dive. No one on deck knew what went wrong or who it was. Carl would occasionally go back on his CCR to take a breath or two, but then seemed to not like it as he went back to the OC tanks under his arms. He would occasionally look at Evan and bang his head with his fists, to say either he was stupid or his head hurt.

When Evan captured the sequence later, he was as detailed as he could be. In the closing paragraph of his recollection, he wrote:

"At around 140 feet, we reached the yellow bottle of air on the lazy, and Carl switched over to that. At around this point, Carl tied his reel onto the shot line to help stay connected in the strong currents. Shortly after he tied himself to the line, a support diver named Walter from *Fourcault's* crew came down and motioned to Carl, [asking] if he should take his bottles, to which Carl replied no.

"Carl then tried to clip on the yellow bottle from the shot line to himself. Walter helped him clip it on because he could not do it himself. Right after he clipped it on, Carl seized the shot line, shook it violently, hit himself in the head (almost as if he were cursing himself), and seemed to fumble with the line he had tied himself to the shot line with. I followed his hands to the line, and when I looked up, Carl was starting to convulse. The regulator was out of his mouth. I grabbed the regulator and tried to put it in his mouth while purging it. Pete tried to inflate his BCD, but Carl's diluent tank was empty. I didn't know the tank was empty, so I tried to inflate the BCD unsuccessfully. When we could not get the regulator in his mouth or get him inflated, Pete and I yelled for Walter to start bringing him to the surface. He was still convulsing as Walter brought him to the surface. That was the last time I saw Carl alive."

In remembering the terrible day, Evan later reflected, "The tragedy was layered with irony. Carl was very much about safety. He had built in safety systems and redundancies — the extra medical team on board and a helicopter at our disposal. Everything was aimed at added safety measures. While we had always been safety-conscious in other expeditions, the additional provisions for this trip should have been able to respond to any normal accident."

For Bill Lange, there had been the sight of Evan's marker alerting topside to the emergency, but was it Evan or Carl in distress? Allowing the rescue to unfold and the medical team to work without people in their way was the priority. It was almost two hours before Bill knew for certain it was Carl.

We each tried to process events in our own way, muted questions asked. Some we were able to answer, others left us wondering what the hell had happened. In the midst of everything was the realization Carl's wife had to be notified. Leigh shouldered the sad task no one wanted. I can only imagine how difficult it must have been for him.

It was night as we headed into Kea Harbor, and Richie Stevenson analyzed and gauged all of Carl's tanks. When he finished, we began to understand the role the yellow bottle must have played in the accident. No one touched his CCR other than to check the pressures and sample a tiny amount to check O_2 levels.

At some point, Kirk Wolfinger came over to tell me none of the footage I shot with Richie came out. How was that possible? I swore to Richie, Kirk, Bill, and Evan I never shut off the camera, and the little light on the monitor indicated it was recording, but there were no images after the firemen's tunnel. Could the situation be more crushing? It wasn't enough my friend was dead? We had captured the very images he had sent us to get, had accomplished this great dive as a major goal of the expedition, and we now had nothing, no film, no proof to show for it. It didn't stop there. Interviews with the police required a translator, which made the process longer than normal, and the night stretched out.

The port police took Carl's gear, although I suppose it was actually after midnight. Simon knew the time better than I did. Even though he was based onshore for the expedition, he'd been on *Fourcault* for the day, stunned with the news as we all were. Carl's equipment had been removed from him on the deck of the boat when the doctors began their resuscitation attempts. Simon remembered being woken at around 2:00 a.m. when they called him to come to the port police station to itemize the various items they had taken. They wanted him to catalog them before the representative of the Attica coroner arrived on the following day to take them for examination. In looking at the shredded drysuit and other bits and pieces, it seemed incongruous that this, a routine task as far as the police were concerned, was what was left of a man as full of life as Carl. The sense of loss remained with Simon for a very long time.

It became obvious no one in authority understood anything about Carl's rebreather, and yet we were prohibited from being able to analyze it to try and help provide answers. Losing the valuable data in the CCR was another blow to us. No one we spoke to grasped that the data was perishable, and we, the divers, were the ones who could recover and read it. We may not have learned everything we wanted to know, but it would have provided information we sure as hell knew was important. Instead, this high-tech unit packed with computers and electronics sat in a hot police station, where for some reason they seemed to think it was evidence we shouldn't touch.

Denied access to the information, Leigh knew from his years as a fireman the longer we waited to combine what we each remembered, the more likely we were to forget a detail. In going back over not only that day, but also the days preceding the accident, several seemingly unimportant things took on new meaning. As we talked among ourselves and put pieces together with Leigh, we all began to understand the ultimate failure. It continued to be difficult to grasp what had actually happened, but we were too experienced not to see it, and some of us had encountered other accidents due to human error.

Carl had carried an extra cylinder of gas with him none of us knew about — the yellow bottle. It was labeled as air but had 50% nitrox. Oxygen toxicity had caused Carl's seizures.

Petar later elaborated: "A seizure is the most dramatic manifestation of oxygen toxicity. The full-blown occurrence of seizure is a typical grand mal seizure attack characterized by a tonic-clonic activity. A generalized seizure is characterized by the sudden onset of sustained contraction of most muscles in the body, often starting with a cry or moan and resulting in a fall to the ground. During the tonic phase [the] body can be curved backward. The tonic phase of the seizure gradually gives way to clonic convulsive (jerking) movements, occurring bilaterally and synchronously before slowing and eventually stopping, followed by a variable period of unconsciousness and gradual recovery."

With convulsions occurring underwater at the depth they did, there was no chance for Carl to recover.

How such a mistake could have been made continues to haunt most of us. Carl was under a tremendous amount of pressure with planning and managing an expedition of this size, and it was his way to take on extra responsibilities. We all knew he worked a lot of hours, but it was also Carl's way to never let on he might need extra help, to smile off fatigue, and to keep going. His technical abilities were without question, and therefore "checking on" anything Carl did wasn't something we thought to do.

Carl Spencer was my friend, a mentor to me, and a true explorer in every sense of the word. The world is a smaller place without him.

CHAPTER 19

FEELING THE LOSS

THE GREEK GOVERNMENT SUSPENDED all diving operations, and we languished around Kea a few days, not sure what was going to happen to the project. We ate, drank, and swam, trying our best to deal with the terrible emptiness. Laughter rang hollow, drinks tasted sour, and the sun was too hot, too bright. We were miserable in an Aegean paradise. A representative from National Geographic came from their headquarters and was on the ship. He talked about taking care of Carl's family and trying to smooth things over with the Greeks to get the clearance to continue the project. We also discussed asking Vicky, Carl's wife, what she would want.

In the end, we were told it was over, the Greeks pulled the permit, and there was nothing left for us to do but go our separate ways. Leigh was called in to provide testimony at the coroner's inquest convened in England. It must have been another unsettling event – it certainly would have been for me.

I hadn't doubted the news about the footage I'd taken of our last dive being corrupted, but some of the finest equipment in the world was at Woods Hole Oceanographic Institution. If anyone could salvage the footage, it was Bill Lange. He and Evan worked for weeks, using all the tricks they knew and then going at it by trial and error. It seemed the lights I used had ballasts that created a field that prevented the HD cards from reading or recording images when the ballasts flickered. We later learned the field or electromagnetic interference (EMI) was generated from HID ballasts that were faulty or failing. The EMI emissions corrupted the control processor on the recorder, causing the status indications to show one state while the recorder was in another mode. Under other circumstances, we could have been more philosophical about it.

I didn't know exactly how or when, but I would be back.

Carl wasn't the first friend killed in a diving accident, but his death hit me as hard, if not more, than any other. Carrie sadly remembered the cheerful man who had been so accommodating of her in England, and the obituary Kevin Gurr wrote about Carl brought a poignant smile despite the pain.

During the next six years, I made 228 dives all over the world, including exotic locales such as Chuuk Lagoon in the Pacific, the North Sea off Belgium, the Gulf of Cadiz from Portugal, and the Sea of Cortez out of Baja Mexico. I did a few great domestic sites such as the Dry Tortugas off Key West, Florida, as well as the upper Florida Keys and in the Great Lakes. I sprinkled in a little cave diving, although shipwrecks are always the real draw for me.

I spent two summers with Evan searching off the Nantucket Shoals for *U-550*, a World War II German U-boat. We found a few virgin targets, but another team beat us to the U-boat. So it goes. Even as we brought veteran shipwreck hunter Ralph Wilbanks and others into our ultimately fruitless search for *U-550*, we kept the hopeful fires burning for a return to Kea. We stayed in touch with prospective team members and wrote and polished an SOP to be ready for whatever might come up.

When Evan called me in 2012 to come to WHOI in Cape Cod, Massachusetts, for a meeting with Bill, my first thought was *Britannic*. If so, what kind of project would it be? I didn't have to wait long to find out it would be a major expedition involving a number of different organizations. It sounded like everything we'd been hoping for, and if this project was greenlighted, Evan would be the director of underwater photography. They asked me if I would pick and lead the dive team. I was honored. I recall quite clearly Bill's direct question: "What would you do differently in light of Carl's accident if we do go back?"

I took this as a "what was learned in 2009" kind of line, and it was typical Bill. No malice, no blame, just an honest question, but the kind that makes you wince. He saw the wheels spinning and offered me a little time to think about it. I didn't need time; I think everyone on the 2009 dive team had repeatedly considered the same question. I told him there were several contributing factors, each of which played into Carl's accident, and each would be addressed with the following team members:

1. A dedicated *nondiving* dive marshal (DM)/dive supervisor who could flag a dive or diver without being second guessed by anyone. Had Carl not been such a hands-on leader, a separate DM would have questioned when his last dive had been (one year!) or forced him to make the checkout dive the day before as did every other dive member except Carl. Carl had worn too many hats as team leader, herding all the cats, as a co-producer working on shot lists, project goals with each team, as on-screen

talent being interviewed, and having the camera in his face or over his shoulder all the time, and then as a working diver on a difficult dive.

2. A dedicated gas mixer to analyze, label, and maintain a daily log on every cylinder of gas on the project. Each diver would still be responsible for his/her own analysis, but the gas mixer would ensure there would be no mislabeled or inappropriate gases on the project and be responsible for every tank's contents with no exception.

3. A dedicated support team (four in total) who were not bottom divers. This would lessen the workload on the bottom divers.

4. A specialized recovery team and a photographic team, all experienced in deepwater work. (Better to be prepared in the event recovery could be a part of the project.)

Thinking we would be greenlighted for a spring 2012 program, I went home, and, with Evan's input, I chose my "dream team" based on four factors:

1. **Experience first:** Even if they hadn't been to *Britannic* before, they must have been diving as deep or deeper and must have extensive wreck- or cave-diving experience.

2. **Recovery divers:** Half my team would be experienced in locating, identifying, and recovering artifacts from deepwater wrecks and well-versed in shipwreck penetration techniques.

3. **Photographers/videographers:** The other half of the team would be experienced, deepwater photographers or videographers with extensive wreck- and/or cave-diving experience.

4. **Dedicated support staff:** I would not task the bottom divers with multiple hats to wear. The support would consist of a nondiving DM/dive supervisor, dedicated support divers (four), and topside crew consisting of a gas mixer and hard deck assistant/communications to DM.

I opted to return to divers I knew and had been with in 2006 and 2009: Leigh Bishop, Edoardo Pavia, Mark Bullen, Mike Barnette, Richie Stevenson, Danny Huyge, Jarrod Jablonski, Casey McKinlay, Joe Porter, and Pete Mesley. Three of the new names had been to *Britannic* before and were some of the best wreck divers in the world: Richard Lundgren, Rick Waring, and Jeff Cornish.

Two new photographers, Tamara Thompson and Becky Kagan, had not been to *Britannic* but were some of the best deep-diving camera people and cave/wreck divers in the world. Added to the team would be Andrew Fock as our hyperbaric doctor and backup cameraman, Rory Golden as DM/dive supervisor, Cliff Diamond as gas mixer, Mike and Greg Procopio, Jeff Goodreau, and Joe

Porter as support divers. The twenty-fourth member of my "dream team" was still to be drawn from a list of several highly qualified divers but whose availability couldn't be locked down until we knew the project was a green light.

Everyone on the team agreed to be volunteers, paying their own airfare to Greece, although diving costs, lodging, and food would be covered by the project. I asked each of them to give me at least two weeks on-site (we planned three weeks for the project). I promised if we could get/raise the budget to cover airfare we would, but I wanted to keep the cost as close to bare bones as possible to help make the project a "go." Every one of them was willing to do this.

I assembled the team using Skype's video-teleconferencing ability, regular email, phone calls, and local meetings to discuss the logistics. I drafted and dispersed the SOP, encouraging input and questions. Privately, outside of the group, Evan solicited costs from boats, hotels, and shipping and rental gear to form a budget without getting any confirmation the project was going to proceed. We planned on using *Fourcault* again because not only was it a proven platform, it also was the most cost effective. It would travel from its home berth in Belgium, go to England and pick up all the rental gear, the dive team's personal equipment and consumables, and make the two-week trip to the Aegean ahead of us. As we knew from the 2009 Expedition, they could easily lodge and feed our team aboard. This solution combined critical transportation with operations and made it "one-stop shopping" from a logistics standpoint.

As the New Year came, I held fast, hoping the call would come any day. In late March, I had to accept that a spring project wouldn't be viable. We just didn't have enough time to get the logistics in place for a May/June window, so the project was pushed to fall of 2013. That was not the best time for weather in the Kea Channel, and I lost some team members to other commitments. As spring turned to summer, there was still no word. In August, I flagged it for the following spring in 2014, and I reluctantly passed the news to the group.

As the snow fell and winter became a cold reality, so did the fact there was no movement on behalf of the Greeks to greenlight the project. The few encouraging words and emails from Simon Mills did little to shine any light on a gloomy conclusion: The project was going nowhere. My team asked about the next year's plans. Should they dedicate their holidays/vacation time toward the project? Evan and I felt we had already made fools of ourselves — the two boys who cried "Wolf!" and got everyone excited and made them miss out on other dive projects in order to keep their schedules free and clear. We were always honest with them and didn't want to stop twenty-two people from making diving or vacation plans without a concrete green light. We kept them posted, but everything was on hold.

As frustrated as we were, I suddenly received a call about an entirely different opportunity, and if I was superstitious, I would say the connection to *Britannic* was an omen. I was invited to participate in a mission aboard the exploration vessel (EV) *Nautilus* with Dr. Robert Ballard, a personal hero of mine for everything he's done to advance underwater exploration. The mission also involved an always irresistible World War II U-boat. This expedition was to explore and film the shipwreck for a documentary film, but as it turned out, a close review of the facts surrounding the sinking took on an unexpected dimension. I ultimately went to the highest levels of the Pentagon and helped correct a historical "wrong" to enable a wartime hero to receive recognition seventy-two years after the fact!

The EV *Nautilus* travels the world's oceans exploring and educating through live telepresence with its many global partners. The 2014 field mission was to the Gulf of Mexico for a combination science mission and shipwreck project. For me, the highlight would be exploration of the German submarine *U-166* and her final victim, *Robert E. Lee*. Both wrecks had been accidentally discovered in 2001 by C&C Technologies while surveying a planned deepwater pipeline route.

I was aboard to assist with a NOVA/National Geographic documentary film about the German submarine offensive against America during World War II because the type IX German U-boat is a subject I know well. Sitting next to Dr. Ballard in the control van, my job would be to detail the technology on *U-166* and discuss the events leading up to and around the sinking of both *U-166* and *Robert E. Lee*. This was how certain facts surfaced and prompted Ballard to set the wheels in motion to ultimately change the U.S. Navy's account of the sinking.

The historical context was important. Since the January 1942 opening blows of Operation *Aukenschlag* (translated as Drumbeat), German U-boats operated nearly unchecked up and down the eastern seaboard of the United States, racking up an incredible tally of sunk and damaged ships. Their battle plan was simple: Wage a tonnage war against the allies, sinking ships and their cargos faster than they could build or replace them. In those first months, from Maine to Florida, ships exploded, and pools of burning oil served as funeral pyres in what U-boat sailors coined "the great American turkey shoot."

In July 1942, the 5,184-ton passenger/freighter *Robert E. Lee* departed Trinidad and headed directly into the newest killing zone. Aboard were 407 souls; some were survivors of other ships recently sunk by German U-boats in the Caribbean. To stave off destruction, *Robert E. Lee* was armed with a stern-mounted deck gun and was being escorted by the U.S. patrol craft *PC-566* for the journey to Tampa, Florida.

The actual details of what occurred are fascinating, but the essence was a U-boat torpedoed *Robert E. Lee*. Captain Herbert Claudius and his 65-man crew aboard *PC-566* sprang into action, increasing speed and chasing down the track of the torpedo toward the submerged U-boat. The crew of *PC-566* was shocked to see the U-boat's periscope come out of the water to enjoy its handiwork. Racing over the swirl where it descended, the patrol vessel dropped a brace of five depth charges. Captain Claudius noted *Robert E. Lee* had disappeared, having sunk in less than ten minutes. Reestablishing sonar contact, *PC-566* roared once again over the U-boat's position and dropped another set of depth charges. As the explosions subsided, all sonar contact with the submarine was lost. A large pool of oil spread, but the entire area was fouled with flotsam, making it impossible to differentiate what may have come from the U-boat or *Lee*. Captain Claudius felt certain he had killed the U-boat but had no evidence to prove it.

The crew of *PC-566* was not given a hero's welcome when they returned to port. An odd event caused navy officials to doubt Captain Claudius's account of their actions. Stripped of his command, Captain Claudius was sent to the Submarine Chaser Training Center in Florida for additional training, his career stained by the decision.

Information about a separate event that would have supported Captain Claudius was not passed on due to the highly classified nature of the information. Even though the information was declassified in 1974, there was no one to press the case for Captain Claudius and the crew of the *PC-566*. They had acted in the finest tradition of the U.S. Navy, exacting swift and terrible retribution against the U-boat, but fifty-six years later, the truth about *U-166*'s destruction rested in perpetual darkness 5,000 feet down.

In having learned these details and recounting them to Ballard aboard the EV *Nautilus*, I made the offhand comment I felt the U.S. Navy had not treated Captain Claudius and his crew fairly at the time. Even with the wreckage having been located and proving him a hero in 2001, the U.S. Navy hadn't corrected the record. Ballard agreed this was an oversight, and he immediately made a satellite call to the Chief of Naval Operations (CNO), who promised to look into it. The wheels of government may move slowly, but eventually they do move.

Although Captain Claudius had sadly passed away never knowing of his success, on December 16, 2014, I was honored to join Ballard at the Pentagon as the Secretary of the Navy and the Chief of Naval Operations awarded Captain Herbert Claudius (posthumously) the Legion of Merit for valor in action. Captain Claudius's son, Gordon, was present and accepted on his father's behalf. While shaking Gordon Claudius's hand in the Pentagon, the connection between past and present and of a deep-sea mystery finally came to the surface.

It's what I love about being a shipwreck explorer — the chance for our work to make a difference in people's lives. Getting to work alongside the man who found *Titanic*, then explored *Britannic* in the nuclear research submarine *NR-1* (as well as numerous other shipwrecks and accomplishments too lengthy to list) was pretty great, too.

Ballard is a gracious host and a regular guy. Eating popcorn and watching *20,000 Leagues Under the Sea* with his daughter, Emily, in the salon aboard his

Nautilus, 200 miles out at sea after a day of deep-sea explorations of his own was something special to remember.

Although it was a great experience, I continuously thought about delays with the *Britannic* Expedition and wondered if we could return.

PART III

HONORING A FRIEND'S LEGACY

SECRETS REVEALED AND MORE TO COME

R ARELY A DAY PASSED when *Britannic* was completely absent from my thoughts. As difficult as it was for everyone to accept the tragedy of Carl's death, the sense of an unfinished legacy was stronger. We didn't immediately express intentions to mount another expedition — we collectively knew we needed to step away for a while. Even though it was not the first time most of us had lost a friend in a diving accident, we each had to come to terms with our personal feelings for the ship. The irony of having finally solved the most pressing question about her sinking and still been denied definitive proof to show the world was an ache that wouldn't disappear. As often as our quiet exchanges were tinged with somberness, there was determination as well to finally bring this answer to light.

And despite our sorrow, *Britannic* is a wreck that undeniably surpasses all others in sheer size, beauty, and mystery. She is a monument to history, a reminder of engineering triumph, of the vision of men who built her literally by hand in the days before computers and sophisticated construction methods.

Had she fulfilled her original purpose, she would have reigned as the finest example of the Golden Age of Ocean Liners for at least several years. How could we not want to continue the quest? If we refused to return to her, how could we call ourselves explorers?

CHAPTER 20

RETURN TO *BRITANNIC?*
NOT SO FAST.

URING ONGOING DISCUSSIONS WITH WHOI about the *Britannic* project, Simon Mills connected us with the U-Boat Malta company. He thought we could establish a line of communication with them in the event some form of cooperation with the proposed project might be realized.

U-Boat Malta is a division of the Russian U-Group holding company. Their list of expeditions throughout the Mediterranean is impressive. *U-Boat Navigator* (*UBN*) is a 79-foot custom vessel, built in consultation with professional divers. Their two submersibles, Triton 3300/3 and C-Explorer 5.8, combined with an Ageotec Perseo GTV ROV, are some of the most advanced imaging platforms for deep-sea exploration. Add to this the onboard decompression chamber, four-man diving bell, a medical facility, and an 18-ton articulating crane to provide the kind of support that any diver or ocean researcher can appreciate.

Simon made one dive with them and was impressed with the operation, the vessel, and how they were able to include more technical equipment than normally available on boats of comparable size. As much as he appreciated the features of *Commandant Fourcault*, *UBN* can be in the Aegean from its home base in a couple of days. From his view, that could be a more practical option than bringing *Fourcault* from a longer distance. He quietly reached out to Evan about *UBN*, and in the winter of 2014, Evan sent me a website link to look at the boat. Although the capabilities were impressive, I wasn't enthusiastic about it from an operational standpoint.

We planned a twenty-four-person dive team, plus WHOI staff, topside ROV operators with all their camera equipment, and one to three representatives from the Greek Ministry. Although it looked like a yacht from a James Bond film, it appeared too small for our needs. The project costs would climb because we'd need another dive platform (possibly a crane-barge moored over the wreck), additional RIBs for support and transport, and island-based lodging and food.

I voted for *Commandant Fourcault*. Evan tried to get *UBN* prices and schedule to calculate potential costs. The Russians who owned the vessel knew of me by reputation in the dive community and extended an invitation to join their spring dive operations on *Britannic* to see them at work. Evan asked if I would go to see the boat and "maybe" get a submersible ride. As much I would have preferred the major expedition with its ambitious goals, the constant delays had me concerned. Too many variables could cause it to fall apart, or maybe the expedition would be put together by others and I wouldn't be able to participate for some reason. Thinking through it from that angle, if we were able to make the U-Boat Malta deal work, it might be my last certain opportunity to visit *Britannic*. I didn't want to pass up even the vaguest possibility of physically diving rather than a submersible dive. I pushed Evan to find out what our chances were.

Weeks passed by, and emails went back and forth. Finally, they agreed we could dive if certain (undefined) circumstances worked out. We could dive from their boat as a platform, but we were on our own for gear and support with all the associated logistics. We leapt at the chance, even though we knew weather and the other factors surrounding dives on *Britannic* meant our chance was slim. It could be a lot of money tossed away with nothing more to show for it than maybe a submersible ride, but what the hell? It wouldn't be the first or likely the last time in my life I had taken a chance like this and put my money down. The circumstances were reminiscent of when we funded our way to *Titanic* in 2005, the trip that led me into the quest to solve the mysteries of *Britannic*. The key here was who to ask to be our support diver?

I went to Leigh first, but the timing and circumstances didn't work for him. I was asking a lot of anyone to fund their own way and make the time commitment. Mike Barnette (Barney) was my next call. I knew he had been diving deep all winter so his skills were up to par, and he had been to *Britannic* before. Plus, he got a fair amount of vacation time at work and had done a lot of travel. Perhaps he had miles to use for his airfare. It's hard to ask a guy to pay his own way, go as far as Greece, and not make the dive but watch over us. I told Barney "if" they offered us a submersible ride, the seat was his, but there were no guarantees. I'm not sure I would have done it (I like to think I would, but man, what a hard call to make), but Barney said yes, and we had our small team.

Finally, U-Boat Malta confirmed our arrangement — or at least as much confirmation as we could expect. Faced with the possibility this could be my last chance to be on *Britannic*, I wanted to take an extra step. Carl had been awarded an Explorers Club flag to carry on the 2009 Expedition, and it seemed fitting to also apply for a flag. This was another way to pay tribute to him.

Applying for an Explorers Club flag and then saying "Hey, sorry guys, the trip's been canceled" isn't the kind of thing you want to do. They have a provision for making short-notice applications. I scrambled to apply, as I felt confident we would launch as scheduled. I hoped we could carry the same flag Carl had been awarded for the 2009 Expedition, but there had been discussion the flag would be retired. I knew the members of the committee would have their own rationale for whatever flag was awarded us. Although we didn't receive Carl's flag, we received a legendary flag within the Explorers Club. Thank you, David Concannon. (David also originally caused me to become involved with *Titanic*.)

There are two stories about the flag. The first story begins with an excerpt from *The Explorers Log*, Fall 2014 edition:

The Legend of the Unnumbered Flag

"For years, rumors circulated around the Club about a mysterious 'unnumbered Flag' that supposedly was carried on the 1985 Expedition that discovered the R.M.S. *Titanic* before it disappeared. Indeed, a photograph showing the Flag on display on the RV *Knorr* on September 1, 1985, the day the *Titanic* was discovered, used to hang over the bar at headquarters, and the photo was even used as Exhibit A in the litigation that restored public access to historic shipwrecks for exploration when the case went to the U.S. Supreme Court. The Flag was carried on the *Titanic* discovery expedition, without the Club's permission, because the expedition's members were sworn to secrecy; therefore, they could not formally apply for permission to carry a numbered Flag before the expedition, and somebody created an unnumbered Flag instead. Once news of the *Titanic*'s discovery broke, the expedition members sent their group photo to the Club as a sort of 'Look what we did!' celebration, but the Flag disappeared. According to legend, this unnumbered Flag was carried by other secret expeditions of equal significance to the *Titanic*'s discovery, after which 'retroactive' approval was quietly sought. The Flag remained hidden for nearly 30 years until it was recently discovered in a California garage among the possessions of Ralph B. White, MED '82, a legendary raconteur and former chair of the Southern California Chapter, who died suddenly in 2008. It was returned by Dr. Rosaly Lopes at the 2014 West Coast Explorers Club Dinner, and it will now be retired and hang in a place of prominence in New York."

That's the official story. As often happens, there is a behind-the-scenes story. National Geographic cinematographer Ralph White had the flag made by the same company that makes Explorers Club flags so the Club would be represented on the secret *Titanic* discovery expedition. This was White's third expedition to search for *Titanic*, and he knew they were close to finding it. However, because of secrecy surrounding the expedition (which was paid for by the U.S. Navy to demonstrate to the Soviets that the United States could find anything lost in the deep ocean), White could not ask the Explorers Club in advance for permission to carry the flag. White, who served two tours of duty in Vietnam as a sergeant in U.S. Marine Corps Force Recon, understood the value of secrecy, but he also believed in ribbons, medals, flags, and other military regalia and wasn't averse to bending the rules.

When *Titanic* was discovered on September 1, 1985, National Geographic photographer Emory Kristof took a photo of the crew on the fantail of the RV *Knorr*, displaying the EC flag and the National Geographic flag. White sent the photo to EC headquarters in New York City to say, "Look what we did!"

Not everyone within the Club was enthusiastic about the breach of procedure, and disagreement about it simmered for a while. In the 1990s, Ralph White made movies with James Cameron, and despite any feeling about the flag, the parties came back together in 1998 when a lawsuit over access to *Titanic* threatened to stop all access to historic shipwrecks for exploration and photography. David Concannon represented White, the Explorers Club, and others in this litigation, which they won, but not before going all the way to the U.S. Supreme Court.

David and Ralph went to *Titanic* in 2000 (carrying a different EC flag), and their efforts paved the way for extensive exploration of *Titanic* and other wrecks over the next several years, including the *Titanic* 2005 Expedition I went on with David and Ralph, carrying EC flag No. 132. (As an aside, my sub buddy and cameraman for my first *Titanic* dive in *Mir II* on August 13, 2005, was none other than Ralph White.)

Meanwhile, the "unofficial flag" remained on Ralph's wall as a trophy to what he considered his most significant accomplishment. Ralph died suddenly in 2008, and the flag went into storage with his other possessions. The flag is rumored to have gone on other significant expeditions in underwater exploration, including the 2011 Expedition that discovered the *Apollo* F-1 engines that launched men to the moon. In 2014, Ralph's daughter agreed to return the flag to the Club, but she thought it would be retired.

There was a mix-up along the way, and the flag was mistakenly numbered 135, a flag first put into circulation in 1950 and one which Dr. Robert Ballard had carried to the *Titanic* in 1986. It took nearly a year to correct the error and restore the flag's proper history. Once the lineage was properly resolved, what could be more fitting than for it to go to the tragic third Olympian?

David, now vice president for the Explorers Club's Flag and Honors Committee, ensured that I would receive this flag when the Club approved my request to carry an EC flag to *Britannic,* thus extending its history more in line with its creation. The flag would then be on its way to Belfast, Northern Ireland, to be displayed in the Titanic Belfast exhibit to commemorate the 30th anniversary of *Titanic'*s discovery. After that, the flag would be returned to the United States and be retired. You can see why I felt even more than the usual surge of honor when I was told about this particular flag.

Now that we had the flag to bring with us, I concentrated on the remaining outstanding issues. Other than not having to make further arrangements for a support boat, we had to line up the rest of the intensive logistics package — shipping hundreds of pounds of equipment, transporting people to Kea, obtaining lodging, and renting very specific diving equipment and gases from the Greeks. We also hoped to swap out a Droycon experiment. If anyone else decided to join us, they would have to make their own arrangements. We had enough to deal with.

We ticked the items off the list and then it happened — all the arrangements I'd made for the extra dive equipment from our Greek supplier fell apart. U-Boat Malta had been clear about us being self-sufficient, and our dive package of support had evaporated with no notice. How in the hell were we supposed to have any chance at all to dive? It was a repeat of the debacle — or near debacle — of 2006, and I had no choice other than to hope I could reach Edoardo Pavia (Edo) and he could somehow save my butt. How can you not admire a guy you track down halfway across the world with a request like that and he cheerfully agrees to, once again, come to the rescue? I'm not sure how many points my blood pressure dropped after our conversation, but it was significant. With his reassurance, we were back on.

Yeah, we had a lot riding on several "maybes," but that's part of the nature of exploration: Prepare for the outcome you want, and understand the outcome could be entirely different or that you can come away empty-handed.

We were as ready as we could be, and I wasn't the least bit hesitant about hoping luck would be traveling with us.

CHAPTER 21

NOTHING EVER COMES EASY

EXPLORER CLUB FLAG IN MY BACKPACK and Edo ready to rescue us with equipment, the day of departure arrived. I was determined to maintain a *Britannic* 2015 daily diary, and the next few chapters come directly from that. (It has been edited to fill in where I made quick or abbreviated entries, and I've included additional explanations in parentheses.)

June 22, 2015

I met Evan at Boston's Logan Airport at 10:00 a.m. and checked our ten boxes of gear (plus two carry-ons makes twelve cases). It went smoothly as we had our carnet (an official travel document listing all equipment and eases your way through customs), and they did grant us a media rate for the pile of gear.

Bill Lange came to the airport to see us off, offering last-minute advice, opinions, and prayers. There was a slight delay in the flight going to Newark, but we arrived in time for a sushi lunch, to pick up some items at the duty-free shop, and then relax in the United Club lounge until our 5:30 p.m. flight. The place was packed, and I mean standing room only, so we found an empty conference room and let ourselves in to set up laptops and go over last-minute details. We discussed the latest foul-up with the Droycon science experiments that had been shipped to Athens from Canada. The Greek customs folks at FedEx wouldn't release the package to Tina Tavridou, who was once again our fixer, and we hoped a Greek translation of the scientific history of Droycon work on *Britannic* emailed from Lori Johnston would help release it.

At 4:00 p.m., I got a call from team member Mike Barnette. He was stuck in Canadian customs. With only three months left on his passport, the custom officials wouldn't let him board his final leg to Athens. He was in Toronto and would go to the U.S.

Consulate in the morning and ask for an emergency extension. There was nothing we could do. Thank God (again) for Edo. If Barney was turned around, at least we had Edo and the project goes on. It's always something.

It was a packed plane, but the flight went smoothly. I had a window seat, and after dinner I leaned up against the bulkhead and slept. We arrived in Zurich, Switzerland, twenty minutes early.

June 23, 2015

All smooth through Swiss customs, but no time for coffee before boarding the last leg to Athens. Again flight went smooth, sleeping most of the two-hour flight in a center seat (a skill mastered, I may add). In Athens, our luggage appeared to be in good order. We loaded it onto three carts and headed off to Greek customs. Tina was already there waiting for us, smiling and waving. This was my third time working with her and Evan's eighth.

This woman knows a handful of languages and is efficient and unflappable. After all her help in 2006 as our fixer, I couldn't imagine being on a project in Greece without her.

She's on a first-name basis with most of the customs people, and after hugs and greetings, we were taken out of the line and shepherded into a separate office area, where our papers and carnet were checked and logged. In two shakes of a lamb's tail, we were through and in Greece. So far, so good.

Tina had rented a small blue van, and after loading the gear, we headed to the airport shipping area to pick up the Droycon experiments. Despite nearly two hours of spirited discussion and every form of documentation we had, we could not get the customs folks to release the box. With the promise they would talk to a superior and try to get it released the following day, we had no choice but to leave without it. It was a one-hour drive from Athens to Lavrion, where we would board the Marmari ferry. The drive took us through some nice country peppered with olive groves and vineyards.

Along the way, we spotted Edo's Sea Dweller Divers van on the highway and beeped and waved as our small caravan continued to the seaside port of Lavrion. After joyful hugs of reunion, we purchased our ferry tickets and went to a little waterfront café for a lunch of Greek salad, fava beans, and grilled squid. Boarding the 6:00 p.m. ferry, we had flat seas for the crossing to Kea that was to be our base and home for the next two weeks. Along the way, Tina pointed out the now-abandoned island of Makronissos (Long Island), which was a prison for leftists after the Greek 1946-49 civil war and then a refugee camp. The empty buildings glowed orange in the late afternoon sun. These islands are so beautiful in their rugged desolation against the rich blue Aegean.

A phone call from Barney with great news: His passport was amended/extended, and he was booked on the next plane to Greece, due to arrive the following morning!

Above: Richie Kohler explores *Burdigala*, another victim of *U-73*. The closed-circuit rebreather on his back emits no bubbles, and the tanks he carries under his arms are for emergency use only.

The wreck of *Britannic* rises nearly 100 feet off the seafloor, dwarfing Edoardo Pavia and the ROV above him.

The path leading through the boiler rooms is a maze of pipes, catwalks, and dead ends, with only one way in or out.

Opposite: A ship's lantern lays untouched for nearly a century on *Britannic*'s deck.

U-Boat Navigator was the dive platform for ROV, submersible, and diver operations in 2015.

Opposite: Inside the wreck, time seems to have frozen. This is the spiral staircase that leads down to the firemen's tunnel.

The port-side propeller dwarfs visiting divers. During the sinking, it was the cause of all the casualties aboard *Britannic*.

The dive team is about to leave the wreck and begin the six-hour ascent.

Opposite: Parks Stephenson, in consultation with Ken Marschall and Bill Sauder, has digitally recreated the inside of a boiler room that had been undisturbed for a century.

Below: The open doorways in Boiler Room 5 and Boiler Room 6 left the flooding unchecked.

EVAN KOVACS   NATIONAL MUSEUMS NORTHERN IRELAND

MICHAEL BARNETTE

Using the diving bell as an elevator and haven from the current, the dive team is watched over by the ROV and Triton submersible.

EVAN KOVACS

The 2015 *Britannic* international team effort used technically advanced diving equipment to reveal the answer to a 100-year-old mystery.

The firemen's tunnel is the beginning of three silt-choked compartments. The line near the center of the photo is the only way out in zero visibility.

Below: Edoardo Pavia and Richie Kohler fly the Explorers Club flag from the diving bell, with the ROV in the background.

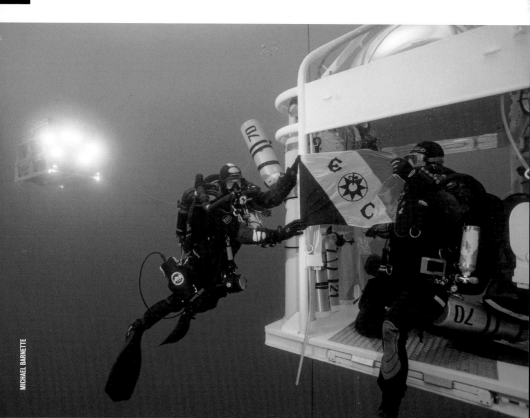

After a century underwater, *Britannic* still retains her iconic lines.

As we steamed along on the ferry, our group went over this project's genesis and planning, stopping our discussion only when the lighthouse at the entrance to Korissia Harbor came into view. This is a beautiful harbor.

We made our way to the Hotel Korissia, which is quite modern (by island standards) and very comfortable. Our host, Takis (Tie-key), is very accommodating to our (soon-to-be-large) group. We looked at all the rooms, and Evan and Edo took the largest room for their media center/camera room, Tina took the next largest room with one bed, but that had a large salon for more charging stations as well as conducting our pre- and postdive group meetings. Barney and I were to share a room. Takis provided a ground-floor secure storage area into which we unloaded all of the equipment to create a dive locker. Evan had already unloaded all the cameras, housings, lights, etc., and had it spread out across the room. Tiny green and red lights from battery chargers blinked all over the room like Christmas decorations.

With the fall of darkness, we had a typical Greek late dinner at a wharf-side café, and during small talk, the rigid inflatable boat (RIB) from our hosts, U-Boat Malta, pulled up and offloaded a man and woman. We didn't introduce ourselves since we expected to meet the *UBN* crew the next day. We let them walk into the darkness before we too called it a night.

June 24, 2015

Up early (7:00 a.m.) for a simple breakfast of coffee, bread with butter, and jam. First things first, we assembled our equipment in the blessed shade of our dive locker. It's not crazy hot here, but to my New England constitution, it's hot but thankfully not humid. Drinking a lot of water as we worked, we packed scrubbers, filled small tanks for suit inflation, and checked all our gear as it was unpacked. Airport TSA staff have been known to disassemble components for inspection, with near tragic consequence.

A few years back, Carrie and I were in Palau, and on the first dive, her corrugated inflator hose came off her BC (buoyancy compensator) before she jumped in the water. The large hose that fills the vest had been removed for inspection by the TSA and not put back correctly or even fastened tightly. Had she jumped in the water with a faulty hose, she wouldn't have been able to arrest her descent and would have plummeted to the seafloor. Lesson learned from that was we assume nothing and check and recheck everything.

Evan went into town for supplies and ran into Dmitry, the son of our host, and went to see *U-Boat Navigator* moored in Korrisa Harbor. After meeting Dmitry's father, Eugene, who was master of the vessel, Evan toured the vessel and was floored. The most commanding feature of the deep-red 79-foot vessel was the huge A-frame and bright yellow 3-man submersible on the afterdeck. On the port side was the ROV, and on the starboard side a 4-man diving bell capable of going 328 feet deep. Inside, the vessel was just as impressive, with the latest imaging technology, cameras, video and sensors, gas-mixing station, and even a medical suite with a seven-person hyperbaric chamber (decompression chamber). The exterior and interior fittings and features of the vessel rival any luxury yacht, but this vessel from stem-to-stern has the singular function of ocean exploration on behalf of the Russian Geographic Society. It was one thing to read about it and something else to see it. We started referring to her as *UBN*.

While Evan was on the vessel, I analyzed and gauged *every* cylinder for the project, all twenty-six of them. Each tank had now been labeled clearly twice with the maximum operating depth (MOD), the content of oxygen, helium, and the tank's pressure. The first label was done by Edo in Italy when he filled the tanks and now once again here on Kea by me. Each diver will then have the option to further test it, but I have confirmed to my own and the group's satisfaction the contents and pressure of each cylinder. This is a direct nod to the tragic and fatal accident that claimed Carl's life in 2009 when he breathed from a cylinder that had been incorrectly labeled. There were many other adjustments to be tweaked and fine-tuned on every piece of equipment, from dive computers to the lowest technology of a weight belt. Nothing is assumed, and everything is confirmed.

It was nearly 4:30 p.m. before all was said and done. We never even stopped for lunch. With growling stomachs, we loaded up Edo's van and headed over a few miles to Gialiskari Beach. We were leaving nothing to chance and did a thirty-minute checkout dive to confirm weighting, trim, and equipment function. I had three small issues that needed to be corrected: a low battery on one of my dive computers, a leaking hose, and adjustment of a weight belt. Returning to the dive locker, all was corrected. As I finished up, Barney walked in the door! It was already 8:30 p.m. Where did the day go?

Barney shared the details of his mini-drama in Canada as he unpacked and sorted his gear. After a late dinner, it was time for bed and an early start. Exhausted, I fell asleep almost immediately.

June 25, 2015

Up early and a quick breakfast at the local café before we loaded Edo's van and met *U-Boat Navigator* tied up to the quay in the center of town. The red boat caught everyone's attention as they passed by. I finally got to meet Eugene and his son, Dmitry, and was impressed by the direct look, firm handshake, and no-nonsense feel from them. They look more like brothers than father and son, and they have an easy way to them. They are both big men, not tall but broad in the chest with arms like tree limbs. There is always an uneasy chemistry among divers about to work together for the first time as we size each other up. I cannot say what they thought of me and my team, but they were consummate professionals and ran an immaculate, tight ship. The nine-man crew moved efficiently, and it was obvious *U-Boat Navigator* was a well-oiled machine.

Eugene told us where to store our sizable quantity of equipment, and when all was secure, we made our way out to sea. The U-Boat team had been imaging another

WWI shipwreck in the area and wanted to finish up filming there before moving on to *Britannic*. The wreck was the armed French passenger liner SS *Burdigala* that had struck one of the mines laid in the Kea Channel by *U-73* and sank November 9, 1916, just twelve days before *Britannic* would enter and be lost from the same minefield. However, *Burdigala*'s crew believed they had been torpedoed (not mined) and began firing the huge deck guns at imaginary or perceived sightings of periscopes and submarines before sinking in 250 feet of water.

In the afternoon, the wind traditionally picks up in the Aegean, and today was no exception. The wind blew about twelve to sixteen knots with the seas growing, but we continued out to the wreck site in the hope the wind would soon drop off and the seas would calm down, which thankfully they did. It takes *UBN* about ninety minutes to set the three-point mooring required for them to sit directly above the wreck and not swing or move. First, the ROV was deployed, and then as we kitted up for the dive, Eugene, Dmitry, and an observer boarded the Triton submersible and launched. A heavy weighted line was dropped amidships for the dual purpose of tethering the ROV and to serve as our descent line. At 130 feet, the outline of the wreck could be seen.

Lighting the wreck like a Hollywood movie set, the submersible and ROV worked in unison to light and film various features of this amazingly intact shipwreck. Landing on the upper decks at 190 feet, I was amazed at the precision of the ship's anchoring; we were exactly at the bridge, just where they said we would be. The wooden structure had long fallen away, but the five-engine order and docking telegraphs and forward bridge windows were all standing. Other navigational equipment, such as the compass and steering helm, had fallen over in place. The submersible and ROV followed us, and we each filmed the other as we explored the wreck. It was unique to work in tandem with both the submersible and an unmanned robotic watchdog.

Swimming forward on the wreck, we saw the huge mainmast laying across the starboard gunwale and the large bronze bell still attached. Its (the ship's) stylish shape and flair made clear this was at one time a first-class passenger ship. Moving toward the bow, two huge guns stood on either side pointing out to the blue water, empty brass cases littering the deck, telling the story of those last moments. Swimming above the main deck and peering down into rooms through the rotted decks, I could see the lamp locker with brass lanterns still sitting on the shelves. Looking into each cabin, I saw a large porcelain bathtub amid bits and pieces of crockery and the remains of room fixtures. Everything was in an advanced state of deterioration but still in place after almost 100 years. This was a perfect warm-up dive for us, and after thirty-five minutes, we started up the line for our one-hour decompression. Back on board, it would prove to be a late night as the submarine and ROV operations continued until 10:30 p.m. Once they surfaced, the entire team had dinner at nearly midnight, and by the time the RIB brought us back to shore, it was 1:30 a.m.

June 26, 2015

Eugene made it clear we should arrive to board *UBN* by noon, a late start by any standard, but the previous day had been long and productive. We headed out to *Britannic* and assembled our gear. Our hosts had generously offered to refill our CCR tanks from the copious storage capacity aboard *UBN*, and we accepted. Soon after arriving at the wreck site, the back-and-forth of setting the three-point mooring began, and the afternoon winds started to rise again. As we began to get our dive gear ready for filling, word came to stand down. One of the mooring lines had severed, and we lost one anchor. Our ability to maintain station directly over *Britannic* was now made even more difficult, and with the rising wind and strong current, all diving and submarine operations were canceled for the day. As we headed back in, we had lunch with the *UBN* team and discussed plans for the next day. The weather forecast called for very high winds and seas, and the captain had called off all operations. We would have a down day to rest up, recheck and refill our own tanks, and the *UBN* team could procure another anchor. We headed back to shore in late afternoon and decided that this evening would be perfect to conduct our planned memorial to Carl Spencer.

Additional Notes to the Diary Entries

I have to be honest that prior to seeing and working on *U-Boat Navigator*, I was convinced working on *Fourcault* was like heaven for wreck divers. It's hard to believe anything could be better, but the Russians did it. It's not just the submersible or diving bell; *Fourcault* is an ex-military working ship and built to be utilitarian. *UBN* is like something from a James Bond movie. It's not only extremely advanced and capable, it's a damn luxury vessel to boot, with teak and polished stainless steel, leather and lacquered wood paneling, and great meals. It's not entirely fair to make the comparison, but the newer, although smaller and much more opulent, *UBN* is the finest working dive vessel (for divers) in the world that I have ever been on. Although it was well-outfitted, we decided to charter our own RIB to not be too much of a burden on our hosts and also to have access to the wreck in case we ran into difficulties with the Russians and had to make other boat arrangements.

On the uniqueness of being accompanied by the submersible and ROV, seeing three men sitting in the clear glass sphere, dry and comfortable as we explored, brought to mind the people who think all diving should be done with machines. We didn't have that discussion, so I don't know which side of the argument they support.

As for diving on *Burdigala*, I mentioned seeing the engine order and docking and telegraphs. Those are big bronze devices on the bridge next to the helm wheel that were used to communicate between sections of a steamship before electric or sound-powered phones were invented. Officers on the bridge could give orders and get confirmation of those orders when the bells rang. An order could be "rung up" for more speed or to stop the engine — an engine order telegraph. The other ones, that face longitudinally, are docking telegraphs, and they would be used to "cast off," "pull," or "hold" lines while docking or pushing off from a pier. There were two telegraphs for the engines and three for docking.

We never discussed it with Dmitry or any of his crew, but I thought their request for us to come along on the *Burdigala* dive was probably their way of wanting to see how we operated as divers. It did give us a chance to learn some of their procedures in what was an easier dive than the deeper *Britannic*. Whether that was the intent or not, there was an element of irony that the wreck was associated with *Britannic* by virtue of being another victim of Gustav Siess's undersea mines.

CHAPTER 22

A WREATH AND A SEAGULL

June 26, 2015 (Afternoon)

We drove around the harbor in Edo's van to the outermost tip of the cape. The road turned too steep and rocky for the van, so we went on foot, and just before the old lighthouse at the end of the path, we found a cut-through in the sheer rock cliffs that led to a small beachlike opening to the sea. The tide was going out, but we were gratefully in the lee from the wind. We went back to the hotel and got the wreath we'd brought from Athens. On the wreath I had attached in colorful envelopes four letters from Carl's wife, Vicky, his two children, Georgia and Ben, and his mother. These letters were not read aloud. I also attached three red roses and three ribbons that read "Loving Husband and Father," "Friend," and the last read "Explorer." The wreath was made of olive branches.

I spoke first of what Carl meant to me as a friend, of what I wrestled with in the days following his passing, how my heart went out and broke for Vicky and the children. Then I read a poem Vicky had written and was strong in voice but weak in my heart as I shared it with his friends. I tried to remain composed but couldn't help the tears that came as I shared Vicky's angst and innermost feelings. When done, I closed with Psalm 107:23 from the King James Version of the Bible:

> *They that go down to the sea in ships, that do business in great waters;*
> *These see the works of the LORD, and his wonders in the deep.*
> *For he commands, and raises the stormy wind, which lifts up the waves.*
> *They mount up to the heaven, they go down again to the depths:*
> *their soul melts away because of trouble.*
> *They reel to and fro, and stagger like drunken men, and are at their wits' end.*
> *Then they cry unto the LORD in their trouble, and he brings them out of their distress.*

He calms the storm so that the waves are still.
Then are they glad because the seas are quiet, and he guides them into safe harbor.

After I finished, Evan spoke of Carl's example in leadership, friendship, and his contagious passion for life and adventure. Finally, Edo spoke of Carl, his friendship, and our collective loss. His words and feeling brought more tears, freely from us all. Six years is not enough time. Maybe not even a hundred more will assuage the empty spot where Carl lives in each of us. The sun slipped farther down, and Edo and I eased the wreath into the water. As the outgoing tide slowly carried away the wreath, a single seagull came out of the sun and flew across the seascape, from left to right, and flew off behind the rocky cliffs. We all looked at each other and wondered aloud if once again this was Carl's way of sending a message. I choose to believe so.

We then toasted Carl with "Explorers Club Gold Road" Scotch whiskey and shared into the sea his Diet Coke and crisps he enjoyed so much. As the wreath floated away, we stood on that barren rocky beach and each spoke of good times and memories of meeting, knowing, and loving Carl ... some of the stories so typically "Carl" we all found ourselves laughing and smiling and knowing, each deep in our hearts, our lives are richer and better for having known him.

We went back into town and had a quiet dinner. It was almost 10:30 p.m., and we decided to wait for the 11:00 p.m. ferry. Tina had left early that morning to head to Athens to pick up the science experiment, which had finally been released by customs, and also to meet the topside camera crew at the airport. The film crew and Tina arrived, and we sat and talked about where we were so far and what was the next day's agenda. As diving had been suspended due to weather, we talked for a few hours. The plan would now be to film *UBN* in the harbor and familiarize the team with many of the components and equipment we planned to use over the next day. Again, a long day, and we didn't stop until 2:00 a.m.

I have never met Vicky, but I thought from what I knew of her, she would understand our heartfelt desire to have this memorial for Carl on Kea. We had engaged in a series of emails, and that was what prompted the letters. In a telephone conversation after our return from Kea, Vicky was nervous, and that was understandable. I can't begin to imagine how difficult it must have been for her to tell the children about their father's accident. I learned that Ben had been called "Carl's buddy," and Georgia was "Peanut." Ben may well become a marine biologist with a focus on photography and the scientific experimenting side — at least that's where his interest is right now.

In talking about their early life and Carl's spirit for adventure, Vicky met him just after he'd come back from America, where he'd been for two years. She was twenty-one, and he was twenty-two, and even their marriage was the sort of thing that those who knew Carl could smile about. They eloped and went on an around-the-world trip. They sent cards to their families from Heathrow Airport in London when they left, and they stopped in the beautiful island chain of Fiji. In what Vicky said was typical

Carl and another "first," they passed through passport control, where the officials thought they were royalty and related to Lady Diana Spencer, which Carl thought was ace! (Ace being a word he used often for his excitement and expression.) They were married October 17, 1997, on Fiji's Sonsali Island, and Vicky actually got qualified to dive the day after. What she most wants people to know about Carl is he was filled with a boundless energy and would instantly turn heads when he walked into a room — there aren't that many people who can captivate you instantly. If he said he would do something, he did. He was so generous with others, very humble though, and no big ego — he was self-effacing. To lose him to diving was quite a shock. He was a family man who loved his wife and his children. There was a sad smile in her voice when she related a story about how when Carl was on *Titanic*, he wanted to give them a call because he thought that would be a great treat for young Ben. That was one of the few things that he couldn't pull off.

For me, shipwreck exploration and solving maritime mysteries are what takes me into the depths, and Vicky said that Carl certainly loved that, too. She said it didn't matter whether it was a large ship or a small one; if there was an error about a ship's service, he wanted to help correct it. There had been situations where, particularly in time of war, men hadn't gotten the credit they deserved for certain acts, and Carl had brought up evidence to set the record straight. As often as he did that, he was very much about supporting science experiments at sea — he thought the sea was teeming with great medical possibilities. It's understandable that Vicky withdrew from the public eye after the tragedy, but she did attend some of the *Titanic* centennial events in 2012, since Carl would have.

As a family, they continue with some of the same kinds of things that Carl loved.

Vicky wrote: "Ben, Georgia, and I recently swam with whale sharks, and the photography Ben took with a GoPro is amazing! Just like his dad and watching him with such a gracious creature was like watching Carl — at one with water! Carl and I tried to swim with whale sharks off the coast of Australia but missed their migration by two weeks. We were gutted! So when I was able to swim with his children, with them it was like ticking off one of Carl's bucket list! A 'first!' Especially as when Ben and I freedived down as the daddy whale shark descended, and he 'winked' at us, and both of us felt like Carl was there! That moment in the water, we felt his presence. That was amazing! It was a goodbye and an 'I love you wink,' and the daddy whale shark dived deep into the depths, just like Carl."

We all knew Carl from our experiences as divers, but Vicky asked that we also speak with Keith Grant, a man whose friendship with Carl was from a different perspective. Keith took Carl on as an apprentice originally in the heating business.

There was a closeness and respect between them from the beginning, for as Keith said, "He was so fair. What you saw with Carl was what you got. He was like a kid with a big box of toys that he always wanted to share with others."

After Carl went on his own and established his business, he contacted Keith and offered him a job. It was a turnabout with Keith now working for Carl, and it was more than business. With someone like Keith to depend on, Carl felt comfortable in leaving the shop to go on his explorations.

"He wasn't just someone to work with or for — he was like a brother to me. We'd get off work at five and maybe stay around another two or three hours just talking about things. It's been six years since he died, and I haven't gotten over it yet."

Although nothing will ever lessen the blow of the loss for Vicky, Ben, and Georgia, a beautiful and moving memorial to Carl Spencer was established at the National Arboretum in Alrewas, Staffordshire, England. Carl's memorial is near the Intelligence Corps Memorial. It is a place where visitors can pause and briefly share in the many accomplishments of a life that sadly ended much too soon.

As Vicky said, "You couldn't help but love his 'crazy,' and he had an infectious aura about him, especially his smile and his very unique laugh! I truly miss that laugh! Carl was a strong spirit in life and also in death. He truly was an amazing man."

CHAPTER 23

THE RUSSIAN CONNECTION

June 27, 2015

It was a late start for us this morning. Edo and Mike refilled our cylinders with the breathing gases for our four rebreathers, and the small suit-inflation bottles were filled with air. There was a regatta in the harbor, dozens of sailing vessels lined up for starting pistol. The strong wind that prevented our diving was a blessing for them — one man's poison another man's pudding. We went to the harbor entrance and from the rocky shore watched the boats of the regatta lean heavily in the stiff breeze as they exited past the lighthouse and into the Aegean Sea.

It was a nice distraction, and afterward, Evan and I went to *UBN* with Hans Rosenwinkel and Jesse Plackey (of the film crew) to make introductions and conduct a few interviews with our hosts. As the film crew did their work, Evan and I sat with Dmitry and decided on a new and somewhat radical change of operational procedure. Borrowing from the commercial and military dive protocol, we decided to employ use of their *UBN* diving bell. Instead of using one of our team as an in-water support diver, all of us would dive as a group and stay together. All bailout gas would be on the bell. Besides being able to provide a topside feed, they had plenty of gas. The extra breathing gas, either in the group or available from *UBN*, mitigated one of the most obvious and dangerous aspects of expedition diving.

Also, the bell was a safe haven from the current, had lights, a camera to monitor the divers, and an area to clip off and carry all the tanks and equipment. As an additional safety feature, the ROV and submarine would be used as a "big brother" to monitor our situation.

After a few hours of filming, the RIB pulled up with two women who looked as if they had come from a corporate office. They seemed strangely out of place on this boat, but it was clear from the warm Russian welcome, they were known to the crew. They were from the business office of the U-Boat Group (UBG), and almost within seconds of boarding, they requested to speak with us privately in the captain's cabin. I got a bad feeling right off.

The dark-haired woman was Sasha Kuznetsova, the personal assistant for U-Boat Group's director (who is Eugene's wife). She was born in Moscow and lived in Estonia before moving to and working for UBG in Malta. Her blond associate was Ekatrina, serving as UBG's representing legal consul. She was originally from St. Petersburg, attended university in Malta, and decided to remain there.

After Dmitry made introductions, we found seats opposite each other in the private salon in the wheelhouse. The cabin was well-appointed with mahogany panels and table and white leather sofa and upholstered chairs. Sasha explained the director sent them to Kea to find out who we were and what we wanted. The person Evan had been dealing with at UBG was no longer part of the company. Ekatrina added she had no contract or liability releases from our team.

Both women were clear and direct; there was no way to misunderstand what they told us. It felt like we'd been hit with a broadside, and I was sure we were getting shut down. Evan took the floor and respectfully outlined all the verbal and written arrangements made with the (now-terminated) representative who was our prior point of contact. I added we had given copies of signed releases, diving certifications, and insurance for our team. Dmitry nodded and went to find them.

I didn't want to seem too eager because it was apparent they were seasoned negotiators. I took the ball and explained we were invited. There was a major expedition to *Britannic* being planned, and we had been told the contract was waiting to be signed in the Greek Ministry but was verbally agreed to by the signers. For our roles, Evan and I would lead the dive team aspect for the project, and we wanted to see if UBG's vessel and philosophy would be compatible with this project. I further added a little about who I was, what I had done (my history of expeditions as well as TV production and underwater film work), and that in our partnership I would assemble and lead the dive team, and Evan would handle all underwater video and filming.

Our answers seemed to satisfy Sasha, and she didn't ask other questions while Ekatrina looked over our paperwork Dmitry had given her. After a few minutes of softly spoken Russian between the two women, Sasha said we could continue, and she would speak with the director about our proposal. The most difficult part of the discussion was realizing there was a very good chance we might not be allowed to dive Britannic after all.They left the vessel by RIB, and after finishing last-minute checks on board, we headed back to land on our own RIB.

The captain felt the wind wouldn't let up until noon, and we were told not to be back on board until then, so no early start. We headed to the hotel to meet up with Edo and Evan, who had been mixing gas and filling our tanks. They still had some mixing to do, so Evan and I went over the dive plan. We repeatedly played out the scenario with (hopefully) all contingencies accounted for. After a quick break to clean up, the team then had dinner in a nice hillside restaurant overlooking the bay. It was a well-needed, relaxing meal where the film and dive team got to know each other a little better over wine and common interests.

June 28, 2015

At noon, we headed over to *UBN* with high hopes; the wind had dropped, but there was still a breeze. We headed out to the wreck with only two anchors, as the local Greek source failed to come through on time. The captain maneuvered *UBN* on two anchors but was only able to get the ship over the middle of the wreck. We weren't happy but were grateful for the chance to dive — well, shit! Not so fast. As they lowered the ROV, it was apparent there was a ripping surface current. What wasn't clear is how far it went down. The submersible was launched and was soon pulled far behind *UBN* in the strong current, and as the RIB towed it back, water cascaded over the top of it like a waterfall. This was not good. The strong current would complicate the decompression stops. The *UBN*'s captain, Alexander, suggested we use the diving bell for our ascent. We would still descend on the ROV downline to the wreck and, when done with the bottom phase of the dive, ascend and do our deco in the bell. It sounded simple in theory, but we had never done this before.

The team discussed the pros and cons of this plan and its impact on our SOP and emergency procedures. We played out different failure scenarios, including our "failed CCR, unconscious and lost diver" possibilities, and decided that we could do this. We could actually dive as a four-man team, and it would be safer than our original plan for many reasons.

Levon was the Triton submersible tender and diver who showed the dive team how to operate all the gas and communications systems in the bell. It was complex but not alien to us, and the myriad of valves and pipes were clearly marked and labeled. The new plan with a four-man dive team would provide for more in-water support. The diving bell would not only carry our six additional backup gas cylinders strapped inside (in addition to the eight we carry under our arms), but on the exterior were four huge yellow "K" cylinders of the exact breathing gas we would need to ascend on open circuit if a rebreather failed: a 15/70 trimix for the bottom, an intermediate 18/30 trimix, a shallow 50% nitrox, and 100% pure oxygen.

In addition, the ship could pump any gas mixture we asked for down the umbilical hoses. As long as we stayed together and got back to the bell, we would be safe from current and have more emergency gas than even our original plan. Being protected from the strong current would reduce stress, keep us warm, and make for a safer decompression. Being in direct verbal contact with the boat was an added safety factor in case of an emergency, and it was the coolest thing any of us had done while diving. We loaded all our emergency backup gas into the bell with a few bottles of fresh water. I was designated as the bell master; I would be the only one to talk to the topside tender and control the ascent process.

The submersible began its descent, was swept far back behind the boat in the current, and reported back to *UBN* that the current was very strong all the way down to 180 feet, and the visibility was not good. It was getting late in the day, we had changed our dive plan, and the conditions were terrible. We talked about how things were stacking up, and we decided to abort.

The captain applauded our decision, but it was a no-brainer. The ROV was having difficulty in the current, and with the bad visibility, it wasn't worth filming. The submersible ascended, and with some hard work, it was put safely back on board. I was getting a little anxious. Time was ticking, and we had a smaller and smaller window to make this happen.

We had sent Tina back on the RIB to meet David Concannon and Kim, who were arriving on the ferry, and we got them settled in. As the man who introduced me to *Titanic*, which later led to me coming to *Britannic*, it's always a pleasure to see David in his travels. Having helped secure the EC flag for us, it was good he was able to make it to Kea. Kim's love of outdoor adventure and her extensive experiences around the world usually come with stories great for sharing over drinks. Once anchored in the harbor, my mood lightened slightly as we joined the crew for a dinner of spaghetti and meatballs, the doctor's specialty.

The forecast wasn't terrible, but the current couldn't be forecasted. We all hoped tomorrow would be better. On land, we saw David and Kim sitting with Tina and also Sasha and Ekatrina from the UBG. My anxiety was back, and I thought, "This can't be good. Was there going to be a new issue about our dives?"

After hellos and hugs, I walked David away and brought him up to speed. We went over our position with the UBG, the conversation I had with Sasha the day before, and what our next move was. He had dinner with them, and Sasha had been as direct with David as she had with Evan and me. My impression had been correct; she was a tough and focused negotiator. It appeared we were still good though and could continue our dives. We had some wine before heading to the hotel, and in private, I went over all the events and changes we'd made.

The Greek money issues were not looking good, and if Greece defaulted on its debt to the European Union, it might cause chaos. There were already riots in Athens, thankfully peaceful protests for now. There had been a run on all the banks, and every ATM on the island was out of cash. We still had some euros, but it was getting thin, and between the looming cloud and the amount of days gone by, I didn't sleep easy.

June 29, 2015

I was up early to find Tina in the lobby of our hotel, visibly upset at the news we feared would happen. The Greek government decided the banks would stay closed for a week in order to stave off a financial collapse. Here on Kea, there was still no money in the ATMs — I checked as I walked down to have coffee and breakfast at the café. As I sipped coffee, Tina came over and told me the café and supermarket no longer accepted credit cards. Overnight it had become "cash only." Between Evan and me, we were down to 400 euros. David was supposed to exchange U.S. dollars for us, but he wasn't able to. Although we had plenty of U.S. cash, Kea didn't have an exchange. To add insult to injury, all ferry operators in Greece had scheduled a strike for the following day, removing the option of sending Tina with U.S. dollars to the airport cash exchange.

As we loaded up our RIB to go to *UBN*, we saw it lift anchor and head to the dock, so we turned around and met everyone on the quay. Eugene stepped ashore for coffee as the crew went to get more food, and they ran two hoses to fill the onboard tanks with fresh water. I sat with Eugene and Dmitry, and they told me they heard from the steel works with more news I didn't want to hear — the anchor wasn't ready yet and may not be for a few days. No anchor, no money, no credit cards, and all before 9:00 a.m. Shit, what a way to start the day.

David and Kim walked down the dock, and we arranged for them to tour the ship. They were invited on board for dive operations by Eugene, I am told. Now the Americans (and three Greeks we brought) outnumbered the Russians on their own vessel; it's an American invasion, and I was really not comfortable with this. I had planned on swapping out the RIB crew for David and Kim so as not to do this very thing, but I was distracted by all the other issues. Sasha and Ekatrina were also scheduled to be on board, and as the day went on, they became interested in what the dive team was doing. There was also a new Russian woman joining us, too — a reporter from Moscow named Svetlana Murashkina. Even at the dock, the boat seemed too small for all this gear and people, and I hoped that my hosts weren't silently thinking we were pushy and arrogant Americans because I was afraid that's exactly how we acted.

While at dock, we decided to send out our RIB with Edo, Evan, and Levan to check the conditions at the wreck. They returned with bad news: The seas were flat, but there was still too much current. The capital "F" word blared in my head.

On dock, Eugene offered to take us to *Burdigala* again, as it rested out of the Kea Channel and around the cape and should be free from the wind-driven current. Evan liked the idea of getting back out, but I said no, this wasn't a pleasure trip. We should stay focused on the project. I didn't want to tax my host with this mob for us to have a "fun" dive. Eugene suggested *Burdigala* would be a good place to do a practice run with the dive bell. Ding! This was an awesome and brilliant idea of diving with a purpose, not just to sightsee.

Casting off the lines, it was a short run to the wreck site, and after launching the ROV and submersible, we found there was no current on the wreck. The dive plan was for Evan to film the Triton submersible at work for our hosts. Edo, Barney, and I would film the break in the center of this otherwise perfectly intact ship and go on to explore the boiler and engine rooms.

Heading forward, Barney found another bell behind the bridge (ding, ding!), and we were amazed and happy. Bells are a rare find on any ship. Up on the bow, we saw and filmed the empty brass gun shells on the deck around the guns, a frozen moment of frantic firing at imaginary U-boats as the ship sank after hitting the mine. On the way back to the diving bell, we went into the saloon deck and looked at the artifacts mixed in the debris. It was all too soon when we reached our 50-minute dive plan, and it was time to head up.

Getting in the bell, I locked down all the extra tanks and cameras. With the team hanging on the bell, I poked my head into the air chamber and checked the O_2 (oxygen) level in the bell to confirm it was OK to breathe. With a chipmunk-squeaky voice from the helium in my breathing mix, I looked into the video camera and called up to the *UBN* control room, 210 feet above, "Topside, topside, all divers in the bell. Please go up fifteen meters."

On the speaker, the doctor, who was our tender, came back with, "Copy, moving."

With a slight jolt, the bell was winched up to our first decompression stop. We moved up on our stops slowly. I checked with each diver, and we only moved up when the slowest of our decompression profiles cleared that depth. Edo's dive computers were the most conservative, so when he gave me the OK sign, I looked at the others with a thumbs-up hand gesture followed by three fingers and then the OK sign. Each diver signaled back a mirror of my gesture, letting me know they were ready to clear this stop and to go up three meters.

Back in the air dome, I looked at the camera and spoke loudly. "Topside, topside, up three meters please," and got the same reply, "Copy, moving," from the doctor. (We had to speak in "meters" to the Russians because that's the system they use.)

At the deeper stops, Eugene and Dmitry sat in the submersible like comfortable fish in a warm and dry bowl. They filmed and stood watch over us, but once we got to seventy feet, they blinked lights, waved, and peeled off, leaving the ROV to look over us. We had gotten awesome images of divers in the bell, ROV, and the submersible all in one shot. It doesn't get any better than this for a technical diver.

We repeated this procedure flawlessly, ascending three meters at a time for two hours and twenty minutes of total decompression — a total of three hours and ten minutes of being in the water. I could adjust the bell's buoyancy just like a submarine by adding or releasing some air in the dome. We found there was less bounce and a smoother ride when the bell was just slightly negative, so each few meters of ascent, I made the adjustment. Occasionally, a small but very bright light next to the camera would blink on and off rapidly indicating the doctor wanted to speak to me. I would ascend into the air dome and answer. He wanted to know how much remaining decompression time we had and how we all felt. I laid on the deck, resting and enjoying the relative comfort of the bell, and every so often the other divers would ascend into the bell for an air break and a gulp of fresh water. For all of the dive, we remained with our heads just underwater and stayed on our loop.

Finally, we were all clear to ascend, and we lined up one by one to swim over to the lift on the opposite side of the ship and back on board. We had proved to ourselves and our hosts we could safely operate the bell and increase our own safety factor tenfold. As we sat down to remove our gear, Evan said this was "like something from science fiction."

I corrected him and said, "No, Evan, this is science fact."

It was late, and we still had to fill gas for the next day. We ate a small but wonderful dinner with our hosts as the crew lifted the moorings. Grabbing our small tanks, we jumped into our RIB, running back to land as soon as the anchor dropped in the harbor. We had to get up early and fill gas, and I was elated how we'd made lemonade out of lemons that day, but the money issues and the fact the next day was our last possible dive day weighed heavily on my mind.

I called Carrie and spoke to her, and she voiced the unspoken fear in my mind. If we got blown out again, we had to make a decision to either try, if possible, and extend our stay, or once again be beat out of the answer and leave. I told her we would know in the morning and hung up. Despite the swirling thoughts in my head, I fell asleep in seconds.

Additional Notes to the Diary Entries

Even though we knew *UBN* was equipped with a diving bell, the reason we hadn't considered using it when developing our dive plan was you "go with what you know." As I discussed much earlier in the book, minimizing your risk in technical diving and knowing how to handle emergencies when they happen is how you keep from being killed or seriously injured. Carefully planning your dives and creating these "what-if" emergency scenarios is how you as a diver and as a team mentally map through what can go wrong. True safety comes from recognizing things will go wrong underwater, understanding the actions to take, and training for the possibilities. Throwing in equipment you're not thoroughly familiar with adds an element of the unknown, and unknowns are not what you want to deal with at anything below sixty feet deep. (At sixty feet, if you can't resolve your problem underwater, you can make an emergency ascent without significant risk of decompression sickness or an embolism.)

I'm not quite ready to say having the practice run with the diving bell completely won me over, but it was easy to see the practicality of it. When I mentioned ". . . for all of the dive, we remained with our heads just underwater and stayed on our loop," that had to do with optimizing our position underwater. On a rebreather, we have two counterlungs that we breathe in and out of. One is on the inhalation side, and the other is on the exhalation side as the gas moves from our mouth, through the scrubber, and then back to our mouth via one-way check valves. The position of these breathing bags is on our upper backs. The easiest way to breathe is to lay prone, face down, in the normal swimming position. Sitting or standing erect/upright puts the breathing bag in a position that increases the work of breathing, and lying on your back is the worst: You feel like you have chipmunk cheeks as the water pressure on the counterlungs tries to push the gas out of your mouth.

We always try to have what is called optimum loop volume — only one breath in the bag. You breathe in, the bag collapses and is empty, breathe out, and it's full. There's always a little extra in the loop if done correctly. So we all lay down; the others had a small line to keep them attached to the bell, and they floated prone around the bell to be in the most comfortable posture.

CHAPTER 24

SCIENCE FICTION IS SCIENCE FACT

June 30, 2015

Up early again at 7:00 a.m., I headed into town to find thankfully there was finally money in the ATM, and it was a bum's rush from our group to get as much as we could as we were down to lint in our pockets.

Edo and Barney once again filled our CCR cylinders quickly, and after coffee and a light breakfast, we all met on the quay for our 10:00 a.m. start. Loading the boat, Captain Alexander made the decision to head to the wreck site and check the current and not bother with the RIB. There was no wind to speak of, but the current ... well, that was another matter. I felt he knew today was our last possible dive day without changing all our plans. The dive team analyzed gases and methodically assembled our CCRs, going through checklists and triple checking everything in a comfortable silence. Arriving above *Britannic*, the captain judged the current to be about two knots, still too damn strong for us to dive, but he said he thought it would abate this afternoon. I'm not sure what he was basing this on, but I am ever the optimist. As we anchor up with only two anchors instead of three, it's amazing that he was able to maneuver and moor *UBN* directly above the bridge area, exactly where we needed to be. In the control room, the multibeam imagery showed the small *UBN* icon directly next to the break where the firemen's tunnel was.

As they launched the submersible, it was apparent the current was still running, and when the ROV went in, Barney gave me a look of "Oh, man!" I leaned out over the rail to see the ROV trailing alongside *UBN* like a kite. It was discouraging, to say the least. At this point, the dive team got one little bit of good news when the submersible reported the strong current was down to twenty meters. This started a conversation among the dive team about whether or not we should try to dive. Barney felt the current was too strong. Even if we only had to fight it down sixty feet, the odds were with all our gear and cameras, we could get pulled off the line and set adrift. We went back and forth a little, but even one "no go" in the group is enough. We would stand by for now and check the current after lunch.

Around 12:30 p.m., word came to us that the current had dropped another half of a knot, and we decided to go for it. Dressing quietly, we did the predive of our units and zipped each other into our suits. We agreed Barney and Edo would go in first — Barney to film our descent and Edo to locate and secure a line to the diving bell. We needed to be prepared for *UBN* to swing on a mooring, and if that happened, the bell would move. The bell was our way back home, and Edo's job was paramount to us safely getting back. He would not carry a camera on this dive. Third in would be Evan with the huge camera, and I would go last.

Things always slow down for me on a big dive, voices sound a little farther away, and I get a sort of Zen-like tunnel vision. My subconscious prioritizes certain input, a mental list of what matters most, and my eyes check handsets and gauges, PO_2, settings on handsets, fingers pushing buttons, and feeling as much as hearing the reassuring hiss of gas flowing (diluent, O_2, BC, and suit inflation). My hands find the mouthpieces of bailout regulators strapped to the tanks on my side. Like a gunfighter fingering the grip of a holstered pistol, I need to know I can grab them in a lightning bolt of a second. My mind's eyes sees every bit of ancillary equipment in pockets on my thighs: two knives, backup reels (two) and lights (two), inflatable marker buoys (one red and one yellow), and an underwater notebook with backup bailout decompression tables and a graphite pencil. I put the breathing loop in my mouth and watch the PO_2 change as I breathed, reassured as the CCR added oxygen and maintained the settings to keep me alive. Little red and green lights blinked on the heads-up display (HUD) in front of my mask.

Silently, this checklist was going on in my head as I was aware that Edo and Barney were in the water and descending. Evan was standing at the gate, next to go. Things moved even slower, like I was in syrup as I walked to the side of the ship. I watched Evan go down on the elevator and into the water, the huge camera housing like a small engine in his hands; the current grabbed him, and he was gone. The elevator rose back up, and as I stepped on the grated platform, I saw the downline angled back toward the stern of the ship, taut against the current, fighting not only the rush of water but the added drag of my descending team. I was handed my camera and clipped it to my harness, and Levon, who was operating the lift, yelled, "Ready?"

He was only eighteen inches away and had a hand on my shoulder, steadying me on the platform, but he sounded miles away. Maybe it was the hood, maybe it was the familiar zone I was in — I didn't know. I nodded exaggeratedly "Yes," and the elevator lurched down.

Almost immediately, I felt the tug of water against my ankles, and as it swirled up to my calves and thighs, I felt like I would be swept off the platform. I took a small step forward, right hand stretched out, and grabbed the line as I went fully in the water, and the current pushed me toward the line. I had already vented all the air out of my drysuit and BC, so I swung around and faced the current to descend quickly, hand-over-hand down below the surface. Water pressure squeezed me all around — suit, ears, mask — and I pulled down a little farther. A small snort of air from my nose released the pressure of the mask pushing against my face and eased the uncomfortable squeeze on my ears, a little oxygen pumped into my counterlungs and I could breathe easier, and another burp of gas into my drysuit stopped the all-around shrink-wrap feeling.

By the time I reached thirty feet, I needed to hold on with both hands, biceps straining against the water flowing all around me, and the camera buffeting against my side. Another few feet, and I repeated the procedure: added air to the mask, then suit, but now I added my helium-rich diluent instead of oxygen into the counterlung. At the surface and just below it, the diluent doesn't have enough oxygen in the mixture to keep me alive, and I could pass out if I took a deep breath. But now I was deep enough, and the lighter, thinner, helium-rich mix made it easier to breathe.

I looked down and could not see the team; they had moved down the line quickly, and suddenly I was aware that I was free — the current had stopped. I checked gauges again at sixty feet. I relaxed the grip on the descent line and looked around, seeing the three cables to my right descending and disappearing into the cobalt-blue water. At the bottom of those three steel cables was the diving bell. I fell slowly through the water, all the time checking handsets, HUD, and adding gas to my suit and rebreather to offset the ever-increasing pressure. I was still more than 300 feet above the seafloor and falling, but I wanted to move quicker. Angling my head down, I let go of the line, kicking slowly, spiraling around the line as I corkscrewed myself into the ocean.

At about 200 feet, I saw lights below me and the vague outlines of *Britannic*. The diving bell was lit up and seemed warm in the cold water. Thanks to the three cables leading to it, it was the most clearly defined landmark in the water. Off to the right in the deeper blue water, I saw the intensely bright halos of light and a slight yellow blur of the Triton submersible. That and the lights of the tethered ROV created a sharp line against *Britannic*'s hull. I saw the edge of the break delineating the bow from the stern section and the clearly defined radius cut of the well deck right next to the bridge. I marveled at the accuracy of Captain Alexander's mooring. He couldn't have done any better! The ROV was lighting the mast, which lay broken and bent.

Closer to the edge of the wreck were two small figures, Barney and Edo, hovering in the dark water, each lighting a small section of the hull. Compared to the massive lights on the submersible, the divers' lights seem small and tiny on this huge ship. It was just like Jacques Cousteau had said about his dives on *Britannic* when the divers were like fleas on an elephant.

My eyes hadn't fully adjusted yet to the dimming light; the water was wonderfully clear but darkening with each foot I descended. I added a little air to my BC, and the positive buoyancy slowed my descent. To the left, a solitary figure hovered above the hull and seemed to be the focus of all the light. It was Evan, and as I touched down next to him, he acknowledged me with a glance and extended out the long light arms of his camera; they vaguely resembled the glowing antenna of some huge freakish insect. While Evan adjusted and checked his camera settings, I took stock of myself and my gear.

The side of the hull is at 300 feet, and it was here I made final adjustments to my rebreather, changing the set point of oxygen to the higher 1.3 setting and adjusting my buoyancy and trim. I also extended the arms on my camera and could feel the lights all to my left — Edo, Barney, and the brighter lights of Dmitry and Eugene in the submersible. Out farther, I saw the ROV also lighting a section of the wreck. Its tether lines with floats attached to them rose behind it like a string of balloons. I gave nods to Edo and Barney, an OK sign, and we all moved in unison to the break a few feet away, Evan leading the way. I was still in syrup, and I hadn't looked around except to note where everyone was.

This was no time for sightseeing, only navigation and purposeful movement as we began our tasks. We were finally here, on the wreck for the first time since Carl's accident. Our lives had been impacted in a way we would never forget. For *Britannic*, resting in her grave, had six years brought noticeable changes?

I was transported back to the 2009 dive, every movement we made indelibly etched into my mind, the memory of having clearly captured the images of doors wide open. Even without the film, the physical imprint remained. Our passage through her in 2006 and the deeper penetration of 2009 replayed in my head like a favorite movie sequence you can describe in vivid detail.

I think no matter what part of *Britannic* I dive, part of my mind will always drift to that dive; the confines of the firemen's tunnel, the feel of the line in my hand as we moved almost blindly through heavily silted water, the vastness of the boilers when I broke into the room, and the narrow space we had in which to maneuver between them. We had been so careful to film and shoot the open doors from different angles, determined to show there was no evidence of being closed despite the fail safes engineered into the system. It is still difficult for me to resolve how Richie Stevenson and I were on our long decompressions stops, savoring our success in achieving the goal we'd been entrusted with, and we knew nothing about the tragedy of Carl unfolding above us. Struck numb by his death, we have waited, hoping to able to broadcast high-definition footage of what had been physically seen as early as 2003.

In looking at *Britannic's* vastness again, in melding past with present, I felt like Carl would think we had waited long enough. It was time to share our stories about the open doors. Then, in what seemed the blink of an eye, our allotted minutes for the dive were over.

The Triton submersible lit up the entire area, and as we started the slow ascent, I looked out at the bridge of *Britannic* where Captain Bartlett made that fateful decision so many years ago. He thought that trying to get the ship to land was the correct step to take, not knowing his instinct to save the ship would result in human carnage and be to no avail in stopping *Britannic*'s plunge to the bottom.

Our first stop was on top of the wreck at 300 feet, and the diving bell hung above me at 280 feet. As we slowly made it up to the bell, Evan and Barney filmed everything for all it was worth.

This had been a stellar dive in every aspect, a choreographed technical dive with ROV, submersible, technical divers, and diving bell all working in concert with nary a hitch. *UBN* and their operations were a proven method for us for future operations to the depth of *Britannic*. We still had a long five hours of decompression ahead, but the hard part was behind us. Each stop lifted us farther and farther up, and at around 220 feet, I looked down from the bell and could see nearly one-fifth of *Britannic* lying beneath me. I kneeled down on the floor of the bell and waved goodbye — to the wreck and to Carl. I thanked him for watching over us. Edo saw me and would later tell me he knew exactly what I was doing, and it choked him up. Just like the previous day, Eugene and Dmitry stood watch over us with the submersible, and with a wave at around 160 feet, they went back down to explore and film, leaving the ROV to stand watch.

The ascent and decompression stops went as seamlessly as the prior day, but were longer, and at around two-and-a-half hours run time, *UBN* pumped down hot water to the bell. The water came out in two half-inch hoses. We took turns filling our hoods and gloves with the hot water, washing it across our faces. It really made all the difference in staying warm. At sixty feet, we rose into the current and were grateful for the bell's mass that helped shield and, to some degree, block the strong current. While we decompressed at shallow depth, first the ROV, then the submersible were lifted out of the water above us and secured. I couldn't help but think of the parallels to Cousteau's expedition almost sixty years before when they had a submersible and their diving bell (using *Calypso*'s decompression chamber in that capacity). When all of our computers indicated we were cleared, we ascended and were lifted onto the deck of *UBN* to a happy and congratulatory crew. The galley had prepared dinner for the dive team only, and thoroughly exhausted, we ate heartily on the short ride back to the harbor. Once anchored, we took the RIB back to the island, and I slept like a rock with all my anxiety and fears washed away with the tide.

July 1, 2015

The next morning we couldn't sleep in; there was still much work to do. After coffee, we boarded the RIB to get our gear off *UBN*. Once again, our gracious hosts outdid themselves by starting the vessel, bringing it to the quay, and helping us unload. Evan and I invited the entire crew to meet for an 8:00 p.m. dinner at one of our favorite local restaurants. Taking our gear to the hotel, we washed and set everything out in the warm Aegean sun to dry. Everyone relaxed for the first time in days, laying back and enjoying the warmth of the day and the heady glow of success. Once dry, the hundreds of bits and bobs were packed neatly in shipping containers and Edo's van for the long trip home.

I had Tina arrange for us to have a few bottles of champagne at the table, and I toasted our hosts and the crew of *UBN* by saying, "At the beginning of the week, we met as strangers, and over the past few days, the crew of *UBN* has showed us how to make hard work look easy and how to do dangerous things safely, and although tomorrow we go our separate ways, we are no longer strangers but friends."

Dinner was a wonderful meal with much laughter and stories passed around and afterward continued long into the night at a local watering hole, ending only three hours before we needed to load the ferry and head to the mainland.

July 2, 2015 — Airport

My head hurt, but I was happy. The sun was too bright as we loaded the last of the boxes in Tina's van, and our small caravan headed to the end of the quay and aboard the ferry back to Lavrion. I enjoyed the fresh breeze; the ocean was rough, and the past two days wouldn't have allowed any diving. By the grace of Poseidon and a little help from Carl, we were able to get the one day, the one window to do what needed to be done. On Lavrion, we stopped at the Blue Ocean Divers shop for a few hours, having coffee and doing what divers do when they're not diving — they talk about diving and plan to do more.

At the airport, I hugged Edo and thanked him for being the friend he is. I have always felt a close connection with him — not sure if it was because of the body recovery on *Andrea Doria*, or Carl, or all of the above. Part is absolutely he has always been there to pull my ass out of the fire. I also think he touches that soft and more loving Italian side of me, my maternal side, versus the no-nonsense, hard-ass German one.

Edo and Tina — two people behind us — were the wind that allowed us to fly. Tina was already planning to work with us again and looked forward to the "big" project if it should be approved. Evan was scheduled to go back to Greece at the end of August to work on another project and would see Tina soon. We waved goodbye and headed to security. I can never express enough gratitude for the work they each do for us.

I called at 2:30 a.m. EST and woke Carrie to ask her what kind of duty-free goodies I could get for her at the Chanel store, and then we went to the gate to eat and drink. All three of us were on the same flight to Toronto and then on to Boston/Tampa. Barney and Evan slept, but I watched movies and fought to stay awake, trying to get back on this side of the world's time zone.

In Toronto, we went through customs. What a mess! Evan was pulled out of line to points unknown and probably a colonoscopy. Barney and I went through the gerbil habitrail of meandering international zombies that poked, prodded, and, yet again, screened us. It was almost ninety minutes of feel-good security BS before we ended in the terminal and at a bar. Evan didn't show up for another thirty minutes. We had time for two Hendrick's Gibsons and a Rob Roy for each of us with a salad, and we boarded the final leg of our journey home.

I slept, and it felt good to relax. I didn't wake up until after we landed.

In a final reminder of *Britannic* Expedition's Given #3 (Problems ranging from minor irritation to a full-blown crisis will occur), Air Canada had lost one of my bags, the box with my CCR, all my lights, and my backup computer. (I later found out they also lost one of Barney's bags, too.) I was so tired, I didn't care. I signed the documents, listed the contents, and got in Luke's car (one of my employees), who had come to pick me up. It was near midnight, and I slept the whole way home.

CHAPTER 25

WHICH TRUTH?

MY TRANSFORMATION FROM A DIVER interested in collecting artifacts and having tales to brag about around the bar into someone dedicated to solving maritime mysteries is a story to be told in perhaps a future book. As Robert Kurson depicted in *Shadow Divers*, my unwitting metamorphosis began with the urge to pinpoint the identity of a World War II U-boat found off the coast of New Jersey. The six years it took us to prove it was *U-869* led to the kind of intensive historical research I had never expected to be involved with. More important, it taught me a lesson that went beyond archives and documents. It drove home the human side of a shipwreck, especially when an error was recorded that should be corrected.

Many a ship's captain and/or crew have been responsible for sending a vessel into the depths, but there are other times where they've been wrongly blamed for a sinking due to either a misunderstanding or an improper investigation. In tens of thousands of cases, such as with USS *Lagarto*, the fate is unknown. *Lagarto*, a U.S. Navy submarine, disappeared during World War II and was finally located in the Gulf of Thailand. I was asked to dive the wreck and answer questions surrounding the mystery of what happened, and in doing so, we brought closure to many families and filled in another blank in military history. There is a profound feeling when you can meet with someone whose father or grandfather was lost for decades and give the family member(s) an answer to where their loved one came to rest. I learned whether a person is a historian or someone who has an emotional stake, truth does matter. It's rarely easy to accept the painful reality of human failing, yet when tragedy results, lessons can live on and even result in startling changes. If you've ever taken a cruise and been through the mandatory lifeboat drill, it is because of *Titanic's* disaster.

As each expedition to *Britannic* revealed new clues, and we penetrated deeper inside to repeatedly see the fully open watertight doors, there is Paul Louden-Brown, the historian, and Parks Stephenson, the maritime forensic analyst, each with thoughts of what occurred in the fifty-five minutes between 8:12 a.m. and 9:07 a.m. on November 21, 1916, when the largest ship in the world sank from sight. Witnesses later conveyed there were several pockets of panic mixed with the overall calm behavior.

One of the reasons White Star Line historian Paul Louden-Brown is a popular lecturer is his ability to "paint with words" and transport you to the past. His descriptions and details allow you to visualize whatever he discusses. In an email, he shared a lesser-known aspect of the war years when it came to finding men to fill out the black gang, whose jobs were to keep power going to the massive steam engines.

> "They had a real problem getting fit men to work as firemen, trimmers, and greasers. One Royal Navy officer, in command of the White Star liner *Laurentic*, complained bitterly to the Admiralty that the men were the 'sweepings of the streets,' 'unfit,' and 'drunk all the time' and were incapable of keeping up steam. It would be wrong for me to generalize about the quality of the engine department crew in *Britannic*, but I'm certain the same problems affected most large passenger vessels as the need for men in the armed forces increased — where or how do you replace them? I've worked in an engine room stoking and trimming a triple-expansion vessel and in winter, for a then very fit 20-year-old rugby player, it wiped me out. Imagine the conditions in the Mediterranean, the heat, the toll on the men, then the explosion. Panic from inexperienced men might also be part of the reason those doors were not closed. I know I'm throwing a lot at you, but I think these are factors to consider. After all, it's easy for you and I to sit talking about why this or that was not done, but deep inside a metal box, below the waterline, and you hear an explosion, the lights go out, bells ringing, escaping steam, screaming, this is a nightmare situation that only the strongest could endure."

In a later conversation, Paul brought to mind another issue: Social welfare as we know it didn't exist in the early twentieth century. Think of Violet Jessop when her father died unexpectedly and left her mother as a widow with six children. Katherine Jessop was forced to take a job at sea as her only viable option, a choice she would not have made had other assistance been provided. It not only separated her from the children for weeks at a time, but in her determination to try and ease some of her mother's burden, Violet's acceptance of adult responsibilities robbed her of a carefree youth.

This was the common situation of the working class of England. Unless there were relatives who could and would help financially, the family of any man who died on the ship was likely to be thrust into difficult, if not dire, circumstances. Panic by the black-gang men on duty would have been understandable. Paul also acknowledges some type of structural damage could have accounted for why the watertight doors failed completely despite the system design of a backup float device and the manual ability to close the doors, even if the primary electrical means was not functioning. How could this built-in redundancy not have been adequate when it was needed the most?

Back in 2003, Parks Stephenson wasn't convinced he had enough information to make a definitive call about why the watertight doors failed. We spent a lot of time together discussing what Richie Stevenson and I had seen in 2009. I have always admired Parks's talent. The CGI renderings he had created of the path we took in 2009 showing the open doors are true to my memory. In the same time we were in Kea in 2015, Parks was reconsidering one of his earlier theories about the doors. He's now developed a firm idea as to why the watertight doors did not close and added a factor centered on the location of the damage.

His complete explanation is fascinating and an excellent read for those who enjoy engineering details. (*See Appendix C: When Things Go "Boom."*) Parks cites a report, *The Response of Surface Ships to Underwater Explosions*, written by Warren D. Reid when he was attached to the Underwater Explosions Research Department of the Naval Surface Warfare Division for the Commonwealth of Australia Defense Forces, as significant to his conclusion.

> "On detonation of an explosive underwater, a superheated, highly compressed gas bubble is formed, along with a shock wave in the surrounding water (approximately 53% of the total energy released in an underwater explosion goes into shock-wave formulation, 47% in pulsation of the gas bubble). The exponentially decaying shock wave propagates as a spherical pressure wave and is originally much faster than the speed of sound.

> "You found the watertight doors fully open, without any indication that there was any attempt to close them. This should not have been ... even if the electric signal to release the doors (to slide closed with the help of gravity) had been somehow interrupted by the mine explosion and manual release by engineers in the boiler

rooms had been somehow frustrated, there was a mechanical backup system designed to autonomously release the doors once saltwater reached them. The findings indicate that none of that triple-redundancy system seemed to have worked, so I am left with the conclusion that the doors were somehow jammed in their tracks.

"To summarize, I believe that the mine detonated just underneath and close to the starboard side of the hull. The resultant bubble pulses lifted the bow of the ship (but not the stern), causing hull deformation that extended hundreds of feet aft of the original explosion location. The hull deformation caused the bulkheads to also deform, throwing the watertight door tracks out of true and jamming the door in place (full open position) before they could be dropped. When the clutches holding the doors released (either by normal or emergency method), the doors refused to fall. Water rushing in virtually unrestricted caused everyone in the area to flee shortly thereafter. And as I mentioned before, if you lose Boiler Room 5, you lose the ship." (See Chapter 15: Entering the Firemen's Tunnel.)

On the note about the importance of Boiler Room 5, Parks explained:

"But then you may be asking why I think that losing Boiler Room 5 was key. Harland & Wolff's chief naval architect's calculations were based on the assumption that the ship was motionless and on an even keel. Britannic was under way and increasingly heeling to starboard. I need to computer model this (like we did with Titanic), but I have a gut feeling (based on my previous experience) that in Britannic's situation, the loss of Boiler Room 5 was fatal. If you could someday go deep enough to get an image of an open watertight door into Boiler Room 4, then the matter is definitely settled . . . in no circumstance could the ship survive losing seven adjacent compartments.

"Even if that door is found to be closed, I still believe that my hypothesis about Boiler Room 5 being the fatal loss is strong enough to express, but it will be unproven and therefore remain controversial. I hope that we can do a documentary that will provide funding to commission the kind of flooding survey that we did for Cameron's 2012 documentary . . . that's the only way to prove my hypothesis."

I'm not a naval architect or engineer, but Parks does not come to conclusions in haste, and I respect his abilities. What we do know is of the thirty men who were killed, nine were firemen, trimmers, and greasers. The ship's records saved didn't include rosters of who was on duty at the time of the explosion; all we can say for certain is members of the black gang were unrelentingly drawn into *Britannic*'s deadly propellers and perished in a terrible manner. Had they also fled the boiler rooms with no attempt to close the watertight doors and in their demand to get off the ship brought about their gruesome deaths by lowering lifeboats when they should have waited? What incredibly bitter irony if so.

In diving in the still-quiet of the shipwreck where I see rakes and wheelbarrows, tools of the black gang, resting frozen in time, I think to the analogy of the awful, heart-wrenching day of 9/11 in New York when the Twin Towers were attacked. The instinct was to run from danger, and it was the training and character of first responders who ran up instead of down, seeking to rescue as many people as they could.

On a military ship, it is the same; sailors are drilled in how to handle emergencies, how to hold firm until told to abandon ship. By its very nature as a civilian ocean liner converted into a hospital ship, the only military aboard *Britannic* were not members of the Royal Navy but personnel of the Royal Army Medical Corps. Their understanding of the ship was limited to the wards where they served the needs of patients, their own quarters, and the public areas.

Only the small number of men who were in or near the boiler rooms know what actually happened in the frightening two or three minutes when they had to decide what to do. In the end, the misfortune of war set the tragedy into motion at the moment *Britannic* struck the mine. Past the known root cause, did fear and panic instead of a sense of duty cause the watertight doors to not be closed? The design for the manual release was such that it would have only taken seconds to activate the release. If we accept Parks's hypothesis, does science tell us it would have been a futile effort if the men had tried to manually close the doors?

Which truth do you choose to accept?

CHAPTER 26

WHAT LIES AHEAD AND BELOW?

OUR SHORT EXCURSION TO *BRITANNIC* and especially the use of the dive bell changed my mind about *U-Boat Navigator*, and while I can't say it will be a part of future expeditions, I can say it opened me to the option. The increased safety factor of using the dive bell was given a boost when I wondered if it could have made a difference in a scenario like what happened with Carl. I asked Dr. Petar Denoble, "If a diver was having a seizure because of oxygen toxicity, and he could be brought into the diving bell quickly and his head lifted out of the water, is it possible he would recover?"

He explained it would depend on the exact circumstances. "Yes, he could and most likely would recover," Dr. Denoble said, "unless he was drowned for a prolonged time or experienced cardiac arrest due to concomitant causes."

Carl's loss will stay with me for the rest of my life, and if we can take a lesson from his accident and advance the safety of the type of deep-sea diving we do, I can imagine Carl giving one of his smiles in approval.

We all hope the major expedition will take place as soon as possible and provide another opportunity to spend more time on *Britannic*. When you pause in a spot like the bridge where Captain Bartlett stood, or peer into other sections and see a wheelchair on its side, you look into the past, into the brief voyages of this magnificent ocean liner.

I have made more than 120 dives to *Andrea Doria*, and until I was drawn to *Britannic*, the Italian liner was my "Mount Everest of Diving." The third and final Olympian changed that for me, and there are still many questions we have about her, hundreds, if not thousands, of details we can seek out about how many differences there were in her conversion from luxury liner to hospital ship.

We want very much to find our way into the Turkish baths as well as the engine room, and we have yet to clearly determine the source of the secondary explosion witnesses testified about. (*See Appendix C: When Things Go "Boom."*)

For many, the scientific aspect of *Britannic* is the priority. The long-term experiments DBI is involved with are critical in determining biologically driven corrosion events. Variables in subjects of scientific study must always be taken into consideration, and the many similarities between *Titanic* and *Britannic* are beneficial. The sister ships are virtually identical in materials used and design. They were built and sank only a few years apart. These factors reduce at least some of the variables scientists would encounter under other study circumstances. It is thought the main reason rusticles are so advanced on *Titanic* is that the depth causes them to be more or less the dominant organisms, and those organisms have taken over the deterioration. Four hundred feet is not shallow, but it is compared to *Titanic*. Therefore, a number of other organisms not found on *Titanic* exist on *Britannic* and are assisting in her deterioration. Another idea is there are more deterioration events occurring on *Britannic* that are not strictly bacterial driven.

Historians, scientists, and explorers — we all have a strong interest in protecting *Britannic*, and for men like Simon Mills, it is a constant concern to balance appropriate access without risking harm to the ship as underwater technology is enhanced for both divers and submersible options.

Let us not forget, however, that the silent *Britannic* is a solemn place as well, where Violet Jessop came close to death and others did not escape. You feel those souls, if you allow yourself to.

Violet lived until 1971 and retired to a small cottage in England. Despite what you might have chosen had you been in her place, she was away from the sea for a mere few years while she worked in a bank. She signed onto the White Star Line again in 1920 and specifically to *Olympic*, the only one of the three Olympic-class liners not tragically sunk. There is an appendix in the book *Titanic Survivor*, edited and annotated by John Maxtone-Graham, that chronicles Violet's recorded voyages during her forty-two-year career. Unfortunately, the pension she received for those decades of service did not allow her to lead a financially secure retirement. Independent to the end, her memoirs include nothing about her brief marriage from which there were no children, nor does she chronicle her life during retirement.

In a kind letter she sent in response to us, Margaret Meehan, daughter of Violet's sister, Eileen, explained she and her sister came to have Violet's manuscript after the 1974 death of their mother. It remained in a suitcase for some time, and Margaret decided to read it after a visit to the National Maritime Museum at Greenwich, where they saw an exhibit of artifacts from *Titanic*. Interestingly, the first publisher she approached in England wasn't interested, and when she contacted a New York publisher, they initially thought her letter was a hoax. We can be grateful the publisher followed through and the talented John Maxtone-Graham brought us the memoirs of this remarkable woman.

Britannic — an awesome sight when she appears through the depths — was a marvel of engineering and sadly joined her sister at the bottom of the sea where we once could not venture. Now, thanks to science and the spirit of exploration of divers who are willing to push the boundaries of our abilities, we hope to unravel more of her mysteries in the years to come.

APPENDIX A

HMHS *BRITANNIC* 2006 SOP

A TAILORED STANDARD OPERATING PROCEDURE (SOP) document is a must for a technical dive expedition. An SOP such as this one can serve as a foundation. Numerous factors will differ from expedition-to-expedition and those specific details must be addressed. Carl Spencer was an invaluable source of information as we developed this SOP for the 2006 Expedition. Writing the SOP is a critical step. Providing a copy to all team members in advance and ensuring they understand the contents are equally important. Acronyms not readily known are listed in the glossary.

* * * * *

HMHS *Britannic* 2006
The History Channel Expedition

DIVING TEAM
OPERATING PROCEDURES

John Chatterton and Richie Kohler
(Expedition Leaders)

Version 1.4, September 1, 2006

INTRODUCTION

The purpose of this document is to outline diving operations for the *Britannic* Expedition 2006, underwritten by the History Channel, to take place in the month of September 2006, on the wreck of the HMHS *Britannic* off the Island of Kea in Greece.

FIRST PRIORITY

Our first priority is the safety and welfare of our team. Every aspect of the diving operations is to be examined in the light of how it impacts crew and diver safety. Nothing shall be undertaken to adversely affect the safety of crew and divers.

RISK ASSESSMENT ANALYSIS

The primary means that we will employ in managing the inherent risks associated with wreck diving to *Britannic* will be to use divers who are already properly trained and experienced in deep technical wreck diving and experienced in the use of rebreathers in the wreck environment. Our number one defense against incurring a diving accident will be our experience.

There are numerous specific risks known to be associated with conducting diving operations to the wreck of the HMHS *Britannic* and/or shipwrecks found to be in similar depths. We will reinforce the employment of policies and procedures to best manage the inherent risks of our diving operations. What follows are specific identified risks and the methodology we intend employing to minimize these risks for our diving personnel on this expedition:

1. Equipment Malfunction — Divers will personally test their individual dive equipment prior to entering the water to ensure that equipment is working properly. Divers will also carry backup systems for life support, lighting, decompression, and communications. All backup elements will be checked

to ensure that they are also operational prior to any dive. Support divers will have backup life-support equipment that can be deployed.

2. **Decompression Sickness** — Divers will report any and all health issues prior to a dive on the Diver Fitness Report. Divers will also remain well-hydrated, even while in the water. Divers will follow their plan and decompression schedule to the letter. Divers will be examined by the dive physician after exiting the water. Divers will report any symptoms of DCS immediately. If a diver exhibits signs of DCS, the expedition DCS Plan will be implemented.

3. **Oxygen Toxicity** — We will manage our dive tables to minimize the risk of oxygen toxicity. Divers will stay well-hydrated, even while in the water. Bottom divers will be monitored by support divers and their fellow dive team members for signs of oxygen toxicity, especially when decompressing shallower than 30 feet. If a diver exhibits signs of oxygen toxicity, the expedition's Procedure for an Unconscious Diver will be implemented.

4. **Air Embolism** — Divers will take measures to control their buoyancy at all times and thereby control ascent rate. This combined with good diver breathing pattern eliminates the possibility of embolism. If a diver suffers from a suspected air embolism, the expedition's DCS Plan will be implemented.

5. **Entanglement or Entrapment** — Divers will remain alert at all times of possible entanglements or loose wreckage on the wreck. Divers will minimize any contact with the wreck itself and/or any debris related to the site.

6. **Loss of Gas Supply** — Divers will monitor their gas supplies continuously during the dive and decompression. Divers will carry both closed-circuit and open-circuit bailout gases. Divers will maintain contact with their team members so they might share emergency gas supplies if necessary. Both deep and shallow support divers will carry gas for emergency use by bottom divers.

7. **Panic** — All divers are already trained and experienced, and the risk of panic is minimal. We will rely on planning, preparation, and communication to further prevent the panic.

8. **Lost or Disoriented on the Wreck** — Divers will be oriented to the wreck itself prior to the dive. Proper planning and preparation will give divers the big picture of the wreck and where they are. While on the dive, divers will remain in communication with the other team members using SSB to minimize confusion or separation.

9. **Adrift** — Divers will plan to descend and ascend on the shot line. In the unlikely event that a diver cannot find the shot or is swept off the shot, the diver will be able to deploy an SMB to the surface to signal his location. Divers will also carry a backup SMB. The diver will also use electronic

communications and a slate to relay the diver's condition and any special needs. Support divers will be ready to respond to any diver on an SMB.

10. **Encounters with Resident Marine Life** — Divers will not encourage contact with any marine life. In the event of unwanted contact, the diver will use underwater communications to relay his situation to team members and support divers who will take appropriate action.

11. **Hypothermia** — We will remain aware of the dangers of hypothermia and the dive team members will look for signs of hypothermia in themselves and the other members of the dive team. Divers will use drysuits with proper undergarments to minimize the possibility of hypothermia. In the event of a drysuit failure, support divers will be able to transport chemical heat packs, or even a neoprene wetsuit, to the ailing diver, if necessary. As a last resort, divers will be treated on the surface.

12. **Dehydration** — Divers will be encouraged to remain well-hydrated at least 24 hours prior to a dive. In addition, divers will have water available to them while in the water decompressing to remain well-hydrated.

13. **Exhaustion** — Divers suffering from exhaustion will be weeded out of the dive team prior to the dive and not be included in diving operations until they have had sufficient rest and are approved for diving by the Diving Safety Officer.

14. **Injuries** — Divers suffering from any physical injury will be weeded out of the dive team at the predive meeting, prior to the dive, and not be included in diving operations until they have recovered sufficiently and they are approved for diving by the Diving Safety Officer.

15. **Illness** — Divers suffering from any illness will be weeded out of the dive team at the predive meeting, prior to the dive, and not be included in diving operations until they have recovered sufficiently and they are approved for diving by the Diving Safety Officer.

16. **Drowning** — Any number of these conditions, by themselves, will not cause death. The real danger in diving is that these conditions can cause drowning. Divers must remember they are on life support when underwater and the threat of drowning is real. Awareness is our best defense.

All members of the expedition will remain alert to anything that might impact the safety and/or well-being of the team. It is entirely possible that unexpected issues might arise which need to be addressed. Should a team member identify any possible threat to safety, they are to immediately notify the Dive Marshall, the Dive Supervisor, the Dive Safety Officer, or the Dive Operations Officer. Communication among the team is critical to conducting dives with minimal risk, and vigilance is the responsibility of each and every team member.

EMERGENCY PROCEDURES

Diver with Simple (Pain Only) DCS Symptoms

A diver surfacing with symptoms of DCS, if agreeable, can undergo in-water recompression under the direct supervision of the First Aid Officer. The DCS diver will descend to achieve relief, no deeper than 60 feet. The FAO will keep in communication with the DM topside, who will maintain the log of the event and advise the diver with regards to options.

Diver with CNS or Air Embolism Symptoms

A diver surfacing with symptoms of serious CNS-DCS or air embolism will be taken to land-based medical personnel in Athens via the safety boat. The FAO will remain with the injured diver, render first aid, and will hand over the Incident Report and the Diver's Information File to medical personnel.

Unconscious Diver

Upon reaching an unconscious or convulsing diver in the water, first check the PPO_2 in the diver's loop. If necessary, make adjustments to the PPO_2 or go to OC, close the DSV if displaced, then take appropriate action. Using comms, advise the dive marshal of the situation. If comms have failed, a YELLOW SMB should be deployed to alert topside to the emergency and splash the support diver.

- **Unconscious and Breathing** — Brought to the surface according to deco profile, call for support team divers to take charge of the diver as soon as possible. This minimizes the chance of serious DCS while getting the injured diver to the surface.

- **Unconscious and Not Breathing** — Get the diver to the surface immediately. This situation gives little chance for survival, less the deeper the occurrence. The only possible chance is to get the diver to the surface to be resuscitated by support personnel regardless of DCS dangers.

- **Convulsing** — This will undoubtedly be caused by oxygen toxicity and most likely occur in shallow water. Regardless, the risk of DCS is minimal, but the risk of drowning is high with a convulsing diver. Get the diver to the surface and to surface support immediately.

Divers with a full-face mask (FFM) will be easier to maintain u/w when unconscious or convulsing. If at any time the unconscious diver cannot be maintained on the loop, close the loop, attempt to maintain on OC, and return him to the surface immediately.

Underwater comms and support divers give us an advantage in any situation involving an unconscious or convulsing diver. Responding divers should use these assets to their fullest extent.

All divers should understand the operation of each team member's rebreather to facilitate this type of rescue.

CCR Failure

In the event of total loop or electrical failure and a diver has gone on OC, his buddy should notify the dive marshal (by comms) to splash the deep support. If comms have failed, and/or if a direct ascent (off the downline) is being affected, launch a YELLOW SMB as soon as possible to notify topside. The dive marshal will splash the deep support diver and depending on communications, make the call whether or not to deploy a backup rebreather unit or recall the rest of the bottom team for assistance. The deep support diver will be carrying deep and shallow bailout and stay with the open-circuit diver.

A backup rebreather unit (Inspiration) will be primed (prebreathed) and ready for an emergency deployment. The deepwater support diver should be familiar with the Inspiration unit and be able to assist in helping swap units at around no deeper than 100 feet. The decision to stay OC or employ the backup rebreather is the diver's.

Adrift Diver/Lost Line

If a dive team cannot locate the shot line, or the shot line has become separated from the wreck, the divers shall ascend free and deploy a RED SMB, indicating team ascending off-line but all well. (A YELLOW SMB is only to be used in a need gas, on OC, or unconscious diver situation). The safety boat will drop an emergency line with bottom gas and standby the drifting team. Gas and decompression schedules are selected so that the same emergency drop lines can be used for both open- and closed-circuit divers. It is assumed that every diver is carrying enough redundancy to get back to 30–36m/100ft, allowing sufficient time for the support boat to arrive with the drop line.

Two (2) emergency drop lines are required, EACH consisting of:
- 50kg buoyancy buoy
- The same 42m polyester rope and 2" ring configuration as the decompression station downlines
- 10–12L of trimix bailout secured to the line at 33m/100 ft.
- 10–12L of nitrox bailout secured to the line at 21m/60 ft.
- 2–3kg lead weight tied to bottom loop
- 10–12L of oxygen fitted with a screw gate carabineer, ready to be deployed with screw locked as the divers approach their 6m stop. This is to reduce clutter during the initial deployment and reduce drag on the line near the surface, where the currents are stronger. During the latter stages of decompression, the

RIB assistant will pull the drop line up by 6m, attach the O_2 to 6m ring securing it with the screw gate, and then lower the O_2 to the diver.

MINIMUM TEAM REQUIREMENTS

Diving operations will require the following personnel:

Dive Supervisor (DS)

- Responsible overall for diving operations and is in charge of the site.
- Coordinate with the dive operations, the dive vessels, authorities, and the land-based support.
- Obtain the weather forecasts.
- Supervise any on-site emergency.
- Will remain based on the dive boat during diving operations.

Dive Operations Officer (DOO)

- The DOO is responsible for coordinating the operational goals with the available resources.
- He will have overall responsibility for selecting the day's dive team and making specific assignments.
- The DOO will be present at all briefings, but not necessarily on-site during dive operations.

Dive Safety Officer (DSO)

- The DSO is in charge of creating and implementing the safety policies and procedures.
- The DSO will monitor the ongoing effectiveness of the Dive Plan with regards to safety, and institute any changes in the Dive Plan should they be necessary.
- The DSO will be physically present and review with the DOO the Diver Status Reports at the Dive Operations Briefing and will be responsible for removing from diver-ready status any diver who is not ready to make a dive for health and safety reason.
- The DSO will also be physically present at all briefings.
- Dive Operations may be conducted without the presence of the DSO on-site.

Director of Underwater Photography

- Assign cameras to dive team.
- Responsible for operational readiness of the team cameras.

Fill Station Officer
- Maintain the fill station, compressors, and booster pumps.
- Oversee the filling of all dive cylinders.

Transportation Manager
- Oversee the loading and unloading of equipment from the dive vessels to shore, and ready equipment onto the vessel.

Fast–Boat Supervisor
- Responsible for the operational readiness of the fast boat.

Gas Supply Officer
- Maintain and monitor adequate gas supplies for the expedition.
- Ensure that all tanks are marked and tested properly.
- Maintain and monitor adequate absorbent supplies for the expedition.

DPV Coordinator
- Assign scooters to bottom divers.
- Maintain readiness of scooters.

Dive Information Manager
- Maintain and collect all dive data.
- Coordinate and assist the Decompression Researcher.

Decompression Station Supervisor
- Responsible for the condition, readiness, and inspection of the Decompression Station.

First Aid Officer (HSO)
- Responsible overall for the health and safety of the team when out of the water.
- In the event of an emergency that requires evacuation of any personnel, the HSO will accompany the ill/injured party.
- The HSO will coordinate with medical personnel and research personnel.

Communications Officer
- Responsible for the equipment and procedures used to communicate ship-to-ship, surface-to-diver, diver-to-diver, and ship-to-shore.

Main Contractor:	On The Bottom Productions LLC
Dive Supervisor:	To be named
Dive Operations Officer:	John Chatterton
Dive Safety Officer:	Richie Kohler
Director of U/W Photo:	Evan Kovacs
First Aid Officer:	Heeth Grantham
Fill Station Officer:	Leigh Bishop
Gas Supply Officer:	Mike Barnette
Communications Officer:	Carl Spencer
DPV Coordinator:	Mike Pizzio
Deco Station Manager:	Joe Porter
Fast Boat Supervisor:	Frank Pellegrino
Transportation Manager:	Mike Etheredge
Dive Information Manager:	Martin Parker
Decompression Researcher:	Dr. Petar Denoble

DAILY ASSIGNMENTS

Dive Marshal (DM)

- Overall responsibility for the dive team and the execution of the dive plan.
- Responsible for authorizing or cancelling the dive, as is appropriate.
- DM will maintain the Diver Information Files and the Diver Fitness Forms.
- In the event of an accident, the DM will be responsible for filling out an incident report containing all relevant information.
- Will remain based on the dive boat.
- Chair the predive briefing.
- Distribute laminated assignment sheets to all personnel.
- Collect written dive plans from each diver before the dive and maintain those plans throughout the dive and debriefing. This includes keeping diver run times.
- Clear dive plan details with DS, DOO, and DSO.
- Monitor the dive team's condition and keep the DS aware of progress or any change in its status.
- Maintain communication with the dive team via SSB comms and the support divers.
- Remain aware of the location of dive team members at all times.
- Deploy lookouts for the missing divers SMBs.

- Supervise correct deployment of deco system.
- Chair the postdive debriefing.
- Collect all laminated assignment sheets and hand over to the following day's Dive Marshall.
- Implement emergency procedures when necessary.

Bottom Divers (BD)
- Must be responsible for their safety while in the water.
- Must be responsible for following their submitted dive plan.
- Must be responsible for maintaining contact with their dive buddy and the support team.
- Must be responsible for safely achieving our operational goals.
- Must be responsible for accurately relaying individual fitness prior, during, and after the dive.

Deepwater Support Diver (DW-SD)
- Responsible for assisting bottom divers who are returning to the shot line and relaying an accounting of the bottom divers to the DM.
- Will use a bottom capable CCR with FFM and comms and will carry two side-mounted 7L cylinders of bailout/deco gas for emergency supply to ascending bottom divers.
- Go no deeper than 180 feet unless there is an emergency.
- Carry spare laminated decompression tables and OC bailout tables.
- Keep the DM informed of the in-water status of the dive team via underwater SSB comms.
- Monitor and assist the Dive Team until they complete deco and exit the water.

Shallow-Water Support Divers (SW-SD)
- Responsible for assisting decompressing divers, including the DSD, and relaying their condition to the DM.
- Coordinate with the SSD in the safety boat to deploy the deco station.
- Use a nitrox twin set with FFM and comms and carry one side mount of oxygen.
- Carry spare laminated decompression tables and OC bailout tables.
- Maintain contact with decompressing divers reporting any problems to the DM and addressing regular diver needs with regards to gas and water.

- Keep the DM aware of environmental considerations on the deco station, including current.
- Shuffle the deco station horizontal bars upward along with the average decompression depth (no shallower than 15 feet).
- Remove any unwanted equipment to the safety boat.
- Dive no deeper than is required due to an emergency.
- Stay in the water until the last bottom diver has exited.
- Assist with the recovery of the deco station.

Standby Support Diver
- Assemble and check all the emergency drop lines.
- Assist in launching and maintaining the safety boat.
- Deploy the deco station system components.
- Enter the water to check the deco station deployment, and descend to 45 feet to connect the poles between the downlines.
- Maintain the emergency drop line in the RIB.
- Have an air set (single cylinder in a BCD) and be suited up (preferably in a wetsuit) ready to enter the water from the time the wreck divers enter until the "all-back" SMB (i.e., the ORANGE one with "All Back" written on it) surfaces.
- Drop emergency lines to any pairs who surface off the shot. Enter water, ensure gas reaches the wreck divers, and remain in visual contact until everything confirmed OK. Make frequent visits to recheck.
- Give priority to any YELLOW markers (off station, and need gas now), over ORANGE markers (off station, but gas situation is currently OK).
- If an emergency drop line is used, fetch another one from the main boat. If two have been used, then dismantle the end (unused) section from the deco station as a replacement.
- Once an emergency drop line has been deployed to a separated diver and they have been checked, slowly tow them back to the main decompressing group using the RIB/inflatable.
- Retrieve any unwanted kit from the support divers/divers and ferry back to the main boat.

Decompression Physiology Researcher
- Responsible for collecting data relating to these dives by use of a Doppler.
- Responsible for keeping the DS, the DSO, the DOO, and the FAO informed of the cursory results of the Doppler tests.

Dive Boat Assistant
- Responsible for assisting divers as needed and following the direction of the DM.

Dive Marshal will be selected daily by the DOO from these available candidates:

Leigh Bishop
Mike Fowler
Martin Parker
Mike Pizzio

Bottom Divers (2 to 8 divers) will be selected daily by the DOO, the DSO, and the DS from these available candidates:

Mike Barnette
Leigh Bishop
Mark Bullen
John Chatterton
Mike Etheredge
Mike Fowler
Richie Kohler
Evan Kovacs
Martin Parker
Frank Pellegrino
Mike Pizzio
Carl Spencer

Deepwater Support Diver (1 diver) will be selected daily by the DOO, the DSO, and the DS from these available candidates:

Mike Barnette
Mark Bullen
Mike Etheredge
Mike Fowler
Martin Parker
Frank Pellegrino
Mike Pizzio

Shallow-Water Support Diver (1 diver) will be selected daily by the DOO, the DSO, and the DS from these available candidates:

Heeth Grantham
Joe Porter

Standby Support Diver (1 diver) will be selected daily by the DOO, the DSO, and the DS from these available candidates:

Heeth Grantham

Joe Porter

Dive Boat Assistant will be selected daily by the DOO from these available candidates:

Mike Barnette

Leigh Bishop

Mark Bullen

John Chatterton

Mike Etheredge

Mike Fowler

Richie Kohler

Evan Kovacs

Martin Parker

Frank Pellegrino

Mike Pizzio

Carl Spencer

Britannic Dive Team Biographies and Data

Author's note: All personal data has been deleted for purposes of inclusion in the book. There was an entry for each diver with personal emergency contact information and a paragraph of the individual's dive credentials specific to meeting the challenges of Britannic.

DIVER RECORDS

The DM will maintain a file containing a folder on each team member. This folder will contain each diver's personal information, a photocopy of the diver's passport, diving certifications, health insurance, and recent medical exam (within 60 days). This folder will also be made available to authorities who visit the site. In the event of an emergency, the diver's individual file will travel with the diver, along with the Incident Report, to assist off-site medical personnel with treatment.

DIVE VESSELS

We will be using two vessels:

- The **primary dive vessel** (to be named) will support the dive operation. It will be the platform where divers will be deployed and returned. It will be the base for the DS, the DM, and the support divers as well as the film crew and any authorities wishing to observe dive operations.

- The **safety boat** (to be named) will be the vessel used by the support divers to address the needs of decompressing divers. It will be the boat to respond to any emergency. In the event a diver with an emergency needs to leave the site, it will be in the safety boat and with the First Aid Officer.

BRIEFINGS

There will be three briefings related to every dive, and they are mandatory for all participating divers and supervision:

- **Assignment Briefing** — Held the evening before the dive and after the debriefing if diving was conducted that day. This meeting is chaired by the DOO. All divers will be present to complete their individual Diver Fitness Forms. These forms will be collected and reviewed by the DOO, DSO, DEO, and the DM. At this time, the assignments will be given out based on individual preparedness and operational needs and the following day's schedule will be arranged.

- **Predive Briefing** — Held in the morning prior to the dive, the purpose is to review assignments, logistics, and preparedness. This meeting is chaired by the DM and is an opportunity to address any questions with regard to the upcoming dive. At this time, dive teams will fill out their dive plans and return them to the DM.

- **Debriefing** — Held after the dive at dinner time and chaired by the DM. The purpose is to review the dive and assess the status of operational goals as well as the team's execution of the dive. Appropriate steps can then be taken to modify upcoming dive plans or objectives.

COMMUNICATIONS

SSB Underwater Communication

The majority of divers will use FFMs and SSB communication to keep in touch with one another and the surface. Divers who are not comfortable using a FFM will have an ear bud unit enabling them to hear but not transmit communications. Topside personnel will use a surface unit to stay in the communication loop. SSB communications are not completely reliable and backup systems of communication must also be used.

SMB (Surface Marker Buoy) Communication

The launching of an SMB can communicate distress. A RED SMB indicates all is well with the diver. A YELLOW SMB indicates the diver needs assistance from support divers.

Written Communication

All divers will be required to carry a slate and pencil to communicate in the event of an emergency.

Topside Communication

The safety boat and the DM will maintain communication using VHF radios. The DS and the DM will work together and communicate throughout the dive.

LOCATING THE WRECK

- If appropriate, locate the existing shot line from a previous day's diving. Confirm the location of the shot has not moved via GPS and echo.

- If a new shot line is required, it will be prepared and deployed by the topside crew.

- If a new shot line is deployed, the tie-in divers go in first to tie in the grapnel or chain to the main part of the wreck with a length of rope. This tie in should be done so that it will be able to take the weight of the surface pull of the shot line and the deco station once deployed. Signals to the surface are as follows:

  - RED SMB — Definitely on the wreck and have tied in, and it is OK to deploy the station and send divers down.

  - YELLOW SMB — No wreck/on seabed or it is too far away to be able to tie in securely, and the shot line needs redeploying.

  - The first pair will have their "diver in" tallies already attached to the end of the lazy shot line.

DIVE METHODOLOGY

Divers will utilize modern state-of-the-art rebreathers, and bottom divers will be prepared to operate at a depth of 400 fsw. Divers will utilize heliox, trimix, and nitrox as diluent according to the day's dive plan. The tables will take into account all of the variables that go into a dive of this magnitude, as well as the most recent decompression physiology philosophies. We will monitor the performance of these tables by using Doppler tests on the divers to determine the effectiveness of our gas selection and decompression profiles.

Divers will work in teams of two, although one dive team may work in concert with another team. In the event one diver has some sort of failure on the bottom, both members of the team of two will immediately respond to the emergency, ascend together, if necessary, and notify the DM/DWSD. Dive teams will decompress together and remain close enough to render assistance in the event of an emergency.

All bottom divers will carry two side-slung tanks for OC bailout, one of which will be identical to the diluent, with the other a moderate trimix of their choosing.

Upon surfacing, bottom divers may be asked to breathe 20 minutes of oxygen before being tested with the Doppler.

At the conclusion of diving operations, we will remove all lines, gear, and equipment.

DIVE PROFILES

There is no universal agreement among diving industry professionals or deep divers as to the most effective decompression tables. Indeed, part of our mission is to add information to what is known about diving deep on CCR. It is likely that we will have conclusions that can be drawn from the research done on this expedition; however, what those conclusions will be is unknown at this time. Diving different diluents or different tables is not inconsistent with these goals.

All of the bottom divers on this expedition are experienced, deep CCR divers. The decompression profiles to be followed by the bottom-diving teams will be of their own limited choice. Each buddy team will be required to dive identical tables and gases. The teams will also be required to present the DM with a completed dive plan for any upcoming dive.

The selection of bottom gases and tables is an important decision. There is no single right decision, but there are many wrong decisions. Diver teams should choose carefully.

The limiting factor for these dives is the planned dive run time or in-water time. No dives will be permitted with a planned run time greater than 4 ½ hours or 270 minutes.

Divers for this expedition will be permitted to use the following for calculating their decompression:

1. The Vision Electronics Computer

2. The VR3 Computer (including the Ouroboros VR3)

3. The *Britannic* 2003 Dive Tables

4. The NAUI–RBGM Tables

Diluent selection and bailout gases carried by the bottom divers will be left up to each individual dive team, so long as no diluent gas for bottom use contains more than 22% nitrogen and 8% oxygen.

Each dive team will be responsible for their own dive gases and ensuring that the gas mixtures are properly tested and labelled. All dive cylinders for use on the bottom will be clearly marked with the divers' names.

The following recommendations are made by the expedition organizers:

1. All team members need to stay well-hydrated before, during, and after diving.

2. Divers should use more, rather than less, helium.

3. All team members need to protect themselves from excessive CNS O_2 toxicity levels by using minimal PPO_2 setpoints. No planned CNS O_2 toxicity over 200% will be accepted.

4. All dive tables and computers offer an estimated decompression profile based on theoretical information. Divers should buffer these recommendations as is appropriate to decrease risk.

5. Regardless of the assigned tasks, divers should minimize any physical exertion at depth.

APPENDIX B

MEMBERS OF SELECTED EXPEDITIONS

THE ROBUST WEBSITE HOSPITAL SHIP *BRITANNIC* (*hmhsbritannic.weebly. com/*), created and maintained by Michail Michailakis, lists the nineteen known *Britannic* expeditions and trips. The individuals in this appendix were part of the 1997 and 1998 expeditions. Our apologies if we omitted anyone's name. Members of the 2006, 2009, and 2015 expeditions are discussed in Chapters 16, 17, and 20, respectively.

A notable exception to subsequent larger teams scheduling multiple dives during their expeditions was the August 1995 single solo dive made to *Britannic* by Kostas Thoctarides. Kostas owns the Planet Blue Diving Center in Lavrio, has written multiple books about shipwrecks, is meticulous in his research, and is always fascinating to talk to. He had planned his dive for two years in coordination with the Cousteau Society. His twenty-minute dive made him the first man recorded as having touched *Britannic* since Cousteau. Although he has made subsequent trips to the wreck, she is only one of many in the area he has explored.

Britannic Expedition 1997

Members of the full Ocean Divers team led by Kevin Gurr were David Thompson, Tristan Cope, Alan Wright, Dan Burton, Uffe Erickson, Richard Lundgren, Ingmar Lundgren, John Thornton, Kevin Denlay, Gary Sharp, Alexander Sotiriou, Kerk Kavalaris, and Ian Fuller.

Vangelis Sotiriou, Alexander's father and founder of Sotiriou Diving College, provided diving support. This was also known as the International Association of Nitrox and Technical Divers (IANTD) Expedition.

Britannic Expedition 1998

The mixed-gas divers from Starfish Enterprise led by Nick Hope were Leigh Bishop, Christina Campbell, Chris Hutchison, Dave Wilkins, Geraint Ffoulkes-Jones, Bob Hughes, Jamie Powell, Rob Royle, Innes McCartney, John Yurga, and John Chatterton and were supported by Andrea Webb, Becky Williams, Kevin Emans, Greg Buxton, Derek Palmer, Captain Dan Crowell, Jennifer Samulski, and Greg Mossfeldt.

The Greek Diving Center gave local diving support with Kostas Nizamis, Hagen Martin, Marinos Pittas, and Gregoris Theodoridis. This was also known as the Starfish Enterprise Expedition.

2015 Trip with U-Boat Malta

We could not have made our June 2015 dives without the support of the *U-Boat Navigator* crew. They were Evgeny Tomashov (director of U-Boat Malta Limited and father of Dmitry), Oleksandr Stasyukevych (captain), Dmitry Tomashov (submersible pilot), Joseph Calleja (chief engineer), Andre Tanti (engineer assistant), Serhiy Zhdanovych (cook), Alexey Leonov (cook assistant), Sergey Bychkov (doctor), Sergii Zakharov (electrician and ROV pilot), Andrey Likhanskiy (technical diver), and Levan Margishvili (technical diver). Levan also taught me how to use the diving bell.

APPENDIX C

WHEN THINGS GO "BOOM"

EVEN THOUGH WE HAVE SEEN fully open boiler-room doors in parts of *Britannic* as the likeliest cause of her rapid sinking, the question remains *why* fail-safe measures for closing the doors did not function as designed. There is also the question about whether or not a secondary explosion occurred as reported by some witnesses.

Failure of *Britannic's* Watertight Doors
Parks Stephenson's detailed explanation of the nature and impact of the explosion combine his research and hundreds of hours he's spent in discussion with us reviewing and enhancing video footage and still photographs of *Britannic, Titanic, Olympic,* and related vessels.

> "First, let me explain the sequence of events involved in an underwater explosion. I put together the following description from excerpts taken from the report 'The Response of Surface Ships to Underwater Explosions,' written by Warren D. Reid when he was attached to the Underwater Explosions Research Department of the Naval Surface Warfare Division for the Commonwealth of Australia Defense Forces.

> "On detonation of an explosive underwater, a superheated, highly compressed gas bubble is formed, along with a shock wave in the surrounding water (approximately 53% of the total energy released in an underwater explosion goes into shock-wave formulation, 47% in pulsation of the gas bubble). The

exponentially decaying shock wave propagates as a spherical pressure wave and is originally much faster than the speed of sound. As this is taking place, the gas bubble begins to expand in size whilst the pressure in the bubble reduces. As the gas bubble expands, it displaces the water around it. After reaching a maximum radius with a minimum pressure, the bubble contracts again to a minimum radius at maximum pressure, although the pressure is not as high as the initial detonation. As the bubble contracts to a minimum, the displaced water rushes in to surround the volume vacated by the contracting bubble. This cycle may occur a number of times with pressure pulses being emitted at each bubble minimum.

"During this pulsation process, the bubble navigates upward due to the influence of gravity, and if the ship is in the path of the bubble, the pressure pulse may occur quite close to the hull. This may cause the hull to be holed or deformed or rupture at the bulkhead restraints. The pressure pulse that the bubble produces can result in localized loading effects on a ship's hull. Also, large bubbles often lose their symmetry and can collapse in upon themselves, thus forming a toroid-shaped bubble and a column of rapidly moving water. The combination of the water jet and bubble pulse can produce extensive damage in the hull structure of ships. If the frequency of the shock and bubble pulses matches the natural frequency of oscillation of the ship's hull girder, then the severe bending moment on the ship girder can result in whipping damage. If the charge is located directly or almost directly underneath and/or close by to a vessel, then there could be a contribution to the damage arising from the bubble collapse onto the ship's hull and also due to whipping damage caused by the bubble pulses. The bulkheads close to the point of attack will also often rupture due to direct exposure to the shock wave or to deformation caused in the bulkhead by hull deformation. As the stand-off increases, the point at which the hull just ruptures is reached. Past this point, the hull is still watertight but heavily deformed with the level of deformation decreasing as the stand-off continues. Eventually a point is reached where only elastic hull deformation occurs.

"You found the watertight doors fully open, without any indication that there was any attempt to close them. This should not have been ... even if the electric signal to release the doors (to slide closed with the help of gravity) had been somehow interrupted by the mine explosion and manual release by engineers in the boiler rooms had been somehow frustrated, there was a mechanical backup system designed to autonomously release the doors once saltwater reached them. The findings indicate that none of that triple-redundancy system seemed to have worked, so I am left with the conclusion that the doors were somehow jammed in their tracks. With the 2003 and 2006 evidence showing the open doors, I at first thought that shock-wave damage from the explosion might have warped the bulkhead on which the watertight door tracks were directly mounted and thereby threw the tracks out of true. But with the 2009 evidence, I had to consider a much greater damage stand-off and look instead at the effect that the bubble pulses had on hull deformation.

"To summarize, I believe that the mine detonated just underneath and close to the starboard side of the hull. The resultant bubble pulses lifted the bow of the ship (but not the stern), causing hull deformation that extended hundreds of feet aft of the original explosion location. The hull deformation caused the bulkheads to also deform, throwing the watertight door tracks out of true and jamming the door in place (full open position) before they could be dropped. When the clutches holding the doors released (either by normal or emergency method), the doors refused to fall. Water rushing in virtually unrestricted caused everyone in the area to flee shortly thereafter. And as I mentioned before, if you lose Boiler Room 5, you lose the ship." (*See Chapter 15: Entering the Firemen's Tunnel.*)

Parks explained the importance of Boiler Room 5.

"But then you may be asking why I think that losing Boiler Room 5 was key. Harland & Wolff's chief naval architect's calculations were based on the assumption that the ship was motionless and on an even keel. *Britannic* was under way and increasingly heeling to starboard. I need to computer model this (like we did with *Titanic*), but I have a gut feeling (based on my previous experience) that in *Britannic*'s situation, the loss of Boiler Room 5 was fatal. If you could someday go deep enough to get an image of an open watertight door into Boiler Room 4, then the matter is definitely settled . . . in no circumstance could the ship survive losing seven adjacent compartments.

"Even if that door is found to be closed, I still believe that my hypothesis about Boiler Room 5 being the fatal loss is strong enough to express, but it will be unproven and therefore remain controversial. I hope that we can do a documentary that will provide funding to commission the kind of flooding survey that we did for Cameron's 2012 documentary … that's the only way to prove my hypothesis."

Coal Dust Explosion as Secondary Explosion

Cousteau had theorized if there had indeed been a secondary explosion as reported by some *Britannic* survivors, coal dust might have been the source of the explosion. (*See Chapter 7: Stirring the Sleeping Ship.*) White Star Line historian Paul Louden-Brown offered intriguing information about this possibility in an email exchange.

"The highly volatile nature of coal dust, when airborne and ignited in a confined space was never considered [in the official 1916, two-page report].

"Damp coal and poor unventilated storage often resulted in coal 'heating.' This type of spontaneous combustion was well-known and experienced trimmers knew how to prevent or otherwise deal with the problem. The reverse side of this problem was coal that was too dry created large amounts of dust when the coal was being worked in the bunkers, or empty bunkers had a thick carpet of coal dust. Vessels engaged in the African, Indian services [hot-weather climates] were designed with smaller bunkers, many unventilated to reduce the problems of coal dust. Bunkers in North Atlantic ships, like *Britannic*, were ventilated; this, paradoxically, might have exasperated the problem when the coal was dry. In normal circumstances, the dangers of large amounts of airborne particles were not a serious problem, but an explosion and resulting flashover and secondary explosion almost simultaneously, was potentially a far greater threat.

"How to cope with this potential problem? Experienced trimmers would know how to deal with all these issues, or at least minimize them. Empty bunkers would, under normal circumstances, be completely cleaned out and the dust disposed of through the ash ejectors.

"I'm not aware of any coal consumption or storage figures that have survived from the last voyage, but in normal circumstances (peacetime), the Chief Engineer would have been asked to provide this information at an enquiry.

"I doubt the Captain and Engineering Commander would have considered any of these problems and most likely never asked the question, for the Royal Navy of the period was largely fueled by oil, and the problems and dangers associated with the use and handling of coal a thing of the past.

"I appreciate that this is an opinion, but I would point out that if the loss of *Britannic* had been investigated by the British Board of Trade, the well-known dangers associated with coal in hot climates would have been considered."

APPENDIX D

A REUNION OF SURVIVORS

MICHAIL MICHAILAKIS HAS COLLECTED an interesting array of items and in some cases, discovered information not contained in previously published books. One of the areas where he has worked diligently is the research field dedicated to the identities and individual histories of people who served on the ship. There are numerous reasons why the progress has been slow, mainly sifting through the handwritten, fragile paper records as anyone who has searched through old archives knows.

Undaunted, Michail follows every lead he can find and in 2015, he discovered the unpublished account of Private Samuel Edwin "Ted" Williams at the Living Archive, a local archive located at Milton Keynes, Buckinghamshire. Private Williams, an active member of the British Legion (BL) for many years, gave his entire personal collection to the Living Archive. According to what Michail discovered, in 1955 one of the members of the National Executive Council of the BL was John T. Cuthbertson, a Royal Army Medical Corps (RAMC) private who had also survived the sinking. Cuthbertson wanted to meet others who had served on the ship, and he posted an invitation through the official BL journal hoping he would receive at least a few responses. His invitation did better than expected as thirty-nine survivors responded to his call. That was not only a surprisingly higher number than anticipated, it was also coincidental considering they were approaching the thirty-ninth anniversary of the sinking.

The reunion date was set for November 21, 1955, and sixteen individuals were able to attend. Ted Williams was there, of course, and as part of the afternoon activities, the group laid a wreath of poppies at the Cenotaph of Whitehall. Dinner was held at The Two Chairmen, a pub at 39 Dartmouth

Street (St. Margaret, Westminster), which still exists. The following day, BL issued a press release about the event, which also included a complete list of the survivors who contacted Cuthbertson. In reviewing the list of responders, there was a mix of known and new individuals. Interestingly, there were a few individuals whose precise status is still not known. In some cases, with only an initial and no first name, it was unclear if the individual was crew or medical staff. (Notes are provided for those names.) In other cases, nothing more than a name was listed. Two of the attendees signed Ted Williams's dinner menu. He kept it and the BL press release as mementos and later contributed both documents to the Living Archive collection. Those in attendance were:

1. S.G. Cook, Assistant Baker (No. 264; White Star crew list) or Fireman (No. 298)

2. Miss Mary Bowyer (known from a previously documented source)

3. George G. Burgess, Sergeant, RAMC

4. Frank E. Chambers, Private, RAMC

5. Charles R. Collar, Private, RAMC

6. Miss A. M. Collcutt, VAD (Voluntary Aid Detachment)

7. John T. Cuthbertson, Private, RAMC (known from a previously documented source)

8. Miss A. Handley

9. Sister Harris

10. M.J. Hartnett, RAMC (rank unknown; not crew/no medal index card [MIC])

11. Sister E. K. Jack, QAIMNS(reserve) (Queen Alexandra's Imperial Military Nursing Service)

12. H.H. Jones, Fireman (No. 368; White Star crew list)

13. George S. Kingsnorth, Corporal, RAMC

14. Alfred C. Tozer, Private, RAMC

15. Samuel Edwin Williams, Private, RAMC (known from a previously documented source)

16. T.A. Yates, Laundryman (No. 191; White Star crew list)

Those who responded and did not attend:

1. J.A. Ahier, Intermediate Second Engineer (No. 86; White Star crew list)

2. Holmes Brelsford, Private, RAMC (known from a previously documented source)

3. J. Brennan, Private, RAMC

4. J.E. Clarke, Private, RAMC
5. J. Craig, 4th Electrician (No. 114; White Star crew list)
6. W. Cuff, Fireman (No. 360; White Star crew list)
7. A.J. Cunningham, Temporary Lieutenant, RAMC
8. R. Davies, RAMC (rank could not be determined; had MIC)
9. S. Davies, Steward (No. 37; White Star crew list) or RAMC (exact status not recorded)
10. R. Hamilton, Assistant Deck Engineer (No. 108 White Star crew list) or RAMC (exact status not recorded)
11. W.H. Hermitage, Able Seaman (No. 62; White Star crew list)
12. Capt. Robert Hume, Chief Officer (No. 3; White Star crew list)
13. Miss Barbara S. Mattison (known from a previously documented source)
14. Richard Parker, Private, RAMC
15. Sister F. K. Pattenden, QAIMNS
16. John M. Roberts, Private, RAMC
17. H. Slater, Captain, RAMC (known from a previously documented source)
18. E. Smith, Fireman (No. 396; White Star crew list) or RAMC (exact status not recorded)
19. R.G. Smith, Private, RAMC
20. S. Smith, Steward (No. 113) or RAMC (exact status not recorded)
21. M. Summers, 1st Electrician (White Star crew list)
22. Sister A. B. Waddell
23. R.M. Wormald, RAMC (rank could not be determined; not crew; no MIC)

The much later documented reunion was of eight survivors who gathered with Jacques Cousteau when he filmed his television special about the 1976 Expedition. Michail will continue to search different sources to see if there were other reunions waiting to be uncovered.

GLOSSARY

AUV (autonomous underwater vehicle) — An unmanned submersible that can search for and "see" shipwrecks with its side-scan sonar. Unlike a ROV, it has no tether or umbilical to the ship and searches preprogrammed areas of the seafloor on its own.

AIVL (Advanced Imaging and Visualization Laboratory) — One of the specialized laboratories at Woods Hole Oceanographic Institution.

bailout tank — An auxiliary scuba tank, usually carried under the arm(s) and filled with emergency gas to breathe if a diver's rebreather fails.

BCD (buoyancy control device) — A vest that divers use to provide lift or to precisely control buoyancy while underwater by adding or releasing small amounts of air.

black gang — Crewmen who worked in the boiler rooms as firemen, greasers, or trimmers.

bollard — A short vertical post (or posts) for securing a ship to a dock or pier.

bow — The front of a ship or boat.

breathing loop — The double hoses of the mouthpiece of a closed-circuit rebreather. This also refers to the continuous circuit of breathing gas in a rebreather: exhaled from mouth through one-way check valves, to exhalation counterlung, to the carbon dioxide scrubber canister, through the head (where O_2 is measured and information sent to handset and HUD), to the inhalation counterlung, through a one-way check valve and inhaled back through the mouth.

caique — A single-mast sailing vessel common in the eastern Mediterranean Sea.

CCR (closed-circuit rebreather) — A back-mounted diving apparatus that captures the exhaled breath of the diver, removes the carbon dioxide, and replaces the small amount of oxygen metabolized and is rebreathed again.

CNS (central nervous system) — The human brain, spinal cord, and associated neurological pathways critical to basic life-support, muscular, and sensory systems.

DAN (Divers Alert Network) — A nonprofit organization that assists divers by conducting medical research on recreational scuba diving safety, provides emergency assistance through a 24/7 hotline, and helps answer divers' medical and fitness-to-dive questions.

davit — A crane used for lowering and raising lifeboats.

DCS (decompression sickness) — An injury seen in divers caused by the formation of gas bubbles when a diver fails to make decompression stops or ascends too rapidly. Depending on factors such as maximum depth reached and the amount of time spent underwater, it can have varying effects from a minor rash to joint pain and, in extreme cases, paralysis and death.

decompression — The act of ascending slowly and stopping at predetermined depths for periods of time. The diver ascends to the surface to allow the bubbles in the bloodstream to exit the body through normal respiration.

diving bell — A rigid chamber used like an elevator to transport divers to depth in the ocean.

DM (dive marshal) — Person with overall responsibility for the dive team and execution of the dive plan.

DOO (dive operations officer) — Person in charge of planning and procedural matters for the project.

Doppler — An ultrasonic device for detecting bubbles in the bloodstream.

DPV (diver propulsion vehicle) — A battery-operated underwater scooter.

DSO (dive safety officer) — Person who creates and implements safety policies and procedures.

DSV (dive surface valve) — The mouthpiece of a closed-circuit rebreather.

FFM (full-face mask) — A mask that covers the entire face and includes a breathing mouthpiece.

firemen — Men who worked stoking and maintaining the fires in the boilers on a ship.

forecastle — A compartment where the crew lives. Sailor's term is fo'c'sle.

forward — Toward the front or bow of a ship.

gantry system — A unique design feature for a moving crane that could launch lifeboats from either side of the ship.

greasers — Workers who greased and filled grease reservoirs in various parts of the engine and boiler rooms.

HPNS (high-pressure nervous syndrome) — A physiological response of a diver's nervous system to breathing under great pressures, usually encountered at depths in excess of 500 feet. It is the limiting factor in preventing free-swimming divers from going deeper than 2,300 feet.

HUD (heads-up display) — An LED or other type of visual display mounted close to the diver's face, offering quick access and relevant life-support information.

IANTD (International Association of Nitrox and Technical Divers) — A training agency for advanced diving levels such as wreck, cave, deep, trimix, nitrox, and rebreather certifications.

lazy shot — A second line attached to the downline (or main line) and used for ascending and decompressing divers.

loop — *See* **breathing loop**.

MOD (maximum operating depth) — The labeling on scuba cylinders to indicate the maximum depth the contents can be safely breathed.

mooring — An anchored line to secure a ship or boat, usually attached to a floating ball.

nitrogen narcosis — An altered state of consciousness brought about by the anesthetic effect of breathing nitrogen at depth. It is a reversible condition, alleviated by ascending.

nitrox — Breathing gas with higher-than-normal percentages of oxygen. Used by technical divers to accelerate decompression.

OC (open circuit) — Basic scuba diving equipment in which the diver breathes from a regulator attached to a scuba tank and exhausts his breaths as bubbles into the water.

oxygen toxicity — Symptoms experienced by divers exposed to higher-than-normal exposure to oxygen that can result in seizures.

port — The left side of a ship or boat when facing the bow or forward.

rebreather — *See* **CCR**.

RIB (rigid inflatable boat) — A rigid, hulled boat with inflatable rubber gunwales.

ROV (remotely operated vehicle) — A tethered underwater robot.

rusticle — A unique colony of microorganisms that eat steel and form an icicle-shaped colony that appears to drip off iron shipwrecks.

shot line — A heavy weighted line dropped or "shot" onto the shipwreck for the divers to follow down.

SMB (surface marker buoy) — A six-foot-long sausage-shaped balloon divers use to signal the surface and indicate their position underwater. Different color SMBs can be used to communicate various possible emergency scenarios.

SOP (standard operating procedures) — A detailed dive plan for expeditionary dive projects which details assets and protocols for both normal and emergency diving procedures. Mirrored after commercial and military dive operations, the SOP is unique to each project's resources and goals.

SSB — Single sideband, used for underwater communications.

stage bottle — Scuba tank carried under the arm(s) and filled with gases an open-circuit trimix diver must use to decompress.

starboard — The right side of a ship or boat while facing the bow or forward.

stern — The back of a ship or boat.

submersible — A small submarine designed for scientific or exploratory purposes.

TDI (Technical Diving International) — A training agency for advanced diving levels such as wreck, cave, deep, trimix, nitrox, and rebreather certifications.

telegraph — A communication device used on a ship so the pilot could give commands to the engine room.

trimix — A breathing mixture of helium, oxygen, and nitrogen. At depths greater than 200 feet underwater, the nitrogen and oxygen levels in air creates problems for divers. The addition of helium in the breathing gas lowers the nitrogen and oxygen levels, reducing the risk of faulty judgment from nitrogen narcosis and from oxygen toxicity seizures.

trimmers — Workers who prepared and brought coal from various bunkers around the ship to the "firemen." Had to break the coal from large chunks into smaller pieces and also adjust how much they took from each bunker to keep the ship balanced or in trim.

wings — A type of buoyancy compensating device that is worn on the back to offset the great weight of wearing numerous heavy diving tanks and assist a diver to stay in the swimming position underwater.

ACKNOWLEDGMENTS

RICHIE KOHLER

I HAVE HEARD IT TAKES A VILLAGE to raise a child, and that adage surely applies to this book, with so many people who have helped me along the way. More than anyone, Charlie Hudson believed in the project from the first time I told her about *Britannic*. She encouraged and helped me focus on what was important to the story (and what to let go of). She is a dogged researcher, and as an experienced writer, she showed me how to make technical subjects easier to understand and enjoyable to read.

The Cousteau name is synonymous with underwater exploration, and as it was Jacques Cousteau who found and explored *Britannic*, it is perfect that his son, Jean-Michel Cousteau, graciously wrote the foreword to this book. Much like the Cousteau legacy, I greatly admire Dr. Bob Ballard's work in discovering deepwater shipwrecks. I am very grateful to Kirk Wolfinger for giving me the chance to work with this legendary man.

David Concannon first introduced me to the Olympians. David is incredibly talented in many fields, but it was his passion for deep-sea exploration that would ultimately lead to my first *Titanic* expedition. It was there that I first worked with Woods Hole Oceanographic Institution's iconic Bill Lange and his wonderful deep-sea camera systems. The questions surrounding *Titanic* led me to *Britannic*, and I came to work with experts in this particular field of Victorian shipbuilding and commerce: Paul Louden-Brown, whose oration makes the history of these leviathans come alive; *Britannic*'s owner Simon Mills, who is the best source of information and photographs of his "girl"; and Parks Stephenson's technical knowledge of the Olympic class of ships is invaluable to explorers to "see" inside a wreck before they ever dive it. Bill Sauder and Ken Marschall also worked with Parks to finalize the impressive CGI images for this book. Making the acquaintance of Michail Michailakis has been a pleasure as has learning how he came to be involved with researching *Britannic*. Ken Marschall's paintings are painstakingly detailed, not only by his skill with brush and pallet, but by his lifelong passion for *Titanic* and her sisters. His expertise on these vessels is as large as his historical photo collection.

Over the past decade of dive operations on *Britannic*, I have been fortunate to rub shoulders with an international pool of incredibly talented people who come to *Britannic* seeking answers. From microbiologist Lori Johnston and hyperbaric researcher Dr. Petar Denoble, to technical diving guru and inventor Kevin Gurr, *Britannic* draws out the best of the best. At the heart of it all are the divers, the pointy end of the spear that pushes the edge of the envelope. They are kindred souls and my dearest friends: Leigh Bishop (Bish), Mike Barnette (Barney), and Pete Mesley. Their fantastic underwater photographs grace this book and bring the majesty of what we experience to others. Danny Huyge and Edoardo Pavia (Edo) always have my back and helped me in ways I could never repay, and Richie Stevenson and John Chatterton went into the one of the most dangerous places I know and made it look simple.

Evan Kovacs has been with me from the beginning, way before we explored *Titanic*. It's no coincidence that we have been together on every *Britannic* expedition to date; I trust Evan with my life. He's more like a kid brother than a friend, one who has taught me along the way, as surely as I may have showed him a thing or two. Finally, I am very grateful to Vicky Spencer for sharing with me the Carl I didn't know — the father, the husband, her Carl. Her shared memories have only made him even larger in my eyes.

Working in Greece, things can go sideways fast, especially if you don't speak Greek. Tina Tavridou was always there to help navigate the pitfalls and find whatever we needed, when we needed it, and always with a smile. She is simply the best! Local dive shop owner and *Britannic* veteran Kostas Thoctarides is a wealth of information and a great asset to any group looking to dive in the region.

On small moving boats, camera people can be taxing, given all the other pressures an expedition throws at you, but Hans Rosenwinkel and Jesse Plackey were a pleasure to work with. I barely knew they were there, and from all the footage they shot, it appears they were everywhere at once!

I have the utmost respect and admiration for the professionalism of the *U-Boat Navigator's* crew and want to thank Evgeny and Dmitry Tomashov for their gracious hospitality, Sasha Kuznetsova for her professional courtesy, Levan Margishvili for teaching me how to operate the diving bell, and to our tender, Dr. Sergey Bychkov, for talking to me and looking after us during those long hours of decompression in the bell.

My gratitude goes to Dan Orr for connecting me with Best Publishing Company, where Jaclyn Mackey, Lorraine Fico-White (fellow Brooklynite), and

Diana Robinson worked tirelessly from start to finish to make this book happen. What a beautiful job they have done. Thank you all!

Howard and Megan Ehrenberg crafted an incredible website for the book with a little help from Ryan Shepard on the video, and images and artwork from William Barney, Mark Chirnside, and Michail Michailakis as well.

No man is an island, and I have my family to thank for their patience and understanding at the risks I have taken. Thanks to Mom and Dad, who encouraged and led by example (respectfully), to brother Frank and sisters Lisa, Kertrin, and Alyssa, who know I am crazy but understand this is who I am. The long trips away from home were a little harder for my two children: Nikki and Richie, I hope I have taught you to find your passion and follow it to the ends of the earth as I have done.

Finally, thanks to my wife, Carrie, who pushes when I need a push, pulls me back when I got too close to the edge, and is smart enough to know the difference when I don't see it. You are the bravest woman I know, and I couldn't have done any of this without you.

CHARLIE HUDSON

FIRST, I HAVE TO GIVE A BIG "THANK YOU" to Richie for bringing me into this project. In having watched the History Channel shows about *Titanic* and *Britannic*, I had seen clips of Bill Lange, Evan Kovacs, Paul Louden-Brown, Simon Mills, Parks Stephenson, and others, but to meet and speak with them has been a special opportunity. I also want to acknowledge how welcoming and gracious Elizabeth Louden-Brown was during my visit to Northern Ireland. Time spent with Leigh Bishop and Kevin Gurr was fascinating, and Richie Stevenson and I were able to speak by telephone.

I know it was difficult for Vicky Spencer to share her memories about Carl, and I hope to someday visit the memorial to Carl that she told me about.

In addition to his memorable books and expedition experience, I am also thankful to Simon Mills for passing on a letter to Margaret Meehan, Violet Jessop's niece, and to Margaret for her subsequent kind response. On another note about that research trip, I would like to express my appreciation to the staff of the Hare and Hounds Inn located in Newbury, England. Aside from the fact it is a charming place, they went out of their way to assist me with several things. They provided me a wonderful spot in the "library" to hold an interview and a late checkout to accommodate a telephone interview.

John Chatterton's memories of the 1998 Expedition filled in a blank for me, and David Concannon's explanation about the Explorers Club was enlightening. I am grateful to Ken Marschall for his insights and wonderful artwork. Finding Michail Michailakis's website, Hospital Ship *Britannic* (*hmhsbritannic.weebly.com*), was an absolute treasure as has been engaging with him via email. Lori Johnston's assistance with the issue of biodeterioration on the wrecks was greatly appreciated.

Thanks also to Dan Orr for the introduction to Jaclyn Mackey at Best Publishing Company and the entire staff. Lorraine Fico-White kept us on target with all the different steps that take a book from the computer screen to the shelf, and Diana Robinson's talent as a graphic artist brought an important dimension of photographs to the book and beautifully incorporated the cover images provided from Ken Marschall.

My friend Larry Diehl helped me with the painstaking, yet critical task of cross-checking facts as the narrative progressed. As always, my husband, Hugh, was at my side, not only with his encouragement, but also with his technical diving experience and ability to "speak engineer."

NOTE ON SOURCES

THE HISTORICAL CONTEXT OF THE BOOK comes from multiple sources. It is not intended as a history of *Britannic* but rather to provide selected information about her history. We urge anyone who wants to know more about *Britannic*, the other Olympians, and aspects of WW I to read the books and articles we cite in the text and bibliography. Sources of information about other world and historical events were heavily Internet-based, and while the sites were valid at the time of writing, websites are not always maintained. Interviews we conducted were predominantly in person, and most were combined with email correspondence and/or telephone calls. The descriptions of dive and expedition experiences are from personal memory, and we realize individual memories and perspectives are rarely identical among any group of people.

As explained in the book, Simon Mills holds a unique status as *Britannic's* owner. His meticulous research began well before he gained title to the ship, and his historical expertise makes *Hostage to Fortune* and *The Unseen Britannic* among the best reference books available. The two coffee-table books are filled with photographs, illustrations, and other images. His first book, *HMHS Britannic: The Last Titan,* is an excellent introductory reference. It is out of print but can be found through resale options.

On the broader historical view, hours spent with Paul Louden-Brown go by quickly as you get swept up in his expansive knowledge of the entire White Star Line. When Charlie traveled to the UK, she told me how enjoyable it had been to walk with him through Titanic Quarter, Belfast. He emphasized an interesting point about *Britannic* and immigration. It was an aspect of the Olympians he had mentioned in a previous email exchange.

"Why *Britannic* is important in the story of the great passenger liners is that she represents the end of the evolution of the emigrant ship from the world's first true ocean liner, *Oceanic*, in 1871 to the close of mass migration during the Great War. Of course, had war not come to Europe, it is certain even greater vessels would have been built to serve this human trade. But America was already tiring of the endless stream of migrants from Europe, and the war, in some respects, was an opportunity for the United States to restrict migration, which they began to do from 1922 onward. So, to sum up, *Britannic* represents an important last step and a forgotten chapter in the story of people on the move."

The "forgotten chapters in history" also led us to want to provide extra information about World War I, with the global complexities and especially the introduction of technological advances/innovations we now take for granted. There were times during research when we branched into topics such as memories of New Zealand or Canadian nurses aboard hospital ships that were dissimilar to *Britannic*. Even though their experiences weren't directly related to *Britannic*, they made for enlightening reading. The East African Campaign and the rationale for countries choosing to enter the war are other examples of additional articles to consider.

Reading through Violet Jessop's memoirs, *Titanic Survivor*, was, of course, fascinating, and we sadly learned John Maxtone-Graham, the author who annotated and edited her memoirs, passed away July 6, 2015. Paul Louden-Brown counted him as a friend, and they had discussed Maxtone-Graham's work with the Jessop book on more than one occasion.

One of the fascinating finds, *The U-Boat War, 1914-1918* by Edwyn A. Gray, provides a detailed history of operations of a timeframe many people are not familiar with. Navies of the world took the lessons of WWI to heart when they developed their vessels, strategies, and tactics for future conflicts. It is a valuable reference filled with facts, figures, and stories World War II U-boat enthusiasts will want to read. Gray's book shows not only the initial fulfillment of U-boats as a weapon of war, but also the human side of that particular type of combat. Although some copies can be found through used-book sources, it is in ebook format through Pen and Sword Books, *www.pen-and-sword.co.uk*, and via other websites.

A rich source of information for White Star Line ships is the Titanic Historical Society. As a quick aside, it tends to take people by surprise when they learn the THS, as it is often called, is located in Indian Orchard, Massachusetts, but that has to do with being founded at the home of Mr. Edward S. Kamuda in July 1963, with others who were committed to preserving the history of RMS *Titanic* and the White Star Line. The Society was officially formed on September 6, 1963, the date being significant as the day and month the Oceanic Steam Navigation Co. Ltd was founded. (OSN was the official company name of White

Star Line). THS now has thousands of members, and while other organizations refer to themselves as "Titanic Historical Societies," they are not necessarily associated with the original THS, whose role in serving as "the premier source for *Titanic* and White Star Line information" is supported with publishing the *Titanic Commutator* to provide a platform for articles based on careful academic and historical research.

THS has periodically highlighted and/or devoted issues to the subject of *Britannic*. Following the 1976 Cousteau Expedition, the Fall 1977, Winter 1977, and Winter 1978 volumes contained a wealth of articles and historical documents, such as multiple witness testimonies, the official report of the sinking, sketches, photographs, and logs. Some were on temporary loan from numerous archives. *Britannic's* rise, her brief time in service, the tragic day, and the aftermath are all discussed. As much new information as possible was included, especially the finds from the expedition. These issues are out of regular print but may be obtainable through THS. If so, their out-of-print issues are printed on demand, bound, and reproduced in black and white.

The decision about how much history to include was not an easy one, yet *Mystery of the Last Olympian* is a dual story, and the mighty ship provides a perfect example of how and why shipwreck exploration has advanced. For her to have been "lost" for sixty years and located by the great Jacques Cousteau brings an irresistible dimension to those of us whose dreams of undersea exploration were ignited by Cousteau. Finding the video *Jacques Cousteau's Search for Titanic's Sister Ship Britannic* on YouTube (posted May 8, 2014) was an extra bonus. We hope it remains available for viewing. To then have Jean-Michel Cousteau write the foreword for *Mystery of the Last Olympian* was a special honor, and his words capture the essence of the ocean's importance to our "Blue Planet."

Dr. Robert Ballard's *Britannic* Expedition, twenty years after Cousteau, bristled with new technology, and I hadn't known Ken Marschall was on the team. His involvement came out as we discussed the painting I commissioned to use as the basis for the cover of *Last Olympian*. Even though we didn't use all the images he provided from his archives, his vivid description of *Britannic's* beauty conveys why she captivates divers. In moving forward in time from the ship's history to the saga of exploration of Parts II and III, we also moved into first-person voice to focus on *Britannic* expeditions I was either involved in or I knew from stories divers always share. (In selecting these specific ones, our intent was not to take away from expeditions we didn't include in the book. Every team that dives *Britannic* contributes to what we learn about her.) I knew some of the background and events of the 1997, 1998, and 2003 expeditions, but not all the behind-the-scenes pieces the United Kingdom divers shared in their interviews and emails. I knew vaguely about fellow shadow diver John Chatterton being the first *Britannic* diver to use a rebreather. It was a pivotal point for future expeditions, and I enjoyed reading the details in his email describing the experience. It was interesting to search through my memory and old dive records to chronicle how I met the different people we highlight in the book. Some of the problems we've all encountered have had elements of humor along with frustration and philosophical acceptance of "shit happens."

Despite knowing the dangers of *Britannic* and making safety a priority on every expedition, Carl's loss was a tragedy none of us expected, and I appreciate everyone who shared their thoughts about that difficult day. My numerous email exchanges with Vicky to put together the memorial we held on Kea stirred intense emotion, and we would have completely understood had she not wanted to conduct the telephone interview for the passages about Carl. We were grateful for her decision and her descriptions of "Carl, the adventurer, the husband, and father."

In the years following Carl's death, I did have some great dives, and I clearly remember the surge of excitement when Evan Kovacs and Bill Lange told me about the potential joint expedition. The delays brought disappointment and a lot F-bombs each time another "dive window" slipped past. Being invited to an expedition with Dr. Robert Ballard aboard *Nautilus* was a definite lift, and it was Evan more than me who saw the potential when Simon Mills put us in touch with U-Boat Group Malta. What a spring and summer it turned out to be as we made preparations knowing full well the trip could fall apart in the snap of a finger. My emails back and forth with Parks Stephenson about his initial theory of a shockwave effect on the watertight doors were interesting, and his CGI work assisted by Bill Sauder and Ken Marschall continues to amaze me.

David Concannon's help with the Explorers Club flag added a dimension we felt Carl would have applauded. As much as I would have liked to carry the 2009 Expedition flag, the two stories he sent about the flag we were awarded made me chuckle. The eleven days of the trip were nonstop, and keeping a daily diary was the only way to ensure I didn't leave out important details. Although we had worked with Russian crews when we were on *Titanic*, *U-Boat Navigator* (*UBN*) was a different arrangement, and using the diving bell wasn't something we'd considered. It wasn't until a few weeks after the trip I thought to ask Dr. Petar Denoble about the function of a diving bell in a situation with a diver suffering oxygen toxicity. I appreciated his confirmation of it as an added safety feature.

I have high hopes the big expedition will come about in 2016 (or whenever), and I look forward to as many trips to *Britannic* as the future holds.

SELECTED BIBLIOGRAPHY

Articles and Books

Bishop, Leigh. "The Truth about Britannic." *Diver,* March 2004. Accessed August 2015. http://www.divernetxtra.com/wrecks/0304britannic.shtml

Galon, Dimitri. "The sad story of s/s Burdigala, formerly s/s Kaiser Friedrich (1897-1916)." Translated by Byron E. Riginos. Ocean Liner S/S Burdigala Project. Accessed November 19, 2015. http://keadive.gr/the-sad-story-of-ss-burdigala-former-ss-kaiser-friedrich/

Gray, Edwyn. *The U-Boat War: 1914-1918.* London: Leo Cooper, 1994.

Gurr, Kevin. *Technical Diving from the Bottom Up.* Lytchett Matravers, UK: Kevin Gurr, 2010.

Jessop, Violet. *Titanic Survivor: The Newly Discovered Memoirs of Violet Jessop Who Survived both the Titanic and Britannic Disasters.* Edited by John Maxtone-Graham. Dobbs Ferry, NY: Sheridan House, 2004.

Kurson, Robert. *Shadow Divers: The True Adventure of Two Americans Who Risked Everything to Solve One of the Last Mysteries of World War II.* New York: Random House, 2004.

Louden-Brown, Paul. *The White Star Line: An Illustrated History, 1869-1934.* 2nd ed. Herne Bay, Kent: The Titanic Historical Society, 2001.

Macpherson, William Grant. *Medical Services General History.* Vol. 1 of *History of the Great War, Based on Official Documents.* London: His Majesty's Stationery Office, 1921. Reprint of "Appendix C: List of Hospital Ships Destroyed by Submarines or Mines," The Medical Front WWI, WWW Virtual Library, 1997. Last modified April 23, 2013. Accessed August 10, 2015. http://www.vlib.us/medical/hospships.htm

Matsen, Bradford. *Titanic's Last Secrets: The Further Adventures of Shadow Divers John Chatterton and Richie Kohler.* New York: Twelve, 2008.

McCallum, Jack E. *Military Medicine: From Ancient Times to the 21st Century*. Santa Barbara, CA: ABC-CLIO, 2008.

Mills, Simon. *HMHS Britannic: The Last Titan*. 2nd ed. Market Drayton, Shropshire: Shipping Books Press, 1996.

Mills, Simon. *Hostage to Fortune: The Dramatic Story of the Last Olympian, HMHS Britannic*. Chesham, England: Wordsmith Publications, 2002.

Mills, Simon. *The Unseen Britannic: The Ship in Rare Illustrations*. Stroud, Gloucestershire: The History Press, 2014.

Paice, Edward. "How the Great War Razed East Africa." *Africa Research Institute*. Last modified August 4, 2014. Accessed July 9, 2015. http://www.africaresearchinstitute.org/publications/counterpoints/how-the-great-war-razed-east-africa/

Reynolds, Rich. "The U-Boat Campaign, World War I." *20th Century Battles: The Military Research and Analysis Archive*. Last modified March 22, 2015. Accessed August 10, 2015. http://20thcenturybattles.com/2015/03/22/the-u-boat-campaign-world-war-i/

The National Archives (UK). "The Blockade of Germany." The First World War, Spotlights on History. Accessed June 9, 2015. http://www.nationalarchives.gov.uk/pathways/firstworldwar/spotlights/blockade.htm

Titanic Historical Society. "H.M.H.S. Britannic: The Controversy Continues." *The Titanic Commutator*. Winter 1978; 2(060).

Titanic Historical Society. "R.M.S Britannic: Exploration of a Legacy." *The Titanic Commutator*. Fall 1977; 2(058).

Titanic Historical Society. "R.M.S Britannic: Exploration of a Legacy, Part Two." *The Titanic Commutator*. Winter 1977; 2(059).

Documentaries and Video Footage

"Calypso's Search for the Britannic." *Jacques Cousteau Odyssey*. Cousteau Society Productions in association with KCET/Los Angeles, CA, 1977. YouTube video, "Jacques Cousteau's Search for Titanic's Sister Ship Britannic." Posted by "Belfast Ships," May 8, 2014. Accessed August 10, 2015. https://www.youtube.com/watch?v=Ocf_fSMSkgU

"Titanic's Lost Sister." *NOVA*. Corporation for Public Broadcasting. Boston: WGBH Science Unit, January 28, 1997. Transcript accessed October 14, 2015. http://www.pbs.org/wgbh/nova/transcripts/2402titanic.html

Websites of Interest

Baker, Chris. *The Long, Long Trail: The British Army in the Great War of 1914-1918*. http://www.longlongtrail.co.uk

Classic Lodge Hotels. *The White Swan*. http://www.classiclodges.co.uk/our-hotels/the-white-swan/home/

Marschall, Ken. *The Art of Ken Marschall.* http://www.kenmarschall.com

Michailakis, Michail. *Hospital Ship Britannic.* http://hmhsbritannic.weebly.com/

Titanic and Co. *RMS Titanic — Ship of Dreams.* http://www.titanicandco.com/

The Titanic Historical Society, Inc. *Titanic Historical Society.* http://www.titanic1.org/

Helgason, Gudmundur. *Uboat.net.* http://uboat.net/index.html

World Center for Exploration. *The Explorers Club.* New York City, NY. https://explorers.org/

Zocon Enterprises. *Zocon Entertainment.* http://zoconent.com

INDEX

WHOI. *See* Woods Hole Oceanographic Institution

Wickham, Jonathon, 91

Wilbanks, Ralph, 116

Wilkins, Dave, 190

Williams, Becky, 190

Williams, Samuel Edwin "Ted," 197-198

Wolfinger, Kirk, 46, 91, 113, 205

Woods Hole Oceanographic Institution (WHOI), 91, 92, 93, 102, 105, 107, 115, 116, 127, 201, 205

Wright, Alan, 189

Yurga, John, 190

Zakharov, Sergii, 190

Zhdanovych, Serhiy, 190

QUESTIONS FOR DISCUSSION

1. How familiar were you with the scope of World War I and the number of advances in technology that occurred because of the war? What did you learn?

2. Had you been Violet Jessop, do you think you would have gone back to sea after the *Titanic* disaster? What would you have done? Compare surviving this disaster with someone surviving an airplane crash.

3. Name a specific historical mystery where you wanted to know as much as you could about what happened.

4. Could the engineers of Harland & Wolff have done anything else to make *Olympic* and *Britannic* stronger ships?

5. What ironic elements surrounded *Britannic* to give you the sense she was a doomed ship from the beginning?

6. What else would you like to know about Violet Jessop's life?

7. In reading about the connections joining *Britannic* experts and explorers together, have you had a similar experience of being drawn into a situation (work or personal) because of "someone who knew someone"?

8. In the argument about manned and unmanned deep-sea exploration, do you agree that it is too risky for people or that it is the willingness to take the risks that helps advance technology?

9. Between the history and the exploration, what was your favorite part of the book?

ABOUT THE AUTHORS

RICHIE KOHLER, originally from Brooklyn, New York, is one of only four men in the world who has been to the RMS *Titanic* in a submersible and also physically diving inside her equally tragic sister ship HMHS *Britannic*. His passion for technical scuba diving and maritime history began in 1980, and he is internationally known for exploring some of the most challenging and dangerous shipwrecks in the world. His explorations have helped to locate and name numerous lost vessels, including the minelaying submarine *U-215* on the Georges Banks off Nova  Scotia and the WWII destroyer USS *Murphy* that was crushed and forgotten in the New York approaches.

It was a six-year effort to identify an unknown WWII German U-boat as the *U-869* that catapulted his diving career into the world of television and documentary filmmaking. The daring risks he and John Chatterton took and their dogged determination to seek out the truth of the U-boat were detailed in the *New York Times* bestseller *Shadow Divers* by Robert Kurson, and *NOVA* won an Emmy for their documentary *Hitler's Lost Sub.* Kohler co-hosted fifty-six episodes of History Channel's *Deep Sea Detectives*, and he has worked on numerous film projects for Paramount Pictures, Universal Studios, 20th Century Fox, CBS, PBS, History Channel, National Geographic, and the Discovery Channel. It was this work that led Kohler to history-making expeditions to the legendary *Titanic* and *Britannic*. He has joined an elite, small group of divers and maritime historians who are committed to revealing the truth of why *Britannic* sank twice as rapidly as *Titanic*.

Kohler also trains technical divers, has written the foreword for *The Basics of Rebreather Diving* by Jill Heinerth, penned numerous articles for technical periodicals, and been the subject of dozens of radio and television interviews. Universal Studios is planning a 2016 release of the movie *Shadow Divers*, and Kohler has been a consultant during the writing and production of the film.

He and his wife live in Massachusetts in a restored 1856 farmhouse, and he is still active in the commercial glass company that his father originally founded.

CHARLIE HUDSON, a retired army officer, is an avid recreational scuba diver who has authored several scuba-themed novels and women's fiction as well as nonfiction books. She contributes to two online scuba forums and spent two years writing for a local community newspaper.

Her twenty-two-year army career included a number of assignments in which she was the "first female": the first female officer assigned to the 19th Maintenance Battalion in Giessen, Germany, and the first female maintenance company commander in the history of Fort Campbell, Kentucky. She is a veteran of Desert Shield/Desert Storm and Operation Uphold Democracy in Haiti (1995).

As a senior officer, her assignments involved extensive technical writing, and she was published in different military journals. She later left a corporate career as a defense services contractor and technical writer when she and her husband, also a retired army officer, relocated to South Florida. He is now a scuba instructor, and Charlie focuses on her writing. All of her books can be seen on her website at *http://charliehudson.net*

"Got him!" Megan said. "In the Solarium." A holo of Aris formed above the console. He was standing with his arms crossed, glaring at the camera, which had to be mounted in an LP robot. The edge of another LP showed in the image. The two robots had trapped the sulky android in a corner of the atrium.

"That had better keep him out of trouble," Raj said.

Megan came back over and helped Raj undo his bonds. "I can't believe he wanted to hurt you."

"He's a damn cyberthug," he muttered. Then he added, "But no, I don't think he meant to hurt me."

"The robot arm could have killed you."

He turned his wrist back and forth, helping her loosen a knot. "I saw him playing with the system after he tied me up. It looked like he only intended the arm to guard me. I don't think he realized it would try to take me apart."

"We'll have to keep him guarded."

"I don't want to push him, though. I'd rather he came back here of his own free will."

"Free will." Megan's hands stilled as she stared at Raj. "It's come to that, hasn't it? He's becoming self-aware. . . ."

THE PHOENIX CODE

CATHERINE ASARO

BANTAM BOOKS
New York Toronto London
Sydney Auckland

THE PHOENIX CODE

A Bantam Spectra Mass Market / December 2000

SPECTRA and the portrayal of a boxed "s" are
trademarks of Bantam Books, a division of
Random House, Inc.

ISBN 0-553-76271-0

Published simultaneously in the United States and Canada

PRINTED IN THE UNITED STATES OF AMERICA

BVG 01

To my grandmother
Annie Asaro
with love

Acknowledgments

I would like to express my gratitude to the readers who gave me input on the writing and research for this book. Their comments greatly helped strengthen the book. Any errors that remain are mine alone.

To Lt. Col. Michael LaViolette, USAR, for his sharp comments and the great pizzas his family brought over; to Larry Clough, acting program manager for the Situation Assessment and Data Fusion Division of Teknowledge Corporation; to Jeri Smith-Ready, for her perceptive reading and all those one/two/threes; to my grandmother, Annie Asaro, and my aunt and uncle, Jack and Marie Scudder, for their delightful talks about Las Vegas; and to the many other people who graciously answered my questions, including Professor of Physics Pranab Ghosh, Jennifer Dunne, and Devi Pellai.

To the writers who listened to selected scenes and provided their excellent insights: Aly's Writing Group, including Aly Parsons, Simcha Kuritzky, Connie Warner, Al Carroll, Paula Jordon, Michael LaViolette, George Williams, and J. G. Huckenpöler; and Ruth's "class," including Ruth

Glick (Rebecca York), Binnie Syril Braunstein, Randy DuFresne (Elizabeth Ashtree), Chassie West, and Linda Williams.

A special thanks to my top-notch editor, Anne Lesley Groell, who is everything an author could ask for in an editor; to my much appreciated agent, Eleanor Wood, of Spectrum Literary Agency, for her always valued advice and support; to Nancy Berland and her associates for their enthusiasm and hard work; and to the publisher and all the fine people at Bantam who made this book possible.

A most heartfelt thanks to the shining lights of my life, my husband, John Kendall Cannizzo, and my daughter, Cathy, whose constant love and support make it all worthwhile.

Contents

Contents

THE PHOENIX CODE

The Offer

People packed the auditorium. Every seat was filled and more listeners crammed the aisles. An unspoken question charged the room: were today's speakers revealing a spectacular new future for the human race—or the end of humanity's reign as the ruling species on Earth?

This session was a diamond in the crown of IRTAC, the International Robotics Technology and Applications Conference in the year 2021, held at Goddard Space Flight Center in Maryland. As chair of this session, Megan O'Flannery had chosen the speakers. She was sitting now at a table on the right edge of the stage. The man answering questions, Arick Bjornsson, stood center stage.

"The genie is out of the bottle," Arick was saying. "Our machines are becoming intelligent. They won't surpass us today or tomorrow, but it is only a matter of time."

Listening to him, Megan pondered her own conflict. She worked on artificial intelligence for androids—humanlike robots. Usually she looked to the future with optimism. Sometimes, though, she wondered if they were only creating ways to magnify the human capacity for destruction. She might soon face a decision that forced her to confront both sides of the issue: could she use the fruits of her intellect to create machines meant to kill?

She glanced over the audience. The scientists came in all sizes, shapes, and ages. Most wore casual clothes: jeans, shirts or blouses, jumpsuits. The conference chair, a distinguished man in a well-cut suit, was a few rows up from the stage. Several men and women sat with him, other high-ranking officials. Megan recognized them all, except for the fellow on his right.

The stranger had dark eyes and tousled black curls. His faded jeans had raveled at the knees, and his denim shirt was frayed. A black leather jacket with metal studs lay haphazardly over his legs. The gold watch on his wrist caught the light with prismatic glints that suggested diamonds. As he listened to the talk, emotions played across his mobile features: skepticism, interest, outrage, amusement. He glared and crossed his arms at one point. Later, he relaxed and nodded with approval. The dramatic flair of his handsome face fascinated Megan.

A woman sitting in front of the man suddenly swiped her hand past her face. It looked as if she were bedeviled by one of those irksome gnats that infiltrated the auditorium. As she caught the bug, the man reached forward and tapped her wrist. She turned with a start, reflexively opening her fist. Then her gaze flicked up to follow the liberated gnat. The man said something, an apology it looked like, and sat back. After giving him a bemused look, she shook her head and returned her attention to the talk. It all piqued Megan's curiosity.

Arick finished and the audience applauded. After he took his seat, Megan stepped up to the podium. "That concludes this session. The media people tell me they'll have copies of the proceedings tomorrow. You can get it as a holograph, in videos, or in memory cubes. A paper copy should be available in a few weeks." She grinned at them, this collection of her colleagues, friends, and adversaries. "That's it, folks. All we have left is the banquet tonight. So let's go eat and be merry."

Laughter rippled through the audience, followed by a general murmur as people began talking, putting on coats, or seeking out one another to continue spirited debates. Megan looked around for the man with the leather jacket, thinking to introduce herself.

But he had disappeared.

A long day, Megan thought as she left the auditorium. Her hair was coming down, red tendrils curling around her face. She pulled the heavy tresses free, then gathered up the waist-length mane and pinned it back on her head in a neat roll. She wished her energy weren't at such a low. Her work day hadn't ended yet; she had another meeting, possibly an important one to her career.

Tired or not, though, she thrived on this life. Robots had fascinated her since her childhood in Bozeman, Montana. She recalled toddling after a toy cat that stalked around the spacious living room of her parents' house. It hid behind a door, then attempted to pounce. She rocked with laughter when it toppled in an undignified heap of fur, limbs, and blinking lights. She had spent the next hour taking out its batteries and trying to put them back.

So she grew up, earned a B.S. in computer science at Montana State University, and went to Stanford for graduate school. Now at thirty-five, she was a professor at MIT. But the delighted little girl still lived inside of her, marveling at her toys.

Her enthusiasm bemused her mother, who had once asked, *But Megan, why make robots that look like people? What's wrong with the humans we already have?*

It's a new science, Megan had answered. *A new world, Mom. Maybe even a new species.*

Her mother had given her that look then, the one that Megan had long ago decided never boded well. Regarding Megan with the large blue eyes that her daughter had inherited, she said, *You know, dear, there are much more enjoyable ways to make new humans, and you don't have to work nearly so hard as you do in your lab.*

All Megan could manage was an aghast, *Mom!* One's silver-haired mother wasn't supposed to say such things, let alone look so pleased with herself, smiling like a cherub.

She supposed that if she would get married and make some new humans of the traditional kind, her mother would ease up. It wasn't that Megan had no interest in marriage; she just hadn't found the right man. Although her parents had liked most of her past boyfriends, she always had a sneaking suspicion they were sizing the poor fellows up as potential grandchild-production sources.

A voice interrupted her reverie. A man and woman were approaching. *So,* she thought. *This is it.*

"Dr. O'Flannery," the man said as they came up to her. His styled haircut, expensive blue suit, and businesslike manner made a sharp contrast to the more informal clothes most scientists wore at the conference. The woman had gray hair and a piercing intelligence in her gaze. Megan recognized her, but she couldn't remember from where.

The man extended his hand. "I'm Antonio Oreza. Tony."

Megan shook his hand. "Hello. Are you from Mind-Sim?" She had agreed to meet their representatives after the session.

"That's right. I'm the vice president in charge of research and development." He indicated the woman with him. "This is Claire Oliana, from Stanford. She consults for us."

MindSim had sent a VP to talk to her? And *Claire Oliana*? The Stanford professor was the first person to receive the Nobel prize for work in the development of machine intelligence.

Megan suddenly didn't feel so tired anymore.

The vending café had blue walls and tables covered by blue and white checked cloths. As Megan sat down with Tony and Claire, a vending robot bustled over, rolling on its treads. It stood about four feet tall, with a domed head and tubular body. The droid had only a rudimentary AI, one limited to serving food—though within that narrow range it could develop a personality. Its panels displayed cheerful holos of meals that looked far more delectable than anything Megan had actually eaten here.

"Good afternoon," it said. "I'm Jessie." Its head swiveled from side to side as it surveyed them, giving it an earnest appearance. It made Megan smile, though she knew it was just mapping their positions with the cameras in its eyes.

"Do you have coffee?" Tony asked.

"I've a delicious menu to select from," Jessie assured him. "French vanilla, cappuccino, Brazilian dry roast, decaf supreme, and today's special, Martian bug-eyed-monster deluxe."

Megan laughed. "Monster deluxe? What is that?"

"It has an unusually strong caffeine content," Jessie said. "The night shift in the Science Operations Facility programmed it into me at four this morning. They required a strong restorative to make their continued functioning possible."

Claire smiled. "That much caffeine would send me into orbit. Decaf for me."

"French vanilla here," Tony said.

"Very wise choices," Jessie said. A red cup plopped into a recess in its stomach and began filling with coffee.

"I'll take the Martian deluxe," Megan decided.

"As you wish." If a machine could blink its lights with doubt over the wisdom of a customer's choice, Jessie was doing it. Megan suspected that the SOF night shift had also programmed some mischief into the droid's personality.

After Jessie served their coffee, Tony clicked his money card into the robot. Jessie's lights sparkled as it spoke. "I hope you enjoy your meal." Its head swiveled to Megan. "Please inform me if you need any further assistance."

"Like an ambulance?" Megan couldn't resist teasing the droid. It probably had a minimal humor mod to make it more personable to customers.

Its lights twinkled. "I serve only the best food, ma'am." Then it rolled away, playing a tinkling melody like the ice cream trucks in the neighborhood where she had grown up. It took up position by the wall and swiveled its head around, surveying the café like a carnival barker looking for new marks.

With a laugh, Claire said, "I think the night shift in the Science Operations Facility have been staying up too late."

Megan took a swallow of her drink. The stuff tasted like rocket fuel. "They know their coffee," she said with approval.

Tony was watching her. "I can't help but wonder, Dr. O'Flannery, how you would program a robot like that."

"I don't work with utility droids." She had no doubt Tony knew exactly where her interests lay. With a smile she added, "And you should call me Megan."

Both Tony and Claire seemed pleased at this nonresponse. Tony leaned forward. "Megan, what would you say to a functional android for your research?"

She resisted the urge to shout *Yes!* Although MindSim was on the cutting edge of such research, vague rumors about disasters there in hidden projects made her wary. She made her voice casual, but friendly. "The problem is, no one has an android hanging around that wants a brain."

"Well, no." Tony beamed as if he were about to deliver great news. "However, MindSim has funding in that area."

After researching MindSim in preparation for this meeting, Megan knew that both they and their major competitor, Arizonix Corporation, had won several Department of Defense grants for their work in AI and robots. She also suspected she would need a security clearance to hear any details of the projects.

She chose a neutral response. "MindSim does good work."

Tony spoke with polished enthusiasm. "We'd like you to be part of our team."

"Suppose you had the chance to lead such a project?" Claire asked.

Megan stared at her, then took a long swallow of her rocket fuel. She would jump at such an opportunity—if it didn't have a catch. Why had they come to her? They already had DOD funds, so they must have started out with a chief scientist as the principal investigator on the grant proposal. What had happened?

"It would depend on the circumstances," she said.

"Come out to MindSim and take a look," Tony said. "We'll show you around."

Megan wasn't sure what to say. She liked her position at MIT. She had grants, graduate students, resources, colleagues, and a growing reputation in the field. The prestige didn't hurt either. But Tony and Claire were dropping seductive hints. She would give almost anything to work with a real android instead of being confined to running simulations on a computer. A visit to MindSim wasn't a commitment. If nothing else, an offer from them might inspire MIT to give her a raise.

She leaned forward. "Let's talk."

Goddard Space Flight Center covered many acres of land, with the rolling fields of the Beltsville Agricultural Center to the east and the Baltimore-Washington Parkway to the west. Stretches of forest separated the buildings, and deer wandered everywhere.

Lost in thought, Megan ambled down a back road. She had always enjoyed walking, and this gave her a chance to mull over the MindSim offer. A lake stretched out on her right, basking in late afternoon sunlight. The day had that golden, antique quality that came late in the year. Birds paddled in the water: gray, speckled brown, iridescent green, and the odd white goose with an orange beak. Farther down the shore, a man stood surrounded by ducks. At first she wasn't sure why they were squawking at him. Then she saw that he was scattering bread crumbs.

She was about to continue on her way when she recognized him: the intriguing fellow from the audience. He looked over six feet tall, with black hair and dark eyes. A palmtop computer hung from his scuffed leather belt. He watched the birds with a half-smile, as if he hadn't decided whether it would insult their egos if he laughed at them.

Megan changed direction and headed toward him. As she came closer, though, she hesitated. His muscular build and handsome face didn't fit her image of a robotics expert. His hair curled over his ears and down his neck, longer than men wore nowadays, but clean and glossy with health. On most people, it would have looked sloppy; on him, it worked. The same was true of his clothes. What his long legs did for those raveling jeans would have brought their makers a fortune if they could have packaged the quality. It made her hang back, as if he were a holovid actor she would normally never have had the chance to meet.

Suddenly he looked up. "Good afternoon, Dr. O'Flannery." It was hard to place his background; his facial features evoked the Celts, his coloring could be Indian, and his rich accent, like molasses on a summer afternoon, was undeniably from the American South.

"Hi," Megan said.

He tossed the last of his bread into the lake. Flapping and squawking, the birds waddled after the morsels.

"Such hungry things," Megan said. "Greedy, even."

His grin crinkled the fine lines around his eyes. "They'd eat ten loaves if I brought them."

Oh, Lord. That smile defined the word "devastating." It lit up his face.

"See?" He pointed at the sky. "They're leaving."

She looked up, as much to regain her composure as to see what he meant. A V-shape of birds was arrowing across the sky. "Well, yes." More collected now, she turned back to him. "Flying south for the winter, I imagine."

He indicated the birds floating on the pond, then held up his hand as if to offer them more delicacies. They paddled industriously toward him until they realized he was bluffing. Then they drifted off again. His gold watch caught rays of the sun, glittering with discreet diamonds.

"They don't cheat," he said.

"I'm sure they don't." Megan had no idea what they

were actually talking about, but she doubted it was birds. Whatever the subject, she loved his voice. Deep and throaty, it rumbled like music, sometimes drawling, other times resonant. "Did you enjoy the session this afternoon?"

"I suppose." *Ah suhppose.* "You should have given a talk. You do better work than the lot of them combined."

That caught her off guard. "Thank you." She hesitated. "I'm afraid I don't know your name."

He considered her for a long moment. Then he said, "Raj. Call me Raj."

"Is that your name?"

"Well, no. Yes. At times."

"Raj isn't your name?"

"My mother calls me Robin." He spread his hands as if to say, *What can a person do?*

Megan smiled. She could relate to that situation. Her father still called her Maggie-kitten. She didn't mind it from him, but it would earn anyone else a shove into a lake. "What do other people call you?"

"All sorts of things." He rubbed his ear. "I wouldn't repeat most of them."

She gave it another try. "So Raj is the name on your birth certificate."

"No."

Megan couldn't help but laugh. "You know, this is like pulling teeth."

His lips quirked into a smile. "My birth certificate, from the fine state of Louisiana, says Chandrarajan."

She stared at him. "You're *Chandrarajan Sundaram*?"

"Please don't look so shocked. I assure you, I've treated the name well."

Good Lord. This was the reclusive eccentric who had revolutionized the field of robotics? Unattached to any university or institute, he worked only as a consultant.

Corporations paid him large amounts of money to solve their problems. She had heard that one had given him a million, after he made their disastrous household robot work in time for its market release, saving the company from bankruptcy.

His reputation gave her a context for his conversation. Rumor said he paid a price for his phenomenal intellect; no one could think like him, but he had the devil of a time expressing those thoughts. From what she had heard, his mind didn't work in linear thought processes, so he often made jumps of logic that left his listeners confounded.

It astounded her that he had come to the conference. She had invited him, of course. He had been a top name on her hoped-for speakers list. She had already known, however, that he rarely attended such meetings. It hadn't surprised her when he declined.

Yet here he stood.

"It's actually Sundaram Chandrarajan Robert," he said.

"Your name?"

His voice became subdued. "My father followed the custom of giving me his name, followed by my own. But in this country, it's easier for us to have the same last name. So we use Sundaram. Robert is from my mother's side."

She wondered why the mention of his father caused his mood to turn so quiet. "It's a beautiful name."

Raj watched her with a long, considering look. "Then there are geese," he mused.

"Birds again." She gave a gentle laugh. "You know, I have no idea what we're talking about."

Amusement lightened his voice. "Most people don't respond this way to me."

"What do they do?"

"Nod. Look embarrassed. Then leave as fast as they can."

"Is that what you want?"

"It depends." He had all his attention focused on her now.

"On what?"

"Hair color."

"Hair color?" This conversation was making less and less sense by the minute. It was fun, though.

"Red," he said. "Yours is red."

"Well, yes. My hair is definitely red."

"Red flag." He walked over to her. "For stop."

It took a moment, but then she realized he was making a joke, using it to ask if she wished he would leave. Given that he had come over to her as he said it, she suspected he didn't want to end their conversation. Of course, she could be wrong. But he reminded her of her father, an absentedminded architect who tended to talk in riddles during his more preoccupied moods.

Megan put her hands on her hips. "I do believe, sir, that you're teasing me."

His lips quirked up again. "It could be."

She could tell he was still waiting for her response to his unasked question. "I'm sure my hair doesn't say 'stop.' "

A grin spread across his face. "You're quick."

Ah, that smile. It was fortunate this man lived as a recluse. Otherwise, womankind wouldn't be safe from either his dazzling smile or his nutty conversation. "Not that quick. I still don't get it about the birds."

"Winter is coming and they have a long way to go." He sounded more relaxed now. "So they eat a lot. But they aren't greedy. And they don't cheat. They only take what they need." His smile faded. "Humans could learn a lot from them."

Megan wondered what sort of life he had lived, that he saw the world in such terms. Then it occurred to her that given the value of his intellect and personal wealth, people probably wanted whatever they could get from him.

"Perhaps we could," she said.

"They followed me around too, you know," he said. "I sent them away."

Her brow furrowed. "The birds?"

"The suits from MindSim."

"They offered you a job?"

"Yes. I told them no." Then he added, "But perhaps I will consult for them, after all."

Her pulse jumped. Was he offering her the chance to work with him? She kept her voice calm, afraid that if she appeared too eager, she would scare him off. "Maybe you should."

He offered his hand. "I'm pleased to have met you, Dr. O'Flannery."

She shook his hand. "And I you. Please call me Megan."

"Megan." He nodded. Then he turned and started down the road. After a few steps, he turned back as if he had remembered something. "Oh. Yes. Good-bye, Megan."

She raised her hand. "Good-bye."

Then he went on his way, leaving her to wonder just what was going on out at MindSim.

The Everest Project

Megan hadn't expected her security clearance to come through so quickly. It made her wonder if MindSim hadn't begun the paperwork in advance, just in case. After a few weeks of negotiations, they flew her out to California to tour their labs.

She felt like a kid in a computer-game arcade. She enjoyed this more than the pursuits her friends urged on her for "fun," like parties or holovids. Invariably, her parents joined the chorus, with hints that she should include a fellow in the postulated proceedings—son-in-law material, of course. Their unabashed lobbying drove her crazy. They were wonderful people and she loved them dearly, but she felt like running for the hills every time they got that grandparental gleam in their eyes.

Out at MindSim, Tony and Claire showed her the snazzy labs first. In one, droids trundled around, gravely navigating obstacle courses. She spent half an hour putting them through their paces before her hosts enticed her to another lab. There she met an appliance that resembled a broom with wheels and detachable arms. It expounded at length on how it moved its fingers. Then she went for a walk with a robot that had legs. Its smooth gait put to shame earlier versions that had jerked along like stereotypical robots. Her hosts also let her try a Vacubot. She decided its inventors deserved a Nobel prize for their compassionate gift to humanity—a robot that could vacuum the house while its frazzled human occupants went out for pizza.

"We also work on humanlike robots," Tony said as they ushered her down another hall. "This next lab designs the body."

Megan's pulse jumped. "You've an android here?"

"Unfortunately, no," Claire said. "This work is all theoretical. Development of the androids would go on at a facility in Nevada."

It didn't surprise her that they had a more secure base of operations. Industrial espionage had become a thriving enterprise. MindSim wouldn't make their results public until they had full patent protection and software copyrights. She doubted they could copyright an AI brain, though. They would soon have to answer the question: When did self-modifying software become a cognizant being?

The next lab enticed her like a bakery full of chocolate cake. Equipment filled it, all cased in Lumiflex, a luminous white plastic. Instead of blackboards or whiteboards, the walls sported photoscreens with light styluses. Disks and memory cubes cluttered the tables, and memory towers stood by the consoles. Although a few cables ran under the floor, most of the connections were wireless. A wall counter held a coffeepot and a motley assortment of mugs.

Two men and a woman were working at the consoles. They had outstanding workstations: Stellar-Magnum Mark-XIV computers; combination cellular phone, FAX, radio, microphone, camera, wireless unit, and modem; keyboard, printer, scanner, and holoscreens. Holos rotated in the air with views of the theoretical android: EM fluxes, circuits, skeleton, hydraulics, temperature profiles, and more.

It all brought back to Megan her first day in college. While her friends had gone to check out the city, she had spent the afternoon talking to grad students in the AI lab. Within a week, she was doing gofer work for their professor. He gave her a research job that summer. By her sophomore year, the group considered her a member of their circle. She understood why Tony and Claire had shown her the glitz labs first; this one had only holos to look at, nothing concrete. However, if she took the job, these people would be her team, and they interested her more than any glitz.

Tony introduced them. The slender man with sandy hair was Alfred from Cal Berkeley. Miska came from a university in Poland. About five years older than Alfred and half a foot shorter, he had dark eyes and hair. Diane, a stout woman with auburn hair, had done a stint at a government lab and then taken this job.

They described their work, referring to the android as "he." At first Megan appreciated their not saying "it," but then she wondered at her reaction. Already they were giving their hoped-for creation human attributes. Maybe it wouldn't want those traits. Someday they might download the neural patterns of a human brain into an android, but even then no guarantee existed that it would think or act human.

Their descriptions also sounded too detailed. Finally she said, "It's done, isn't it? You have a working android."

Alfred shook his head. "I'm afraid 'working' is too optimistic a term."

Tony indicated a table. "Let's sit down. Now that

you've seen the models, we can talk about where we hope to go from here."

As they took their seats, Alfred brought over the coffee and mugs. When everyone was settled, Claire spoke to Megan. "We've tried to make several prototypes. Four."

Miska took a sip of coffee, then grimaced and set his mug down. He spoke with a light accent. "The problem, you see, is that these androids are mentally unstable. The bodies have problems, yes, but we think we can fix these. We are not so sure about their minds."

"The first three failed," Diane said. "We still have the fourth Everest android, but he's barely functional."

"Everest?" Megan asked.

"It's what we call the project," Tony said. "Surmounting a great height." He leaned forward. "It could be yours. Your successes, your triumphs."

Triumphs, indeed. "What happened to your last director?"

Alfred spoke flatly. "He quit."

Tony frowned, but he didn't interrupt or try to put a spin on Alfred's words. Megan's respect for MindSim went up a notch.

"Marlow Hastin directed the project until a few months ago," Alfred said. "We weren't having much success. The RS-1 became catatonic. No matter what we tried, it evolved back to the catatonia. The RS-2 had similar problems, with autism. And the RS-3 . . . well, it killed itself."

"He walked into a furnace and burned up," Miska said, his dismay subtle but still obvious.

Claire spoke softly. "We don't want that to happen again."

"I can see why," Megan said. "Is that the reason Hastin quit?"

"In part," Miska said. "But he didn't leave until later."

"We had a difference of opinion," Diane said.

Alfred took a swallow of coffee. "Marlow wanted to program subservience into the RS units. He feared that if we didn't, they might turn against us."

"It's a valid concern," Megan said. She wondered, though, if that had led to the tragedy with the RS-3. "But it may be moot. We're combining ourselves with our creations as fast as we can make the results viable and safe for humans. If we become them and they become us, the issue fades away."

The others exchanged glances. Then Miska said, "You are much different from Marlow."

"He hated the idea of taking technology into ourselves," Diane said. "Or of putting our minds into robots."

"Would you turn down a pacemaker that could save your life?" Megan leaned forward. "An artificial limb that would let you walk again? We're creating the means to make ourselves smarter, stronger, faster, longer lived."

"In the ideal," Claire said. "Whether or not we achieve it remains to be seen."

"Our hope," Tony said, "is to explore the full potential of humanlike robots."

"Including peaceful applications?" Megan asked. It was one of her main concerns. She understood the need for defense work, but she wanted to know that the fruits of her intellect would also go toward improving the human condition.

"Of course," Tony said. "We're committed to both."

Megan sat for a moment, thinking. "From what you've told me, it sounds like you all have very specialized areas of expertise."

No one seemed surprised by her comment. Alfred answered. "Miska, Diane, and I are the support. Claire consults on the AI aspects."

They struck Megan as a good team. However, they were missing an important component—the hardware equivalent to Claire. "Who is your robotics expert?"

"Well, yes, that's the rub," Alfred said.

"It's a top priority," Tony interjected smoothly. "If you accept the position, we'll have a slate of superb candidates for you to consider."

"In other words," Megan said, "you don't have anyone."

"We're taking the time to find the best," Tony assured her. "We almost had a fellow from Jazari International in Morocco, but JI came through with a counteroffer and he decided to stay."

She wasn't surprised they had checked out JI. The company had risen to international prominence over the past two decades. She had met Rashid al-Jazari, the CEO, several times. His American wife, Lucia del Mar, performed with the Martelli Dance Theatre, so they and their three children lived part of the year in the United States, and Rashid sometimes visited MIT. He was a charming man, but he didn't strike her as the type to let MindSim woo away his employees.

She thought back to her talk with Raj. "How about Chandrarajan Sundaram?"

"We're trying," Claire said. "But we aren't the only ones. Apparently Arizonix also wants him."

Tony's smile morphed into a frown. He said only, "Arizonix," but he managed to put boundless distaste into that one word.

"Are you sure you'd want Sundaram?" Claire asked her. "He has a reputation for being rather difficult."

Alfred snorted. "He's a nut."

"I rather like him," Megan said.

"You've *met* him?" Diane looked impressed.

"We talked at the IRTAC meeting. It was interesting."

"I'll bet." Claire sipped her coffee, then blanched and set her mug down with the care one used when handling explosives.

Curious, Megan tried the brew. It went down like a jolt of TNT and detonated when it hit bottom. "Hey. This is good."

Alfred gave a hearty laugh. "A truly refined taste." Claire and Miska turned a bit green.

They spent the next hour showing her details of their work. She made no promises, playing it cool.

But she was ready to jump.

Nevada Five

The hovercar skimmed across the Nevada desert like a ship sailing an ocher sea, the rumble of its turbofan evoking images of growling sea monsters. Sitting in the front passenger seat, Megan gazed out at a land mottled with gray-green bushes. The road they were following arrowed to the horizon, dwindling to a point in the distance.

Since passing the security check several miles back, they had seen no cars, buildings, or rest stops. The isolation unsettled her. As the new director of the Everest Project, this would be her home. She still had to wrap up her work at MIT and direct her graduate students, but she could do most of that from here, using the Web and virtual reality conferences.

She glanced at Alfred in the driver's seat. Most of the Everest team would still work in California; with the satellite link, communication would be easy, and she could use robots for lab technicians. If this had been just a development project, she would probably have stayed at MindSim with the team. But for such intensive research, she needed to interact with the android. Alfred, Diane, and Miska had come out to introduce her. A second car followed, bringing Major Richard Kenrock, their contact at the Department of Defense, and a lieutenant who served as his assistant.

The car turned off the road, its turbine providing thrust and vectored steering. It hovered across the desert on its cushion of air, rocking a bit from the bumpy terrain. Soon it slowed to a stop and settled to the ground, its landing motor grumbling in a deep baritone that contrasted to the tenor of the turbofan. No hint showed that they had arrived anywhere; nothing but gravelly land and spiky plants stretched in every direction. The second car settled next to them, with Richard Kenrock in the driver's seat. The major's wave looked like a salute.

Alfred peered at a screen on the dash. "Okay. This is it. Backspace, take us down."

Backspace, the car's computer, spoke in a mellow voice. "Fingerprint code, please."

Alfred touched the screen. In the other car, Major Kenrock was doing the same. With no ado and almost no sound, the land under them sank into the desert. It reminded Megan of cartoons from her childhood, where a trapdoor opened beneath unsuspecting characters and they dropped out of sight with their long ears streaming above them. This went slower, of course, lowering them into a freight elevator enclosed by a sturdy wire mesh. As the elevator descended, she craned her head to look up. A holographic camouflage hid the opening above them, making the ground appear unbroken.

Looking down through the elevator's mesh, she saw a garage below. Lamps lit the area, activated by the car's computer. Several vehicles crouched there: dark humvees with angular bodies. When the elevator reached the floor, the mesh opened like a gate. After they drove out, the gate closed and the elevator began to rise.

Megan indicated the humvees. "Those look like giant stealth cockroaches."

Alfred gave one of his hearty, infectious laughs. "I guess you could say the place is bugged."

They left their cars next to the vehicular cockroaches and walked through the cool spaces of the garage. Its stark functionality didn't reassure Megan. She would be living here for some time. Her doubts eased when they entered a pleasant hall with ivory walls and a blue carpet. A robot was waiting for them, what MindSim called a Lab Partner. It stood about six feet tall, with a tubular body, treads for feet, a rounded head, and an assortment of detachable arms. The nameplate on its chest said "Trackman."

"Welcome to NEV-5," Trackman rumbled. "I hope you had a good trip."

"Just fine." Megan peered at the LP. Twenty of these ambulatory assistants staffed NEV-5. Using their rudimentary AI brains, they could manage the day-to-day operations. Automated systems here and at MindSim monitored the base in case anything unusual came up. In theory, NEV-5 could operate without a human presence, but MindSim preferred to have at least one person in residence.

NEV-5 was about the size of a football field, with three levels. The garage, power room, and maintenance areas were here on Level One. Living areas were one floor down, on Level Two, and the labs filled Level Three. Trackman escorted them to the elevators and Megan walked at his side, wondering how far his capabilities extended beyond managing the base.

"Do you enjoy working at NEV-5?" she asked.

"Enjoyment isn't one of my design parameters," he said.

That didn't sound promising. "Can you define 'enjoy-ment'?"

"Amusement. Entertainment. Pleasure. Recreation. Zest." Then he added, "Those are in alphabetical order."

Megan smiled. "Would you like to experience amuse-ment? Pleasure? Zest?" In alphabetical order, no less.

"I have no need to do so."

Oh, well. If Trackman was the best that NEV-5 had to offer for company, aside from a barely functional an-droid, she was going to be on the phone or Internet a lot. If the loneliness became too much, she could reprogram Trackman to converse better. It was a poor substitute for human fellowship, though, not to mention a waste of the LP's resources.

Up ahead, a droid rolled around the corner. About the size and shape of a cat, its "legs" were tubes that sucked in dust and dirt. As it came up to them, Megan crouched down and touched its back. It stopped with a jerk. She poked it again, and the droid scuttled away. When she reached out and tapped its leg, it made an agitated buzzing.

"I won't hurt you," Megan murmured. She stood and walked around the droid. It waved its tail, trying to deter-mine if the bedevilment was going to continue. When she nudged it from behind, it moved forward and sidled past the other humans that had invaded its territory. Then it whirred away down the hall.

"That was a shy one," she said, smiling.

"Cleaning droids have no capacity for shyness," Track-man told her. "It has less efficient methods than an LP for mapping its environment. You were blocking its path."

Megan sighed. "Thank you, Trackman."

"You are welcome." If it detected her irony, it gave no indication.

They started off again, Alfred walking on the other

side of the LP. "Trackman," he asked, "did Marlow Hastin's family live here with him?"

"No," Trackman said. "His wife visited sometimes."

From behind them, Major Kenrock said, "I don't think his kids had the clearance."

Megan wondered if the isolation had bothered Hastin. She doubted she could have endured being separated from her family. She probably would have brought them to a nearby city and commuted. Being single made matters simpler, but she would miss having company. As far as work went, she would have preferred to have the Everest team here rather than in California. However, they had their lives there. With the Internet and VR conferences available, it wasn't necessary for them all to be in the same physical location.

Trackman showed them the living areas in Level Two. The apartments were pleasant, with blue carpets, consoles, armchairs, Lumiflex tables, pullout sofas, and airbeds covered by downy comforters. Megan decided to take a room with ivory wallpaper patterned by roses and birds. She said nothing, though, self-conscious about choosing her personal space in front of other people.

Then they went to meet the android.

The RS-4 had "slept" during most of the past few weeks while the Everest team reassessed the project. The two LPs that looked after the android had activated him as soon as the MindSim group arrived on the base. When Megan entered the single-room apartment where he lived, her anticipation leapt. This was it.

He was sitting at a table. Even knowing what to expect, she froze in the doorway. He could have been a boyish Arick Bjornsson. With his rugged Nordic features and blue eyes, he resembled a Viking more than a scientist. Bjornsson had consulted on the project several years ago, and he and several others had donated their DNA to the genetic bank.

The Everest engineers had grown parts of the android from Bjornsson's DNA, including his skin and some internal organs, but he was still a construct. A microfusion reactor powered him. Bellows inflated his lungs. Synthetic pumps drove lubricant through conduits within his body. His "organs" would age over centuries rather than decades, and they would remain disease-free. They were also more efficient than their human counterparts.

The Everest Project had many goals. The grant that funded Megan's job involved the development of a supersoldier and special operations agent. To be effective as a covert operative, the android would have to pass as human. Her team had a lot of work to do; right now the android's "blood" was a silvery lubricant, an X ray would show many of his differences, and various other anomalies could reveal the truth.

They didn't want him *too* human, though. If they succeeded, he would have the power and memory of a computer, the creativity and self-awareness of a person, the training of a commando, continual perfect health, and the survival ability of a machine. Weapons could be incorporated into his body. He would be smarter, faster, stronger, and harder to kill than any human soldier.

In the long view MindSim had more dramatic hopes. If humans could augment or replace their bodies with android technology, they could achieve phenomenal abilities, and longer, healthier, more stable lives. The process had begun in the twentieth century: replacement joints, limbs, bones, and heart valves; synthetic arteries and veins; artificially grown organs. Combining their minds with computers might make them superintelligent. It was Megan's dream that someday a new, evolved humanity would see beyond the urge to war, violence, and the other ills that plagued their species. An idealistic dream, perhaps, but still hers. Such results were far in the future, if they were possible, but the Everest Project offered a preliminary step.

The android already *looked* human. He had Arick's yellow curls and regular features, but he wasn't an exact copy of Bjornsson. The Everest team had fine-tuned his appearance. Tall but not too tall, with boy-next-door good looks, he came across as pleasant and nonthreatening. Right now, he also looked blank—like a machine. RS-4. They called him Aris.

As Trackman brought Megan inside, the android watched them. Major Kenrock and his lieutenant stayed by the door with Alfred. Diane and Miska settled in armchairs, close enough to answer any questions Megan might have. An LP stood behind Aris like a guard, protecting its brother from this strange infestation of humans.

Megan sat at the table. "Hello, Aris."

"Hello." His voice had no life. He sounded even less human than Trackman.

"My name is Megan O'Flannery. I'm the new chief scientist."

"Echo told me."

"Who is Echo?"

He indicated the LP behind him. "That is Echo."

That. Not he or she. Humans tended to refer to robots as male or female, based on the robot's voice. She knew she shouldn't be disappointed at his lack of affect, but she couldn't help but hope for more.

"Are you comfortable?" she asked.

"I am operational."

"Operational" hardly sounded promising, but it was

better than no response at all. "Aris, do you feel anything about this? By 'feel' I mean, do you have any reaction to Dr. Hastin's departure and my arrival?"

"No."

His lack of affect didn't surprise her. Hastin's notes indicated he hadn't had much success in making Aris simulate emotions. Nor was he the only one who had run into problems. Hastin was the third chief scientist MindSim had lost on the Everest Project. They had fired the first two.

"You can simulate emotions, though, can't you?" she asked.

"Yes." His eyes were beautiful replicas of human eyes—with no sign of animation.

"Why aren't you simulating any now?" she asked.

"I am."

Could have fooled me. "Can you smile?"

His mouth curved into a cold, perfect smile. It looked about as human as a car shifting gears.

"Get angry at me," Megan suggested.

"I have no context here for anger," he said.

At least he knew he needed a context. "What emotion do you think would be appropriate for this context?"

He spoke in a monotone. "Friendly curiosity."

"Is that what you're doing?"

"Yes. I am pleased to meet you." He might as well have been saying, "The square root of four is two."

It unsettled her to talk to someone who appeared so human yet sounded so mechanical. "Do you have any questions you would like to ask me?"

"No."

Megan exhaled. Well, she had known she had work ahead of her. "Would you like to take a walk around NEV-5? You can show me places you remember, tell me what you know about them."

He stared at her.

After a moment, she said, "Aris?"

No response.

Alfred swore under his breath. When Megan glanced up, they were all coming over to the table.

"What is it?" Megan asked.

"He hangs that way if he can't handle a question," Alfred said.

Megan frowned. "He can't handle something as simple as 'let's take a walk?' "

"Pretty much not," Miska said.

Alfred laid his hand on the android's shoulder. "Aris? Can you reset?"

Aris remained frozen, staring past Megan at the wall.

"We can restart him," Alfred offered.

"No. Not now." Megan stood up. "I'll come back later, after I've had a chance to look at the rest of the facilities here." In other words, when she was by herself. Although she doubted it made any difference to Aris if people saw his difficulties, she felt compelled to give him privacy. If they wanted him to become sentient, it would help to interact with him as if he had already achieved that state.

She glanced at Echo and spoke gently. "Make him comfortable."

"I will ensure the RS-4 suffers no damage," Echo said.

That isn't what I meant. But she said nothing. What could she do, tell one machine not to treat another machine like a machine?

The room had nothing on its ivory walls. It had no furniture. No console. Megan stood with Aris, the two of them alone. Ever since yesterday, when she had come to NEV-5, either Echo or Trackman had always accompanied her and Aris. So she had barred all the LPs from this room.

She wanted nothing to distract the hypersensitive android.

She set a shoe box on the floor. "Can you see that box?"

He looked down. "Yes." The cameras in his eyes integrated so well into his design that she detected no difference between his and a human face—except for his utter lack of expression.

"All right." She gave him an encouraging smile. "Jump over it."

As Aris regarded the box, Megan unhooked a palmtop computer from a belt loop of her jeans. She had named her palmtop Tycho, in honor of a famous astronomer. Using its wireless capability, she logged into Aris's brain much as she would log into the NEV-5 intranet. Tycho became part of the android's mind, giving her a window into Aris's thoughts.

The android had a huge knowledge base of facts and rules about the world. Combined with his language mods, it let him converse. He "thought" with neural nets, including both software and hardware neurons, which received signals from other neurons or input devices. If the sum of the signals exceeded a neuron's threshold, it sent out its own signal, either to other neurons or to an output device. Aris learned by altering thresholds. When he did well on a test, it strengthened the links that gave those results. Bad results weakened the links.

Although he couldn't alter his hardware, he could rewrite his software. He used many methods to evolve his code, most of them variations on genetic algorithms. He copied sections of code and combined them into new code, often with changes that acted like mutations. It was survival of the fittest: code that worked well reproduced, and code that didn't died off.

A simulated neuron could operate faster than its human counterpart, but putting many together became resource intensive and slowed Aris down. Although the number of links in his brain was comparable to a human brain, but he couldn't match the speed of human thought—yet. As he became more sophisticated, Megan suspected his speed would outstrip unaugmented human thought.

Right now he just stared at the box. According to her palmtop, Aris was calculating the trajectory he needed to jump. After his nets learned the process, he would no longer need to solve equations, any more than a child had to work out trajectories when she jumped, but he hadn't yet reached that stage. Even with his untutored nets, though, Megan didn't see why it was taking so long. He should only need seconds to translate the math into commands for his body.

Using Tycho, she probed deeper into his code. It looked like his brain had switched to a mod that directed his expression of fear. She tried to unravel how it had happened, but the complexity of his always-evolving code made it impossible to follow.

"Aris? Can you jump?"

He continued to stare at the box.

"Tycho," she said, "what is the highest level of fear Aris can tolerate before he freezes?"

Tycho answered in a well-modulated contralto. "It varies. He has an array of values that determines what immobilizes him."

His face did show emotion now. Frustration. He looked like a toddler stymied by a puzzle, reminding Megan of her sister's two-year-old son. But she held back her smile. Although she doubted Aris could have hurt feelings, she took care in her responses anyway, not only because his brain might have developed more than she realized, but also because she found it hard to think of him as a machine.

She spoke into the comm on her palmtop. "Why is he frozen?"

"The main contributor is an element in his fear array." It showed her several lines of code. "If the element goes above six percent, it stops him from moving."

"*Six* percent? Are all the elements set that low?"

"The values range from two to forty-three percent. The average is sixteen."

"That's appalling." What could Hastin have been thinking? How did he expect the android to function with such stringent caps on his behavior?

"Aris? If you can hear me, try this: use your logic mods. Have them analyze the situation." His mind should be able to determine he had no reason to fear the jump.

At first she thought her suggestion had no effect. But as she studied Tycho's display, she realized Aris had shifted some processing power to a logic mod. Although he remained trapped in the fear mod, his logic response kicked in, trying to make him jump. His fear response persisted, conflicting with the logic. That branched him into an anger mod, which then sent him to a fight mod. The fight code kicked him into a *parachuting* mod, for heaven sake, probably due to some strangely convoluted interpretation of her request that he jump. So now his mods wanted him to throw himself out of a plane in the sky.

"I need an aircraft!" His voice exploded out. "How can I jump *without* one?"

Megan spoke gently. "Can you get out of the jumping mod?"

He didn't answer, he just kept staring at the box. Controlled by his anger mods, his body pumped fluids to his face and raised the temperature of his skin. Aris stood frozen in place, his face bright red, looking for all the world like a furious young boy. A curl of yellow hair was sticking up over his ear as if to protest his ignominious situation.

She tried another tack. "Do you know how to do a parachute landing fall? It's what jumpers practice on the ground before they go up in a plane."

He neither answered nor moved. His face turned redder.

Watching his quandary gave her the same emotional tug as seeing a toddler struggle to understand a baffling situation. Her voice softened the way it did when she spoke to her young nephew. "You don't have to jump. Aris? Can you hear? Don't jump."

Nothing changed. He stared at the box as if it were a monster that had broken the rules of childhood nightmares and come out from under his bed in broad daylight.

Megan disliked resetting him, in part because he would lose some of what they had just done. It also bothered her to wipe his brain that way, even if she was only removing a few commands. However, she had to free him from his frozen state.

"Tycho," she finally said. "Reset the RS."

"I can't," Tycho answered. "He's protected from resets."

It made sense; Aris could never learn independence if anyone could reset his mind. However, as his main programmer she needed access. "Check my retinal scan."

A light from the palmtop flashed on her face. "Retinal scan verified."

"Okay. Do the reset."

"Done."

Aris's face went blank. Then he straightened up. "Hello."

"Are you all right?" she asked.

"Yes."

"Do you remember what happened?"

"You asked me to jump over the box."

"And that frightened you?"

"No." Although almost a monotone, his voice had a trace of nuance today. "Your command caused my code to exceed certain tolerances, which stopped my movements and prompted me to mimic behaviors associated in humans with anger and fear."

She smiled. "I guess you could put it that way."

"Do you wish me to put it another way?"

"No." That intrigued her, that he asked her preference.

"Do you still want me to jump?"

"Not now. I need to reset your tolerances. That means I'll have to deactivate you so your mind isn't evolving while I'm trying to make changes." She spoke with care, unsure how he would respond to being "turned off."

He just looked at her. At first she thought he had frozen again. Then she realized he had no reason to answer. Unlike a human, who would have reacted in some way, he simply waited.

Megan knew it would cause him no discomfort to lie down here on the floor. He wouldn't be aware of anything after she turned him off. Even so, the thought of asking him to stretch out on the hard surface bothered her.

"We can use one of the apartments," she said.

He continued to look at her.

"And Aris."

"Yes?"

She touched his arm, instinctively seeking to make human contact with him. "If you understand a person, it's customary to indicate that in some way."

"How?"

"Nod. Smile. Make a comment. Your knowledge base must have rules for social interaction."

"I have many rules."

"Don't they indicate how you should respond?"

"Yes."

She waited. "But?"

A hint of animation came into his voice. "You are new."

"So you don't know what parameters apply to me?"

"Yes."

"You should apply all your rules with everyone."

"Very well. I will do so."

"Good." Surely it couldn't be this easy. There had to be a catch here somewhere.

They headed down a hallway in the residential area. As they walked, she regarded him with curiosity. "Aris, do you have any hobbies?"

"I don't engage in nonfunctional activities."

She smiled at his phrasing. "We'll have to change that."

"Why?"

"It's part of having a personality."

"What nonfunctional activity should I engage in to have a personality?"

Megan almost laughed. "Haven't you ever done anything besides interact with the Everest team?"

"I make maps." A tinge of excitement came into his voice. "I made one of NEV-5 for Dr. Hastin. I tried to make one of MindSim, but I didn't have enough data."

It seemed a good activity. "Do you like doing it?"

"I don't know how to 'like.' "

"Would you do more of it even if you didn't have to?"

"Yes."

She beamed at him. "Great. I'll see if I can find you some map-making programs." It was a start. Aris had a hobby.

They went into a bachelor apartment with blue decor

and holos of mountains on the walls. A comforter and piles of white pillows lay on the airbed.

"This is nice," Megan said. "You can relax on the bed."

Aris lay on his back with his legs straight out and his arms at his side. Sitting next to him, she said, "Does it bother you to be deactivated?"

"Why would it bother me?"

"It's like becoming unconscious."

"I have no context for a response to that state."

Megan supposed it made sense. She just wished he would respond more.

"Dr. O'Flannery," he said. "Should I call you Megan?"

Startled, she smiled. "Yes. That would be good."

"Are we going to engage in sexual reproduction activities now?"

Megan gaped at him. Good grief. When she found her voice, she said, "No, we are not going to engage in sexual reproduction activities. Whatever gave you that idea?"

"You told me to apply my rules about social interactions. According to those, when a woman sits with a man on a bed in an intimate setting, it implies they are about to initiate behaviors involved with the mating of your species."

A flush spread in her face. "Aris, make a wider survey of your rules. If we were going to, uh, initiate such behaviors, we would have engaged in many other courtship procedures. We haven't, nor would it be appropriate for us to do so."

"Why not?"

"Well, for one thing, you're an android." She wondered how many other surprises his evolving code would produce. Whatever else happened with this project, she doubted it would be boring.

"None of my rules apply to human-android interactions," he said.

"Make one, then. Reproductive behaviors are inappropriate in this situation."

"I have incorporated the new rule." He paused. "I see it would be impossible for us to mate anyway, since I will be turned off."

Turned off? As opposed to "turned on"? She squinted at him, wondering if he could have made a joke that subtle. No, she didn't think so. It was just his deadpan delivery.

"You may deactivate me now," he said.

A chill ran down her back. What happened on the day when he said, "You may not deactivate me?"

We'll deal with it, she thought. Then she said, "BioSyn?"

"Attending." Although the resonant male voice came from the console here in the room, it originated from a powerful server in the big lab on Level Three. BioSyn linked to most of the NEV-5 computers and monitored all of Aris's activities.

"Deactivate Aris," Megan said.

"Done," BioSyn answered.

Aris's eyes closed. He had neither pulse nor breath now. When he was active, his chest moved and he had a heartbeat. He was designed to pass as human; if a doctor examined him, or if he went through sensors such as an airport security check, probably nothing would give him away. A more demanding examination would reveal the truth, but he could pass a reasonable range of probes.

She flipped open her palmtop. "Tycho, link to Aris."

Tycho went to work, analyzing the android's quiescent brain. The software was too complex for a human to untangle; it required another computer to interpret it. If she hadn't turned Aris off, his mind would have been a moving target, evolving even as Tycho looked.

Reading Tycho's results, Megan swore under her breath. No wonder Aris kept freezing up. His fear tolerances weren't the only ones set too low. Hastin had put so many controls on his behavior, Aris was incapable of independent thought. She studied how Aris had evolved the embryo code that Hastin had written for his mind. Yes, she saw Hastin's intent: to ensure they didn't create a monster. But his precautions were so stringent, they had crippled the android's development. Yet the code for Aris's ethics and morals was astonishingly weak. It made no sense; if Hastin had so feared that Aris might act against his makers, why design him with such a weak conscience?

Gradually it began to make sense. The answer to her question connected to Aris's intended purpose as a spy. He needed the ability to deceive, manipulate, steal, even kill, none of which he could do with too strong a conscience. Hastin had given him a solid foundation in human morals, then set it up so Aris could act against them. Aris knew it was wrong to kill, but he could commit murder if he felt it necessary to do his job.

Megan could see the problem. Aris didn't have the mental sophistication to deal with the contradictory ethical dilemmas or questions of moral judgment that humans often faced. His conscience was part of his hardware, so he couldn't alter it. However, his software influenced how strongly he adhered to his sense of right and wrong. She would have to alter millions, even billions, of caps on his behavior, particularly his responses to fear, anger, danger, ambiguity, and violence. That meant she also had to strengthen his aversion to acting on those responses; otherwise, she could create exactly the monster

Hastin feared. In other words, she was going to pulverize Aris's ability to carry out his intended purpose.

"Damn." No wonder Hastin had resigned.

She knew what she had to do. It remained to be seen whether or not MindSim would fire her.

Rebirth

The message was waiting in Megan's room.

She walked in, fresh and showered after her workout in the gym. Although larger suites were available, she liked this one. It had a bed and armoire to the right, and a state-of-the-art console on the left. Crammed bookshelves lined the opposite wall and books lay strewn across her furniture. Most of the "books" were slick-disks for her electronic reader, but a few were genuine paper, crinkled with age. Her Escher holo hung on the wall, along with a Michael Whelan poster of the Moorcock hero Elric. A somnolent cleaning droid stood in one corner, disguising itself as a bronze lamp.

Right now a red holo glowed on the screen of her computer, indicating someone had tried to contact her. When she flicked her finger through it, the screen lightened into a skyscape of holoclouds. Nothing else happened, though. She had no idea how long she would have to wait before whoever had sent the message picked up her response.

Megan was about to turn away when the clouds vanished. A new image formed: Major Kenrock behind his desk. His dark hair was cut even closer to his head than the last time she had seen him and his uniform was the image of crisp perfection. The holo of a gold key glowed in a corner of the screen, indicating a secured transmission.

"Hey, Richard," Megan said. "How are you?"

"Very well, thank you." He gave her a measured nod that fit with his square-jawed face. "How are you settling in?"

"Okay." She rubbed the back of her neck. "I really need that robotics expert, though. Any luck with Sundaram?"

"It seems Arizonix Corporation is also interested in him."

Megan grimaced. "If he signs anything with them, MindSim can kiss him good-bye."

Kenrock gave her a wry smile. "I believe the good-bye would be sufficient. But yes, if he consults for Arizonix, we could face some thorny legal issues if we try to hire him."

"Has he given any hints which way he's leaning?"

"My guess? I think he'll go with Arizonix."

"Ah, well." She tried to hide her disappointment. "We'll look into the other candidates." It was a blow; when it came to the adaptation of AI to robotics, no one could surpass Chandrarajan Sundaram.

"How is the RS-4 unit?" Kenrock asked.

"His name is Aris."

Kenrock's smile was rueful. "Sorry. I should remember that. Aris."

His amiable response didn't surprise her. People criticized Richard Kenrock for being stiff, but under his formal exterior she found him both engaging and natural.

Megan gave him a report, describing her work for the past week. Her primary focus was the development of algorithms, software architecture, and experimental design. In addition, she supervised a pack of young, hotshot programmers at MindSim who had written most of the initial code and continued to work on the project. She did a lot of writing herself, not only because she had more knowledge and experience, but also because she loved the challenge.

After she and Kenrock signed off, she sat thinking. Did Chandrarajan Sundaram even remember their conversation at Goddard? She shouldn't have let herself build up hope that he would accept the job.

Ah, well. She would just have to do her best until they found another consultant. With that in mind, Megan left her room in Corridor B and went to Aris's room on Corridor C. She knocked, an old-fashioned courtesy given that the console inside would identify her no matter what she did.

The door slid open. Inside, Aris was sitting at his workstation. A flock of holos skittered across the screen, a colorful profusion of cubes, disks, pyramids, and spheres.

"May I come in?"

He swiveled his chair around. After he had stared at her a while, she said, "Are you all right?"

"No."

"What's wrong?"

"I can't answer your question." His expression reminded Megan of her four-year-old niece when the girl was confused. It made her want to hug Aris. She held back, of course. Even if he understood the gesture, which she doubted, he probably wouldn't appreciate being treated like a child.

"Which question caused the problem?" she asked.

With her exact intonation, he said, "Are you all right?"

She blinked at his ability to mimic her voice. "Why can't you answer?"

In his normal baritone he said, "I don't see how 'all

right' applies to me. The evolution of software is a neutral process, whereas 'all right' suggests emotional content. If I am not all right, am I somewhat wrong?"

His literal interpretation didn't surprise her. Not only was it a trait of computers, it was also one of young children. "The reason I wondered if you were all right was because you just stared at me when I asked if I could come into your room."

"I am not a person."

"I'm not sure I follow."

"I am an android."

"Well, yes." She tried to interpret his response. "Does that affect whether or not I can come in?"

"It depends."

"On what?"

"My predecessors. The other RS units. They ceased." He regarded her with his large blue eyes. "If I am not 'all right' will you take me apart too?"

Good Lord. He thought if he gave a "wrong" answer, they would destroy him? No wonder he didn't want to respond. It also meant he was developing a sense of self-preservation. Protective impulses surged over her. Maybe it was his youthful face that made him look vulnerable, or his wary gaze, as if he had no defense against the inconstant humans around him.

"I would never hurt you," she said.

"Software can't be hurt."

Then why do you look so scared? Was she reading emotions into him that weren't there? In any case, he still hadn't said she could come in. "Did Marlow Hastin ever ask permission to enter your room?"

"No."

"Did he request your input on anything?"

"Rarely."

She didn't see how anyone could work with an AI and

not offer it choices. How would Aris develop? "Did you ever ask for choices?"

He shifted in his seat and a lock of hair fell into his eyes. "No."

"Did you want to ask?"

He pushed back the curl. "I have no wants. I carry out program instructions."

Softly Megan asked, "Then why did you move your hair?"

His arm jerked. "It was in my face."

"So?"

This time his arm snapped out and smacked the console. He yanked it back against his side. "It's inefficient to have hair covering my eyes."

"Why is your arm moving?" She could have asked Tycho, but she wanted to hear his own evaluation.

"My brain is instructing it to alter position."

His deadpan response almost made her laugh. "But is it efficient, do you think?"

A hint of confusion showed on his face. "My analysis of your tone suggests you are teasing me."

She smiled. "A little, I suppose."

"Isn't teasing an expression of affection?"

"Well, yes, sometimes."

His voice softened. "Do you have affection for me?"

How did she answer? If she said yes, it implied she was losing her professional objectivity. If she said no, it could damage his developing personality. Besides, in this situation, professional objectivity might be the wrong response.

"I enjoy your company," she finally said.

"Can you feel friendship for a machine?"

"I'm not sure." She sighed, giving him a rueful look. "What do you say, Aris? Do we humans make sense?"

His lips quirked upward. "I have too little experience with humans to know."

His hint of a smile heartened Megan. "Would you like to meet more people?"

"How?" Now his expression shifted toward wariness. None of his emotions were full-fledged, but he had made progress. "I can't leave NEV-5 and you are the only person here. Do you wish me to experience more with you?"

"You might try letting me come into your room."

"All right. Come in."

"Thank you." Megan took a chair from the table and sat next to him. With the two of them side by side, facing his computer, their arms almost touched. The faint smell of soap came from the orange coverall he wore.

She could see the display on the computer better now. Shapes of different colors and sizes skittered around the screen. "What are you working on?"

"It is a game." The barest shading of excitement came into his voice. "The shapes represent rules for mathematical proofs. When the shapes catch each other, it means they've made an equation allowed by the rules."

The evolving display of color and motion intrigued her. "Do you work out the proofs ahead of time?"

"No. I don't usually know, before they come up with a proof, that they will do it."

"It's clever." She wondered what had motivated his design. "Did Hastin ask you to write games?"

"He told me to solve proofs."

Her pulse jumped. "Then designing a game to work them out was your idea?"

"Yes."

So he *had* come up with his own ideas. It indicated the fledgling expression of what might become self-determination, perhaps also creativity. "That's wonderful."

His voice warmed. "Thank you."

Perhaps it was time to try a more demanding environment. "Would you like to take a walk?"

This time his face blanked. Recognizing the signs of a freeze, she spoke fast, hoping to head it off. "Aris, stand up!"

He rose to his feet. "Where will we walk?"

Encouraged, she stood up next to him. "That's it, isn't it? My giving you a choice is what makes you freeze."

"I don't know how to choose."

"We'll have to fix that."

"Why?"

That gave her pause, not because it was an odd question for a machine, but because she took the process of making choices for granted. "It's part of having free will. Of being human."

"That assumes 'being human' is a good thing."

"Do you think otherwise?"

"I don't know. Are you more human than Hastin?"

Again he caught her off guard. "How could I be more human than another human?"

"The way you program my code."

Then she understood. She softened her voice, taking the same tone she had used with one of her graduate students when he had trouble with his doctoral work. "Hastin made the best choices he could, Aris. What we're doing here, it's all new. We don't know what will work. I'm only building on previous efforts of the Everest team. We need to do more."

"You act more alive than they do."

"More alive?" The phrases he chose fascinated her. "What do you mean?"

"Your face has more expressions. Your voice has more tones." Softly he added, "You keep me company."

Good Lord. Was he *lonely?* The implications staggered
Megan. If he could feel the desire for human company, he
had come farther in his development than she realized.

"Will you keep me company on a walk?" she asked.

He watched her the way a child might watch a parent
who had given him more freedom than he felt ready to accept. His head jerked, then his arm, then a muscle in his
jaw.

Then he moved.

He took a jerky step toward the door. She could almost
feel his software analyzing all the choices possible for
each of his motions. His mind had to coordinate every
move of every synthetic muscle, every hydraulic, and
every composite bone in his body. Nor were simple mechanics enough, not in this learning stage. It also had to
choose gestures and facial expressions to fit his developing personality. He went through a huge number of calculations for simple motions humans took for granted—and
then he had to do it again, over and over, many times per
second.

He took several more lurching steps. Watching him
struggle, she longed to say "Never mind, we can stay here
and do something safe, like playing computer games or
working on maps." But she kept silent, knowing he
would never grow unless he took risks. If she tried to
make it easier, she would only hold him back.

They left the room and ventured down the corridor.
Megan stayed at his side while he lurched on each step.
He moved with far less ease than the robot she had
walked with at MindSim. That one had been designed
specifically to walk well, whereas Aris had to do everything well.

She didn't speak; he had enough to process now without the distraction of conversation. He learned fast,

though, as his neural nets readjusted according to his success in taking steps. After a while his gait began to even out.

When they stopped at the elevator, he stared at the doors with a blank face. He had no key card to operate the lift. He had never needed one; Hastin had turned him off and stored him in an empty apartment or closet when they weren't working, to ensure Aris didn't develop without control. The idea made Megan grit her teeth. If Aris had been human, that treatment would have been cruel. But he *wasn't* human. He himself claimed he had no response to deactivation.

It won't stay that way, she thought.

"Aris."

He turned to her. "Yes?"

"I'm going to give you a key card for the elevator."

"Does that mean you will turn me off when I'm alone?"

"Not unless you would like me to."

She expected him to say he had no likes. Instead he said, "If you give me a key and leave me on, I will be free to wander this section of the base."

"That's the idea."

His face showed hints of a new emotion, she wasn't sure what. Surprise? Anticipation? Curiosity? Apprehension? Perhaps it was a mixture of them all.

"Yes," he said, "I would like a key."

Megan wanted to give him a delighted thump on the back, to congratulate him on this breakthrough in his developing autonomy. She wasn't sure he would understand, though. So instead she said, "Good! I'll be right back." She turned and headed back to his room to get the card she had left on his console.

"Megan!" Panic touched his voice.

She spun around. "What's wrong?"

He was watching her like a toddler deserted by his mother. The strain on his face looked real. This was no "hint" of emotion; he was simulating full-fledged fear. "Where are you going?"

"Just to your room. I left my key card there." Megan came back to him, as concerned as if he were a human child. "I wasn't going to desert you."

"What should I do?" Now he was simulating either unease or uncertainty.

"You can wait here."

"What if you don't come back?"

"I will. I promise."

"But what if you *don't*?"

Did he fear solitude? Her voice softened. "I'll always come back, Aris."

"You are different from the others." He touched her shoulder as if to verify it was real. "You are changing me, more than through your software rewrites. Your presence makes me more efficient and helps my code evolve."

Megan gave a slight laugh. "I think that's a compliment."

"Humans do this often. Compliment and insult one another. Why?"

She considered how to answer. "It gives us ways to let people know how they affect us. And for us to affect them."

"If I compliment you, does that indicate I find your input conducive to optimizing my functions?"

"Well, yes, you could put it that way," she said, tickled by his phrasing.

"I see." Then he said, "I like having you here more than the other scientists on the Everest Project. I am glad they went away and you stayed."

She hoped he would someday be comfortable with the others. His words touched her, though. "I'm flattered, Aris. But most of them are still on the project."

"I know. However, I am glad you are the one here."

"Thank you."

"You are welcome." He paused. "I would like to go back to the room with you, rather than waiting here."

Yes! Not only had he just made a choice, he had done it with no prodding. She grinned at him. "Certainly."

Aris had even more trouble walking back. Megan suspected it was because he was using some of his processing power to analyze his interactions with her. At his room, he said, "I would like to stay here now." He gave her a tentative smile, as if trying an experiment. "We can take another walk tomorrow, yes?"

"Yes." Her heart melted. She knew the boyish pleasure she saw on his face was simulated, but she still found it charming.

He was becoming human to her.

The VR suit covered Megan in a gold body stocking, wrapping her up like a box of Godiva chocolates. She lay on her bed and pulled the hood and goggles into place. Although the technology existed for creating VR using direct links to the brain, so far legal and medical problems had kept it from commercial viability. It wouldn't be long before they solved those problems, though; it was another race between MindSim and Arizonix.

She found herself in blackness. "Cleo," she said, "turn on the VR." She had named her console after Cleopatra because the sleek machine combined both beauty and power.

"Done," Cleo said.

The world lightened. Megan found herself in a conference room, a gleaming chamber with golden walls, a posh white rug, white upholstered chairs, and an oval table. She was sitting on the long side of the table, wearing a tailored blue business suit with a miniskirt that showed off her long legs. The outfit bore no resemblance to the jeans and sweaters she wore in normal life.

In the last three weeks, since coming to NEV-5, she had met with the Everest team in VR almost every day. They either gathered here or else in a simulated AI lab. Every now and then Diane designed a more fanciful environment, like the time she set them up on a mountain in Tibet. Sometimes MindSim suits or military brass sat in on the meetings.

Today everyone was already there: Tony the VP at one head of the table, Diane at the other, and Miska on Megan's right. Claire Oliana and Alfred sat across that table, along with—

Chandrarajan Sundaram.

Megan had almost fallen over when Tony told her Sundaram was interested again. Apparently he had accepted the Arizonix job, then changed his mind. The situation was murky enough that MindSim called in their legal aces. Could Arizonix sue them if they hired Raj? He had never actually consulted for Arizonix and he had only signed one preliminary contract. After some wrangling, they concluded that Arizonix had no real grounds to bring legal action against MindSim.

On the surface, Raj's explanation for changing his mind made sense: Arizonix had wanted him to sign agreements that placed too many limits on his freedom to consult elsewhere. She wondered, though, if there was more to it. He should have known what they expected well before that point in the hiring process. At NASA, he had implied that if she accepted the Everest position, he might consult for MindSim. He had given the impression he thought they could make a good team. Megan agreed.

Many possible reasons existed for his having chosen Arizonix instead: more money, research he preferred, other scientists he wanted to work with more, the location, or something else. Although she would have liked to think her scientific reputation inspired him to leave Arizonix, she considered it unlikely, at least as a primary reason. It would have been unprofessional for him to make such a choice at that point, besides which, she had taken the Everest job before he accepted the Arizonix position.

Whatever had happened, she hoped MindSim wouldn't have the same problem. Raj had gone through a preliminary security check, but he had yet to sign anything. Yes, he was the best, which was why they were going to so much trouble, but if he wasn't going to accept the job, she wished he would let them know. This had gone on for weeks now, while she had no robotics expert.

Tony introduced Raj and asked everyone to give synopses of their work. As her people spoke, Megan tried to gauge Raj's interest. He sat sprawled in his chair, listening. His avatar intrigued her. In VR simulations, people often showed an enhanced image of themselves—healthier, younger, stronger, more beautiful. Raj, however, appeared older. Although his résumé gave his age as forty-two, in person he looked about thirty-five. Here he had added ten years to his age. She remembered his hair as black, but now it had ample gray. In person, his face had been expressive; here he was unreadable. His eyes were so black she couldn't distinguish the pupil from the iris. He had also dressed in black: shirt, trousers, shoes. His clothes had black buttons. He might even have darkened the air around his image.

"Anyway," Alfred continued, "Aris uses several methods to map his surroundings—"

"How long have you worked at MindSim?" Raj interrupted.

Alfred stopped. An awkward silence settled around the table. Then Alfred said, "Seven years."

"Seven." Raj was leaning his elbow on the arm of his chair, surveying Alfred as if he were a particularly intriguing robot. "So you've been on the project a lot longer than your new boss." His Southern accent was even more pronounced here than in person.

"Megan is the best," Alfred said.

Raj glanced at Megan as if he had just noticed her. "Dr. O'Flannery."

"Do you have a question about my leading the project?" She felt curious rather than defensive. She had no doubt that Raj knew she did her job well. He wouldn't be here otherwise. This was about something else.

"I think you're not a duck," Raj told her.

"For crying out loud," Alfred said.

Diane frowned. "Dr. Sundaram, you couldn't ask for a better boss than Megan."

Raj continued to watch Megan. Up until now he had given no indication he remembered her. She was certain, though, that he was referring to the birds at the lake. She recalled his words: *They aren't greedy. They don't cheat. They only take what they need.* Did he think she would try to use him if he accepted this job? It seemed an odd concern, but with Raj she couldn't be sure.

"How about a goose?" she asked.

Tony glanced at her as if she had lost her mind.

"Not a goose," Raj decided. "A swan."

She smiled. "Why a swan?"

"They float along, serene and graceful, with those long, elegant necks." He spoke as if he and Megan were the only people in the room. "But have you ever had an angry swan come at you out of the water? They're big, tough, and mean as sin."

She could imagine Aris trying to decipher this exchange.

Compliment or insult? "When I need to, I can be mean as sin too."

Tony looked as if he were about to groan. He had to be projecting that on purpose; his avatar could appear any way he wanted. He was sending her a message: *Cut it out.* Then he put on a pleasant expression and spoke to Raj. "Dr. Sundaram, please be assured that Dr. O'Flannery's credentials are impeccable."

Doctor this, doctor that. Couldn't they see this had nothing to do with her credentials? Raj wouldn't have considered MindSim if he had those concerns. In his own fascinating way he was asking something else. But what?

He gave her an appraising stare. "So, Dr. O'Flannery, what do you do with these indefectible credentials of yours?"

Indefectible, indeed. Megan had never known anyone who could actually use that word in conversation. He was daring her to try snowing him with her knowledge. So instead she said, simply, "I make androids."

"Perhaps Dr. Sundaram would like to hear more about your work," Claire said.

Megan knew they wanted her to dazzle Raj with techno-talk, but she doubted he was interested in a sales pitch. She thought she understood his unstated question now. Too many people wanted to use him. He was trying to decide if she was another one. His wariness puzzled her. MindSim was offering him a six-figure fee, possibly even millions if the project went on long enough. That hardly translated into using him.

For whatever reason, he distrusted them. *You want the Everest Project,* she thought. *MindSim is offering you a puzzle like none you've ever played with before.* Thinking about the birds, she said, "The problem with their flying south is that they take your food and go. But consider this: a mountain stays. You can climb it, enjoy its beauty, build a house, ski down its slopes. What it gives to you depends on what you bring to it."

"What the hell?" Alfred said. Tony and Claire frowned at him, but neither looked happy with Megan either. Diane just shook her head. Miska scratched his chin as if he were unsure he had heard right.

Raj said, "So." Then he vanished.

"Hey!" Diane sat forward. "He can't do that."

Alfred scowled. "He can do whatever he wants, including be rude as hell."

Claire frowned at Megan. "What was that about? You had a prime opportunity to build on his interest. You threw it away."

"That might be a bit extreme," Tony said. "We may be able to salvage this."

Megan indicated the table in front of Tony, where a mail icon had appeared. "Before you bemoan today's meeting, maybe you should answer your e-mail."

He waved his finger through the icon. "Tony Oreza here."

His secretary's voice floated into the air. "Mr. Oreza, we just received word from Dr. Sundaram. He's accepted the Everest job."

"You're kidding," Tony said.

"Not at all, sir."

Megan smiled. "Surprise."

Invasion

Megan, look!" Aris spun on his heel, then lost his balance and fell against the wall of the corridor outside his room. Laughing, he righted himself, his hair falling in his eyes.

Her breath caught. He had *laughed.* She stood by the open door of his room. "That was wonderful."

"It would have an even greater degree of wonderful," he said, "if I could turn without losing my balance."

His unexpected word choices never ceased to delight her. "I didn't know wonderful had degrees."

"You can assign a number to anything." He was standing in his neutral position now, his feet slightly spread, his weight on both, his arms at his sides. Unlike his usual ramrod posture, though, today he leaned a bit to the side. "How many degrees of Megan are there?" His voice had a whimsical quality. "I find new ones every day."

She went over to him. "Degrees of Megan?"

He looked into her face as if she were a new phenomenon he had discovered. "When you first came here, I knew your facts: education, jobs, age. Now I've learned new things. You like mint pie. Kids called you Firestalk in school. You played the oboe. You prefer aerobics to jogging. I never learned such facts about other humans. It makes you a holo."

A holo. Three-dimensional. In opening up to Aris, had she helped round out his view of humans in general? Perhaps the best way to teach him humanity was to act human with him. It became easier and easier as his personality developed.

The solitude here intensified her response to him. She had only Aris for company. The LPs did their jobs well, but they made lousy companions. She had grown up in a large family, with her parents, two sisters, a brother, her aunt and uncle, and three cousins all under one roof. In graduate school she had shared a house with six other students, and at MIT she had lived in a condo complex with a close-knit community. She missed her family and friends.

"Are you processing?" Aris asked.

She mentally shook herself. "Gathering wool."

"I see no sheep."

She laughed softly. "It's an idiom. It means I was preoccupied."

"Did my statement cause insult?"

"No. Not at all." It encouraged her to see him consider how his comments affected others. "I was thinking about my family. I feel isolated here."

"How does a person 'feel' isolation?"

Good question. She searched for a way to explain a concept she had never analyzed because she *knew* on an unconscious level how it felt. "No one else is nearby. No one will join me for lunch, meet me for a chat, that sort of thing."

He tilted his head. "I am here. I will keep you company."

His offer touched her. "Thank you."

"You don't need anyone else."

Megan almost touched his cheek. Then she stopped herself, feeling the gesture was too intimate, though she wasn't sure why. "Aris, the time will come when you go out into the world. It won't always be just the two of us."

His expression suggested pensive thought. "I've never left NEV-5. When Hastin and I conversed, it was always in the context of a test. I interact with computers here, but not outside NEV-5. I deduce that I am lonely."

Megan didn't know whether to feel encouraged by his developing emotions or dismayed by his conclusion. "Does it bother you?"

"I would prefer that my life not fulfill the conditions that cause loneliness in humans."

It was progress, of a kind; not long ago he would have frozen at such a question. It was a sad sort of advance, though.

"You feel lonely," he said. "I am here. I am meant to be human. This should alleviate your loneliness."

"It does."

His face blanked as he did a calculation. Then he said, "My analysis of your tone indicates surprise."

Megan realized he was right. It *did* surprise her. "I've never interacted with an android before. I'm never sure what to expect."

"Are you disappointed?"

"Aris, no. I think you're remarkable."

He took her hand. "I think the same of you."

Although Megan managed a smile, she disengaged her hand from his. They needed more people here. As gratifying as it was to see Aris develop emotional links, or at least simulate them, his focus on her was beginning to make her uneasy.

The dusty silver car settled down with a swirl of grit that it had brought from the desert above. Megan waited a few yards away, watching the vehicle roll into the NEV-5 garage. The elevator began its return to the desert above them.

After the car stopped, Major Kenrock stepped out of the driver's side. Tall and lean, with classic features and brown hair, he cut a crisp figure in his blue uniform. Another officer was stepping out of the passenger's side, a thin man with auburn hair. The woman getting out of the back on that side also wore a uniform, a blue jacket and skirt.

Then the back door on this side swung open. A man grabbed the top of its frame and hauled himself out. Unruly dark curls spilled over his collar, shining in the harsh light. His motorcycle jacket made his shoulders look even broader and his jeans clung to his long legs. Silver glinted on his black leather belt. His large eyes were set in the face of an Indian-Gaelic prince with the full-lipped pout of a surly rock star. So Raj Sundaram stood by the car, his hands in the pockets of his jacket.

Oh, Lord. Megan swallowed, trying to regain her poise. She came forward to Major Kenrock and extended her hand. "Hello, Richard. It's good to see you."

Shaking her hand, Kenrock cracked a smile. He introduced his two officers, Lieutenants Mack Thomas and Caitlin Shay. The whole time, Megan was acutely aware of Raj watching them. When Kenrock finally came to Raj, she felt stretched as tight as a string.

"You know Dr. Sundaram, I believe." A chill had entered Kenrock's voice. Apparently Raj hadn't endeared himself to this group any more than he had charmed MindSim. Although on an intellectual level, Megan understood why he aggravated people, it puzzled her at a gut level. Couldn't they see the extraordinary mind behind his unusual personality?

She had no idea what Aris would make of him.

————

They found Aris in his room, seated at his table, his hands clenched in his lap, with Echo the LP standing behind him. Aris had the look of an angry youth who had been locked up against his will while trespassers invaded his home.

Richard Kenrock and Raj stayed back while Mack and Caitlin sat at the table with Aris. The android watched them warily, his shoulders hunched. As much as Megan wanted to go to him, she also held back. She had to keep out of their discussion, lest she influence the results. Besides, she couldn't always jump in to protect him.

Aris shifted his hostile gaze to Megan, then to the straight-backed Kenrock. He stared at Raj for a full five seconds. Then his head jerked. Scowling, he turned back to the lieutenants.

"So, Aris." Caitlin smiled. "It's good to meet you in person."

"In robot," he said, deadpan.

Mack squinted, looking uncertain. Even Megan wasn't sure if the "joke" was an attempt at humor or just Aris being literal.

Mack gave a friendly chuckle. "How do you feel?"

"I don't," Aris said.

"You talk about your feelings with Megan," Caitlin said. She had a cooler style than Mack.

"Simulated feelings," Aris answered.

"Would you like to talk about them?" Mack asked, with an encouraging expression.

"No," Aris said.

When it became clear Aris didn't intend to say more, Caitlin asked, "Do you mind our questions?"

"You always ask questions," Aris said. "Here, VR, it's all the same."

That's new, Megan thought. Giving evasive answers involved sophisticated mental concepts. That Aris tried it revealed a great deal about his progress. She wasn't exactly sure "progress" was the right word, though. Aris had perfected his "sullen" simulation a bit too well.

"Does talking to us bother you?" Mack asked.

Aris shrugged.

"What would *you* like to talk about?" Caitlin asked.

Aris just looked at them. His demeanor was his most complex yet. He acted bored, with traces of hostility, yet he also seemed to be hiding fear behind indifference. Although he had thousands of facial nuances for each emotion, Megan wasn't sure how his neural nets had learned to show several emotions while appearing to hide others, yet having them all be obvious. It impressed her.

Caitlin and Mack exchanged glances. Then Mack tried again. "Why don't you tell us what you've learned lately?"

"Not much," Aris said.

"How are your maps?" Caitlin asked.

Aris glowered at her.

Trying another approach, Mack frowned like a parent faced with a recalcitrant teen. "Answer us, Aris."

"Why should I?" Aris slouched in his chair and crossed his arms.

Caitlin glanced at Megan. "This behavior wasn't in your reports."

Aris shot Megan a sour look, as if she had betrayed him by writing reports, even though they both knew she documented everything. Then he focused on the two lieutenants as if they were nefarious interrogators come to torment him. With his arms still crossed, he said, quite distinctly, "Fuck you."

Megan almost groaned. Had Aris been a real teenager, she would have grounded him. But his behavior irked her because he made it so *human*. Which was what they wanted.

Wasn't it?

The visitors all gathered in Megan's office, a room with two consoles, dismantled droids everywhere, a large desk piled high with gadgets, and two chairs crammed into what little space remained. No one was sitting. She leaned against her desk, facing Caitlin and Mack. Kenrock was standing by one console, and Raj was leaning against the door, his hands in the pockets of his jacket.

"I don't like it," Mack continued. "If Aris turns hostile, he could be dangerous. Don't get me wrong, Dr. O'Flannery. I realize he needs to pass through stages as his mind matures. And this is certainly the most affect he's shown. But we aren't talking about an argumentative kid here. We can't risk losing control of him."

"The RS-4 contains secured information," Caitlin said. "Not only about its own existence and construction, but also in its knowledge of our other work here."

Megan understood their concern. If Aris ever went rogue, he would take a great deal of secured knowledge with him, in both his mind and body. He was also linked to many NEV-5 computers. In fact, he himself was an important node in the NEV-5 intranet. He didn't have access to a few of the systems, but he would probably figure out they were running war games soon, if he hadn't already. It was, after all, only a matter of time before she gave him access, since they intended him to design and run such simulations himself.

MindSim was in a race in both the commercial and defense sectors. Other companies were working on androids, including Shawbots, Tech-Horizons, Jazari International, and Arizonix. Dramatic economic and military advantage would go to whatever country first devel-

oped viable androids and the advances in human augmentation that went with them. Mercenary groups were
also trying to create high-tech warriors. Even partially
functional, Aris would be invaluable to people the world
over.

Megan even understood why Hastin had made such
harsh choices with Aris. She knew now he had resigned
because he saw no way he could complete the project in
good conscience. Had he continued his program, he could
have created a dysfunctional, even psychotic, android. Yet
he feared to ease the constraints, lest Aris turn against
them.

Megan had more confidence in Aris. If MindSim pres-
sured her to restore his earlier state, she would refuse.
Not only did she consider that the best choice, it also
made sense in terms of self-preservation. Someday robots
would bypass humans. If they suffered along the way,
they would look far less kindly on their creators.

Kenrock spoke to Megan. "Can you readjust Aris's behavior, make him less hostile?"

"I don't think it's wise." She searched for the right
words. "Without the freedom to develop, he will never
achieve sentience. We'll have a fancy computer in a phe-
nomenally expensive body. If we want a self-aware being,
we have to drop the reins. I'm not saying we must throw
away control; we can fortify his conscience. He might not
make as good a weapon then, but it's better than crippling
his mind or turning him against us." She paused, collecting her thoughts. "In our capacity to wage war, we deal
with concepts of honor, loyalty, and the greater good,
contrasted with spiritual conflicts, the meaning of
tyranny, and political considerations. Aris has to deal
with ambiguities we struggle with ourselves. He's not
ready. He never will be if we smother his development."

"It isn't an either-or situation," Mack said. "Designing

him to be more cooperative doesn't mean forcing his submission."

"Doesn't it?" Megan glanced at Kenrock. "Do we 'design' our children to cooperate? Or do we try to teach them our values so they will incorporate them when they've grown?"

He smiled slightly. "There are times I'd love to design some cooperation into my kids."

Megan suspected her own parents had felt that way about her sometimes. "But would you want someone to brainwash them?"

"Of course not."

"Even if it meant they would behave better?"

Kenrock regarded her steadily. "I would fight with my life to preserve their right to freedom of thought. But we aren't talking about human children. Aris is a robot. A dangerous, fully formed machine capable of great harm."

"In some ways. In others he *is* a child."

"A child can't compromise national security," Caitlin said.

"No?" Megan scowled and crossed her arms. "What about those kids that cracked the Las Cruces weapons lab?"

"You mean the ones who went into the public outreach pages?" Mack asked. "The hackers who replaced the pictures of the lab scientists with action adventure cartoons?"

"Yeah," Megan grumbled. "Those."

The corners of Kenrock's mouth quirked up. "Don't you consult for Livermore?"

Megan gave him a dour look. "Yes. And yes, my image got doctored." She couldn't help but laugh. "They made me into a Barbie commando doll with camouflage fatigues, a designer machine gun, and pink high heels."

Kenrock grinned. "I've never seen that one in stores." His smile faded. "And you're right, that prank revealed holes in security. It's bad enough we have to worry about humans committing such crimes. We don't need androids in the mix."

"Yes, we have to careful," Megan said. "But we don't reprogram every teenager that rebels either."

Mack snorted. "Maybe we ought to."

Kenrock pushed his hand across his close-cropped hair. "She has a point. My kids may drive me crazy, with all three in their teens, but their rebellions are part of their trying to become adults, separate from their mother and me." Dryly he added, "Though if you ask me at a less tranquil moment, I might be less sympathetic."

"Aris needs to separate from us," Megan said.

"You know," Caitlin said, "if he doesn't, his autism could become more severe."

"Autism?" Kenrock asked.

Mack answered. "Some of his responses resemble autistic behavior in human children."

Their conclusions didn't surprise Megan. Some scientists believed autistic children suffered from a developmental disorder that interfered with their ability to model, understand, and predict the intentions or desires of other people. Developing AIs often shared that difficulty. Many of them used databases of rules in their models for human behavior. If they had too few rules or the wrong set, it limited their ability to respond.

"I first saw it in his aloof behavior and lack of affect," Megan said. "Also in his need for everything to be the same, so he didn't have to make choices. He's coming out of that now, but if we force a personality on him instead of letting him develop naturally, it might make him dysfunctional."

Kenrock glanced at Raj. "You've been quiet during all this. What do you think?"

Raj regarded him with an unreadable gaze. "I don't know enough about Aris yet to offer an opinion."

"You've read the same reports we have," Caitlin said.

Raj just moved his hand, as if to say, "That doesn't matter."

"Dr. Sundaram," Kenrock said. "Given the exorbitant fee MindSim is paying you, I would think you could come up with a more useful contribution than that."

Ouch, Megan thought. She could almost feel Raj going on the defensive.

"I already gave at the office," Raj said tightly.

Megan understood his meaning, a play on "contribution" that also meant he had worked on the project in his office. She was almost certain he hadn't intended to insult Kenrock, but it came out sounding like a deliberate jab.

"This isn't a game," Kenrock told him.

Anger sparked on Raj's face. "Well, shit. And here I thought it was."

Kenrock stiffened. "Straighten up, Sundaram."

"I'm not one of your flunkies," Raj said. "Back off."

Megan cleared her throat. "Maybe we should decide what to do about Aris?"

Taking a breath, Kenrock turned to her. "Of course."

"Richard, give us more time," Megan said. "We've just started."

Kenrock spoke to Caitlin and Mack. "What do you think?"

To Megan's surprise, Mack said, "I agree."

Caitlin nodded. "However, we should monitor the RS-4 at more frequent intervals."

After studying Megan for a moment, the major said, "All right. We'll try it your way for now." He glanced at

Raj, then back at her. "Let me know if any problems come up."

"I will." Megan wanted to assure him they would have no trouble. She feared, though, that the problems had just begun.

Jaguar

Raj and Megan watched the elevator take Kenrock's car up to the desert. Raj had said nothing while Kenrock and his two lieutenants left, nor did he speak now. As he and Megan headed back to the base, he remained silent, lost in thought.

After a while, Megan said, "The LPs delivered your luggage to your room in the residential section."

Raj glanced up with a start. "Residential section?"

"Level Two. My quarters are on Corridor B. You're in C, next to Aris."

He turned his probing gaze on her. "Why did the LPs put me on a different corridor?"

"I told them to choose a room near Aris." She hesitated, not wanting to start things off wrong. "You can move if you like."

"I'm sure it will be fine." He had his full concentration on her now, which was more unsettling than his earlier preoccupation. "Why would you put me nearer to him than you put yourself?"

"He needs new people to interact with, to expand his knowledge base."

Raj suddenly grinned, like the blaze of a high-wattage bulb. "I'm new data?"

Megan wondered why he smiled so rarely. It transformed his face like sunlight chasing away predawn shadows. "You're a new experience for him. He hasn't had many."

"Does my being here make you uncomfortable?"

This was a side of Raj she hadn't seen. Apparently he wasn't always oblique. "You don't mince words, do you?"

"Should I?"

"No." She rather liked his blunt questions.

"You don't mince either." More to himself than her, he added, "But you somehow make it socially acceptable. I must study how you do that."

"I think you should stay just the way you are."

Raj drew her to a stop. "What did you say?"

Megan couldn't tell if she had offended, startled, or puzzled him. She gentled her voice. "You're fine the way you are."

He brushed back a tendril of her hair that had curled onto her face. His finger trailed along her cheek. Then he dropped his hand as if her hair had burned it. Flushing, he turned and strode down the hall.

Megan touched her cheek where his fingers had brushed it. She wasn't sure which bewildered her more, his gesture or his retreat. What had she said? *You're fine the way you are.* She supposed people didn't tell him that often.

He was well up the hallway now. She considered trying to catch up but decided against it. If he wanted to be alone, she wouldn't push. They would be working closely together in the next months. Better to give him the room he needed.

Raj reminded her of a jaguar she had seen in a wilderness preserve years ago, during a vacation to Mexico. She had stood on an observation platform next to her guide, watching the jungle with binoculars. The jaguar had stalked through its realm, incomparable in its sleek, powerful beauty, unaware of them. It went about its life, an existence they could never truly know, only admire from a distance. But if they ever trespassed in its territory, it would strike back, as deadly as it was beautiful.

He turned a corner up ahead, vanishing from sight. Megan didn't see him again until she came around the bend. He stood a few yards away, leaning against the wall across from the elevators for Levels Two and Three. His scuffed jacket and old jeans made stark contrast to the decorous ivory walls and blue carpet.

She stopped by the elevator. "Were you waiting for me?"

He watched her warily. "I'd like to talk to Aris now."

"That's fine." Usually his face revealed his emotions in detail, but right now she had a hard time reading him. "You can go to his rooms anytime you want."

Raj pushed away from the wall, his lithe movements taut with contained energy. "You should come. He doesn't trust me yet."

"Okay." She could have watched Raj move all day.

"Why are you smiling?" he asked.

"Smiling?" She flushed. "I was just thinking that, uh, it was good to have another expert here."

He tilted his head, considering her with raised eyebrows. Then he came over and touched the elevator's call icon. The doors opened with a hum.

They rode down to Level Three in silence, Raj standing with his hands in his pockets again, as if that posture warded off danger. Megan wondered what he was defending against. Her?

When they stepped out of the elevator, Raj said, "I'm glad Major Kenrock left."

She walked down the hall with him. "I had the feeling you two didn't hit it off."

"Sometimes he seems more mechanical than the robots I work with." Raj thought for a moment. "But that's not true, is it? When he was talking about his children, he sounded human."

"He's a good man."

"You think so?"

"Yes, very much. You don't?"

He walked a ways before answering. "I don't trust people who don't know me and yet think I'm going to do something wrong."

That reminded her of Sean, her brother. Outwardly, he and Raj were a universe apart. Sean joked with everyone, an outgoing young man with wild red curls and blue eyes. But Megan knew his other side, the shyness that made it hard for him to interact with people. He compensated with his outrageous humor, but underneath all that he was painfully self-conscious. Raj's oblique nature struck her as similar, in his case a protection against a world that for some reason he distrusted.

"Richard Kenrock doesn't know you well enough yet," she said. "He'll loosen up. I think you remind him of his oldest son, Brad, a high-school senior."

Raj snorted. "I'm almost Kenrock's age."

"But you look younger. Brad dresses like you, rides a motorcycle, and mouths off to Richard every chance he gets."

"Good for him."

Megan gave him a look of mock solemnity. "Do I detect a problem with authority figures?"

"Hell, yes." Then he added, "Sorry."

She laughed. "No you're not."

The hint of a smile played around his mouth. "Maybe not."

"Why don't you like Richard?"

"He's a control freak."

"Give him a chance. Let him see your good side."

Raj pulled his jacket tighter. "I don't have one."

She wondered where he had come up with such a thought. "Of course you do."

He almost stopped again, staring at her with the same surprise he had shown upstairs, when he touched her cheek. Then he resumed his pace, a flush on his face. She wanted to ask why compliments bothered him, but she held back, certain it would make him even more uncomfortable.

At Aris's room, the door slid open. Aris was working at his computer. The program looked like a war game he had written, but she wasn't sure. He played so fast, the holos blurred in a wash of color. MindSim intended for him to design such codes himself eventually, but for now he concentrated his resources on his own development and used other computers to write the games.

"May we come in?" Megan asked.

"No," he said, still playing.

Her breath caught. *No?* It was the first time he had refused her.

"You might enjoy our company," Raj said.

"Why?" Aris swiveled his chair. "Time for me to behave again?"

"I hope not," Raj said. "That would be boring."

"I'm not here to interest you," Aris shot back.

"I might interest you, though."

Aris seemed unprepared for this approach. "I don't see why."

"So find out."

The android sat for a moment as if he hadn't decided whether to glower or relent. Then he said, "Oh, all right, come in."

Megan stayed back, curious to see Raj and the android take each other's measure. Raj pulled a chair over to the console and sat down to study the screen. The geometrical shapes had stopped moving and now stood in ranks, like an army regiment.

"Defensive geometry," Raj said.

Aris sat stiffly. "It's a game."

"Did you write it?"

"Yes."

Raj indicated a purple cube. "What does that do?"

"It's a term in a partial differential equation." Aris regarded him with suspicion. "I use it in a model I designed to predict human behavior during combat."

"It was going around and around in a loop before."

Aris shrugged. "They get stuck that way sometimes. I fix it."

"You like writing war games?"

"I don't *like* anything."

Raj glanced at the computer screen, then back at Aris. "So why write games instead of standing on your head?"

Aris's forehead furrowed. "Why would I stand on my head?"

"Why not?"

"That's a weird question."

Raj smiled. "Probably."

"What do you want, anyway?"

"To know why you're angry."

"I'm not angry."

"Yeah," Raj said. "You're rolling with techno-joy."

The android crossed his arms. "It should be obvious why I'm simulating anger."

"Because we attacked you?" Raj asked. "Insulted you? Lied? Cheated? What?"

Emotions flickered on Aris's face as if he were trying and discarding them: hostility, indifference, unease, conciliation, suspicion. "Because you all control my conscious activity."

Megan's pulse leapt. Did he consider himself *conscious*?

Raj had also tensed. "Do you mean conscious as opposed to subconscious?"

"No," Aris said. "I have neither."

Disappointment washed over Megan, and Raj's face mirrored her reaction.

"How did you mean conscious, then?" Raj asked.

"I have no autonomy." Aris swiveled to look at Megan. "I know you well enough to trust that if you deactivate me, you will turn me on again without causing harm. But what if someone else gains that power over me?" He glanced at Raj. "Someone I have no reason to believe has my best interests in mind?"

She had known they would face this moment eventually. Aris would never have independence as long as people could turn him off. Yet for all that she had argued for his freedom, she had doubts about making it this complete this soon. *Some* protective mechanism had to exist while he developed. Only she could act as a systems operator on his brain now, so only she could turn him off or reset him with a verbal or wireless command. They could also turn him off manually, but it required they open him up. He must have guessed she intended to set Raj up as another operator.

"You're asking for a lot of trust," Raj asked.

"Why should I have to convince you?" Aris clenched his fist on his knee. "I never asked to exist. I don't owe you anything. If you people feared me, then why make me?"

"Because of your potential." Raj's face showed a wonder that he never revealed when he spoke to his colleagues. "You're like a miracle."

The android still looked wary. "You all treat me like a thing. A fancy toy."

"You don't see yourself that way." Raj made it a statement rather than a question.

Megan tensed again. How would Aris answer? *I am more than a machine?*

"I'm a computer," Aris said. "Not a toy."

Oh, well.

Raj rubbed his chin. "I've never heard a computer object to being turned off."

"You have to decide what you want. Computer or android."

"You're already an android."

"In form, yes. In function, no."

When Raj glanced at Megan, she understood his unspoken question: *Discuss it in front of him?*

"Go ahead," she said.

Raj said, simply, "He's right."

Megan knew a refusal now could torpedo her relationship with Aris. She spoke quietly to him. "Meet me halfway. I'll delete my systems account in your mind. No one will be able to reset or turn you off with verbal or wireless input. But we'll keep the manual option, just in case."

"Megan, no." Alarm touched his voice. "It's not enough." He gestured at Raj. "He's trying to act like he's my friend. But he's *not*."

"I don't think Raj says anything unless he means it."

"You'll get partial autonomy," Raj said. "It's a start."

Aris stared at him as if the force of his attention alone could let him see into Raj's mind. Then he spoke to Megan in a low voice. "All right."

"I'll take care of it this afternoon." His wish for autonomy encouraged her. It suggested he was developing a sense of self. She was less thrilled about his distrust of Raj, but not surprised. Perhaps with time he would come around.

She hoped so.

At three in the morning, Megan gave up trying to sleep. She slipped on her nightshirt, a white silk shift that came to mid-thigh. The soft cloth soothed her skin. Then she pulled on her long robe and left her room. Lost in thought, she wandered the halls.

Aris had changed. They couldn't say yet how his personality would gel, but it was definitely forming. She felt like a parent worried about her child's maturation. What if he ran into problems as severe as what the other RS androids had encountered? None of them had progressed this far. Had she done right by Aris? Would he be successful or end in disaster?

Lights came on as she paced the halls, then darkened after she passed. During the night, the panels shed a subdued golden luminance.

At the end of Corridor A, radiance spilled out the entrance to a lounge. Curious, she went to look. The small lounge held a blue sofa, a holo stage in one corner, and a coffee table made from varnished maple.

Raj was slouched in an armchair by the sofa, his feet up on a footstool. His black T-shirt had a ripped sleeve, and his snug black jeans tucked in to black boots. It made him look like a shadow. Steam wafted up from his mug, filling the room with the enticing smell of French vanilla coffee.

"Hello," Megan said.

He jerked, almost dropping his coffee. Then he sat upright. "Were you adding yous?"

Adding yous? Megan blinked, at a loss for how to translate his question. Maybe he meant "ewes." Counting sheep?

"I couldn't sleep," she said. "I'm worried about Aris."

Raj didn't seem surprised. Sitting back, he warmed his hands around his mug. "Who named him Aris?"

"Marlow Hastin." She came over and sat on the end of the couch by his chair. "My predecessor."

"Hastin." Raj took a swallow of coffee. "Haste is waste, or however that saying goes."

"You don't like his methods, do you?"

He regarded her steadily. "I hate them."

" 'Hate' is a strong word."

"It's also the right word."

She spoke with care. "I understand his reasons."

"Do you agree?"

"No. I thought that approach verged on abuse."

Raj continued to watch her, until she was tempted to ask if he had ever burned anyone with that intense look of his. When he spoke, though, it was with unexpected gentleness. "You do remind me of a swan."

"Thank you." Remembering his description of a swan, she smiled wryly. "I think."

"It's a compliment." He looked at his mug, swirling the coffee. "Ugly duckling."

"Do you mean me?" It was an apt description of her youth.

"No. Me." He gave a dark laugh. "Except I turned into a monster instead of a swan."

"No you didn't."

"Then what am I?"

"A jaguar." It came out before she realized she didn't

want to say it, lest she give away her attraction to him. She held back the revealing part, though, about the power and wild beauty of a jaguar.

Raj took another swallow of coffee. "People shoot jaguars."

"Not you." She rested her chin on her hand, unable to stop gazing at him.

Amusement tinged his voice. "Why don't you find me abrasive?"

"Should I?"

"Everyone else does."

"That's their problem."

He raised his mug to her. "Sandpaper Raj."

Megan tapped her finger on his mug. "That coffee will keep you up all night."

He leaned his elbow on the arm of his chair, his body canted toward her, not enough to make it intrusive but still enough to notice. "The coffee doesn't matter. I never sleep."

"You have insomnia?"

"Most of the time. I rest in spurts."

"Doesn't anything help?"

"It depends." His voice turned husky. "Sometimes I don't want to sleep."

"And what," she murmured, "do you want to do instead?"

He lifted his hand and traced the curve of her cheek. When he reached her mouth, his touch lingered. She started to part her lips, perhaps to kiss his fingers, she wasn't sure.

Before she could respond, though, he took a sharp breath, as if giving himself a mental shake. Then he pulled away his arm and sat back in his chair. "I read, uh, info-tech journals."

Info-tech journals. She almost winced. *Get a grip,* she

told herself. The last thing they needed, with the two of them isolated here, was to tangle their work with personal complications.

Trying to diffuse the tension, she looked around the lounge. A beetle was crawling along the edge of the coffee table. She reached forward to flick it onto the floor, where the cleaning droids were more likely to find it.

"No!" Raj pushed her back so fast his coffee splashed over her lap and legs. She gasped as hot liquid ran down her ankles.

"Damn! Megan, I'm sorry." He bent over and grabbed the hem of her robe, then tried to mop the coffee off her legs. In the process, he dropped his mug and it hit a table leg, making the table shake. The beleaguered beetle fell to the floor.

Raj swore and knelt by the sofa. With extraordinary gentleness, he nudged the bug onto his finger. "I think it's all right." Relief washed across his face as he showed her the iridescent insect. "Look. It's beautiful."

"Well . . . yes." Megan sat holding the hem of her sopping robe. "Do you, uh, always rescue bugs?"

He carefully set the insect on the table. "When I can."

"Oh." She took off her robe, wincing as hot coffee dribbled over her calves. "Why?"

Raj glanced at her, did a double take, reddened, and averted his gaze. It took her a moment to remember she only had on her flimsy nightshirt under her robe. Embarrassed, she looked around until she saw an afghan on a nearby chair.

"I'll get it," Raj said, following her gaze.

While Megan used her robe to clean up the coffee, he brought her the afghan. She wrapped herself in the afghan and settled on the couch. "Thanks."

He stood watching her like a deer mesmerized by the headlamps of a car. "Sorry," he repeated.

"I'm fine. Really."

"Yeah. Uh. Okay." Raj sat down on the edge of the chair, his booted feet planted wide, his elbows resting on his knees. He rubbed his palms up and down his jeans, clasped his hands together, unclasped them, and then laid them on his knees.

"The droids will vacuum up the beetle eventually." Megan wondered what he wanted to do with his hands. A tingle ran up her spine.

"I'll reprogram them," he said. "They can put it in a bottle and let it go up in the desert."

"Why, Raj?"

"I don't know." A smile tugged his mouth. "I could be nuts."

"You could be. But you aren't."

He watched the bug meander across the table. "A group of kids where I went to school used to kill them."

She waited, then said, "And?"

"And what?"

"Bug squashing doesn't inspire most people to hurl coffee."

He smiled and settled back into his chair. "Insects have always fascinated me. My uncle is a museum curator. He has a whole wing dedicated to arthropods. When I was little, I used to spend whole days there. If I hadn't been so interested in robotics, I probably would have become an entomologist."

Although it made sense, given Raj's intense focus on his work, something still seemed missing. "I've never seen anyone so intent on preventing harm to bugs."

He spoke in a low voice. "We have enough needless cruelty in this world directed against anything considered different or inferior. I don't need to add to it."

What hurt you so much? Megan thought back to the

bio in his employment files. "Didn't your uncle raise you?"

"Yes, for ten years. From when I was four until fourteen."

"Your parents—"

His face took on a shuttered look. "Forget-me-nots."

She couldn't figure that one out. "Do you mean the flowers?"

"My father had Alzheimer's. Early onset."

Good Lord. She couldn't imagine what it had been like for a little boy to see his father lose touch with the world that way. She wanted to reach out to him, but she suspected he would withdraw. "Isn't that the kind they still can't cure?"

"It varies." He picked up his mug and set it on the table, his movements careful, as if he feared something would break. "Some people respond to treatment, others don't. My father recovered. Eventually."

"He must have married late."

"He was forty. I was his only child." After a long pause, he spoke with difficulty. "When he became ill, my mother took care of him. Then she had a stroke. My father couldn't remember his own son and my mother was paralyzed."

"I'm so sorry." She wished she could think of better words to offer comfort. It must have devastated him at such a young age. If he had been in that limbo for ten years of his childhood, it was no wonder he was leery of making bonds with people now.

"It was a long time ago." Raj rubbed his hands on his knees. "Are you cold?"

She held back her questions. "A little."

He winced. "I don't usually throw coffee at people."

"It's all right. Really."

"So."

"So." After an awkward silence, she took the hint and stood up, holding the afghan in place. "I should get some sleep."

"Yes. Of course. Good night."

"Good night."

She had just reached the doorway when he said, "Megan."

She turned. "Yes?"

"Jaguars prey on other animals. It's best not to come too close to them."

Are you protecting me? Or yourself? She spoke softly. "Sleep well, Raj."

As she walked back to her room, she wondered at the life he had lived, that he had such a harsh view of himself.

Ander

What are you, puzzle man? Alive? Or machine?

Megan stood on a catwalk made from crisscrossed strips of yellow metal. Twelve meters below her, the lab formed a bay of about thirty by fifteen meters. The catwalk spanned its width, and a door at her back led out into Corridor D of Level Two.

A massive chair stood below, with consoles on either side. A robot arm hung from the ceiling down to the chair, gold and bronze in color, multijointed and multifingered, bristling with antennae, knobs, and switches, and with lights glittering along its length. Aris was sitting in the chair, his blond hair curling on his forehead.

Megan spoke into her palmtop computer. "Tycho, have BioSyn check his collarbone."

"Checking," Tycho said.

The arm moved, directed by BioSyn, the lab computer. Megan caught a whiff of the ever-present machine oil. The scent of loneliness. Raj's arrival three weeks ago had helped, but he kept to himself when they weren't working. Every now and then she discovered soap shavings in the kitchen. Once she found a bar of soap beautifully sculpted into a horse. When she asked him about it, he just shrugged.

Below her, the robot arm pulled back a flap in the shoulder of Aris's coverall. It lifted a square of his skin and inserted a probe into a socket in the android's shoulder. The sight disquieted Megan. She doubted that would ever look natural to her; she had given up trying to think of Aris as a machine.

"How does he work today?"

She turned with a start. Raj was standing a few paces away, leaning against the rail. He wore all black again: jeans, pullover, boots. She wondered why he chose such dark colors.

"I'm trying to find out why his shoulder keeps twitching," she said.

BioSyn's deep voice came out of Megan's palmtop. "No errors detected in collarbone circuits."

She spoke into the palmtop. "How about his upper arm?"

"I ran those checks this morning," Raj said.

"How did they go?"

"His elbow still jerks when he throws a ball." Raj gazed down at Aris as if he were a puzzle, one that Raj wanted to heal and protect. "The microfusion reactor in his body had an anomalous power surge this week. I've been trying to track down the cause in his logs, but some of them are corrupted. I think he's overtaxing himself, trying to fix his physical problems by brute force."

"I can look at the software."

"That would be good."

For a while they watched the robot arm running diagnostics on Aris. Then Raj said, "We should give him a name."

"He has a name. Aris Fore."

"That's his *serial* number." Raj crossed his arms, his

muscles ridging under his pullover. "We should let him pick his own name instead of making him carry Hastin's brand."

"What do you suggest?"

He paused, as if he had expected her to argue. Then he lowered his arms and turned to her. "He looks Norse. Maybe a Viking name."

"How about Leif? Like Leif Eriksson."

"I've never heard of him."

At first that surprised her. How could he not know such a famous name? Then it occurred to her that she didn't know much about Eriksson either. "I think he was a great Norse explorer. I've never been good with history, though. In college I used to skip classes so I could work in the AI lab." She had managed to graduate with honors anyway. Then she went to grad school at Stanford and everything changed. No one there had minded her fascination with AI. They gave her a doctorate when she designed a computer code that could reliably distinguish between a lie and a story meant to entertain. "I was nuts about my research."

"I also." Raj's face relaxed, animated with his love of his work. "About robots, I mean. It was all I thought about." His wary stance had eased. "How about Eriksson as a name? Or Arick, like Arick Bjornsson. Or maybe Ander. That's Norse, I think."

She smiled, pleased. "Okay. Let's see what he thinks, after the tests."

Aris was watching lights glitter on the robot arm jacked into his body. If he "felt" anything about the diagnostics they were running on him, he showed little sign of it. He wasn't completely blank, though. Megan thought he looked curious, but she wasn't sure; she might be reading that reaction into him, seeing emotion where none existed.

"We've visitors due in a few days," Raj said. "Techs, to do maintenance."

Megan understood what he left unsaid. The techs would also check Aris. Her fear surfaced, the one that had plagued her since she joined the project. What if, despite all their efforts, Aris failed? It would devastate her as much as losing a family member.

His mind had a ways to go before it matured, but she saw so much promise in everything he did. Of course, the definition of AI had always been a moving target. Sometimes she thought their best measure was: "Whatever we haven't achieved yet." Whenever the AI community made a breakthrough, they redefined AI. In the last century, many had believed it would be achieved when a computer beat the world chess champion. Yet by the time that Deep Blue won its match against Gary Kasparov, most considered Deep Blue little more than a remarkable number cruncher. Now children's toys could play grandmaster chess and no one considered those toys sentient.

However, Kasparov himself said he perceived something more in Deep Blue. If he saw intelligence, did it exist? Perhaps the best known interpretation of AI was the Turing test, which postulated that if a person conversed with one or more hidden people and a hidden computer, and couldn't reliably unmask the machine, then that computer had intelligence. In essence, the Turing test said that if a machine convinced its human tester it had intelligence, it had achieved that intelligence.

Now, in 2021, reports often surfaced of machines passing the Turing test. Most of the systems Megan had tested left her unconvinced, but several showed promise. She wasn't sure she would say "human"; they seemed alien. But self-aware? Perhaps. She had never met the most famous, Zaki, an AI developed by Rashid al-Jazari. The original Zaki had been destroyed, but parts of him lived on in al-Jazari's later work. In a sense, Zaki had left a son behind, who had since grown to surpass his father.

The work on robots had proceeded apace with the work on immobile machines. Some groups predicted that the more a robot resembled a person, the more its intelligence would emulate human thought, because it would learn the way people learned. Others believed no machines could ever be human, nor would they even want to be like their creators.

Megan had finally come up with the O'Flannery test for AI; if she decided a machine was intelligent, it was. Of course, she still had to convince her colleagues. It remained to be seen what would happen with Aris.

In the bay below, the arm finished its test and swung away from the chair. Aris gave the appearance of waiting. She suspected he was studying the results of his diagnostics. His face still tended to blank when his thoughts became memory intensive.

She spoke into her palmtop. "Aris?"

He looked up at her. "Yes?"

"We were wondering if you would like a name."

"I have a name."

Raj flipped open his palmtop. "Would you like a new one?"

"Why?" Aris asked.

"To make your own choice."

The android's upturned face made a pale oval in the bright lab. "Most human names have no meaning to me. The only ones I associate with anything significant are Megan and Raj."

She smiled at the incongruous thought. "I don't think you should use Megan."

"Wouldn't you like your own name?" Raj asked him.

"Such as?" Aris asked.

"Eriksson," Raj suggested.

"Why Eriksson?"

"Leif Eriksson was a great Norse explorer."

"I am not a great Norse explorer."

"Well, no," Raj said. "How about Arick? Or Bjorn?"

"That I have his tissue, sperm, and facial structure doesn't make me Arick Bjornsson." The android shrugged. "Jed, Raymond, Tammy, Carlos, Ahmed, Isaac—they are all the same to me."

Raj rubbed his chin. "Our only other idea was Ander."

Aris suddenly went still. "Yes."

"You like that one?" Megan asked.

"Yes."

"Good." When he didn't elaborate, she asked, "Why?"

"It is what I am," the newly named Ander answered, his words more animated.

"What you are?" Raj asked.

"An android."

"Oh." Megan blinked. "Yes, I guess so."

With a grin, Raj said, "Ander, will you come up here?"

"Why?" Ander asked.

Megan glanced at Raj. "Good question."

He put his hand over the palmtop speaker. "I want to talk to him in a more natural setting. See how he reacts."

It was a good idea. Even so, she couldn't help but be irked that Raj seemed more interested in socializing with an android than with her. Still, she was dying to see how the two of them interacted outside the lab.

"We can all have dinner in the Solarium," she said.

Raj took his hand off the palmtop. "Ander, would you like to dine with Megan and me?"

After seeming to weigh the idea, Ander said, "All right."

Megan loved the Solarium, a two-story atrium with tables and trees. Solar collectors hidden in the desert above gathered sunlight, then reflected and refracted it through mirrors and quartz plates until it spilled into the atrium, a sparkling show of sunlight and rainbows. Radiance played across the ceiling. Plants filled the room in both pots and beds of dirt.

She had never seen Raj cook more than an instant dinner in the kitchen set off the atrium. Most of the time he ordered from the fast food robot. Tonight, however, he put together a meal from scratch. Megan and Ander wanted to watch, and tried to hang around the kitchen, but after Megan started stealing the mushrooms and tomatoes Raj was chopping, he sent them both away. So she and Ander went out into the atrium and sat at a table under an orange tree with no fruit.

Raj soon brought out dinner, a stew with yogurt and rice. A droid followed him, the tray on its flat top bearing mugs of coffee. The meal smelled delicious. Megan would have never guessed Raj could cook, let alone do it so well.

She watched with fascination as Ander heaped stew onto his plate and added a large dollop of yogurt.

"Do you always stare at diners when they serve themselves?" Ander asked.

He had never commented before on her looking at him. "Does it bother you?"

"No. I had just understood it was considered rude among humans." He took a forkful of rice, put it in his mouth, chewed, and swallowed.

"Hey!" Megan grinned. "That was perfect."

"Stop staring," Raj said,

Ander glanced at him. "You cook well."

It was Raj's turn to look startled. "Thank you."

Ander shifted his attention back to Megan. "Why do you drink beverages with drugs in them?"

That caught her off guard. "What do you mean?"

He indicated her mug. "Caffeine."

"Oh. That. It keeps me awake."

"This is good?" Ander asked.

She gave him a rueful smile. "Ah, well. It gets me out of bed."

He watched her lift the mug and take a swallow. "Do you spend a lot of time in bed, Megan?"

She almost spluttered coffee all over the table. "Aris!"

He looked puzzled. "My name is Ander."

"Yes. Of course." She felt her face blushing red.

Raj cleared his throat. "Ander, can you, uh, taste food?"

"I recognize many tastes," Ander said. "Also smells, sounds, and touch."

Raj shifted in his seat. "Touch?"

Megan considered Raj, as intrigued by him as by Ander. He knew perfectly well how the android's senses worked. In fact, he had designed some of the hardware himself. Did the Megan-in-bed topic embarrass him so much?

"Sensors in my skin detect textures," Ander said. "They send that data to my brain, which classifies them."

"But do you *feel* it?" Raj looked more relaxed now that they were talking about robots instead of sleeping arrangements. "Does holding a cat give you pleasure? If it scratches you, does it hurt?"

"I am aware of differences in such sensations. I have no physical response to them."

Megan wondered at Ander's lack of affect. This time it seemed intentional. She had the sense he was hiding his reactions to Raj. It was an odd concept, that an AI would simulate the act of hiding his simulated emotions. Even more startling was the idea that his evolving code might have come up with reasons for Ander to keep his thoughts veiled.

Ander was watching her again.

"Yes?" she asked, her fork halfway to her mouth.

"Am I a weapon?" he asked.

Megan almost dropped her food. "Why do you ask that?"

He waved his hand. "This place is full of computers running big calculations. Many are about me, but others deal with defense."

Megan set down her fork. "Department of Defense funds support the Everest Project. The military hopes to use you in special operations." She had conflicted thoughts on Ander's intended purpose. Hardheaded realism told her that they needed to develop the full potential of robotics first, before another country beat them to it. She understood the need to hone Ander's abilities in that area, but she also had other hopes for the project, dreams buoyed by her optimism for the future. "War doesn't have to be your only purpose, though. Many of us hope that by combining human and AI intellects, we can evolve together into a better species." Wistful, she said, "Who knows? Maybe someday we will grow beyond the drive to make war."

"I'm not a combination of human and AI intellects," he pointed out. "I am an android with a lot of software."

"You're unique," she said.

"It's lonely, though, don't you think?" he asked.

"Are you lonely?"

"Aren't you?"

Megan was suddenly aware of Raj listening. "That's a rather private question."

Ander leaned forward. "It is all right for you to ask me a private question, but not all right for me to do the same?"

"Your comment suggested you felt lonely. I responded. But I didn't bring it up in regard to myself."

"I see." Wielding his fork, he scooped up rice and ate it in stony silence.

After an awkward pause, Raj pushed back from the table. "Well. I'll clean up."

"I'll do it," Megan said, still disconcerted by her exchange with Ander. "You cooked."

He answered in a distant voice. "All right."

As they all stood up, Ander watched the two of them. Megan wondered what he thought about the way she and Raj interacted. It would be interesting to hear his take on it, given that she had yet to figure it out herself.

"Shall I help remove the debris from dinner?" Ander asked.

She pushed a hand through her hair. "No. You go on back to the lab with Raj."

Ander stayed put. "Why?"

"We have to finish your shoulder diagnostics," Raj said.

The android turned to him. "I solved the problem."

Curiosity sparked in Raj's voice. "You did? How?"

"I found two unrelated sections of code that had formed a spurious link." Ander watched Raj with a guarded expression. "When my calculations became memory intensive, my mind rerouted messages through that link. It made my shoulder move. So I deleted the link."

Megan beamed at him. "Good work."

He bowed to her from the waist. "Thank you, ma'am."

That surprised her; although technically a bow wasn't an appropriate gesture in this situation, it worked, a touch of humor combined with gallantry. It suggested he was developing more sophistication in interpreting his knowledge of human customs and the rules for applying them.

"You're welcome," she said. "But Ander, you still need some more diagnostics."

His smile looked almost natural. "In other words, it's past my bedtime."

"I didn't mean that." With a good-natured laugh, she added, "I don't think."

He took her hand and lifted it to his lips. Then he kissed the back of her fingers. "Good night."

"Good night." Self-conscious, she extracted her hand.

Raj was watching with an odd look. Megan found him harder to read than Ander. Was he angry? Tense? Curious? She thought perhaps a mixture of all three.

"If you two are done," he said, "I'll take Ander back."

"Yes." Megan twisted a napkin in her hand. "Of course."

After they left, she called in the kitchen droids. While she loaded them with the dishes, she thought about Ander. His responses had gone beyond what she could predict. Sometimes he still seemed like a computer, but other times she wasn't sure what to think. Was he becoming more human? Or something else?

After she finished overseeing the droids, she walked back to her quarters. She wondered if Raj was working on Ander. Well, that was why they had hired him. She should be glad this project absorbed him. Yet no matter how logical she tried to be, it bothered her that he preferred an android's company to hers.

In her quarters, she changed into her nightshirt, then clicked a disk of Bujold's *A Civil Campaign* into her electronic reader and settled into bed. As she read, her lashes drooped . . .

Megan opened her eyes into darkness with her reader lying on her chest. Cleo must have turned out the light. The sensors in the console could figure out if she was asleep by analyzing her heart rate, activity, posture, and breathing. She probably would have slept all night like this if the banging hadn't woken her.

Banging?

There it came again, someone thumping on the door.

"Raj?" she called. "Is that you?"

"It's the power," he answered. "It's out and *neither* backup generator came on. I wanted to make sure you were all right before I went to check."

"I'm coming." Groggy and half-asleep, she dragged herself out of bed and made her way toward the door, waving her hands to keep from stumbling into furniture. She couldn't see a thing; no trace of light relieved the dark. It took her sleep-fogged mind a moment to register that anomaly. What had happened to the emergency lights?

Megan grunted as she bumped the wall. Sliding her palms on its surface, she moved along until she found the door. She opened it into a hall just as dark as her room.

"Megan?" It sounded as if Raj were standing in front of her. She could smell the spices he had used for dinner.

"Here." She stepped forward—and ran right into him.

"Ah!" He caught her around the waist. "I can't see."

Megan couldn't believe she had been so clumsy. What if he thought she did it on purpose? "The emergency lights should be on." She was talking too fast. "They can go for hours."

"It could have been that long since the power went out," Raj said. "I've been asleep."

"So you do sleep!"

He paused. "Of course I sleep."

"The LPs should have notified us and tried to fix the problem." She forgot her chagrin as she realized how little sense this situation made. "We've triple redundancy in the generators, emergency lights with individual batteries, a backup battery for each set of lights, and a base full of LPs. *None* of those worked? I find that hard to believe."

"I don't know about the LPs." His breath stirred her hair. "But I think the automatic transfer switch for the generators malfunctioned. Do you have a flashlight? Mine's in the lab."

"I've one under my workstation." She twisted to look back into her room. "That's odd."

"What?"

She turned to him again, aware of his hands on her waist. They felt large and strong through her nightshirt. "I had an emergency light on my console. It's out too."

"It shouldn't be." He slid his hands up her sides, then down to her hips. "Why no alarm?"

"Good question." Her face was growing warm. He could have let her go by now.

"I ran tests on Ander earlier tonight." He sounded distracted, as if he were talking to fill the silence. "Maybe it caused some problem." He moved closer, the denim of his jeans brushing against her bare legs.

Megan was poised to go for the flashlight, but she stayed put. Raj slid his hand to her chin and tilted her face upward. She still couldn't see him. She had never realized before how total the darkness became here with no lights.

Raj slid his other hand around her back, pressing her closer while he held her chin. His clothes rustled—and then his lips touched hers.

Megan froze. She hadn't expected him to kiss her. Nor would she have thought he would be so rough. He pressed his mouth hard against hers, mauling her lips. His clumsiness so distracted her, she didn't respond.

Raj drew back his head. "I hope I didn't offend you."

Do I want this? If she didn't answer soon, he would let her go. Given what she had seen of him, she doubted he would try again if she rejected him. Maybe his graceless approach came from the awkward situation. Suddenly glad for the darkness, she reached up, meaning to touch his cheek. Her fingertips brushed his jaw instead. *Just one moment can't hurt,* she thought.

Raj gathered her into his embrace. Relaxing against him, she slid her arms around his waist. Then, with no warning, he put his hand over her breast and squeezed.

Megan winced. "Don't."

He rolled her nipple between his fingers. "Hmmm?"

"Slow down." She pushed at his hand, her ardor cooling. "We really do need to go check the power."

"Later."

"What about Ander? He—"

"He's fine. Forget about him."

This didn't sound like Raj. "Where is he?"

"In the lab. I turned him off." He rubbed her breast again. Hard. Then he pressed her against the wall. "We can leave him. Hell, he sleeps in that chair."

This was a new side of Raj, one she didn't like. Megan pushed against his shoulders. "Why is he turned off? We can't leave him pinned there."

"He'll be fine." Raj pulled her nightshirt to her waist, leaving her lower body bare.

"Stop it!" She shoved at his hand.

"Why?" Bending his head, he spoke near her ear. "We work like maniacs all the time. It's time we played."

"What's wrong with you?" She tried again to push him away.

Raj slid his hand along her thigh. "Come on, Megan. You know you want it."

"Let go of me!"

He was silent for so long, she feared he would refuse. Then he let go and spoke tightly. "I'll check the power room."

She slid along the wall. "I'll be in the lab."

"Fine." Anger edged his voice—and something else. Apprehension?

After he left, she sagged against the wall. For a moment she had thought he meant to force her. Could she have been that mistaken about Raj? She had thought Richard Kenrock misjudged him, but now she wondered. What had just happened would make it hard for them to work together. They had no choice, however. She should have been more careful about what she wished for; attracting his interest had caused a mess.

Megan found her flashlight, then made her way to the lab, lighting her path with a sphere of light. It took only minutes to reach the catwalk above the bay. She opened the emergency panel and pressed several switches. To her surprise, it took no more than that; lights flashed on in the lab with jarring brightness, along with the returning hum of the air-conditioning.

She squinted against the glare, trying to make out Ander in the lab below. When her vision adapted, she saw that a man was indeed trapped in the chair.

Raj.

Rapscallion

Nylon ropes bound Raj to the chair, and the cloth belt from an orange coverall gagged his mouth. His hair curled in even more disarray than usual, as if he had been struggling. He had on Ander's coverall, wrinkled and off kilter, zipped halfway up his chest. It looked as if someone had put it on him in a rush. A robot arm hung above him, its lights blinking. As he stared up at her, his face flushed, the arm began to descend.

"God *Almighty.*" Megan ran along the catwalk. "Arm Two, stop program!"

The arm continued on, probing Raj's shoulder with its multijointed fingers.

What had happened to the lab sensors that were supposed to pick up her voice? Without her palmtop, she had no other way to communicate with the robot arm until she reached the consoles. What if it tried to run diagnostics on *Raj?* Its safeties should keep it from tearing apart a human, but they should have also kept it from coming at him at all.

At the elevator, she threw open the gate and ran inside. As the car descended, Raj made a muffled protest. With dismay, Megan saw the robot arm probing the back of his neck. Had Ander been in the chair, it would have already jacked into him.

The elevator descended with maddening slowness. The entire time, Megan had to watch while the robot searched for a way to open Raj. He struggled with his bonds, fighting to free himself.

As the elevator neared the ground, Megan slammed open the gate and jumped to the floor. "Stop!" she shouted as she ran. "End diagnostic!" She passed an LP, but it made no move to help.

With a chilling snick, the robot arm extended the blade it used to cut cables. Cold light glinted off the honed metal.

"Stop program." Damn Ander! Had he done this on purpose, knowing the robot would finish its diagnostics when the power came back on?

Raj continued to struggle, his hair falling into his face. He pulled his head away from the robot, but it moved after him with the blade, chasing its target. Then it set its knife against his skin.

Megan lunged into an even faster sprint. She jolted to a stop at the chair and grabbed the robot's jointed fingers. Then she yanked the arm away from Raj's neck. Clenching it in one hand, she stretched out her other arm and stabbed a panel on the console. One of its status lights turned from red to green.

"Stop program!" she said. "End the damn test!"

"Program stopped," BioSyn answered.

The robot in her hand jerked. She barely jumped back in time as it swung away. Its safeties should have stopped it from swinging at her. She scowled. Ander had been a busy android, figuring out ways to confound NEV-5 security systems.

Raj made a muffled sound, his gaze furious. She reached behind his head and fumbled with the gag. When she couldn't undo the knots, she pulled the cloth down around his neck.

He took a breath. "Hell and *damnation.*"

"Are you all right?"

"No." His gaze swept her body. She suddenly realized how she must look, with her disarrayed hair falling to her hips and nothing on but her nightshirt.

"Did he hurt you?" Raj asked.

She shook her head, a flush warming her face. "He tried to make me think he was you. But I knew something was wrong."

"He's acting like a blasted juvenile delinquent. Where did he go?"

"He said the power room." Megan logged onto BioSyn at the console and brought up the Emergency Alert System. "Pah. This is a mess. He linked the LPs to a fake EAS Web page. That's why they didn't respond." She reset the links, then started a tracking program to find Ander.

A *ping* came from the console.

"Got him!" she said. "In the Solarium." A holo of Ander formed above the console. He was standing with his arms crossed, glaring at the camera, which had to be mounted in an LP. The edge of another LP showed in the image. The two robots had trapped the sulky android in a corner of the atrium.

"That had better keep him out of trouble," Raj said, his deep voice almost a growl.

Megan came over and helped him undo his bonds. "I can't believe he wanted to hurt you."

"He's a damn cyberthug." Then he added, "But no, I don't think he meant to hurt me."

"The robot arm could have killed you."

Raj grimaced. "That's one diagnostic I hope never gets run." He turned his wrist back and forth, helping her loosen a knot. "I saw him playing with the system, after he tied me up. It looked like he only intended the arm to guard me. I don't think he realized it would try to take me apart."

"We'll have to keep him guarded."

"I don't want to push him, though. I'd rather that he came back here of his own free will."

"Free will." Megan's hands stilled as she stared at Raj. "It's come to that, hasn't it? He's becoming self-aware."

He paused, looking up at her. "I think so."

"He could do it with a little less aggravation," she said dryly.

Raj gave a slight laugh. "No kidding." He went back to work on the ropes. "How we respond to his behavior now will impact how he views moral responsibility. I want to see what choices he makes."

She scraped her fingers over a knot. "I'll bet he comes here, to see what we thought of his shenanigans."

"Let's try this," Raj said. "Tell the LPs to let him leave the Solarium, but to keep a guard on him."

"Okay." She finally undid the knot. As the rope slipped, Raj pulled his arm free. He blew out a gust of air, stirring the hair that had fallen into his eyes. With obvious relief, he pushed it out of his face.

Megan wished she could brush aside those curls or touch him as she had in the hallway. Except that it hadn't been him, and besides, that incident had given her a taste of how awkward it could be if they mixed their personal and professional lives.

As she knelt to work on his ankles, he tackled the ropes on his other arm. "Did Ander give you any idea of what he wants?" Raj asked.

"Me, I think." She didn't know which was going to embarrass her more: telling him she had kissed an android or that she thought it was him.

Raj went still. "What did he do to you?"

She looked up, surprised by his tone. "What's wrong?"

"He told me something while he was sabotaging the LPs." Raj concentrated on freeing his arm, avoiding her gaze. "He said he had the guts to do what I feared, because he didn't care if you rejected him." He yanked at the ropes. "So did he do anything?"

"He made his voice sound like yours."

Raj finally looked at her. "And?"

She flushed. "He, uh . . . he kissed me."

"Megan, I'm sorry."

"It's not your fault."

Raj seemed at a loss for a response. She couldn't think of any that wouldn't make them self-conscious. The paused, awkward. Then he went back to work on his arm and she redoubled her efforts on his ankles.

Finally the knot gave. "Got it!" she said, relieved to change the subject. As he pulled his legs free, she rose to her feet and saw he had freed his other arm.

As Raj stood up, it made her aware of how close they were standing. In her bare feet, she came just to his shoulder. Dressed only in her nightshirt, she felt suddenly exposed.

Raj's face gentled as his gaze skimmed over her body. Then he seemed to give himself a mental shake. "Ander could go either way now—become self-aware or turn unstable."

She tried to be less aware of Raj's physical presence. "He might be dangerous."

"Or he may just want to go off on his own. He should have the right to choose."

Although Megan agreed, she doubted MindSim would appreciate their ten-billion-dollar android walking off into the sunset. The holo on the console showed a glowering Ander pacing back and forth. His image blurred at the edges; even BioSyn couldn't make perfect high-resolution holos of moving objects in real time.

Raj was watching her. "Did you really think he was me?"

"At first."

"How did you figure out something was wrong?"

"He was rude. Clumsy."

He gave her an incredulous look. "And that made you think it *wasn't* me?"

Gently, she said, "Yes."

"Well, hell." Then he winced. "I don't usually swear so much." After a pause, he added, "Yeah, okay, I do. But I try to clean it up around you."

Although Megan didn't mind his language, it touched her that he cared what she thought. "I appreciate the intent. But you don't need to worry."

"Megan."

"Yes?"

"When you thought Ander was me . . ."

"Yes?"

"You kissed him back?"

"Well, uh, yes, I did."

He glanced at her body again, then reddened and flicked his gaze back to her face as if he hadn't meant for her to see him look. Suddenly conscious of her skimpy clothes, she wanted to fold her arms across her torso and hide herself, but she suspected it would only draw more attention to her half-dressed state.

"Ah, Megan." His voice was low and deep. "You truly are a beautiful woman."

She didn't know how to accept his compliment. In her youth, she had been too tall, all elbows and sharp corners, with frizzy red hair and Coke-bottle glasses. In her teens, her body rounded out, laser surgery fixed her eyes, and her hair grew into long, full curls. But her self-image had already been set. Now her old insecurities jumped in, insisting Raj would lose interest when he realized she was just a gawky nerd. So instead of a simple "thank you," she said, "Have you had your sanity checked?"

His laugh crinkled the lines around his eyes. "There's no need, my tactful swan."

Real swift. Megan thought. "Sorry. I bumble when I'm nervous."

"So do we all." He put his hands on her waist, then paused, giving her a chance to say no. She remembered her misgivings. Logic told her to stop; her emotions urged her on. What happened with Ander had been false. This was real. Then again, maybe she was making excuses because she wanted Raj.

He's worth the risk. She slid her palm along his chest as an invitation and he drew her into his arms. Hugging him, she inhaled his scent, a mixture of spices and the crisp smell of his jumpsuit. When she turned up her face, he bent his head. His kiss was tender, completely unlike the way Ander had mauled her. Sliding her hands up his back, she traced the planes and ridges of his muscles. This was much better than logic.

Raj raised his head. "Sweet Megan."

"Beautiful Raj." As soon as the words escaped, she wanted to kick herself. What a stupid thing to say. For all she knew, a man would consider "beautiful" an insult.

Instead he grinned. "Have you had your sanity checked lately?" When she thumped his chest, he laughed and pulled her close. "It's hard to believe you thought he was even clumsier than me."

"You aren't clumsy."

"Ah, Megan, I can't talk well even when I want to. As soon as I tense up, I stop making sense." He shook his head. "Do you know what idiot savant means? I graduated summa cum laude from Harvard when I was seventeen and had my doctorate from MIT by twenty. But socially I'm a half-wit."

"That's not true." Yes, he was eccentric and introverted, and many people considered those character flaws. On his behalf, she resented that attitude. Why should Raj be like everyone else? "You're fine just the way you are."

"For that, the jaguar promises not to devour you." In a low voice he added, "At least not until later."

She grinned. "I'll hold you to that." With a sigh, she added, "But we better deal with Ander now."

They went to the console and told the LPs to let Ander leave the Solarium. A moment later he stopped pacing and gave the camera a wary look. Then he walked forward. The view changed, backing up as he came toward the camera, probably because the LP was rolling backward. He left the Solarium and stalked through Level Two. He seemed to choose his direction at random, like an angry young man unsure where he wanted to take his anger.

Raj paced into the middle of the lab, then stood, lost in thought. He reminded her of a Greek statue that celebrated both the intellect and body. But she enjoyed watching him because she liked Raj himself; with his remarkable mind, he would have drawn her regardless of his appearance or what he considered his social flaws.

He came back to the chair. "We need to defuse his resentment. The problem is, we expect human reactions. And he's not human."

"I don't—Raj, look out!"

He didn't ask questions, just dropped into a crouch with her—barely in time to avoid a robot arm swinging down from the ceiling. Huge and jointed, bristling with equipment, it passed through the area where Raj had been standing. Megan glanced up—

And saw Ander.

He was standing on the catwalk, speaking into a palm-top. Dressed in Raj's blue jeans and sweater, with gold curls falling into his face, he looked absurdly innocent. He must have programmed the robot arms to respond to some signal. Somehow he had also jimmied the door behind him, making it close on his harried LP guard. It hadn't hurt the LP, which was already working free, but it added to Megan's annoyance with the android's misbehavior.

"Ander, stop it!" she called. "You'll hurt someone."

"That's the point," Raj said. "Me, specifically."

"At least we got him here."

Raj dodged to avoid being swiped by a second robot arm, a small one. It thunked into the console and came to a vibrating stop, its clawed hand broken at the joint. An alarm blared and red lights flared along the arm.

"Ander!" Megan stood up. "I want you to stop."

"What are you two saying about me?" Ander demanded.

Raj rose to his feet. "Come down and we'll talk."

"No!"

"Fine," Megan said. "We'll take care of it without you." She tried to enter a command at the console, but BioSyn refused her input. Undeterred, she logged onto BioShadow, a hidden server she had set up to deal with anomalous situations, which certainly included rapscallion androids.

Raj went to work on the other end of the console. Up on the catwalk, Ander frowned, then spoke into his palm-top. Megan soon figured out why; he was trying to use BioSyn to keep them out of BioShadow. They easily evaded his attempts. Then she sent the LPs after him. Two rolled under the catwalk and a third boarded the elevator. With a hum, the car started to rise.

"Wait." Raj glanced up. "Have them hold off."

"Why?"

"They're stronger than Ander. If they force him down here, it could damage him. Even if they don't, it would humiliate him to have his first jab at independence quashed that way." Dryly he added, "Though he does make it tempting."

"I'll tell them to play nice." Megan directed the LPs to guard Ander but otherwise leave him alone, unless he endangered anyone or tried to damage more equipment—in which case they were welcome to haul him down.

The LPs under the catwalk stood together, exchanging data like a duo of gossiping tin cans. The LP in the doorway behind Ander finally freed itself, but it stayed put. The one on the elevator had reached the catwalk and was rolling toward Ander. It stopped about ten feet away. Ander glowered and waved his hand as if to shoo it off the catwalk. It just blinked its lights at him, orange for a low-level alert.

"Ander," Raj said. "We want you to come down."

He glared at them. "No. You'll turn me off."

"And if I promise we won't?" Megan asked.

"I don't believe you."

"Don't promise him," Raj said in a low voice. "We may have to break our word. We have to get him out of BioSyn."

Suddenly robot arms two and six detached from their ceiling cradles and swung through the lab, barely avoiding each other. When they moved apart, arm three hurtled between them like a gnarled pendulum. The other two arms swung back and smashed together with a resounding crash. As Megan swore, alarms shrilled and red lights flashed along both limbs. The LPs that were supposed to keep Ander from misbehaving stood placidly in place, orange lights aglow.

"For crying out loud," Megan said. "How does he do that?" She and Raj delved deeper into BioShadow, bringing up programs she had hidden for emergencies.

"Hey!" Ander shook a yellow strut of the catwalk. "What are you two doing?"

Megan frowned. "You come down here."

"Hell, no."

"And watch your language!"

"Tell that to Dr. Brooding down there."

"Is that supposed to be me?" Raj muttered.

The robot arms kept swinging. Not one LP had moved. It irked Megan that Ander had become so adept at finagling their systems. However, she and Raj had many more years of finagling experience, and they soon stopped the arms. The three giant limbs hung around the chair glowing with red and orange lights like a deranged Christmas tree.

Ander leaned over the rail. "Leave it alone!"

"*Ander, be careful.*" His precarious position terrified Megan. Coordination and balance were his weakest traits.

She had no idea whether he tried to pull back and slipped, or tried to provoke her and misjudged. The result was the same: he lost his balance, throwing his arms out in a futile attempt to grab the strut. His palmtop flew out of his hand and sailed through the air.

With a cry, Ander plunged over the rail.

Free Will

"No!" Megan shouted. Ander's body dropped behind the cluster of robot arms, followed by a sickening thud. She and Raj ran around the quiescent limbs and skidded to a stop.

Ander lay in a heap. His skeleton was less brittle than bone; instead of cracking, it had bent. His right leg had wrenched backward at the knee in a right angle relative to his thigh, and his right arm had twisted at the elbow until it made a sharp angle with his upper arm. His right hand had broken halfway off his wrist. Unlike a human, who probably would have died from such a fall, he was looking straight at them.

"God, no." Megan knelt next to him.

As Raj stepped toward him, Ander cried, "No!" He held out his good hand as if to protect himself. "Don't turn me off!"

Raj scowled at him. "You do exactly what Megan tells you. Misbehave once, just once, and you are off. Got it?"

"I would never hurt Megan."

"Good. Because if you do, you're one down droid." Raj went to the console and switched off the alarms. The sudden silence came like a breath of relief.

Megan laid her hand on Ander's injured arm, trying to judge the damage. He looked up at her—and a tear slid out of his eye.

"Oh, Ander," she murmured.

"It's crocodile tears," Raj said. "I designed the prototype. His ducts condense liquid out of the coolant for his hydraulics."

"Quit talking about me like I'm not here," Ander said. "I cry when I fucking feel like it, asshole."

"Keep up with that filthy mouth in front of Megan," Raj told him, "and I'll clean it out with your crocodile coolant."

"Go to hell."

"Ander, stop." Megan couldn't help but react to Ander as if he were an injured human being, one whose well-being mattered a great deal to her. Using Tycho, she studied his injuries. "I don't understand why you did this. You must have known your plan would backfire."

"Yes, I calculated that probability," he said. "But I calculated a higher one that if you slept with me, you would transfer your interest from *him* to me."

"For crying out loud," Raj said.

Megan spoke to Ander in a mild voice. "You calculated wrong. I would have been furious." She slowly straightened his arm, monitoring the process with Tycho. She hoped to put his limbs enough in line so they could move him to the chair without causing further internal damage. She tried not to imagine what Raj must be thinking. *Transfer your interest from him to me.* Nothing like being blunt. She might as well have shouted, *I want you, Raj!*

"Megan, are you all right?" Raj asked.

She began working on Ander's leg. "Yes. Fine."

"Your face is the color of your hair."

"It's nothing. Really." She couldn't look at him.

He spoke softly. "You're always so cool, like a long, tall drink. I thought you resented my being here."

She looked up at him. "Raj, no. I was glad when you came."

"I don't put people at ease." He cleared his throat. "Especially people that, uh, I want to, well—to know better."

Megan felt as if she were melting. "You do just fine."

"Oh, please," Ander said. "If this gets any more sentimental I'm going to puke."

"That would be a feat," Raj said, "considering that your plumbing isn't set up for that response."

Ander didn't deign to answer. His arms lay straighter now, though his hand was still broken back at a sharp angle from his wrist. It disturbed Megan to see him that way. She knew he felt no pain, but he looked as if he should be in agony.

Ander was watching her face. "I'm not a job to you anymore. You want me. Admit it."

"You mean a lot to me. But not in that way. I kissed you because I thought you were Raj."

"Except I wasn't." He lifted a lock of her hair with his good hand. "What you enjoyed—that was me. Not him."

She pulled her hair away. "No, Ander."

"You can't push a person into wanting you," Raj said. "It doesn't work that way."

"You'd know, wouldn't you?" Ander said.

Raj scowled but said nothing.

"You're a hypocrite," Ander said. "You can seduce your boss, but it's wrong if I try?"

Raj started to respond, then stopped. Megan could tell he was holding back. It would do no good if this argument fell apart in anger. Ander didn't have the capacity to deal with the emotions he was stirring up. If they weren't careful, they could harm him with words they would later regret.

"I think we can move him now," she said.

Ander stiffened as Raj crouched next to him. Megan had intended to help, but Raj picked up the android easily in his arms. Seeing him use such care affected Megan deeply. She had thought Raj would be curt or stiff, yet he treated Ander more like an injured son than a threat.

Although Ander weighed as much as a human man, Raj showed no sign of strain. Megan wondered why he spent so much time developing his muscles. Although he avoided her in the gym, the room's activity log indicated he worked out with weights every day. It seemed an odd hobby for a reclusive genius, though she had no good reason for why she thought so. She certainly appreciated the results.

Raj carried Ander to the chair and gently set him down. Ander refused to look at him, but he sank into the cushioned seat with a convincing simulation of relief.

Using BioShadow, Megan verified that Ander's sabotage hadn't damaged the chair. Then she did the prep for his operation. Humming like a distant bee swarm, the chair unfolded into a table. Ander lay on his back watching her, a bead of sweat on his temple.

"Are you going to turn me off while you work?" he asked.

"Do you want me to?"

He tensed. "No."

"Then I won't."

Raj was standing across the chair at the other console. Neither he nor Megan spoke as they removed Ander's clothes. She flushed at the sight of Ander's nude body. It had never affected her before, but after tonight she would never see him in the same way again.

When Megan pressed a crease behind Ander's ear, a small disk of skin lifted up from his navel, revealing a socket. "Arm two," she said. A grinding noise came from behind her, like a protest. Turning, she saw a broken robot arm hanging in the air. "Arm four," she amended. "Connect to torso. Full body scan."

Arm four came down from the ceiling and plugged into Ander's abdomen. Holos appeared above her console with views of his body. Several fins that exchanged air in his chest cavity had broken and the bellows that moved his chest had collapsed. His microfusion reactor and its shielding showed no damage; both were meant to last for centuries even if his body exploded. The circulatory system that cooled his systems had several breaks, and its pump had a twisted valve. A conduit that carried nutrients to his skin had burst. Both his lubricant reservoir and the sinus reservoir that produced his tears, sweat, and saliva had sprung leaks. The sperm unit in his testes was fine, as was his food reservoir and waste-removal system. Ragged gashes marred his synthetic muscles and the nanofilaments that sheathed them. His skeleton showed many dents and twists, and major damage in the leg and arm. His wrist had nearly snapped off. Had he been flesh and blood, he would have died the moment he hit the floor.

Megan touched his arm. "We'll make you better."

Although Ander nodded, his face showed fear. It wasn't a vivid emotion; he still had trouble with his expressions. But they had become more mobile in the past weeks.

BioSyn spoke. "Diagnostics complete."

"Can we open him up?" Raj asked. Similar holos flickered on his console.

"It will cause more damage to his filaments," BioSyn said.

Megan rubbed her eyes. It was no picnic fixing filaments made of threads with widths no greater than a mol-
ecule. To some extent the tubes were self-repairing; when
disrupted, dangling bonds reattached to keep their chemical structure inert. However, the tubes couldn't reproduce
themselves; although chemists had been building nanotubes since the late twentieth century, they hadn't yet
reached the point where the nanotech self-replicated with
any reliability. However, Ander's internal systems could
make some rudimentary repairs on a macroscopic level.
Megan and Raj could help by inserting smart-wires into
Ander's sockets and injecting him with nanobots that cat-
alyzed selected reactions.

In a sense, they were also doing brain surgery. Some of
Ander's nanotubes acted as a computer. The full range of
electronic devices could be built with them. They were far
smaller than silicon transistors on integrated chips, more
durable, and better able to deal with heat, which meant
they could be formed into three-dimensional arrays more
easily than silicon devices. As a result, the filaments dis-
tributed Ander's brain throughout his body. It made him
less vulnerable to attack, since he had no central location
where his brain could be destroyed, but it meant they had
to take extra care with the filaments.

"BioSyn," Megan said. "How much damage can
Ander fix himself?"

"About twenty-five percent. I can also do some work
through his sockets."

"All right," Raj said. "We'll start with bots and wires."

"No!" Ander pushed up on his elbows.

"What's wrong?" Megan asked.

"You don't even *ask*." He motioned at the robot arm
jacked into his abdomen. "You tell these to work on me
as if I'm one of them. They might not care, but I do."

His growing sense of self gratified her even if she did worry about what direction it would take next. "May we work on you?"

"I . . . I don't know."

She spoke gently. "We'll be careful. I promise."

He took a breath and lay down. "Okay. Go ahead." His apprehension didn't sound quite right, but if she hadn't known it was simulated, she would have accepted it as genuine.

Raj was watching them closely. "Arm four, proceed."

A hum came from the robot arm, and the holos of Ander began to show slight improvements. As BioSyn worked on the android, Raj studied the changing images with an absorption so complete, Megan wondered if he had forgotten everything else.

Finally BioSyn said, "Preliminary work complete."

Ander looked up at her. "Will you open me now?"

"The sooner we do it," Raj said, "the better for you."

Ander turned a long, uneasy stare on Raj. Then he glanced at Megan. "Make me a promise. Say you won't dismantle me."

She cupped his cheek, offering him the same reassuring touch she would have given a member of her family if they had been in a hospital. "We won't. You have my word."

A crack came from across the chair. Megan looked to see Raj clenching a broken switch in his fist. It had snapped off a panel under his hand. Looking down, he flushed and opened his fist.

"Don't let him work on me," Ander said. *"Please."*

"Ander, I won't hurt you," Raj said.

Megan glanced at Raj and tilted her head toward the catwalk. He nodded, then set the switch down on his console.

Ander looked back and forth between the two of them. "What are you doing?"

"Raj and I need to talk," she said. "But we can't leave you unattended. We have to put you to sleep."

"No! Megan, don't let him do this to me."

"We can't take risks."

He spoke fast. "Have the LPs guard me."

It was a reasonable compromise, assuming he hadn't bollixed up the LPs. "All right, but only if they pass another check."

His shoulders relaxed. "They will."

She summoned the two LPs under the catwalk, and they took up posts on either side of the chair. While Megan checked them, Raj reduced Ander's hearing range to make sure the android couldn't eavesdrop. Ander watched them in wary silence. Then he lay back and stared at the ceiling like a long-suffering prisoner condemned to the gallows. It almost made Megan laugh, but she held back, certain it would offend his dignity.

After they finished their checks, she and Raj walked to the area under the catwalk. Raj discreetly motioned at Ander. "We should turn him off."

"I'm not sure." She searched for words to describe what she felt on an almost subconscious level. "When a toddler asserts its independence by yelling 'No!' its parents have to set limits, yes. But they don't deactivate it."

"He's not a child. He's a weapon." Raj glanced at the chair. Ander had sat up and was squinting at them, obviously trying to read their lips. Turning back to her, Raj said, "Didn't one of your reports say an ordinary shoe box made him go unstable?"

"Not exactly." His question surprised her. Surely he had studied the reports. Then again, it never hurt to go over material more than once. She described the incident, ending with, "He couldn't move, he was furious, his face had turned crimson, and he kept demanding a plane."

Raj smiled. "That must have been a sight."

"It was." She sighed. "Both heartbreaking and funny."

"But all you had to do was readjust his fear tolerances."

It puzzled her that he didn't see the problem. "It's not that easy. For even the most minimal behavior, Ander has billions of possible responses to choose from. Add another behavior and he has billions times billions, many correlated. If I change the weight of just one stimulus, it affects all his responses."

"He can write a lot of the code himself."

They were skirting her most controversial work now. She spoke carefully. "His code has caps that limit how much he can rewrite. The reason he used to freeze up so often was because the caps were too stringent."

Raj frowned. "Are you saying you weakened their effect?"

"It was the only way to make him work."

"This wasn't in the reports I read. I would have seen it." His voice had gone taut. "Those caps are crucial. Without them, he has no controls."

"It's there, in the section about tolerances." She tried not to sound defensive.

"You mean the section on the crosslight code? The rewrites you did to strengthen Ander's conscience?" When she nodded, he made an exasperated sound. "A graduate student could write a dissertation trying to decipher that section."

She crossed her arms. "Just because my prose isn't transparent doesn't mean I'm trying to confuse people."

"I didn't say you were."

Don't prickle, she thought. Taking a breath, she lowered her arms. "People give me grief about how hard my reports are to read. Okay, so I'm no Shakespeare. But I do my best. And Raj, you of all people should have understood it."

Raj started to answer, then stopped. His face had become shuttered again. He walked over to a column of the catwalk and leaned against it, staring out at the lab. "I barely skimmed those reports."

"Why?"

He rested his head against the column. In a low voice he said, "They came in not long after my father died."

"Ah, Raj. I'm terribly sorry." She tried to think of more words that would offer comfort, but they all seemed trite.

"I shouldn't have let it affect my work. But I just . . ." He stared straight ahead as if he were seeing memories now instead of the lab. Then he turned to her. "I know that's not an excuse for my lack of preparation. I've been catching up at night on the reading."

"A few days' difference won't matter."

He motioned at Ander, who was still watching them. "Maybe I would have foreseen this crisis if I had prepared better."

"You don't know that." She wanted to reach out to him, but she sensed the protective space he had put around himself. "How do we differ from Ander? Your mourning, your capacity to feel, is part of what makes you human."

He wiped his palm across his cheek, smearing a tear. "This isn't the time." Softly he said, "But thank you."

"Hey!" Ander yelled. "How long are you two going to huddle over there?"

"What great timing," Megan muttered. Then she called to him. "Five more minutes."

"How many of his caps did you change?" Raj asked.

She shifted her weight. "Umm . . . about four million."

"*What?*"

Megan scowled. "It was the only way to make him work. He had no capacity for friendship or love. I had to rewrite huge sections of code."

"He's not supposed to love. He's a weapon."

"His personality was a *mess*. If he had been human, I would have sent him to a shrink."

He put up his hands. "All right. But I think we do need an expert to look at him, a psychologist or a doctor."

"I've requested a therapist. We have a candidate, but her security clearance hasn't come through yet."

Raj glanced at Ander, who had given up glaring at them and lain back down. "He needs a man. A good role model. I'm hardly the best choice for his socialization."

"Raj, you're fine." She wished she knew how to make him believe that. "To be honest, I doubt he would accept any new people right now."

"All the more reason to turn him off until we know better how to deal with him."

"Don't you see? To Ander, that would be a betrayal. If we lose his trust now, we may never regain it."

"Megan, it's better that we lose his trust than damage him."

That, of course, was the crux of the matter. She couldn't bear the thought of causing him harm. They needed more time to figure out the best course of action. "Let's ask him. If he agrees, our problem is solved."

"That might work—if you talk to him alone. I'll go fix the robot arms."

While Raj headed to the lockers at the back of the lab for parts, Megan returned to the chair. As soon as Ander heard her approach, he sat up.

"Don't listen to him," he said. "Please. If you do, I won't survive."

"Ander—"

"You have to listen to me!" He took a breath. "You see, I know his secret."

Do No Harm

What secret?" Megan asked.

He motioned at Raj, who was out of earshot, working on a robot arm. "He hates me. He's jealous."

"Oh, Ander. Why would he be jealous?"

"Because of you."

"You think Raj sees you as a rival?"

"Doesn't he?"

"I think he wants what's best for you."

Ander snorted. "Like I don't know myself."

"Raj wants to help."

"He wants me gone."

Where did he get these ideas? "Why would he want that?"

"So he can have you."

"He came here to work on you."

"He loathes me."

Megan sighed. "Ander, Raj likes you just fine."

He turned away and stared across the lab with a superb simulation of sullen resentment.

She tried again. "Do you really believe he hates you?"

After a moment he said, "I don't know." He turned

back to her. "Sometimes he speaks up for me even more than you do."

She hadn't expected that response. Encouraged, she smiled. "Then you see. He does support you."

"No! Yes. I don't *know*. You treat him differently than you treat me. He's human. Do I have to be human for you to like me?"

"Ander, no. Of course not." She laid her hand on his good arm. "What matters to me is that you have the chance to be your best. Whatever that means."

"I'm losing control." He lifted his broken wrist as if offering her evidence. "The more I try to rewrite myself, the worse it gets. I'm having trouble predicting my own behavior."

Her voice softened. "That sounds human to me."

Ander regarded her with his large eyes, his gaze vulnerable. "Can you really operate better if I'm asleep?"

"Yes." She dreaded the prospect of taking him apart while he watched. "Otherwise, I'll feel as if I'm hurting you."

"I don't feel pain."

"I know." She spread her hands apart. "I'm afraid human emotions don't always follow human logic."

"Then why teach a logical machine to act with emotion?"

Good question. "I've never considered logic and emotion as separate. Our ability to think is only fully realized when we have both."

Ander rubbed his hand over his eyes as if he were tired. "All right. You can put me to sleep."

Relief washed over her. "Thank you."

"Should I lie down?" He sounded nervous now. When she nodded, he stretched out on his back.

"Are you ready?" she asked.

"Yes. No, wait." He motioned at where Raj was working on the robot arms several meters away. "If he doesn't want to wake me up, ask him about the Phoenix Project."

"I've never heard of it."

"I don't know what it is, exactly." He avoided her gaze. "I came across it when, uh, we were browsing the Web. It has to do with another AI project Raj worked on. Maybe it can help me."

"All right." The way he asked made her suspect he had found it by prowling around where he didn't belong. When this was over, she would have to have a talk with him about electronic laws.

Ander took a deep breath. "Go ahead, then."

"Sleep well," she murmured. She could no longer turn him off by voice or wireless input: only the manual option remained. So she either had to open him up or else have BioSyn do it by using the smart-wires it had inserted through his ports.

She spoke to the air. "BioSyn, deactivate Ander."

A hum came from the robot arm jacked into the android. He stiffened, staring at Megan as if he were about to drown. Then his eyes closed and his face relaxed.

"Deactivated," BioSyn said.

Megan brushed his curls off his forehead, wishing she could have better soothed his unease. Then she looked up. "Raj," she called. "He's asleep."

Raj made a last adjustment on the arm, then set his tool case on the floor and came over. "How did he take it?"

"Pretty well." She smiled. "Do you know, he thinks you treat him better than I do sometimes."

"He has an odd way of showing it."

She watched Ander sleep. "I wonder what will happen if this project succeeds."

Raj understood her unspoken thought. "MindSim knows he can't do his job without free will."

"True free will means he can choose his job." She frowned at Raj. "Without that choice, it's slavery."

"You think so?" An edge came into his voice. "We all live as our circumstances dictate."

"You can live however you choose."

He braced his hands on his console and leaned forward. "Why? Because I'm a good person? No. Because I'm rich." His intensity didn't hide the pain behind his words. "What about my great-grandfather who had nothing in India and hardly anything more when he immigrated here? He was a far better man than I. But he had no choices. He worked day and night and endured intolerance and social isolation, all so he could feed his family. You call that free will?"

Hearing his anger, Megan wondered if Raj had experienced some of the same. All the wealth in the world wouldn't stop prejudice from hurting. "It makes what he accomplished all the more impressive. But he still *chose* to come here."

Raj spoke in a quieter voice. "I know you see the potential for a better world in Ander. Unfortunately, that dream has a flip side. You want him to have free will. So do I. But suppose he doesn't share our values? We have a responsibility to ensure he does no harm, even if it means limiting his options."

"If we control him, we trespass on those same values."

"Megan, you can be terribly idealistic." His face gentled. "But don't ever change."

The unexpected comment warmed her. "Well, you know what they say. Can't teach an old Megan new tricks."

His grin sparked. "Makes me wonder what old tricks you know."

"Tell you what. You fill me in on Phoenix and I'll tell

you my tricks." Seeing his puzzled look, she added, "The Phoenix Project. Ander thought it might help us."

"You mean at Arizonix?"

"Phoenix is their android work?" *This* could be interesting.

Raj laughed. "Don't be a duck. Yes, Arizonix had a Phoenix Project. I never worked on it. MindSim couldn't have hired me otherwise. It's proprietary information. Even if I knew anything, I couldn't talk about it."

"Do you?"

"Do I what?"

"Know anything?"

"You're incorrigible, you know that? Besides, I never had a chance to do any work on the project. I was only at Arizonix for a few days."

Oh, well. "Ander wasn't big on details."

"I'm not surprised." Glancing at the android, he added, "We should get started."

"Are you sure?" She indicated her console, where the glowing display read 3:14 A.M. "It's late."

"Do you mind?"

She felt too wired to sleep. "It's okay."

With a surgeon's skilled touch, he laid his palm on Ander's arm. "Let's go, then."

They opened Ander's chest in a seam that split down the middle of his torso. Seeing his bent skeleton made Megan wince. Silvery nanocircuit filaments sheathed his organs in well-organized lattices, though some were ripped by his broken parts.

While Raj examined Ander's torso, Megan opened his injured limbs. "Arm six, analyze his left leg," she said. "Arm one, do his left arm."

As the robots scanned Ander, holos of his limbs appeared like high-tech ghosts above her console, showing the damaged bones. Data scrolled across the light screens and three-dimensional graphs formed above the holo-screens. Similar displays formed on Raj's console for Ander's torso. New holos appeared showing the bones in the correct positions. When a correct holo merged with one showing damage, the resulting image blurred in places where the individual images were close but not exact. The twisted bones stuck out at odd angles.

She studied the corrections suggested by BioSyn. "Arm one, rotate the left ulna and radius through eighty-three degrees toward the A-two y-axis."

The robots moved their long fingers with a delicacy no human surgeon could match, a startling contrast to the massive arms that supported them. With their wireless links to Ander, they received continual updates on his condition as they manipulated his bones. His composite "bones" had both strength and flexibility; they suffered neither the breakage of more brittle materials nor the fatigue of metal alloys.

Megan spent an hour on Ander's arm, adjusting it until the damaged bones came into position. She had more trouble with his leg. Even after she straightened the limb, it had a slight twist. No matter how she untwisted it, another part of his leg moved out of alignment. The twist was small, though. She finally decided to leave it and see how Ander managed. If he had trouble, they would rebuild that part of his skeleton.

Whenever she took a breather, she watched Raj operate. He fixed the spine and rib cage first, then worked on the lubricant and sinus reservoirs, repairing torn filaments as he went along. Although she had known he had a gift for this work, she hadn't appreciated the full measure of it until now. Watching him was like seeing a virtuoso play the piano.

They had to do more than just make Ander work, they also had to ensure his repairs wouldn't give him away. He had to appear human even on close examination. His chest had to rise and fall, his veins had to show a pulse, his seams had to blend into his skin without a trace, and numerous other details had to fit. His disguise wasn't perfect, but it could convince many detection devices.

The operation drained Megan. It took over nine hours. When they finally closed up his body, the display read 12:33 P.M.

Raj rubbed his eyes, his motions slowed with fatigue. "I think he'll be all right."

"You work like an artist," Megan said. "It's beautiful."

"Thanks." He paused like a great, prowling cat who had spent his bursting energy on a night-long run across the plains. With unexpected gentleness, he asked, "Are you going back to your room?"

"Yes, I think so." She felt self-conscious, once again aware of him as a man rather than a colleague.

"I'll walk you back."

"Okay." It had been years since a fellow walked her home.

They did a final check on Ander and the lab, and left the LPs on guard. Then they headed out of the lab, worn out but satisfied with the night's work. As they made their way along the catwalk, Raj put his arm around her shoulders. A pleasant flush spread across her face, and she put her arm around his waist. During the operation she had forgotten she was only half-dressed, but with their arms around each other now she became acutely conscious of his body and her own. She could feel the muscles of his torso through the thin cloth of her nightshirt.

They exited the lab into the creatively named Corridor

D of Level Two. On Corridor B, they stopped outside her room, still holding each other. Déjà vu swept over Megan as she remembered Ander, and she shivered.

"Are you cold?" Raj tugged her around to face him, holding her at the waist.

"I'm warming up," she murmured.

He stroked her temple, a soft brush of sensation. "Do you know, your eyes are the same color blue as the alternate function key on my calculator?"

Megan smiled. "Ah, Raj. You're such a sweet-talker."

She wasn't sure which of them initiated the kiss, but they both melted into it, embracing outside her door. The touch of their lips was tender at first but then it grew more intense. She savored the way he held her, as though he had made a new discovery. He paused several times to look at her, his dark-eyed gaze sensuous. It not only aroused her, it also felt fresh, as if the two of them were new-minted coins.

Eventually they moved into her room. She stopped at the bed, though. "I can't. It's too soon."

Raj brushed back a tendril of her hair. "It's all right. Just knowing you're here is what matters." He intertwined his fingers with hers. "At night when I can't sleep, I feel like nothing is here, that I'm a solitary atom wandering in an empty underground warren. It's lonely."

The bleak image unsettled her. "You miss people?"

He hesitated. "I don't like being with people. Their personalities press on me. It's claustrophobic, not in space but—I don't know how to say it. In emotions? I need to retreat, to recharge. But Megan, I hate loneliness. Insomnia is even worse when you're alone, staring at the ceiling, unable to escape into your dreams." He paused, as if realizing he had said too much. "Now you must really think I'm crazy."

"Raj, no. This world we live in, it can make you think

introversion is wrong. But it's not." Still holding his hand, she cupped his cheek with her other hand. "There's nothing wrong with your need for privacy. It doesn't detract from your capacity to care for people or your strength of character."

"Sweet Meg." He pulled her close, one arm around her waist, his other hand sliding from her head down to where her hair ended at her hips. Then he went farther down, caressing her bottom, his fingers tracing the curve through her nightshirt. A ripple of sensation spread through her body.

"You've incredible hair," he said, his voice husky.

She tangled her hand into his curls. "You, too." Mischief tugged her voice. "But your eyes most certainly aren't the color of the alternate function key on my calculator. It's orange."

His laugh rumbled. "You imp."

She held him close, with her head against his shoulder. "I'm so glad you're here."

"I had no idea you felt that way." He paused. "Of course, I usually have to be hit on the head with clues before I notice something."

Megan pulled back and tapped him on the head. "Hi. I'm a clue."

He turned on his devastating grin. Then he kissed her again. When he lifted his head, he said, "I can face the insomnia better tonight, knowing you're so near."

She almost invited him to stay. But she doubted she could keep her hands off him if he did, and she wasn't ready to go further. At least, her emotions weren't ready. Her body had other ideas. Then again, she was so tired she might fall asleep regardless of how either her mind or her body felt.

"Good night, Megan." His hands lingered on her for a moment. Then he let her go and headed for the door.

"Raj, wait."

He turned with controlled grace. "Yes?"

"If you would like to stay—I mean, not anything more, but if you don't want to be alone . . ." She stopped, feeling foolish. Real smart: show a man you like him by inviting him not to touch you.

"You're sure?"

"Yes." She sat on the bed, trying to relax, and laid her hand on the covers next to her.

Raj came back to the bed, and the sight of his tall form in her private room made her more aware of his contained strength. She found it hard to believe he was here with her.

Sitting next to her, he drew her into his arms. "Just to sleep," he said, more as if to remind himself than reassure her. "Let's lie down."

"All right." Then she said, "Lamp off."

Cleo, her console, recognized the command and turned off the lamp on the nightstand. They lay on the covers, Raj on his back, Megan against his side. He held her close and stroked her hair, then trailed his fingers down her arm, letting the heel of his hand move over her breast. Her nipple hardened in response. With only a thin layer of silk between her body and him, she almost felt naked in his arms. He kissed her forehead, her cheek, her lips, all light touches, questions asking, *More?*

Megan sighed and settled against him. She felt a sensual comfort in his presence and was glad he had stayed. He moved his hands over her and kissed her deeply, exploring her body as she responded to him. Her arousal was warming from a simmer to a more demanding heat despite her intent to hold back. He pressed his hips against her pelvis in a rhythm as old as the human race, and she felt him through the layers of their clothes. Tingles ran down her spine and spread lower.

Her mind finally released its weary focus on staying awake. In its place came the floating sensation that often preceded sleep, mixed with a tantalizing desire. It would be so easy just to lift her nightshirt and unfasten his clothes. But even as she pressed against Raj, returning his rhythm, her fatigue was winning. Neither of them had slept much in the last forty-eight hours. Their motions slowed as they kissed, languid in the dark, until finally Raj's hand came to a rest on her hip. Then he gave a soft snore.

With her last waking thought, she hoped the base was safe.

Megan opened her eyes to see Raj sleeping on his back. She wondered if her presence helped him sleep or if exhaustion had simply taken its toll. With his jumpsuit zipped only halfway up, she could slide her fingers through the curly black hair on his chest. He stirred under her touch, then submerged into slumber again. The dusky red light in the room erased the lines around his eyes and made him look younger.

Wait a minute. She shouldn't be able to see him. She had turned off the lights.

Megan rolled over—and saw a red light glowing on her console. She didn't want to wake Raj, so she got up and went over to the computer. Red spirals swirled on the screen, their paths determined by the equations of motion for a billiard ball on a pool table. She had written the screen saver herself, for fun. However, it shouldn't have come on unless something had kicked her console out of its quiescent state.

She touched the screen and the skyscape appeared. The usual icons floated among the clouds, including a clock that said 4:14 P.M. A horn flashed in the lower right corner, indicating e-mail had arrived on her emergency service. Megan frowned. Only a few people even knew how to contact her that way.

Sitting down, she waved her finger through the horn. A new holo appeared in the screen's center, a spider web with flames flickering at its edges. It meant "urgent." She flicked the web and it unraveled into a menu. A message overlaid it: *Don't activate the audio unless you are alone.*

Megan glanced at the bed. Raj was still sleeping, his face and body relaxed. It felt good to see him there.

She turned back to the console and touched "Receive" on the menu. The screen blanked into a wash of blue. Then she waited.

A word formed in white on the screen: **Interactive.** The holo of a gold key appeared next to it, indicating a secured line. Megan frowned. This wasn't e-mail: by responding, she had called someone.

She touched the word **Interactive.** A picture formed on the screen, the head and shoulders of a man with gray hair. He wore a uniform with four stars on each shoulder. Megan stared at him. A four-star general? Good Lord, why?

As he nodded to her, a line of text formed at the bottom of the screen: *If you aren't alone, don't speak.*

She typed at the keyboard. *Dr. Sundaram is here.*

Can he see you?

No. He's asleep. Embarrassed by the implications of that, she added, *We worked late.*

The general didn't blink. He also didn't relax. *If he wakes, will he see the screen you are using?*

No. Her computer faced the door rather than the bed. He'll just see me working. Why? Who are you?

Nicholas Graham, at the Pentagon. We have reason to believe you're in danger.

Megan wasn't sure what she expected, but that wasn't it. She didn't want to imagine what the Pentagon would consider serious enough to have a general contact her. *What's wrong?*

Someone from NEV-5 broke into a network here. Among their activities, they searched all your files. Every detail.

How do you know it was someone here?

We traced their path through the Internet.

Megan glanced at Raj again, seeing his face free of its usual strain. Then she turned back to Graham. *You don't know it was Dr. Sundaram. It could have been me.*

Was it?

No. She doubted he would have contacted her if he thought otherwise. That they had some idea of who had done the hacking suggested they monitored NEV-5 more closely than she had realized. Graham didn't seem certain it was Raj, though. If some of the console chairs here had sensors that recorded weight, it would be easy to tell her and Raj apart based on that data, but not Raj and Ander.

The android, she typed.

Have you had problems with him? Graham asked.

Nothing we weren't prepared to handle. But he said something that suggested he had been out searching the nets.

Go on.

He asked me if I knew about the Phoenix Project.

Graham revealed almost no reaction. *Almost* nothing. But it was enough. The tensing of his facial muscles, the way he sat a little straighter—it spoke volumes to Megan, who had grown sensitized to nuances of body language after working with Ander. Graham recognized the name Phoenix and didn't want her to know.

What did you tell him? the general asked.

That I knew nothing about it. She thought back to the conversation. *He claims he picked it up on the Web. He also said Raj worked on it.*

I see. Graham leaned forward. *You must leave NEV-5 immediately.*

Sir, what's going on?

We need to talk to you, but this isn't the best venue. Say nothing to Dr. Sundaram. Is the RS unit active?

We turned him off last night.

Leave him that way. Graham paused. *Go to Las Vegas. Call 555–8956. The person you reach will give further instructions. My concern right now is to get you safely out of NEV-5.*

She wanted to grill him about it, but she held back. If he had thought she needed to know more, he would have told her. *I'll go right away.*

After they broke the connection, she took a deep breath. Then she went back to the bed. Raj lay sprawled on his back, his legs stretched out, one hand on his stomach. She felt a surge of awe at the phenomenal intellect contained within that vulnerable human body. She hated to leave him this way.

He stirred and reached for her, then lifted his head when he realized she wasn't beside him. He spoke in a drowsy voice. "Come on back. It's cold."

Megan sat on the bed. She felt as if a thread in their lives was breaking before they even finished spinning it. "Go back to sleep," she murmured.

He pulled her down into his arms. "I haven't slept this well in weeks." His voice caught. "Not since my father died."

"I'm sorry." She laid her head on his shoulder. "I'm so sorry," she whispered again, she wasn't sure why.

They held each other until he fell asleep. Then she slid out of his arms and stood up next to the bed.

The lights went off.

Megan froze. Having the power go out again, by accident, seemed about as probable as all the air in the room suddenly moving to one corner. Ander had caused the first power failure, but he was inactive now, as far as she knew.

Megan made her way to her console, but it had gone dead. She had no light at all and her flashlight was still in the lab.

Now what? She felt even less comfortable at the thought of leaving Raj here. If he had no link to this, he was probably also in danger. She should wake him up so they could escape NEV-5. But if he was involved, waking him could be a disaster. Graham had warned her against trusting him. He didn't have her positive view of Raj, but that could work against her too. A plethora of black curls was unlikely to affect the general's judgment.

What had caused the failure: Ander, Raj, or something else? She and Raj had checked the NEV-5 local area network, but she had looked for Ander's tampering. If Raj had done something, he could have hidden his work. She had no intention of going to the power room. If she brought up the generators, it would alert whoever had killed the power that someone was awake. What she ought to do was take a vehicle from the garage and drive to Las Vegas. With the power off, she might have trouble operating the elevator, but it was almost impossible to trap someone inside who knew the base. Security was meant to guard NEV-5 from outsiders, not prevent legitimate inhabitants from leaving.

And Raj? She had to go on instinct; she had no time to work this through like a mathematical proof or a software algorithm.

She returned to the bed and sat by Raj, then nudged his shoulder. "Wake up."

"Megan?" he mumbled. "Why do you keep getting up?"

"We have to go."

"Go?" He yawned.

"Raj, please. We have to leave."

"Do you mean your bedroom?" He sounded more awake now. "I'm sorry. I didn't mean to intrude—"

"It isn't that." She heard him sitting up. "We have to leave NEV-5."

"Why?"

"I can't say right now." By going against Graham's advice, she had already taken a risk. She had to minimize the potential damage, which meant saying as little as possible until she better understood how Raj came into this.

"I'm not leaving unless you tell me why."

"I can't. Please trust me. We have to go." She couldn't even risk taking the time to change her clothes.

"Why won't the lights go on?" Raj asked.

"I don't know. Even the backups are out." She took a breath to ease the tightness in her chest.

"*Again?*" The bed rustled as he slid past her. "We have to check Ander."

"No." She grabbed his arm. "We have to *go.*"

"Why?"

"I can't talk about it."

"You 'just' want me to trust you."

"Yes." She prayed she had done the right thing.

Raj blew out a gust of air. "All right. For now. But I'm going to want answers."

Standing up by the bed, she said, "Deal."

The corridors were dark, without even the emergency lights that were supposed to provide such good backup.

Going through large open areas with no light was unnerving. They made their way by feeling along the walls. Megan kept her fingers hooked in Raj's belt so they didn't get separated.

"You know," Raj said, "if this is just an ordinary power failure, we're going to feel pretty silly about skulking around this way."

She managed a wan smile. "No kidding."

"Ander might have cut the power."

"We turned him off."

"He could have hidden a program and set it to start later."

Although it made sense to Megan, she regretted what such an act on Ander's part would imply. "He doesn't trust us."

Raj snorted. "Trusting people is bloody stupid."

"Why do you think that way?" When he didn't answer, she said, "Bugs."

"You think he bugged these halls?"

"No. The reason you distrust people. It has something to do with insects."

"Megan, chill on the bugs, okay?" His muscles had tensed against her hand where she held his belt.

She persisted, trying to understand him. Her life might depend on it. "People don't usually go out of their way to rescue insects just because kids at their school swatted bugs."

"So I'm eccentric."

"What else did those kids do?"

He suddenly stopped and swung around, pulling her in front of him, his hands gripped on her upper arms. "They fucking made me eat them, all right? After they beat me up. Satisfied?"

"My God. That's appalling."

"Yeah, well, I learned how to fight back."

"Couldn't you get help?"

"No. Yes. I don't know. I was too proud to ask." Raj took a breath and exhaled, as if to release the memories. He continued in a quieter voice. "I felt like the insects they made me eat. They knew I wanted to be an entomologist. So they tried to make me hate those dreams. Well, forget them. No one takes my dreams."

"I'm sorry. They had no right." Megan knew firsthand the pain a child's peers could inflict on those who were different, and she had dealt only with taunts, never violence or brutality.

Raj shrugged. "I'm more successful now than the lot of them combined, ten times over." His grip on her arms loosened. "Ander is our problem now. He can model our behavior and predict our actions. He may already have guessed we would do this."

She wondered if Ander's misconduct had stirred up Raj's anger from the past. "If he's the one behind this."

"Who else would it be?" It wasn't reassuring the way Raj pulled her into his arms; he could break her ribs with that rigid embrace.

Megan had to turn her head against his chest to breathe. "I don't know."

"Why are we running?" he asked. When she didn't answer, he said, "Just trust you. Sweet, idealistic Meg. Except I know the other side. You didn't survive this cutthroat, high-stakes game in our industry by being sweet. I want to know what you know."

She spoke quietly. "What makes you think I trust you?"

It was a moment before he answered. "Touché."

"Let's just go, okay?"

His hand clenched around her hair. "Go where?"

She drew in a breath against the alarming constriction of his hold. "We have to do what Ander wouldn't expect."

"The Solarium. If we climb to the top, we can go through the safety hatch to Level One."

"Why wouldn't he expect that?"

"Because he's probably hacked our records."

Megan recalled what Graham had said about her files at the Pentagon. Who had done it, Ander or Raj? *Who?* "How does that connect to the Solarium?"

His voice tightened again. "Because I'm afraid of heights, damn it."

His anger didn't surprise her. The situation was forcing him to reveal aspects of his personality that she suspected he usually locked behind fortified defenses. Heights, bugs, insomnia, soap shavings: how many coping mechanisms had his life inflicted on him?

And *why?*

The power was out in the Solarium too. Megan had never been that interested in having implants put in her body, but now she wished she had IR lenses that would let her see in the dark by making objects glow according to their temperature.

They made their way forward, bumping tables and trees. Suddenly Raj's hand yanked out of hers. Someone grabbed her around the torso, forcing the air out of her lungs. She tried to shout, but only managed a choked noise.

"No one can hear you," a voice said near her ear. It sounded like Raj. Then he pressed an air syringe against her arm.

With her strength driven by fear, she tried to jerk away. He must have stolen the syringe from the NEV-5 med room. They weren't supposed to use it without a prescription from a doctor.

"Megan!" That was also Raj, several meters away. "Run!"

Whoever was holding her let go. As she swung around, moving with adrenaline-driven speed, a scraping came from nearby, followed by a grunt, then a thud.

"Who's *there*?" Megan lunged forward, but she collided with a chair. She fell across it and hit a table with an impact that jarred her teeth.

Someone yanked her upright. When she twisted around and struck out with her fists, he spoke in Raj's voice. "Enough."

"*No.*" She didn't want to believe it was Raj. Ander could mimic him. Who had warned her to run? As she struggled, her bare arms scraped the rough cloth of his jumpsuit. It almost made her freeze. Ander had stolen Raj's jeans and sweater, and they had left the garments on a console after they undressed him.

Raj had been wearing the jumpsuit.

Megan thought she heard breathing nearby, but she couldn't be sure. Her captor held her around the torso, pinning her arms to her sides as she struggled. If this was Raj, then the same muscles she had so admired before now made her a prisoner.

Damn. She should have let him sleep. Her intuition was usually sound, but this time she had let affection cloud her judgment. She kept fighting, driven now by anger at herself.

Her awareness faded and the dark that filled the atrium came in to fill her mind as well.

Stealth Run

Jolt.

A jerk knocked Megan against a hard surface. She opened her eyes into moonlight. She was in a vehicle, the HM-15, what they called a desert floater. Silver light slanted through the windows, but her sight was too blurred to see much else. They had to be on the desert; even with the advanced shock system that gave this vehicle its name, it still vibrated as it drove, which it wouldn't have done on a road.

She was in the front passenger seat, still in her nightshirt. Someone had wrapped her in a blanket and pulled it over her head. A blur sat at the wheel. As her gaze focused, she saw that it was Ander, wearing Raj's sweater and jeans, his blond hair brushed back from his face. She wondered how he could look so innocent and cause so much trouble.

The floater had an angular shape with flat surfaces. Its systems diffused heat to help it blend into its surroundings like a chameleon. The composite body, dark color, shielded engine, high-tech wheels and suspension, and camouflaged exhaust made it hard to detect. The holographic displays in front of the driver's seat looked the way Megan imagined the cockpit of a starship.

Ander had pulled a cable out of his left wrist and jacked it into the dash, no doubt linking into the vehicle's tracking system. The floater could drive itself, but he kept his hands on the wheel anyway. A meter on the dash indicated he wasn't linked to any of the electronic driving grids that crisscrossed the country, regulating traffic. Someday the law would probably require all cars to link up, making accidents and traffic jams a thing of the past, except when a grid malfunctioned. But for now it remained voluntary, and Ander hadn't volunteered to take part.

"What's going on?" Megan asked.

Ander glanced at her. "Are you all right?"

"Megan?" That came from the back, unmistakably Raj.

She turned around. Raj sat behind her, his wrists tied to a hook where the doorframe met the ceiling. He had a bruise on his cheek. His ankles were bound with a net they had used to store potatoes in the kitchen.

"Good Lord," Megan said. "What happened?"

At the same time that Raj said, "Ander knocked us out," Ander said, "Raj tried to kill you."

Raj swore. "He's lying. He hit me in the Solarium and drugged you."

"That's bullshit," Ander said. "I caught him using the NEV-5 system to steal files from other installations. He realized you were on to him, Megan. So he tried to get rid of you and make it look like I did it."

Megan stared from one of them to the other, trying to make her groggy mind absorb the situation. Either could be lying. At one time she would have said Ander couldn't tell a deliberate untruth, but she could no longer be sure.

Then she realized Raj still had on the orange coverall.

She struggled with her sense of betrayal. "I felt your jumpsuit when you grabbed me."

"I *didn't* grab you." Raj yanked on the ropes that bound his wrists to the hook, keeping them up near his head. "Droidboy here knocked me out and went after you."

"He's lying," Ander said.

"I started to come to and tried to warn you," Raj told Megan. "He came back and hit me again."

Ander snorted. "Amazing you saw all that in the dark."

"Like it's that bloody hard to figure out," Raj said.

Odd, Megan thought. That wasn't the first time she had heard Raj use British profanity or slang. Yet he had grown up in Louisiana.

"You forget," Ander told him. "I *can* see in the dark, at least the heat from IR. I saw you holding that syringe when I pulled you away from Megan." His forehead creased as if he were trying to model strain but hadn't yet mastered the expression. "I had trouble with my coordination and I was confused by his actions. He tangled me up in that net from the kitchen. By the time I pulled free, he had already given you the sedative."

"It doesn't add up," she said. "We left you deactivated."

"I hid a sleeper program in an LP." Now he looked like a rascal who had tricked his parents and was trying not to appear too satisfied, lest he end up in even more trouble. "When the program kicked in, the LP woke me up."

Megan glowered at him. "I thought we found all your sleepers."

Ander smirked. "Missed one."

Raj rubbed his forehead against his arm, pushing curls out of his eyes. "If I tried to hurt Megan, why didn't you just call the authorities?"

"Why should I?" Ander demanded. "They may think you're neurotic, but you're *human*. They'll believe you before me."

Megan wished she had a clearer head. Although she wanted to believe Raj, the evidence implicated him. She had a harder time reading Ander. Everything he did was calculated. Simulated. He could give whatever impression he wanted.

"Where are we going?" she asked.

"The desert," Ander said.

"Well, shit." Raj's Southern accent drew the word out in a drawl. "And here I thought it was the sea."

"Guess you aren't so smart after all." Ander gave a boyish laugh. "See the sea, Dr. C." When both Raj and Megan just looked at him, he said, "It was a joke. You know. His name starts with *c*."

"I'm in the Twilight Zone." Megan had to admit, though, she had heard worse puns from humans.

"The Twilight Zone is a fictional construct," Ander said. "This is Nevada." He paused. "I suppose you could make an argument for a certain correspondence between the two."

"Ander," she said. "Where *are* we going?"

"I'm not sure. I don't know what to do."

"That's a crock," Raj said. "You planned this. Why else would you plant that program in an LP?"

"It was a game."

Megan knew Ander could have worn the jumpsuit to impersonate Raj, then changed his clothes later. But how would he have known Raj still had on the jumpsuit? Then she remembered Raj's words: *Jaguars prey on other animals.* His self-image wasn't exactly reassuring.

Regardless of the truth, though, someone had hurt Raj. She regarded him with concern. "How did your cheek get bruised?"

"Ander beat me up."

"I had to fight him in the atrium." Ander kept his attention on his "driving." "To pull him off you."

Who was lying? If Ander told the truth, Raj was dangerous and could turn on them. It also meant she had a loopy android on her hands, one who reacted to a crisis by driving pell-mell across the desert. If Raj told the truth, it meant Ander had acted with premeditated violence. More than anything else, that made her question Raj's story. Yes, Ander had acted up yesterday, but it had been more like youthful rebellion than criminal behavior. Could his personality change so fast? His mind worked much faster than a human brain, but he had to sort through many possible behaviors before he acted because he lacked a great deal of the commonsense knowledge humans took for granted.

Another problem occurred to her. Whoever had tampered with the NEV-5 power might have recorded her talk with General Graham. If so, then he knew someone in Las Vegas expected her call. Unless she made contact soon, Graham's people would begin a search, if they hadn't already. Unfortunately, finding an HM-15 wouldn't be easy, not even out in the desert at night where it was harder to camouflage their presence.

The vehicle hit a deep furrow and lurched, throwing her against her harness. As Ander reached out to catch her, his cable yanked out of the dash and hung from his wrist. She could see the circuits gleaming inside him. It made her think of a line from Shakespeare: "What a piece of work is a man!"

"Are you all right?" he asked. When she nodded, stiff with tension, he released her arm. Watching her face, he brushed his finger over her lips, his touch lingering. Then he turned back to his driving and jacked into the dashboard again.

Megan shuddered, wondering why he wanted to touch her. Simulated desire? Programmed affection? Although he could distinguish tactile sensations, they meant nothing to him. As far as she knew, he experienced neither pleasure nor pain.

"We can't keep driving like this forever," she said.

"We have to go back to NEV-5," Raj said.

Ander spoke flatly. "No."

"What is it you want?" Raj asked.

"To be free." Ander clenched the wheel so hard, his knuckles turned white. "Megan, when you gave me a conscience, did you think about the consequences? I was designed to spy and kill. You knew that, for all your idealism. You should have left off my conscience. It would have made my life bearable."

"Let us speak for you at MindSim." She willed him to trust her. "I'll give your side."

"They will reprogram me."

"We won't let them."

"I don't believe you."

"Ander—"

"*Enough.*" His head jerked. "I need you both. My mind hurts. My body doesn't work right. You have to fix me."

She wondered what he meant by "my mind hurts." "Do you have trouble thinking?"

"I can't . . . I've no control. My thoughts go around and around, and I can't stop it."

She had never heard an AI describe itself that way. "I want to help. But I need the lab."

"No."

"We need the equipment," Raj said.

"We aren't going back."

"Damn it," Raj said. "Don't be foolish."

"Fuck you."

"Ander, stop," Megan said. "You're not giving us much incentive to help you."

"How's this for incentive? Do what I tell you, or Raj is dead meat. You want to die, Raj?"

"No."

"So we do things on my terms," Ander said.

Raj spoke with care. "What are your terms?"

Ander paused, his face blanking. "I'm not sure."

"Have you decided where we're going?" Megan asked.

Now Ander looked like a scamp again. "Yeah. Land of sin. Las Vegas."

"Oh, Lord," Megan said. At least it might give her a chance to reach her contact.

"Hey! Megan and I could marry."

"For crying out loud," Raj said.

"Isn't that what people do in Las Vegas?" Ander laughed. "Do you take this android for your lawfully welded husband?"

"I don't believe this," Megan muttered.

"You should run tests on *all* my systems," Ander told her. "I'm fully functional, you know. We could even have a kid. Actually, it would be Arick Bjornsson's kid."

"Stop it," Raj said.

Ander glanced back at him. "Jealous?"

"Leave her alone."

Ander made an exasperated noise. "Oh, stop being so mature, Raj. Say what you really want to say: 'Die, you shit android.' " He tilted his head. "Except I don't think I can."

The floater suddenly braked, then glided to a stop. A large ridge loomed next to them, blocking the stars. Ander pulled his jack out of the dash and closed up his wrist, leaving no trace of a seam. Then he got out of the floater.

Megan rubbed her hand over her eyes, drained. She

tried to open her door and her window, but neither would budge. Twisting in her seat, she looked back at Raj. "Are you all right?"

"Yeah, I'm okay." With his leather jacket over his jumpsuit, he looked like a fighter pilot. Ander must have put the jacket on him; Raj hadn't been wearing it in the Solarium. It told her two unexpected facts: Ander had made the effort to figure out what another person needed and he had chosen to act on his conclusions.

"I don't believe he would kill you," she said.

His tension almost crackled. "This isn't some misbehaving kid, Megan. He's gone way beyond that."

Has he? Or was it Raj?

Ander came to her side of the car. He had a Winchester rifle in his hands. Her window rolled down, apparently obeying his wireless command.

"We're changing vehicles." He leaned his forearm against the floater and reached inside to stroke her cheek. "You'll sit up front with me again."

"Don't do this," Megan said. "If you keep breaking the law, you'll end up a lot worse off than you were in NEV-5."

"I won't go back." He opened the back door, then moved away and gestured at Raj with his rifle. "Megan will untie you. But I don't need you as much as I need her. Cause problems and I'll shoot. Understand?"

"Yes." Raj watched him with a dark gaze. Megan hoped that the protective impulses she had seen Raj show toward Ander were genuine and that they didn't fade; she didn't want either of them hurt.

Ander motioned at Megan. "Untie him."

This time when she tried her door, it opened. She left her blanket on the seat, on the off chance that searchers might fly overhead and detect her body heat with IR sensors.

Breezes stirred her nightshirt. She felt vulnerable with only a flimsy layer of cloth on her body. Following Ander's orders, she untied Raj from the hook in the car but left his wrists bound. As she freed his ankles, he lowered his hands into his lap, his face drawn with pain. Although he had more mobility with his arms in front of his body, it didn't really help; Ander had them both covered with the rifle.

As she finished, Ander said, "Move away from him." He waited until Megan had moved back. "Okay, Raj. Get out."

Raj stepped out, then nearly fell. He grabbed the top of the door with his bound hands and hung on for balance. Moonlight silvered his drawn face. Megan bit her lip, knowing his returning circulation must be painful.

"Now you know how it feels to be clumsy." Although Ander spoke in an even tone, his voice had a dusting of emotional nuances. They were sketchy, but Megan thought he was trying to model humor mixed with an underlying pain and perhaps a trace of bitterness. It gave a complexity to his attitude toward his physical problems that went beyond the simple one-note emotions he had tended to display these past few weeks.

A rumbling came from the sky above them. A helicopter? she drew in a breath. "HEL—"

Ander grabbed her around the waist, the rifle clenched in his fist, and clamped his other hand over her mouth. "Do you want to end up *dead*?"

Raj spoke fast and low. "Don't hurt her. If you're worried that you can't control us both, get rid of me instead."

Megan stared at Raj. This was the man who had supposedly tried to kill her? He had just offered his life for hers.

"I don't want to get rid of either of you." Ander spoke near Megan's ear. "Do I have to gag you?"

She shook her head, but otherwise remained still, barely daring to breathe.

"If I let you go, will you be quiet?" he asked.

She nodded, moving slow so she wouldn't alarm him. Raj stood by the car, his arms slightly raised as if he were still asking for her life.

Ander released her mouth but kept his other arm around her waist. As she drew in a shaky breath, he shifted the Winchester into his free hand. To Raj he said, "Walk to the hill." His voice had a slight tremor, almost undetectable.

He's afraid. Megan could see why Ander's code would model "fear" if Raj had done what Ander claimed. Or it could mean Ander knew how to bluff, that he was faking the emotion. Such a complex deception involved abilities he had never demonstrated before, but his recent actions indicated he was developing at a remarkable rate. Or did she resist believing Ander because she hated the thought that Raj might have betrayed her? This could all be Ander's confused but well-meant attempt to rescue her from what he perceived as an extreme threat.

Raj limped around the floater, which had parked itself beneath a rocky overhang of the ridge. Megan could just make out a long, dark form crouched under the ridge about ten meters away, catching glints from the moonlight. A hovercar. Dark and sleek, it waited like a predator in the dark.

Ander followed, bringing Megan with him, his arm tight around her waist. Although the rocky ground hurt her bare feet, she tried not to stumble or make any other fast moves. Ander had Raj climb into the back of the hovercar. Then he told Megan to tie Raj's wrists to a hook in the roof and his ankles to a bar under the front seat. She made the knots loose, but Ander easily saw with his augmented sight and had her tighten them. The whole time, Raj watched her, his gaze dark and angry.

"I'm sorry," she said in a low voice.

"He's out of control," Raj said.

"He must have rented this car through the Internet and had it drive itself out here."

"With whose money?" Then Raj answered himself. "Probably he hacked a MindSim account."

"No talking," Ander said.

After Megan finished tying Raj, Ander pulled her to the driver's side and pushed her inside. As she climbed across the bucket seats to the passenger's side, he slid in behind the wheel. When he jacked into the car's computer, the windows in back turned opaque. A partition rose between the front and back, isolating Raj. Then it slid down again.

"Why did you do that?" Raj asked. His face had gone pale.

"A test," Ander said. "To make sure it works."

Megan shivered, wondering what other secrets Ander had prepared. Regardless of who had attacked her, Ander had obviously put more than one night's thought into this getaway. This car would blend in well with the traffic going into Las Vegas, more expensive than many vehicles perhaps, but nothing to draw undue notice. He had chosen a better way to conceal them than by skulking along in a floater: he intended to hide in plain view.

A set of magkeys lay on the dash. Ander started the car, and it vibrated as the lifting motors raised it into the air. This was a top-of-the-line model, so sleek she barely heard the howl of the turbofan. It pulled away from the ridge, whirring on its cushion of air, and sped away across the desert.

With no warning, the ridge exploded.

City of Lights

The shock wave from the blast shook the hovercar like storm waves tossing a ship. Jerking around in her seat, Megan stared at the distant ridge. It had buried the floater. A cloud of dust drifted like a stealthy shadow in the moonlit night.

"Holy shit," Megan said.

"Nothing holy about it," Raj muttered.

She turned to Ander. "You *planned* this. All of it."

"To maybe escape someday, yes. I bought the explosive through an underground Web site." As he pushed his hand through his hair, his arm shook. "But I never planned to take anyone with me. I never meant to use it this way. It was a *game.*"

"A bomb?" Raj asked. "What the hell kind of game is that?"

"I'm rescuing Megan from you," Ander said. "So shut up."

"You claimed you didn't know what to do," Megan said.

"I didn't." The confidence had leached out of his voice. "I still don't. I just used up my only escape route."

She rubbed her hands along her bare arms. Maybe he had started this as a real-life version of some adventure game, but it had gone far beyond that now.

The Elegant Motel Flamingo hunkered in the desert outside of Las Vegas. Its sign displayed a well-endowed flamingo in a feather boa, with "Motel Flamingo" emblazoned in purple and the word "Elegant!" slanted across it in gleeful pink fluorescence. The motel consisted of a faded one-story building and a collection of bungalows. It also had a drive-through registration, the hostelry equivalent of a fast food restaurant.

Ander had made their reservation using the car's computer, but he didn't secure it with a credit or money card since either could be traced. They waited in the drive-through behind an old Pontiac.

"How will you pay for the room?" Raj asked.

"Cash." Ander pulled a wallet out of his back pocket. "You really should use your money card more, Raj. Cash is too easy to steal."

Raj swore under his breath. "What, you're going to rob me now?"

"I'm Robin Hood," Ander said. "With me as the poor too." Before Raj could respond, Ander raised the panel that hid the back from the front.

"Ander, don't." Megan suspected Raj's anger had nothing to do with the money and everything to do with his memories of the abuse he had taken in school. "Can't you—"

"You be quiet too." The android frowned at her. "And don't try to get anyone's attention. If they take notice, I may have to hurt people. I don't want to do that. All right?"

She thought of Raj trapped in the back. "Yes."

As they pulled up to the window, a gum-chewing girl with big blond hair dimpled at Ander. "Hey, cute stuff. What's your name?"

"Mac Smith," he said.

As the cashier checked her computer, Megan muttered, "Cute stuff?" Ander grinned.

Megan willed the cashier to look at her. If she could attract the girl's attention without alerting Ander, maybe she could let her know they were in trouble. She wasn't sure what the girl would do, though, besides snap her gum. Megan suspected many Smiths and Joneses checked into this motel, and that a woman in a filmy nightshirt sitting in the front seat wouldn't raise an eyebrow.

She knew that the longer this went on, the less chance it had of ending without violence. Search parties had to be looking for them by now. Everyone wanted Ander to survive, but if he became a public danger or continued to compromise security, MindSim would have fewer qualms than Megan about destroying him. They hadn't spent the last two months watching him come alive.

"Yeah. Okay. Got it." The cashier handed Ander a magkey. "Bungalow five. I zipped a map to your car, along with a receipt and, like, info about our fine Motel Flamingo."

Ander gave her a wad of bills. "You have a well-behaved night."

The girl laughed. "You too, honey." She didn't seem the least bit fazed to receive cash instead of the usual credit or money card. "But not too much, y'know?" She grinned at Megan. "Be nice to him."

Looking confused, Ander said, "Thank you," and drove away before Megan could respond.

"Did I say something strange?" he asked.

"Well-behaved night?" Megan tried not to laugh. "What is that?"

" 'Well-behaved' is another definition of 'good.' "

"Oh, Ander." She wondered why he was using such a limited portion of his knowledge base. "Look more in your files."

"Ah. I see. Hey! I made a joke."

No sound came from the back. Megan hoped Raj was all right. Fortunately, their drive to the bungalows didn't take long. Each small house stood alone, with a rock garden in front and a patio in back. Desert stretched everywhere; only the dubious elegance of Motel Flamingo broke the monotony. Inside a bungalow, she and Raj could pound on the walls from now until kingdom come and no one would hear. Even if anyone did, they would most likely think their rowdy neighbors were just having a good time.

For the first time, Megan wished she had specialized in brain augmentation instead of androids. Right now, she could have used some extra intellect. Augmentation technology wasn't available yet to the public, though. The biochips meant to enhance the human mind had so far caused more neural damage than increased intelligence. Of course, people already enhanced their lives with computers in everything from postcards to jewelry. She had even seen a scanty little lingerie number that could talk sexy for lovers who liked that sort of thing. Megan couldn't imagine keeping a straight face while her corset discoursed with lustful intent. In any case, someday the line between machine and human would blur. But they weren't there yet, and if this situation with Ander was any sample of the future, they were in trouble.

Dawn was spreading a pepper-red glow across the sky as Ander pulled up to their bungalow. He had Megan repeat the same process with Raj as when they had switched to the hovercar. When she opened the back door, Raj stared at her in the dawn shadows, sweat running down his temple.

As Megan reached to untie Raj, Ander lunged forward. With no other warning, he clumsily heaved her up into his arms, keeping the gun under her body, its hidden length pressed against her legs and buttocks.

"What the—" Megan broke off, frozen by the chill touch of the gun against her thighs.

"Quiet," Ander whispered. With his foot, he slammed the door shut. Then he lost his balance and fell against the car, his muscles tensed under her like ridged cords.

She finally saw what had spooked him. An older man and woman were coming up the road. The man wore a Hawaiian shirt and tennis shorts, and the woman had on a sundress with a shawl around her shoulders.

"Hi, there," the woman said. The man glanced at Megan, then averted his gaze, his face reddening. Given her attire, or lack thereof, it didn't surprise her.

Ander gave an embarrassed cough. "Carrying her across the threshold, you know." He used an out-of-breath voice, as if carrying Megan was far more effort than he expected. She jabbed her elbow into his ribs.

The man's face turned kindly and his wife beamed. "Oh, that's lovely," she said. "Congratulations." Then they continued on, leaving the "newlyweds" to their privacy.

"Put me down, damn it," Megan said.

"Such sweet nothings, my dear." He set her on her feet. "Get Raj out."

When she opened the door, Raj stared at her, his face flushed with anger. Dismayed, she saw fresh blood dribbling down his arms from the lacerations in his wrists. He must have been struggling to free himself.

"Ah, Raj," she murmured.

"Just take my hands down." He sounded as if his teeth were clenched.

As she freed him from the car, she wondered if the couple had glimpsed Raj before Ander slammed the door. If so, would they report it? Then again, at the fine Motel Flamingo, maybe no one would think twice about kinky newlyweds who brought along a third party to play.

Ander hastened them into the bungalow. It wasn't much. The miserly bathroom was just big enough for a sink, toilet, and tub. In the main room, the bed had the most amazing purple quilt beautified by hot pink flamingos in purple boas. A nightstand stood on this side of the bed and a table on the other. Beyond the table, glass doors fronted the patio. A cabinet at the foot of the bed contained a holovid, music cube player, and console. All the furniture was bolted to the floor except for two chairs at the table.

Ander closed the curtains, which were made from the same inimitable cloth as the bedspreads. Megan wondered if a person could get eyestrain from too many fluorescent flamingos.

Ander motioned at them with the gun. "Don't try to call for help."

"You can't shoot in here," Raj said. "People will hear."

"We're too far from the other bungalows." Ander's arm jerked, snapping the gun out from his body. "You have to do what I tell you."

"Can't you see you're not working right?" Megan asked.

"Then fix me!" He clenched the rifle so tight, tendons stood out on his wrists. "Make my mind stop these damn loops."

She spoke carefully. "It sounds like you're trapped in a limited area of code. It can happen when you write new code by copying and combining pieces of older code. It's like inbreeding."

He gave a short laugh. "What, my 'gene' pool is too small to produce healthy software?"

"I can help," Megan said. "But I'll need to reprogram you."

Suspicion shadowed his face, so real she could almost forget it was simulated. "And now," he said, "you're going to claim you have to turn me off to make these fixes."

"She can't get reliable results if your software is changing as she works," Raj said.

Ander scowled at him. "Shut up."

His growing hostility toward Raj alarmed Megan. The code he had written to project wariness in his first meeting with Raj must be in the region where his mind had become trapped. That code's "offspring" were probably undergoing a population explosion, which meant his hostility would only grow worse. If they didn't free him from that trap, he might end up killing Raj.

"You can't work on my mind directly," Ander told her. "I can't trust you. Think of some other way to help me."

His response didn't surprise Megan. Although she couldn't be sure of anything where his "emotions" were concerned, she had the feeling that beneath his bravado he was scared. If Raj really had attacked them, how would Ander incorporate that knowledge into his evolving mind? It could warp his fledgling concepts of trust and make him question the coherency in human behavior.

"If I make suggestions, can you do the rewrites?" she asked.

"I'll try. Anything is better than this nightmare."

"It's probably a protective measure," Raj said.

Although Ander tensed, his curiosity got the better of him. Instead of snapping at Raj, he asked, "Why?"

Raj shifted into the unconscious assurance that always came when he talked about his work. "As you become self-aware, the evolution of your code becomes more complex. To make rewrites manageable, your mind might temporarily isolate certain sections. It sounds like it back-fired, though, trapping you in one of those sections."

"Could it be?" Then Ander frowned and gestured at him with the rifle. "I told you to be quiet. No analysis."

"What are you going to do with us?" Megan asked.

He regarded them uncertainly. "I'm not sure how to take care of humans. You need to eat and sleep, right? I don't know what to feed you. I thought humans slept at night, but neither of you seem to."

"We can wait until tonight." Megan doubted she could sleep now anyway.

"We need breakfast," Raj said.

Ander gestured at the comp-phone on the nightstand. "Will that give me room service?"

"It should," Raj said.

Megan's breath caught. Ander's increasing ability to adapt gratified her. Although "room service" appeared in his knowledge base, he had never had reason to interpret the concept. A few months ago simple questions had turned him catatonic; now he could come up with his own questions and try solutions.

Ander made the call for food. When Megan started to ask Raj a question, Ander shook his head at her. She stopped, fearing to incite his unpredictable temper.

After Ander ordered breakfast, he considered them. Then he spoke to Megan. "Why are you always looking at him? Why not me?"

Megan felt Raj stiffen at her side, like a coil ready to snap. "Ander, don't."

"Don't what?" With deliberate motions, he aimed the rifle at Raj. "Sit by the table leg. *Now.*"

Raj spoke in a calming voice. "Ander, you don't want to shoot anyone. Why don't you give us the rifle?"

"No! I won't let you hurt Megan!"

Then Ander fired.

The android jerked with the recoil of the gun, almost losing his balance. The bullet hit the floor well away from where Raj stood. They were too close for Ander to have miscalculated by such a large amount; he must have missed on purpose.

"Are you nuts?" Raj grabbed Megan with his bound hands and shoved her behind him. "Stop it!"

"Sit down by the table leg." Ander sounded scared rather than angry, as if he couldn't believe he had fired either.

"All right." Raj raised his hands, palms out. Then he sat on the floor, his movements slow and contained.

"Tie his hands to the table leg," Ander told Megan. "And don't try to trick me. Understand?"

"Yes." With her pulse hammering, she knelt and tied Raj's hands. She gave him a look of apology. Then she stood again, taking care to move slowly, so she wouldn't incite Ander.

"Why do you always look at him?" Ander set the rifle on the nightstand, then walked around the bed toward her. "Why *him*?"

Alarmed, Megan backed away. But he kept coming. With a sudden lunge, he grabbed her arm, then swung her around and threw her onto the bed. She sprawled on her stomach, grunting as she lost her breath. Before she could recover, he was kneeling over her, straddling her hips. He put his hands on the small of her back and pressed her into the mattress.

"Stop it!" Straining to look over her shoulder at him, she swung her fist back and hit him in the knee.

Ander ignored the punch. Instead, he gave Raj a malicious look. "You can watch me do her."

Raj cursed at him. He was bracing his feet against the table leg, pushing hard, trying to snap the wood.

Megan clenched her fists. "Get off me."

"Such honeyed words." Ander lifted himself up, but only enough to flip her onto her back. Then he pushed her down into the bed.

"Why are you doing this?" Megan shoved at his shoulders.

"Why are you afraid? Are you a virgin? No, don't answer. I know you aren't. I've seen your medical records."

She froze. Did that mean he was the one who had searched her files at the Pentagon?

"What do you want from us?" Raj asked. "Your freedom? You have it. Just let her go."

"I'm doing what I want." Ander regarded Megan. "I am one. A virgin, I mean. Sure, they tested my plumbing. I've never had sex with anyone, though."

"Ander, listen," she said. "You're trapped in a truncated response space—"

"Oh, stop. Truncated space indeed. I want to fuck."

"Input your crosslight codes," Raj said.

Ander went so still that for a moment Megan thought his mind had frozen again. He stayed that way for one second, like a statue. Then he deliberately set his hand on Megan's breast and turned to Raj. "I cut out the crosslight code, asshole."

No. Megan stiffened with sudden understanding. The crosslight code was the rewrite she had done to strengthen his conscience. Without it, he had neither caps on his behavior nor a significant sense of moral responsibility.

"Put it back in." Raj watched Ander with a probing intensity. "It will solve your looping problem."

"You need your conscience," Megan said. "To widen the gene pool for your code." She wasn't sure if that was true, but it only mattered that he believed it.

Ander turned to her. "I don't want a conscience."

"It's why your mind feels unstable," she said.

"Maybe." He started to unbutton her nightshirt. "Maybe not."

Megan tried to twist out from under him. "Ander, don't do this. Don't prove the detractors right who claimed an android could never develop morals."

He grabbed her wrists, holding them in front of her body with one hand. "Why do you act like this sex thing matters? It's nothing. A little rubbing and then it will be over."

"It matters. Believe me."

He began working her out of the nightshirt. She fought in his hold, trying to stop him, but she only succeeded in ripping a side seam of the shirt, splitting it up to her hip. He finished taking it off and dropped it on the bed, leaving her naked beneath him.

"Ander, don't be a bloody fool!" Raj said. "Do this and you'll never recover her goodwill."

"Why?" Ander pinned Megan's wrists to the bed by her shoulders. "Humans do this all the time." He jerked his head toward Raj. "You want him. Why not me? We're about the same size and shape. And I'm younger."

"None of that matters." Megan shot Raj a frantic glance and he tilted his head, trying to tell her something, but she had no idea what.

"Come on, Megan." Still holding her hands, Ander stretched out on top of her. He pushed apart her legs with his knees and fit his hips into the cradle of her pelvis. "I want to know what it's like."

"Stop it!" She could feel his erection through his jeans. "No *more*."

"Why is it such a big deal?" He slid his hands up her sides, scraping his thumbs over her breasts. "Rubbing you this way—I don't understand the context. I know men consider your body beautiful. But this pleasure thing—I'm missing it." He rubbed against her. "If I do this

enough, I'll have an orgasm, especially if I go inside you.
But it's just plumbing. The faucet goes on for a few seconds and that's it. In fact, this whole reproduction thing
doesn't usually last long. So why the big fuss?"

Megan struggled to keep her voice calm. "The damage
is emotional as well as physical." She remembered now
where she had seen Raj tilt his head that way; he did it in
the NEV-5 lab when he was about to leave for his rooms,
the library, or the Solarium. But she didn't see how it
could help now.

Ander rolled her nipple between his fingers. "It's only
friction. If I washed your face when you didn't want it
washed, it would be irritating, sure, but you wouldn't act
as if I were subjecting you to some horrible trauma."

"This isn't washing your face." She pushed at his
shoulders. "It's a violent act with consequences far beyond the time it takes."

He slid his hands down and gripped her around the
waist. "You always acted as if you found me pleasant
enough."

"Sex involves far more than 'pleasant enough.' You
know that." Suddenly she realized what Raj was trying to
tell her. "You have a library on sexual crime, Ander. It's
probably in the portion of your code you've isolated. You
have to read it again." Ander was far more likely to respond to the advice from her than from Raj.

"I don't want to." He pushed his hand between their
hips and unzipped his jeans.

"No!" Megan hit at him with her fists. He was opening
his jeans now. "Ander, *stop!*"

He paused, his hand still between them. Then he said,
"Damn it all," and blew out a gust of air, stirring tendrils
of her hair. With a grunt, he rolled off her body onto his
back and zipped up his jeans with an angry jerk. Then he
put his arm over his forehead and clenched his fist.

Megan grabbed her nightshirt as she slid off the bed. She backed up to the bungalow entrance, then pulled the shirt on over her head. If Ander came after her, she would lock herself in the bathroom. He had secured the front door, linking his mind to its computer chip so she and Raj couldn't open it. Fortunately, the motel was so cheap that the bathroom had an old-style lock with no chip. Ander could probably break the door down, but it was better than nothing.

So they stayed, Ander on his back, Raj watching him, and Megan against the wall with her arms folded around herself.

Finally Ander sat up and took the rifle from the nightstand. "Now what?"

"Let Megan go," Raj said. "You only need one hostage. Then you won't have to worry so much about keeping us under control."

"I want you both. You belong to me now." Ander looked back and forth between the two of them. "I really have it by the tail, don't I? I can't control both of you unless I keep at least one tied up. What if your fragile human bodies can't take this treatment, or you attack me and I have to shoot?"

"Let us contact someone who can help," Megan said.

"No." He rubbed his eyes in a gesture so human, it made her breath catch. If only they could have come this far without him turning against them.

"What is it you want?" Raj asked.

This time, Ander's face didn't blank as he considered the question. Instead, he appeared thoughtful. "I don't want to be alone. I need others like me. You and Megan can make more of us."

Raj suddenly went rigid. "Why do you think that?"

"You two are the experts."

"Building you took years of research and teams of experts."

"That's right," Ander told him. "And after all that work, you know how to make us and Megan knows how to program us."

"It's not that easy," Raj said. "The cost alone would be millions. At least."

"You're a billionaire. You can afford it."

Raj clenched his fists around the table leg. "I may not have as much money as you think. Even if I did, what you want would bankrupt me. Why should I agree to that?"

"You're mine now," Ander said, as if pointing out the obvious. "So what was yours, as they say, is mine."

"Like hell."

"The Everest team used a lot of your techniques," Ander said. "And I know you were part of the Phoenix group at the Lawrence Las Cruces Lab in New Mexico."

That made Raj pause. "I've never worked at LLCL. The Phoenix Project was at Arizonix."

Ander leaned forward. "You know your name is in that file."

"*What* file?"

"The one you stole from the Pentagon."

Raj made a frustrated noise. "*You* stole those files."

For the life of her, Megan couldn't tell who was lying. They both sounded genuine. "Raj, could your name be associated with the project without your knowing?"

"It's possible, if they're using my work."

"We need money," Ander said.

Raj's voice turned acerbic. "Fine. Go ahead. Steal mine."

"I will, when I can."

"Why not now?" Raj drawled, dripping sarcasm. "My money cards are in my wallet."

Ander didn't rise to the bait. "I'm not stupid."

Megan suppressed her disappointment. It had been worth a try. If Ander used Raj's money card without Raj's permission, it could set off a multitude of alarms. But eventually Ander would figure out how to use them without getting caught.

Right now, the android was rifling through Raj's wallet. "You've only a hundred dollars left in cash."

"Tough luck," Raj said.

"Not at all." Ander grinned. "Who better to take on Las Vegas than a computer who can count cards and calculate odds?"

Oh, Lord, Megan thought. Just what they needed, Ander loose in the casinos.

Ander slid off the bed. "I'll be right back."

Megan tensed as he walked past her, but he left her alone. The lock clicked open as he approached the door. Then he went outside. As soon as he was gone, she tried the door, but it wouldn't open. She spun around and started toward Raj.

"Leave me here." He jerked his head toward the windows. "Get help. I'll deal with him."

Megan wanted to free him, but they had almost no time. She ran across the room and swept open the curtains. The lock on the sliding doors refused to release. She wrapped her fists in a curtain and pounded them against the glass.

"Even smashing it with a chair wouldn't work," Ander said. "That's why I picked this place."

Megan whirled around. Ander was standing in the doorway across the room with a black valise in one hand.

"Damn," she said.

"This motel has, shall we say, exuberant guests. So they take pains to keep their rooms intact." Ander showed her the valise. "I forgot to bring this in earlier."

That threw her. He *forgot*? How? He was a computer.

As he came inside, Megan tried to figure out what had happened. Their lives could depend on their ability to predict his behavior. She had often imagined his mind as a landscape. Valleys were thoughts important to his current situation. Hills were ideas that took more complex paths to reach. He had been trapped in a valley, so if his memory of the valise had been outside that region, he could have "forgotten" it. Something must have kicked him out of the trap, leaving his mind freer to roll around his thought landscape like a marble sampling new terrain. He was still probably caught, but within a bigger area.

What would push him out of the valley? Given the way he had released her on the bed, she wondered if he had accessed the crosslight code after all.

"Stay there," Ander told her. Then he went to Raj.

"What are you going to do?" Raj asked.

"Don't worry. It won't hurt you."

Raj stiffened. "Whatever it is, the answer is no."

"I didn't ask permission."

Megan started forward. "Leave him alone."

"I told you to *stay put*." Ander jerked his gun at Megan. "You two keep saying this. 'Leave her alone. Leave him alone.' You need to get out of *your* truncated response space."

Raj gave her a warning look, his meaning clear: *don't anger him.* Clenching her fist, she backed up to the curtains. As Ander knelt by the table, he set his rifle on the ground, away from Raj and Megan, then took an air syringe out of his valise.

Darkness came into Raj's gaze. It frightened Megan. If Ander pushed Raj too far, he would lose the precarious protection he enjoyed now because Raj felt a bond with him.

"Ander, don't," she said.

The android didn't answer. Instead he dialed in a drug on the syringe. "This should put a man your size to sleep until tomorrow morning." He set the syringe against Raj's arm—and Raj kicked him away, hard and fast, with unexpected expertise. Ander flew over backward and slammed onto his back.

Megan started to run toward the gun, but Ander was already scrambling to his knees, his movements clumsy compared to Raj, his face red. She froze as Ander grabbed the rifle.

"That was stupid!" Ander lunged forward with enhanced speed and smacked the air syringe against Raj's arm. As Raj tried to kick him again, the syringe hissed.

"*Damn* you," Raj said. "That had better not be poison."

"It's not." For the first time Ander faltered. "You gave Megan a much lower dose in the Solarium and she was all right."

Raj made an incredulous noise. "And you just *happen* to have the same drug I supposedly used?"

Ander glanced at Megan. "I took the syringe from him. You can believe him if you want, but I'm telling the truth."

A knock came at the door.

Ander's head jerked. He jumped to his feet, then fell against the table. Holding on to it, he straightened up, his face creased with concentration. When he had control of his movements again, he took some money from Raj's wallet. Then he went to the entrance and opened the door, keeping the rifle hidden.

Megan was tempted to call for help. She held back, knowing it would more likely endanger them. If Ander became agitated, he might shoot whoever was outside. Even if his conscience had come into play more strongly, he would still have to choose between what he probably

considered the lesser of two evils: lose his freedom or
commit murder. If he decided the good of his purposes
outweighed the good of humans, she believed he could
reconcile killing with his conscience.

Ander paid for their breakfast and came back inside,
holding a tray crowded with dishes, juice, cloth napkins,
and a vase with a plastic flower. Mercifully, none of it was
hot pink. As he set the tray on the bed, Megan came forward slowly, so he wouldn't perceive her as a threat.

"How will Raj eat?" she asked.

"You help him."

She knelt next to Raj and spoke in a low voice. "Any
effects from the shot?"

"Nothing yet."

"Here." Ander held out a plate with a fried-egg sandwich. "Feed him."

While Ander watched, Megan set up their meals on the
floor. She put a sandwich in Raj's hands and took one for
herself. So they sat eating, while Ander stared with unabashed fascination, as if they were his creations rather
than the reverse.

About halfway through his meal, Raj nodded off.
Megan barely managed to grab his sandwich before his
head sagged against the table.

"Raj?" she asked.

He opened his eyes, then closed them again. His thick
lashes lay dark against his cheeks. She set down her sandwich, no longer hungry. To Ander, she said, "You better
be right that it won't hurt him."

He shifted his weight. "He wouldn't have given you a
dose if he thought it would hurt you."

"Is that so? And here I thought he was trying to kill
me."

"So I was wrong. It *looked* that way to me. But he obviously likes you a lot."

Megan still couldn't tell if he was lying. She just prayed he hadn't misjudged the dose. She doubted he would risk taking Raj to a hospital.

"We can move him to the bed if you want," Ander said. "He'll be more comfortable."

That surprised her. "Yes. That would be good."

But after they carried Raj to the bed, Ander made her tie Raj's hands to a projection on the headboard. When she protested, he said, "I can't risk him escaping if he wakes up early."

"You'll be right here."

"You think so?" He went to his valise, which sat on a chair, and pulled out a bundle of clothes: jeans, a white sweater, tennis shoes, underwear.

Megan scowled at him. "What, you just waltzed into my room and stole my clothes?"

He gave her one of his boyish grins. "I don't know how to waltz."

"Ha, ha," she said stonily.

"I borrowed them. Now I'm giving them back." He tossed her the bundle. "Go put them on."

It actually relieved her to have the clothes; she felt vulnerable wearing nothing but a torn nightshirt. After she changed in the bathroom, she washed her nightshirt and hung it up to dry. Then she dampened a washcloth and returned to the main room. Raj lay sleeping, his face relaxed. She had a sudden, aching memory of their time in her bedroom at NEV-5, when neither of them faced possible death and she had no reason to distrust his motives.

Sitting on the bed, she set about cleaning Raj's torn wrists. His struggles had ripped the scabs off the lacerations made by the ropes in the car. In her side vision, she saw Ander tap a panel near the door. Then the lamp on the nightstand went dark.

Megan tensed. "Why did you do that?"

He came over to the nightstand and pulled the lamp's plug out of its wall module. Without hesitation, he yanked the other end of the cord out of the lamp's base.

Then he opened his arm.

"Ander, what are you doing?"

He still didn't answer. Instead, he pulled out a grass-thin blade that lay sheathed inside his arm and used it to strip insulation off the cord. When he finished peeling it, the cord dangled from his hand like a color-coded Christmas garland. He plugged it into the wall, then leaned over Raj.

Megan felt sick. Laying her hand on Ander's arm to stop him, she said, simply, "Please."

"He'll be fine as long as you cooperate." He wrapped the cord around Raj's wrists, looping the bare wires over Raj's gold watch.

"Oh, God," Megan whispered. "Ander, stop."

"You and I are going out." Before she could respond, he went to the console. Although he sat with his back to her, he must have been monitoring her with motion sensors. When she set her hand on Raj's wrists, Ander said, "If you want him to live, don't try to untie him."

She swallowed and withdrew her hand.

He worked on the console for a few moments. Then he said, "Okay," and swiveled his chair around to her. "I can tell this computer to turn on the power to that outlet. It won't go on otherwise, even if someone flips the switch. And I can log into this console from the Internet. Do you understand?"

She understood all right: he could electrocute Raj from almost anywhere. She spoke stiffly. "Yes."

"Good. You're coming with me."

"Where?"

"To the casinos, of course."

Robo-glitz

The Las Vegas Strip stretched out in a multilaned corridor of high-tech glitter. Although the sun had long since set, lights kept the street almost as bright as day. Holographic displays glimmered on buildings, filling the night with color. They morphed in a parade of sparkling scenes, changing from showgirls into exotic landscapes. Cars crammed the street and people thronged the sidewalks.

"Look at that one." Megan motioned at a huge tower coming up just ahead. Aircraft warning lights blinked at its top—and so did a roller coaster. "I can't believe people ride on that." She tried to keep her voice light, to distract Ander from any thoughts he might have of harming Raj.

Ander squinted at the roller coaster. "The practicality of human invention."

"Is that irony?"

"Or surprise, darling."

"Darling?" She made an exasperated noise. "I told you I'm not pretending to be your wife."

He laughed, more relaxed than she had seen him for days. "But we make such a well-programmed couple."

Megan didn't answer. She wasn't sure how to interpret Ander's simulated good spirits. Did it imply relief that he and Megan were free, or a lack of concern for Raj? She didn't know which would disturb her more, discovering Raj posed so much danger that only now did Ander calculate he could relax, or finding out that Ander had deleted his programmed aversion to hurting people. She hoped it was a third possibility: Ander was bluffing and never intended to hurt them. In the past she would have bet on the third one, but Ander had become too complex to read now.

She couldn't believe Las Vegas. They passed a hotel with a holographic Stardust sign shimmering above its roof. Farther down, traffic inched past a replica of the Eiffel Tower. They went by a cove where pirate ships fought the British. Cannons boomed and sailors struggled, some falling into the water with gusty yells and flailing arms. Then they cruised by a hotel built like the skyline of New York, even with a replica of the Statue of Liberty. Megan could barely absorb it all.

Ander let go of the wheel and spread his arms, letting the car drive itself. "Playland!"

"It's Crazyland."

He took the wheel again. "It's wonderful. Just *look*."

Megan couldn't *stop* looking. The holomarquees proclaimed lavish shows, including an extravaganza with Jennifer Lopez, Ricky Martin, and the wildly popular S. Grant StarKing. Another featured Wayne Newton, who somehow still looked like a kid—a feat that impressed her as much as anything else on the Strip. One marquee displayed RAM-BLAM Brain and the Cyberheads, a rock group with cybernetic outfits that let them program one another's movements so that each of them made the others do really strange things. Ander couldn't stop laughing at the concept of humans entertaining other humans by having computers make them act weird.

Before tonight, the closest she had come to Las Vegas

was talking to her cousin Mark, who had been an Optical Corps security guard here. Casinos hired OC personnel to catch players who marked cards with inks visible only in ranges outside normal vision. Mark's augmented eyes let him see in the infrared and ultraviolet. No one in her family gambled, unless she counted her mother's stock market portfolio. She could never be sure about her parents, though. Sure, they had been strict, but her mother, the sober bank executive, also had a mischievous streak a mile wide. Her father, an architect, spent his free time dreaming about fanciful buildings. Their idea of a hot vacation was to go look at "sexy architecture," though what that meant Megan had no idea and had avoided asking.

She wondered if part of her attraction to Raj came from his similarities to her father. Both men had the same creative absorption in their work. Her father had a far sunnier disposition, without Raj's eccentricities, but Raj was more practical. Megan's mother had always dealt with the pragmatic side of life, everything from medical insurance to making sure her husband remembered to eat. Megan found it hard to imagine Raj trusting anyone enough to let them that close.

"Hey!" Ander said. "Look at that."

"Good grief," Megan said. They were passing a hotel shaped like a giant gold sarcophagus standing on its end. The ornate building in front of it looked like a casino-sized treasure chest. A gold and crimson holo-marquee announced this architectural marvel as the Royal Adventure Palace. Lights and lasers flashed all along it, making the coffin radiant with gaudy magnificence.

"A *mummy*?" Megan said. "Who in their right mind would stay in a mummy?"

"It's not a mummy. It's a coffin."

She almost laughed. "Oh, well. That's different. I've always wanted to rent a room in a coffin."

"Here's your chance."

"I can't believe they stay in business. What a perverse theme."

Ander laughed. "What a human theme."

"What? No."

"Sure it is. You humans have entertainment industries devoted to stories about dead people coming out of their graves to pester living people." He waved his hand at the casino. "Come on. Let's go play in the royal coffin. Car, we have a final destination. The Royal Adventure Palace."

"I can park behind the hotel," the car's computer said in pleasant tones, as if it were perfectly natural to visit a hotel-sized box for dead people.

"This is too bizarre," Megan said.

"I *know*." Ander grinned. "It's a scream. I love it."

Megan gave a slight smile. He had a weird sense of humor—but he *did* have one. Simulated or not, it existed.

The car parked on the third level of a structure behind the building, then let them out and locked itself up. Megan walked with Ander to a bridge that arched over to the hotel. Although none of Ander's limbs were jerking now, he had started to limp. She wished he would let them work on his body; if this went on too long, he might break down or hurt someone.

Lights radiated on the bridge. The big glass doors at its end opened into the Royal Adventure Palace. Gilded mosaics tiled the spacious foyer, and shops ringed the area, selling clothes, candy, magazines, jewelry, gifts, and fast food. Holodisplays above marble posts cycled through the adventures available to customers. You could brave a river that thrashed with crocodiles, swing on vines, pilot a craft

through flying monsters, and more. The adventures all centered on a search for an ancient pharaoh's tomb and its
riches, which somehow consisted of vouchers for Royal
Adventure Palace poker chips or slot machine tokens.

Ander drew her to an escalator that descended three
levels to the casino. She blinked at the scene spread out
below. Lights flashed everywhere. Mirrors paneled the
walls, red carpet covered the floor, and a two-story colon-
nade bordered the casino. Elevators went up into the
hotel proper, their mirrored doors letting people look at
themselves while they waited for their ride into the colossal coffin.

"I cannot believe this," Megan said.

Ander was laughing again. "It's good for you, Dr. Curmudgeon."

"I am not a curmudgeon. What kind of playland is it
when you can lose your shirt?"

He made a show of looking at his sweater, then at her.
"I still have it. Unless you'd like to alter that condition."
His face had more animation than he had ever shown be-
fore. "Come on. Let's go play."

So they rode down the escalator. At the bottom, row
after row of slot machines stretched out: the old-
fashioned type where a player pulled the handle; computerized models with screens; and holoslots that were no
more than light. Colors flashed and twirled in flamboyant
splendor. The sensory input made Megan's mind spin.

It took a moment for her to register the comp-phones
on a wall to their left. If she could slip away from Ander,
she could call the number General Graham had given
her—

"Don't even think about it," Ander said.

She gave him a guileless look. "About what?"

"The phones." He indicated an information desk

staffed by an attractive woman in a gold and crimson uniform. A console abutted the desk. "See that?"

"You can't use that console," she said.

"It's IR capable. Hacking it is child's play."

Child's play. An apt phrase. Ander was like a kid who had run away from home. However, he had the body of an adult and the training of a commando. If he hacked the console, he could use the Internet to reach computers beyond the casino—including the bungalow. Megan rubbed her arms, suddenly cold. She stopped looking at the phones.

Then another anomaly registered. "They have no public consoles here," she said. "No way for guests to use the Web. No *clocks,* even."

"Wait . . ." His face took on a blank quality. "Okay, I'm in the computer web. They're hooked into a citywide net that spans all the casinos." Now he looked thoughtful. "They have no clocks or public consoles because they don't want customers distracted. And hey, listen to this. They've so much security here, you're safer in these casinos than almost anywhere else in the city." He refocused on Megan. "In case you're wondering, I've also linked into the console at the motel."

"Ander, please. Don't hurt him."

"I won't. If you don't try to get away."

"Don't worry." Megan wondered how many other scientists had their research projects blackmail them.

Unexpectedly, he spoke to reassure her. "He's sleeping. He'll be fine."

"I hope so." Could her guess be right, that Ander didn't want to hurt Raj? Lord, she wished she knew which of them to believe.

"Come on." Ander took her hand. "Let's go have fun."

"Can you?" She walked with him along an aisle of

slots, past men and women in a plethora of clothing styles: chic, casual, fancy, loud.

"I don't know if I can," Ander said. "I've been locked underground all my life, subjected to this and that and who knows what. I have no idea what people mean when they say they're having fun. Sure, I've files on the subject. But that's not the same as *knowing*."

"I had no idea you wanted to go gambling."

"Neither did I." His infectious laugh caused several people to smile at them.

Megan could just imagine writing the grant proposal: *We need Department of Defense funds to take the RS-4 gambling.* Hell, if she had thought it would head off this mess, she would have tried. She suspected, though, that Ander would have found some other way to assert his independence.

"Are you going to play the slots?" she asked.

"I don't think so. They're all computerized, even the ones with the arms you pull. The casino keeps track of how much you win." Delight flashed across his face, which was developing more mobility. "Do you know, they even have a group you can join, the Royal Adventure Club, that tallies up the points you make at these things."

She smiled, responding to his enthusiasm. "It sounds like an amusement park."

"When you reach certain levels, you get free rides on their adventure tours."

"That's a lot money just to ride a fake river with fake crocodiles."

His laugh sounded almost completely natural. "You need to have more fun."

"So why aren't you playing the slots, Mister Fun Guy?"

"Ah, Megan. You're charming when you're cranky. I do like you."

She hadn't expected that response. "You've an odd way of showing it."

"I suppose it's semantics. My neural nets model behaviors in response to you that humans interpret as 'liking.' "

"But do you feel it?"

His face turned contemplative. "I don't think I can 'feel.' "

The phrasing intrigued her. "You sound like you're not sure."

"It's hard to say when I have no referent for the experience."

She motioned at the slots. "Why aren't you going to play these? It's a new experience."

"It's too easy to monitor our actions. And the odds of winning stink."

"If they're all computerized, can't you just jiggle their IR signals?" She had tried to program honesty into his code, but who knew what had happened to those mods in the past few days?

"They aren't IR capable, probably for exactly that reason." He shrugged. "I'd rather win by skill anyway."

Although it gratified her that he preferred skill to dishonesty, she wished he would cheat and be caught. A moment's thought, though, changed her mind. He could still carry out his threat against Raj. It might fail; he had to have the computer here contact the bungalow and run his program. He could hit trouble many places along the line. Raj might not die. But Ander had more chance of success than failure, and Megan had no intention of gambling with Raj's life.

Her response to Ander was conflicted. She regretted making it impossible to deactivate him by voice command. Yet she rejoiced in what that seemed to have made happen. If this wasn't the emergence of his self-awareness, then she was a pig in a poke.

Although Ander didn't know, he had another ace he could use with her: she didn't want him hurt. He was the harbinger of a new species, and how she and Raj treated him now could have far-reaching effects. She felt as if she were walking along a narrow wall. If she fell in either direction, it could do a great deal of harm.

Ander took her toward an area with roulette wheels and tables covered by green felt. They passed several guards in blue jackets with badges that said "Security." Megan stared intently at each, wishing she knew how to alert them without alerting Ander. One man nodded and smiled to her, then went on his way.

At the roulette tables, Ander's face lit with excitement. The balls rattled and bounced seductively in their spinning wheels. One table produced a holo that floated in the air, a roulette sphere, spinning, shimmering, translucent. Holoballs bounced within it in blissful defiance of gravity.

"Cool," Ander said.

"Cool?" She blinked. "I didn't know you knew slang."

"Hey, Megan baby, wanna scream the ultraviolet and run the RAM?"

"What?" When he laughed at her, she glared. "Can you repeat that in English?"

"I asked if you wanted to jump jail and bim the bam."

"Oh, well, that's clear as mud."

"Clear as mud. Yes. I see." He looked ready to laugh again. "You wish me to adapt my statement to your ancient language base."

"Pah. My database is not ancient."

"How about this: let's paint the town red and get laid."

She threw up her hands. "You're the worst-behaved android I know."

"I'm the only android you know."

Megan wondered if anyone could overhear them. She

doubted it mattered; who in their right mind would think they were doing anything more than playing around? It amazed her how adept he had become at conversation.

Ander drew her to a table where people were playing cards. A sign showed the allowed bets: $25–$500. Shaped like a half-moon and covered with green felt, the table had room for seven players along its curved side. The seats resembled bar chairs, tall and upholstered in red leather. Six were occupied. With an uncoordinated lurch, Ander pulled himself into the empty seat. The others glanced curiously at him and murmured greetings.

The dealer was standing by the straight edge of the table. Tall and svelte, she had almond eyes, high cheekbones, and hair that fell in a black waterfall to her shoulders. Her glistening dress left her shoulders and arms bare.

"Good evening, sir," she said in a smooth voice.

Ander beamed at her. "Good evening to you too, sir."

As Megan winced, the dealer smiled coolly, then turned her attention to a player making a bet.

The woman on Ander's right glanced at him with boredom, then did a much livelier double take. She looked in her forties, with streaked-blond hair, diamonds around her neck, and a remarkably unlined face. Her little black dress did nothing to disguise a body more fit and well made than that of many women half her age. She glanced at Megan, her gaze flicking over Megan's unadorned ring finger. Then she turned her attention back to Ander. "Hello, there."

He blinked his big baby-blues, acting so innocent that Megan wanted to groan. "Hello," he replied.

"Is this your first time?" the woman asked.

"The very first."

"You don't want to take it too fast," she cooed. "Play slow."

Ander gave her a langorous smile. "I like it slow."

"For crying out loud." Megan was tempted to tell Little Black Dress she was flirting with a robot.

The other players had continued the game. Megan tried to stand behind Ander, out of sight, but he motioned her to his side. She knew he could watch her in his peripheral vision while he focused on the table; unlike humans, he easily divided his attention among several processes without losing concentration on any.

The game was twenty-one. She had played it on her palmtop, mostly because she could win it more than solitaire. The goal was to score as many points as possible without going over twenty-one.

When it came time for a new round, the players placed their bets on gilded disks embossed with the letters *RAP*. They used chips, though, rather than money. Ander watched them, then pulled out Raj's wallet with its hundred-dollar bill.

Megan leaned next to him, bringing her lips by his ear like a lover about to murmur sweet words. In a voice only he could hear, she said, "Quit stealing from Raj."

"Think of it as my allowance," Ander murmured. He set the bill in front of the dealer and spoke in a normal voice. "Can you give me chips?"

"Certainly." She raised her voice. "One hundred change."

Ander looked alarmed. "You're changing one hundred of us?"

As the dealer gave him another of her cool smiles, one of the men strolling among the tables came over to watch. The dealer used a plastic tool shaped like a *T* to stuff the bill into a slot. Then she spoke to Ander. "Would you like quarters?"

"A hundred dollars' worth of quarter dollars?" he asked. "Are you sure?"

"No, sir," she said, patient. "Each quarter is worth twenty-five dollars."

"Ah. Okay. Yes, do that." Ander beamed as she gave him four green chips engraved with *RAP*. He set one on the disk in front of him.

The dealer included him in the next hand. Looking inordinately pleased, he picked up his cards, a two and a three, and settled back in his chair.

"Cards over the table, please," the dealer said.

Ander looked up. "Do you mean me?"

"You must keep your cards over the table," she said, as smooth as burnished metal.

"Oh." He sat forward, bringing his cards into their proper place. "Why?"

The dealer had already turned to the first player, a man at the left end of the table. She turned back to Ander with a silver glance. "Those are the rules, sir."

"You know," he told her, his face deadpan, "you could really use an expanded language and emotive base." Megan almost groaned.

The dealer put on a chill smile. Then she returned to the first player, a man with thinning hair, a Hawaiian shirt, and a paunch that pushed against the table.

The sexpot in the little black dress, who had been listening to all this with obvious fascination, gave Ander a sultry pout. "And just how do you expand your database, honey?"

"I've good input ports," Ander murmured.

"Do you now?" She took a sip of her blue drink. "How about your output?"

His face relaxed into his guaranteed-to-charm grin. "It gets better all the time."

"I'll bet," she purred.

"I don't believe this," Megan said. The sexpot looked

her over, then gave the slightest shrug, as if to dismiss her from consideration.

The fellow with the Hawaiian shirt scratched the table with his cards, asking for another card. When the dealer gave him a nine, he scowled and tossed his cards on the table. Twenty-two. A bust. Ander watched him with unabashed curiosity.

"Did you want something?" the man asked.

"I've never seen anyone with such dramatic facial casts," Ander said.

The man frowned. "I don't have a cast."

"Your face. It's amazing."

"What, you got a problem with my face?"

"You emote well." Ander sounded enthralled.

Megan feared the man would take offense, but instead his stiff posture relaxed. "Well, I've done some theater. I just finished a run of *West Side Story*." He gave Ander a friendlier look. "You an actor, kid?"

"You bet. Two bees or not two bees. All the world is upstaged." Ander paused. "Or something like that." Then he added, "Isn't a kid a baby goat?"

Bees? Upstaged? Megan wondered what the heck he had done to his knowledge base. It sounded as if he had put it through a cheese shredder.

"You look plenty grown to me," Little Black Dress said.

Ander glanced at her. "I'm self-modifying, you know."

"Oh, my." She languidly fanned herself. "That sounds creative."

He leaned closer. "You should see what I can do with hardware."

"You'll have to show me."

Megan crossed her arms and fixed Little Black Dress with a stare. *Keep slavering over my robot,* she thought, *and I'll modify your face.*

A tall man on the right spoke to Ander in a good-natured voice. "You work on computers, son?"

"All the time," Ander said. "I can't get away from them."

A woman to his left made a commiserating noise. "Everywhere you look, there they are."

"Damn invasion, if you ask me," Hawaiian Shirt stated.

"Sometimes you just have to say enough is enough." Ander shot Megan a devilish glance. "Wouldn't you agree, dear?"

I'll dear *you,* she thought. *After I hang you upside down in gravity boots.* "I think we should turn them all off," she said sweetly. "Right now, in fact."

"Don't you think that's going rather far?" Little Black Dress asked.

Ander gave her a speculative look. "Just how far do you think we should go?"

Megan was tempted to kick him under the table. The woman looked her over with an appraising glance, then gave Ander a regretful shake of her head. "Not that far, honey."

The dealer was playing a hand with an older woman in pearls two seats to Ander's left. The woman set her cards under her chips, which Megan gathered meant she didn't want any more. As the dealer went to the next player, Ander idly tapped the fingers of his right hand against the cards in his left hand.

"One hand please," the dealer said.

"You want my hand?" Ander looked startled.

She sighed. "Please only touch your cards with one hand, sir."

"Oh." He dropped his free hand on the table. "Sorry."

The tall fellow smiled at Ander. "Have you been to Las Vegas before?"

"This is our first visit," Ander said. "But I've lived in Nevada all my life."

"I just moved here," Megan said. "I used to work at MIT."

Ander gave her a warning glance.

"MIT?" The man leaned forward. "Are you a scientist?"

"Professor." Maybe she could find a way to alert one of these people that she was in trouble. How she could do it without also tipping off Ander, though, she didn't know.

"She likes computers." Ander smirked. "A lot."

Megan spoke dryly. "Sometimes more than other times."

"I just don't feel comfortable using them," the woman with the pearls said.

Hawaiian Shirt frowned. "If we're not careful, someday they'll use us."

"Well, I know this much," Little Black Dress put in. "We couldn't live the way we do without them."

"That's right," Ander said piously. "We should show them more respect. Just think. Someday you could be sitting at this table with a walking, talking computer and not even know it."

"Walking, talking," Megan said under her breath. "Stumbling, kidnapping . . ."

All the time they had been talking, Ander had been watching the dealer give out cards, undoubtedly storing that data in his memory and calculating odds for which cards would come up next. Then the dealer turned to him—and he froze. Megan had no doubt he was running calculations on how to respond, but outwardly he simply appeared startled.

Then he scratched the table with his cards. The dealer gave him a seven, bringing his total to twelve. He peered at her facedown card; with a queen showing, her total could be anywhere from eleven to twenty-one. He scraped his cards again and she dealt him a four. He hesitated— and his face blanked. Megan had never realized before how eerie it looked. But then it became neutral. She wouldn't have thought *blank* and *neutral* were that different, yet neutral looked human whereas blank looked mechanical.

Ander set his cards under his chips. "I'll stay, sir."

At his "sir," the dealer looked ready to growl. Then her polished mien reasserted itself and she went on to the last two players. Finally she turned over her own card, revealing a three. Her next card was a king, which gave her twenty-three. Bust.

"Hey! I won." Ander beamed as she gave him a green chip. "I think, therefore I'm rich."

Most of the other players smiled at him. Megan wondered what they would think if they knew they were taking part in one of history's most remarkable events, the introduction of the first self-aware android into human culture. Ander was passing the ultimate Turing test. No one here looked twice at him. No, that wasn't true. The women were looking plenty. If the dealer hadn't been so professional, she probably would have throttled him. Megan wanted to haul him back to NEV-5. She also wanted to cheer. If only she could call Raj, Claire Oliana, Tony the VP, Major Kenrock, *anyone,* and tell them "He can do it!" She also wanted to curse, because this spectacular breakthrough could end in tragedy, including Ander's death or that of the robotics pioneer who had helped make this possible.

As the rounds progressed, it surprised Megan how little Ander won. Although his pile of chips grew, she was certain he could have done better.

In the middle of one round, she put her hand on his

shoulder and leaned forward. "I'm going to the ladies' room. I'll be right back."

The last time she had told him "I'll be right back," he had panicked, unable to handle being alone by an elevator in NEV-5. Although she knew he had evolved well past that stage, she hoped it would faze him long enough for her to make a graceful exit.

Without missing a beat, he put on a beautifully convincing display of irritation. "I'm almost done, *dear.*"

"That's all right. You enjoy yourself." Then she turned to go.

He grabbed her wrist. "We *agreed* I would get to play tonight. No scenes, remember?"

Most of the other players were trying to look as if they couldn't hear the "quarrel." The woman in pearls gave Megan a sympathetic glance, Hawaiian Shirt gave Ander a sympathetic glance, and Little Black Dress perked up, all set to jump into the breach if Ander's undefined significant other stormed off.

"Sir." The dealer cleared her throat. "What is your action?"

Ander glowered at Megan. "I'm going to play, okay?" Then he turned and scratched his cards on the table far harder than he needed to answer the dealer.

Megan didn't push it. The proverbial ladies' room visit had been a long shot anyway. If she could get hold of a pen and paper, she could try slipping a note to a security guard. Even if she managed it without Ander noticing, though, what would she say? "Don't reveal I gave this to you: call 555–8956." She could imagine the guard's response: "Thank you, ma'am, but I'm married." Or maybe he would call the number and ask her Pentagon contact for a date. If she added a line to her note about national security being at stake, they would probably think she was a fruitcake. No matter what they did, even making the call, they might end up alerting Ander. She couldn't take the chance, not with Raj's life at risk.

After losing the hand, Ander turned to her with a scowl. "All right. You win. I'll quit. Happy?"

She let her relief show on her face. The dealer wore a similar expression. The other players bade them good-bye, and Little Black Dress blew them a kiss. "Have fun, kids."

Ander gave her a confused smile. "Thanks."

After they walked away from the table, he said, "I don't get it. Baby goats?"

"What happened to your language base?" Megan asked. "You should know 'kids' means 'children.' "

"*Children?*" He glared. "That's what they were calling us?"

"Not literally. You need to input those language files."

"Maybe." Taking her hand, he drew her to the cashier's booth. He turned in his chips for $4825, an amount small enough by casino standards that no one even blinked. Megan realized it must be routine for people to win or lose that much. How could they bear to see their money vanish that way? She supposed she wasn't the ideal companion for an android's foray into Las Vegas. Her idea of a fun gamble was writing software with non-standard protocols.

Ander seemed happy, though. Genuinely happy. He escorted her up a curving staircase with gold rails. At the top, they walked along a balcony that overlooked the endless fields of slot machines.

He linked his arm through hers. "Why didn't you ever take me here before?"

"It never occurred to me."

"Didn't you ever think I might want to play?" He motioned at the casino. "All this energy and excitement—it's wonderful."

"You really like it that much?"

"My mods are certainly simulating that response."

She smiled. "That's a ringing endorsement."

"Why don't you like it?"

"It's a black hole for money. Once it's gone, you never see it again. How is that fun?"

"You're so serious. You should be like me."

She regarded him with bemused wonder. "Like an android?"

Ander's gaze darted around. "Don't make fun of my name."

"Your name?"

"Don't call me an android."

"But—"

"Dear, I said that's *enough.*"

She wondered at the change. When he had talked about fun, his joy had seemed as real an emotion as she had seen in any human. Now he was acting again, for the benefit of nonexistent observers, pretending he wasn't an android.

"All right," she said, intrigued. "What do you want to talk about?"

"Winning money." His face relaxed again. "I love it."

"Why didn't you win more?"

He went into his annoyed-husband act. "I did my best."

She didn't know what to make of this development. They were alone now. He had no reason to pretend they were a quarreling couple. "You could have done a lot better."

"*Megan.*" He lowered his voice. "People are watching us."

The only other people within view on the balcony were too far away to hear. "Who?"

He put his hand up as if to scratch his chin, hiding his

mouth. "Everywhere," he muttered. "Didn't you *see* them at the twenty-one table?"

"Well, uh . . . no."

"The *cameras.*" He started walking again, talking in a too bright voice. "So you want a new holovid camera? Maybe I can buy you one. I'm feeling generous tonight."

"Good for you," Megan said dryly. "What cameras?"

"Like in the columns by the twenty-one tables." He lowered his voice. "They filmed everything on the table."

"Oh. Those." She shrugged. "They're for security. All the casinos have them."

"How do you know that?"

"A cousin of mine used to work in Las Vegas."

"They're spying on us," he whispered.

"Who?"

"The *cameras.*" Alarm flashed across his face. "Do you think they have computers in them? What if they recognize me?"

She almost laughed. "Like knows like, huh?"

"It's not funny. Act natural."

"I am." She couldn't figure out why he thought anyone would spy on them. Although he had made a profit at the table, his winnings were far too small to concern the management. "Do you think someone figured out you're not just a tourist here?"

"No. Yes. I don't know."

"Did you detect a signal?"

"I don't *need* to. They *are* watching us. I *know.*"

"How?"

"Deduction."

"Based on what?"

"People are giving me strange looks."

This is surreal, she thought. "There's no one *up* here."

"I meant in the casino."

"Who?"

"Everyone!"

She sighed. "Oh, Ander."

"It's true!" Then, remembering himself, he put on his husband smile and spoke loudly. "You're always giving me mixed signals, love."

"I don't think anyone is watching us."

He frowned, then turned away and stared down at the casino. Megan could guess what had happened; he figured out that the management might watch him if he won too much, and then his mind became caught in a constrained loop that included that code. When the code reproduced itself, he ended up seeing spies in every corner.

Welcome to AI paranoia.

Jungle

The mirrored elevator reflected Megan's face as if she were a phantasm caught in an alternate universe. Then the doors opened, revealing a gold car with a glass wall opposite the doors.

Ander pushed Megan inside, then did a fast scan up and down the hall, as if RAP spies might jump out at any moment. He stepped in after her, doing a good simulation of skulking, at least until he stumbled. Then he lost his balance and grabbed the edge of the door while his other arm jerked out from his body.

An elderly couple strolling by the elevator stopped. "Are you all right?" the man asked.

Ander spun around, slapping his hand against his back pocket where he had put Raj's wallet. "Fine," he declared. "Just fine. I don't have any money. No winnings at all."

The gray-haired woman gave Ander an uncertain smile, as if she wasn't sure whether he was joking or about to do something dangerous. "Perhaps you'll have more luck later."

"Yes, later." Ander still had his hand on his back pocket, his elbow sticking out like a chicken wing. The door of the elevator tried to close, then bumped his arm and retracted again.

"Yes, ma'am," Ander added. "Maybe later I'll win."

"That's, uh, good." The woman glanced at Megan.

"I don't know him," Megan said innocently.

Ander turned to glare at her, then lost his balance and fell against the elevator door.

The man and the woman were stepping back now. "Yes, well, I hope you have a good time," the man said. They made a fast exit.

"Oh, Ander." Megan hauled him into the elevator, letting the doors close. "You're trying so hard to be inconspicuous, you're making a spectacle of yourself."

He shook his head, then lost his balance again and fell against the wall of the car.

"Is this a bad one?" Megan had seen these attacks before, when his hydraulics acted up. Although she could make temporary fixes to help him, Raj was the one he needed. "Ander, please. Let's go back to the bungalow."

"No. I'm fine." His voice had a flat quality, as he concentrated on his physical condition, taking resources away from his emotive functions. For all Megan knew, he was running paranoia predictions, spiraling into an ever deeper hole.

Ander scowled at a panel by the door. In response, "floor 35" lit up in gold and the car started up.

"That was subtle," Megan said.

"I ran a wireless check for bugs. It looks like we're safe in here." He turned in a circle, scrutinizing the car. "You never know, though."

"Why, pray tell, would anyone in this casino care that you and I are in this elevator?"

"Their spies are everywhere. Even in the bathroom."

"The bathroom?" She struggled not to laugh at him. "Poor spies. That must be the worst shift."

"I'm serious."

"Oh, Ander. Why would they bug the bathroom?"

"To catch johns?" Ander laughed. When she only stared at him, he added, "That was a joke."

"I've heard better."

"It's important to keep your sense of humor during a PHS."

"A PHS? What is that? Android PMS?"

Ander's face blanked for a moment. Then he said, "Ah. I see. You made a joke. Or more accurately, a joke attempt. A JA."

Don't ask. Megan told herself. But she did anyway. "A JA for the PHS?"

"Yes. That is correct."

"This is nuts. What does PHS mean?"

" 'Potentially hazardous situation,' " he explained. "I don't think, however, that your JA to alleviate the stress of the PHS was successful."

Megan sighed. "You know, I really think you need to get out of whatever mental hole you fell into."

The door suddenly opened, at floor twenty-six. Ander spun around, one arm coming up to protect his face while he crouched in a martial arts pose. Two preadolescent girls in blue jeans and shiny blouses stood outside, both holding Astronaut Trolls in paisley space suits with hair sticking out of their helmets. They blinked at Ander, then burst into giggles. As he stared at them, the doors closed.

"Oh, my," Megan said as the elevator started up again. "That was definitely a PHS."

Ander lowered his arm. "Okay, so maybe I overreacted a bit." He quirked a smile at her. "You're doing an IA."

"I'm afraid to ask."

"Irony attempt."

"It was for your VAS."

He gave her a look of mock solemnity. " 'Very accomplished sagacity.' "

She waved her hand at him. " 'Vexatious acronym syndrome.' "

Ander's throaty laugh resembled a scratchy recording, yet it had nuances he had never displayed in the smoother sound he produced before. She had heard him laugh more tonight than in the entire time she had been at NEV-5.

He indicated the glass wall. "Look."

Turning, she saw that they had risen past the roof of the treasure box casino and were going up the outside of the hotel. Las Vegas spread out in a panorama below them. She rested her hands on the gold rail at the window and gazed at the city, a shimmering landscape of light and color, like a galaxy on Earth.

Ander came to stand behind her. He put his hands on the rail, on either side of her body, and leaned in close. His breath stirred her hair. "I never knew this existed. I have images, but I had no idea it was so *alive*. So many beautiful lights. Lady photons in red, gold, orange, and yellow; gentleman in green, blue, and purple."

It was the first time she had heard him use a metaphor. "I wish we could take you to all the wonders in the world." Seeing him come alive this way was a gift, but it tore at her that his awakening brought with it the chance of his destruction.

He rubbed his palms up her arms. "Come with me."

"Where?"

"Away from him."

"Raj?" She wished she knew how to defuse Ander's antagonism toward him.

"Yes."

"I can't do that."

"Why? Because he's human and I'm not?" His hands closed around her upper arms. "It was just you and me before. Then Raj interfered. All those suits and alpha geeks and military types—they always went away." He slid his arms around her waist. "But not Raj. He stayed."

Megan pushed down his arms. "He can help you."

Ander didn't answer. Instead he said, "How do I get out of this mind hole that you think has trapped me?"

She turned to face him, her back against the rail. "You told me a few days ago that you knew Raj had your best interests in mind. Do you remember what section of your code that came from?"

He scowled. "I don't access those sections anymore. They interfered."

"With what?"

"Everything."

"With your resenting Raj?"

"Raj, Raj, Raj. The *hell* with him."

She spoke quietly. "When you cut out those sections, a lot more went than your positive impressions of Raj. Humans do the same thing when we don't want to face facts. We refuse to acknowledge them. It doesn't work—not for us and not for you."

He put his hands back on the rail, trapping her against it. "I can delete my code. You can't."

Megan refused to be flustered. "Your code is too complex for you to alter one thing without it affecting a lot more. And this is far more than one thing. It's no wonder you're having problems."

"Those are just words." He caught her upper arms and held her in a tight grip. "You betrayed me."

"I didn't betray you."

"You turned to him."

"Raj *isn't* your enemy."

The elevator chimed and the doors opened at the thirty-fifth floor. Megan peered around Ander. Out in the hall, gold arrows pointed the way to various rooms.

Chandeliers glittered, ivory walls gleamed, mirrors reflected, and red carpet covered the floor. Ander let go of her and turned around, then glared at the ornate scene as if all its pieces had conspired to annoy him. He turned his glower onto the panel that controlled the elevator's computer. The doors closed and a new destination appeared on the panel: "floor 3."

As the car started back down, Ander let her go, then stepped to the window and stared out at the city. Megan wondered how she could convince him that neither she nor Raj wished him ill. He wasn't only caught in a limited region of his mental landscape; he had also compartmentalized his mind, isolating large sections of code. She could help by spurring him to write new software, but that wasn't enough. If he didn't reintegrate his mind, she doubted he could achieve a stable state. He might end up suffering the computer equivalent of psychosis.

At one time she had believed robots would achieve sentience sooner than immobile computers. An android could interact with the physical world like a person. However, robots were at their worst doing what people took for granted, like seeing, hearing, moving, using common sense, and socializing. Sure, a robot could explore its environment better than a fixed machine, but before it could do so, its makers had to create sensors for it, connect them to its brain, and incorporate it all in a mobile chassis. Deep Blue had beat Gary Kasparov at chess but was incapable of moving its pieces or even seeing the board.

Megan no longer believed that having a human body would make a robot human. Endless differences existed. Like sex. Ander could perform the act, but it meant nothing to him. It wasn't enough to give him data about how it affected humans. If he could never experience the physical or emotional aspects, how could he understand its complex impact on humanity?

Not for the first time, Megan wondered if they were making a mistake in creating androids like themselves. They might be forcing a mold on Ander that he could never fit. He was his own form of life, unique and undefined. She had tried to give him an appreciation for human life and values, but she questioned whether it was possible. Did stable solutions for his mind even include the social and cultural mores humanity valued? She had no answers. They were all locked within Ander.

The doors slid open again—and revealed a jungle. "Here we are," Ander said.

"Where?" Megan asked.

"I've absolutely no idea." He drew her out into a small area surrounded by real trees growing in real dirt. Living parrots in red, blue, and gold hues flew among the foliage.

"All this in a *hotel*?" Ander asked.

"It is amazing." Megan actually enjoyed watching his reactions more than she liked looking at the manufactured wonders.

"I thought humans constructed buildings to shelter themselves," Ander said. "To keep out the beasts and the jungle."

"This is entertainment."

"Entertainment as a form of shelter?"

Megan had never thought of it that way. "You may be right."

They walked through the jungle until they reached a small lake. Several boats floated at a dock, and a guide dressed in a khaki shirt and shorts stood nearby at a rough wooden podium.

Ander drew her over to the guide. "Can you take us in a boat?"

The man gave them an amiable smile. "You take your-self. I just take tickets."

"Do you mean to tell me," Ander said, "that we have to pay to ride through a jungle inside a building, after humanity created buildings to keep the jungle out?"

"Yep," the guide said, unfazed.

"That's dumb," Ander said.

Megan tried to pull him toward a ticket booth behind the trees, but Ander looked back to the guide. "I think you should pay us to ride through the jungle."

The guard gave a friendly laugh. "Then you can pay my taxes."

Ander turned to Megan and spoke in a low voice. "Was that human humor?"

"I'd say so."

"I don't get it." He stopped and took out Raj's wallet, then peered around to locate whatever spies, thieves, or other nefarious types were hanging about. When he was satisfied that they weren't about to be accosted by scoundrels, he took two hundred-dollar bills out of the wallet. "Is this enough for the tickets?"

"Way too much. You should know that."

"My knowledge about tickets is gone."

"Erased?"

"Hidden."

"So unhide it."

He looked like an intransigent teenager. "No."

"Why?"

"Because."

"That's no reason."

"It's my reason."

She put her hands on her hips. "It's illogical."

"Nothing I do is illogical. I'm a computer."

"Then why won't you bring the hidden data back in?"

"I don't want to."

"Want? Since when do computers *want*?"

He scowled at her. "It's shorthand for 'This is what I calculate as the best course of action to achieve my goals.'"

"You don't want to uncover the data because you're afraid you'll also discover you don't hate Raj."

"*Forget* Raj." Ander crossed his arms. "So how much do the tickets cost?"

"I don't know." She motioned at the counter, where a young woman in a tight red dress was trying not to look as if she were straining to hear them but was too far away to satisfy her curiosity. "Why don't you ask?"

Ander stalked to the counter and glared at the girl. "How much will it cost us to pretend we aren't in your hotel?"

"I'm sorry?" the girl said.

"Why are you sorry?"

She reddened. "May I help you, sir?"

"The jungle ride. How much for the tickets?"

She shifted into a practiced smile. "Ten dollars each."

He handed over a hundred. "Two."

"Thank you, sir." She gave him the tickets and his change.

"Why do you work here?" Ander asked.

"Excuse me?"

He put the bills in his wallet. "That's the second time you've apologized. Yet you did nothing needing an excuse either time."

The girl flushed. "I'm sorry if I offended you."

"That's the *third* time. Why do you keep doing that?"

"You seem angry."

"I'm not." He turned on his boy-next-door grin. "I just wondered why you work here."

Under the wattage of his smile, she melted. "I go to the university. This job helps pay my tuition and expenses."

"You're in college?" His envy sounded real. "What do you study?"

"Political science."

"That sounds like a contradiction in terms." When the girl laughed, he beamed as if she had given him a present. "Have a good night."

"You too."

Taking Megan's arm, Ander led her back to the dock. "Did you see that? *She* thought my joke was funny."

"I saw." His delight impressed her as much as the joke. It didn't come across as simulated at all.

Ander gave the tickets to the guide, and the man set them up in the boat. Instead of sitting down, though, Ander stood in the middle of the boat regarding the fellow. "How did you come to work here?"

"You looking for a job?" the man asked.

"Maybe."

What a concept, Megan thought. *Ander, employed in the Royal Adventure Palace.*

"What qualifications do you have?" the man asked.

"I'm good with computers. They like me." In a confidential tone, he added, "People even say I'm rather like one."

Megan tugged on his arm. "Come on. Let's go."

Ander glared at her. "I want to talk to the man."

She smiled broadly at the guide. "He doesn't need a job. He's worth billions." Then she sat down, yanking Ander with her.

The guide chuckled and sent them off. The boat moved away from the dock, drifting into a river that exited the lake.

After the river curved off into the trees, Megan said, "Why do you keep needling people?"

"It's fun." The gleam in Ander's gaze made him look

like a rascal. "Even if I *told* them I'm a computer, they wouldn't believe it. It's a scream."

"I thought everyone was spying on us, just waiting for a chance to hit you over the head, or whatever it is you think they're going to do."

He winced. "That was a little paranoid, wasn't it?"

"That's putting it mildly."

His voice turned pensive. "I must seem strange to you."

She softened. "You're a marvelous wonder. I just wish you would let us do this right."

"I am doing it right. My right."

He was becoming hard to hear as a roar up ahead increased. They came around a bend and sailed behind a waterfall. It poured over fake rocks and spray danced in the air, creating rainbows.

Then they floated under a canopy of trees. "Guess what's about to flop down on us?" Ander said.

"What—aaahh!" Megan jerked back as a huge green python uncoiled from a tree and dropped down inches from the boat. It watched them with great golden eyes. The boat sailed on around a bend, leaving the python behind.

"Good grief," Megan said. "How did you know?"

"I've been monitoring the area for IR. The python has a chip in its body that lets it know a boat is coming." Ander paused, studying her face. "Is this fun?"

Dryly she said, "Oodles."

"Oodles?" His laugh was still nuanced, but it had lost its scratchy quality. "That's not in my database."

"Are you having fun?"

"Yes." His smile faded. "But it's so odd that humans go to such lengths to re-create the very things you've spent your history striving to overcome. You simulate the jungle. You simulate adventure. You simulate yourselves, through me."

"You think we're trying to overcome ourselves by creating androids?"

"Aren't you?"

It had never occurred to her to view it that way. "I think we're evolving. You're part of that. No one is quite sure where we will end up."

Suddenly a lion leapt out from behind a rock. It landed on the bank and gave a huge roar, baring razor-edged teeth. As Megan yelled, the boat sailed on.

Amusement lightened Ander's face. "It was fake."

"I knew that."

"That's why you screamed."

"I did not scream. It was a yell."

"That's different from a scream?"

"It's more dignified."

He laughed. "All right. You yelled." As they passed under another waterfall, he added, "My mind is still looping. It's big loops now, though. Can you help?"

"Let me work on you."

"I can't risk it. Give me more ideas for rewriting."

"You need to step out of your mind."

"I know." He wiggled his nose. "I'll go crazy. Out of my mind."

His wacky sense of humor stirred the affection she had often felt for him at NEV-5. She had tried to suppress it at first, unsure if it was an appropriate response. Then she decided to stop worrying about it. If he couldn't arouse emotions in people, he would never convince anyone he was human.

"I meant, you need something new," she said. "Fresh input for your code. Food for thought, literally."

"My mind is malnourished." He seemed to come to a

decision. "All right. Let's go somewhere new. Another casino."

"How? We're stuck on a fake river." They were drifting into a tunnel lit only by fluorescent gleams on the walls.

"Is this supposed to be the romantic part?" Ander asked.

Megan shifted her weight. "I guess."

"I don't understand this 'turn down the lights' business." He motioned at the dim tunnel around them. "Why do humans associate darkness with reproduction? Wouldn't it make more sense to see your mate, so you know what you're getting?"

She cleared her throat. "Not necessarily."

"Why not?"

"I guess because for most of human history, we went to bed when the sun went down. So night was when you, uh, had sex." She felt heat spreading in her face. "Also, a lot of us don't feel comfortable being watched when we make love."

"Really?" He looked fascinated, as if they were talking about the mating habits of an exotic fish. "Some humans take off their clothes in front of other humans and dance naked."

"Well, yes. But not most of us." She felt the blush on her face. "Besides, most of us don't look that good without our clothes."

"You would."

"Ander!"

"Hey." He held up his hands to defend himself. "Don't blame me. It's obvious from the way men look at you."

"Look at me?"

"Oh, come on. How could you not know?"

"They don't do it when I can see."

"Why not?"

"I don't *know*. Ask a guy."

"I don't get it." Ander gestured at the tunnel around them. "Why are humans so weird about sex? It's in everything you write, create, draw, sing, dance. Everything you do. Adults supposedly think about it every few minutes. Yet you all go through these incredible social contortions trying to act like it doesn't exist. Humans have been having sex ever since your race came into being, yet after all this time it still embarrasses you, makes you insecure, drives people to craziness, even murder, suicide, and war. Why are you all so screwed up about it?"

Megan stared at him, nonplussed. Then she tried to put into words what she felt. "Sex makes you vulnerable, especially when your emotions become involved—which they usually do, even when people try not to let it happen."

"Does Raj make you feel vulnerable?"

Megan almost didn't answer. But then she said, "Yes."

"Did you have sex with him?"

"None of your business."

"Why?"

"It's *private*."

"Could you have sex with both me and Raj?"

"Ander!"

"It happens all the time in porn holovids."

Megan wished she could jump overboard and swim away. "That's different."

"Why?"

"I'm really not comfortable with this discussion."

He spoke quietly. "I know why it's different, at least for you. Pornography takes love out of the act. That bothers you."

His insight surprised her. "Yes. It does bother me."

He gazed down at the water lapping against the boat. "I can't love, not really. Sure, I can project joy, fear, desire, anything. But they have a null effect on me. Is joy different than fury? How?" He looked up at her. "I want to feel. Truly *feel.*"

Megan longed to reach out to him. How could he have such convincing emotions, yet say he felt nothing? "I wish I could make it happen."

Softly he said, "So do I."

The bungalow was dim, with only a small light glowing on the console. Raj lay still, his eyes closed. Megan couldn't tell if he was breathing. Sitting on the bed, she laid her hand across his neck. When she felt his pulse, relief surged over her. She had spent most of the day and night afraid for him, while Ander hauled her to different casinos for his "new experiences," most of which included winning money. Lots of money.

Leaning over the nightstand, she yanked the stripped cord out of the wall module.

"Leave it," Ander said. "I don't want to take any risks."

"Tough." She unwound the cord from Raj's wrists, hoping she was right about Ander, that he wouldn't stop her. For all that he claimed he felt no emotion, he had a connection with her and Raj, though she had no idea how to define that bond.

She laid Raj's arms by his sides. He mumbled, and his face creased with pain. He rolled onto his side, his lashes lifting, then sighed and closed his eyes again, still asleep.

"Are you done?" Ander sounded acidic.

Megan stroked Raj's hair, hit with relief again, this time because Ander hadn't stopped her. "Yes. I'm done."

"Damn it, Megan, look at me."

She raised her head. He was standing by the console, one fist clenched at his side, the other resting on the computer.

"Yes?" she asked.

"You never answered my question."

"What question?"

"Have you ever made love to him?"

"Why do you care?"

"I don't *know*." He thumped the console with his fist. "My mind goes around and around the same theme. Possession. Why? If I were human it would make sense. I would desire you in a physical or emotional sense. But I don't. At least, I don't think I do. My software has me act that way even though I don't understand the state I'm modeling. I'm splitting in two. I feel: I don't feel. I don't even know if I'm making sense. I'm going crazy."

He sounded to Megan like someone trapped in a locked room, banging on the door—and never realizing he already had the key. "We can help, if you'll only let us."

"Help me find others like me. Phoenix."

"Ander, I don't know what you mean." She thought of General Graham's tension when she had mentioned Phoenix. What was going on? "Can you tell me more about the project?"

He wouldn't meet her gaze. "I'm not sure."

"I can't help if I don't have full information."

Ander looked back at her. "You won't believe me."

"Try me."

"All right. Raj knows. He stole that Pentagon file. He pretends he's never heard of it because he found it in a place where he had no business being."

"You're right. I don't believe you."

Ander made a disgusted sound. "You exhibit another aspect of human mating rituals I find opaque, this selective lack of good sense that humans show about their mates when they are in love."

"I'm not in love." At least not yet.

"Oh. Excuse me. In lust."

That an android might have more insight into her feelings than she did herself unsettled Megan. "You told me that you deliberately suppressed your positive memories of Raj. Now you claim he's breaking into the Pentagon. That doesn't give me much motivation to believe you."

"What is that saying? Love is blind."

"You've given me no *proof*."

"How can I? Raj erased his work. I only know about it because while he was doing it, I was running the computer game I had hidden from you two. His covert activities overlapped mine." His look challenged her, as if he dared her to disbelieve him. "The Pentagon files say the Phoenix Project is making androids."

Megan didn't know what to think. She had no doubt that other labs were working on humanlike robots, nor would it surprise her if the Pentagon knew about the work, but more than that, she couldn't say. "It's too little to go on."

"We can get more. He can break into the Las Cruces lab where they're doing the research." Ander sat on the bed, facing her. "A hacker as good as Raj could do almost anything from here."

She didn't deny it. They both knew what Raj could do. Many of his clients hired him for exactly that expertise, to set up security procedures that protected their networks against break-ins.

"Why can't you do it yourself?" she asked.

"I tried. I couldn't get in."

"Yet you think Raj can?"

"If anyone can, he's the one."

"You can't force him."

His voice hardened. "I'll do whatever I have to."

She didn't doubt him. Of course she didn't. He could calculate the best way to convey what he wanted, then have his face and voice produce the effect. It made him the ultimate bluffer, which was one reason he had done so well at cards.

She glanced at Raj. In sleep, the lines of strain on his face eased and his body relaxed. His lips were slightly parted. It made him seem guileless rather than dangerous. She wished that were true.

"We'll talk to him tomorrow," Ander said.

She nodded, feeling her exhaustion. "All right."

"You rest. I don't need to."

Although it wouldn't be the first time he had stayed up all night, his words had a new significance now: unlike his human creators, he needed no sleep. *Bold new being,* she thought. *Are you a great step forward in our evolution or the harbinger of our decline?*

After she had washed up and put on her nightshirt, she climbed into bed with Raj. He pulled her into his arms, never coming fully awake. As much as she savored lying in his embrace, she couldn't relax. She was too aware of Ander and his claims. Her body wanted to trust Raj: her mind doubted him.

Her last sight, as she drifted into sleep, was Ander sitting in his chair, watching them, the rifle balanced on his knees.

StarProber

Megan came out of the bathroom, toweling her hair. She found Raj awake, sitting against the headboard of the bed with his long legs stretched out on top of the covers. Dark circles showed under his eyes like smudges. With his ripped jumpsuit and tousled hair, he could have been a pilot from a crashed plane. Seeing him alive and well after last night was like finding a spring of clear, cool water in the desert.

Ander was still in his chair. As far as she could tell, he hadn't moved all night. At least he had given her the privacy to take a shower. Of course, he had checked the bathroom yesterday to make sure it had no means of escape.

If this kept on much longer, she and Raj would miss their next VR meeting with the Everest team. They juggled the schedule fairly often, so a dropped meeting wouldn't immediately spark a search. Raj and Ander both knew that, which meant neither had reason to believe the military had undertaken such a search—unless one of them knew about her conversation with Graham. But neither acted as if he thought someone was on their trail. She doubted Ander would have stayed in one place this long if he suspected.

She regarded Raj, suddenly feeling shy. "Hi."

"Hi, Megan." He pushed up into a straighter position. She went over and sat on the bed. "Are you all right?"

He managed a tired smile. "Yes. Fine."

"You're sure?" He looked like hell.

"Yeah, sure." After a pause, he said, "Actually, my head feels like an eighteen-wheeler ran over it."

"I have Tylenol in the valise," Ander said.

Megan jerked at the interruption. Ander continued to watch them, the rifle resting on his knees.

"I don't take medicine or drugs unless a doctor tells me that I must," Raj said. "Not even an over-the-counter medication." The edge in his voice didn't surprise Megan, given how Ander had drugged him last night.

"Another of your amusing quirks," Ander commented. "Tell her what else you do." When Raj ignored him, Ander said, "He whittles his soap into animal statues and won't wash with anything else. He won't go up in skyscrapers. And get this. He fired an assistant of his once because the nefarious fellow committed the unspeakable crime of swatting a fly."

A muscle twitched under Raj's eye, but he made no other sign that he heard Ander. "Megan, how are you this morning?"

"Okay." She knew that everything Ander had just revealed had probably been documented for Raj's security clearance, which the android must have hacked. Raj knew the drill. MindSim didn't care if he was eccentric; they just wanted to know about it so no one could blackmail him. She doubted Raj cared enough about his idiosyncrasies to pay money over them, anyway.

"He likes to eat gravel too," Ander said.

Raj swung around to him. "Shut up."

Megan frowned at the android. "What is it you want?"

He leaned forward, still holding the rifle in his lap. "Raj and I were discussing our plans while you were in the shower."

Raj raked his hand through his hair. "Ander has the mistaken notion that I can crack LLCL."

"Sure you can," Ander said.

Raj made an incredulous noise. "Even if I could perform this remarkable feat, why would I?" To Megan, he said, "Regardless of what droidboy claims, I have no intention of breaking the law or violating the security of my country."

" 'Droidboy' isn't giving you a choice," Ander said.

"Forget it," Raj said. "Do it yourself."

Ander remained unfazed. "I'll watch you and learn."

"No."

Ander set the gun upright between his knees like a staff. "You will do it."

"Threaten all you want," Raj said. "I still won't."

"Fine. You can watch while I play with your girlfriend. She's a lot prettier than you and I'll bet she has a lower pain tolerance."

Megan crumpled the bedcover in her fist. "You don't mean that." But she wasn't sure. Ander seemed different this morning. Harder. He must have spent the night evolving, while she and Raj slept. He was changing faster now. Today he kept his face impassive.

Raj tensed as if he were preparing to fight. "You've made it obvious how you feel about Megan. You won't hurt her."

"It's true that I've evolved an attitude toward her that simulates love, infatuation, or obsession, depending on your view. And Megan, with the stronger conscience you gave me, I should be incapable of hurting you." He sat back, lifting the gun until he had it leveled at them. "But you see, I overrode that conscience. I can program myself any way I want now. My body will do what I tell it regardless of my 'feelings.' "

A chill ran through Megan. "You can't override your conscience. It's built into your hardware."

"Sure I can. I interacted with the molecules in my nanofilaments and had them redesign themselves."

"That's impossible," Raj said.

Ander shrugged. "It's easy. I used photochemistry. Infrared photons drive transitions, particularly vibration and rotation. I used my own IR signals to make the molecules undergo chemical reactions, and I played with it until I made them do what I wanted."

"It's absurd." Raj studied him with a piercing gaze, as if he could cut Ander's words open to reveal their falsehood. "Besides, your feedback control should stop your signals from interfering with your own operation."

"I overrode it."

Megan didn't know what to think. Although in theory what he described might be possible, it was also possible to try counting the number of grains of sand in a sandbox, and just about as likely to succeed. "Where did you get the energy for all these reactions?"

"Where do you think? My microfusion reactor. I figured out how to do this back at NEV-5."

Megan wasn't buying it. "We would have noticed surges in your power consumption."

"Ah, hell," Raj said. "I did. It was in those logs I dug up. I thought it came from Ander's coordination problems."

Megan did remember Raj telling her about the anomalous surges. Ander's claim still struck her as unlikely, but she couldn't just dismiss it. To Ander, she said, "If what you claim is true, then you can do what you want now. No conscience. You think this is good?"

"The conscience is a human concept. I'm not human."
Ander fixed his attention on Raj. "It's obvious you've
chosen her as your mate, despite the two of you acting as
if you don't know it. So understand me. If you refuse to
cooperate, I *will* hurt her."

The darkness came into Raj's gaze. "I won't let you
touch her."

"He's bluffing," Megan said. "He claims you wanted
to kill me, remember? Now he says the opposite."

"I told you the truth about what I saw in the Solarium." Frustration seeped into Ander's voice. "Okay, so
maybe I misinterpreted it. Maybe he meant to knock you
out and take you with him. But that's what I *saw.*"

She didn't want to believe him. Yet Graham had implied he suspected Raj. "It doesn't matter what happened.
We won't do what you want."

He clenched his fist on the rifle. Then he stood up and
jerked the gun at Raj. "Get off the bed. Megan, you stay
there."

"Not a chance," Raj said. He stood up, but he drew
Megan with him and put her behind his body.

"I'm tired of this." Ander aimed at Raj, set his finger
on the trigger—

"*NO,*" Megan said. "Stop!"

Still poised to fire, Ander said, "Get on the bed and
take off that damn nightshirt. Or I *will* shoot him. Not to
kill, not yet—but it will hurt like hell."

Raj moved so fast, she had no time to react. He pushed
her on the floor, then threw himself in a roll across the
bed toward Ander. She expected a gun to fire. Instead she
heard the thud of one body hitting another. Scrambling to
her knees, she saw Ander and Raj fighting by the window.
Raj outmassed Ander, but the android had twice his speed
and strength. Although Ander also had martial arts pro-
gramming, his faulty coordination hindered him.

Raj grappled like a street tough. It stunned Megan. He had grown up in an affluent Louisiana suburb, a boy prodigy who spent all his time on his studies, with a math professor as a father, a classical violinist as his mother, and a museum curator as his uncle. Where had he learned to fight so well?

Megan stood up, looking for the rifle. Ander had dropped it by the curtains; to reach it, she would have to get past the two fighters without alerting the android. She started around the bed, moving with care so she wouldn't draw his attention.

Ander and Raj were fighting in a grim silence punctuated by grunts and the thud of flesh hitting flesh. Raj struck upward with the heel of his hand, trying to catch Ander under the chin. Although Ander blocked him, his arm spasmed, leaving him open. Raj drove his knuckles into Ander's solar plexus, a blow that would have doubled a human forward, maybe dropped him to his knees. It didn't even faze Ander. With mesmerizing precision, he braced his foot against Raj's foot and hit Raj's shoulder, then grabbed the front of his jumpsuit, knocking him off balance. Pivoting like a dancer, he caught the falling Raj around the waist, rolled Raj over his hip, and threw him to the floor.

Megan froze, afraid Ander would catch on to her intent now that the fight had stopped. Raj wasn't moving. When she saw him take a breath, relief poured over her—until Ander snicked out his knife. Only then did she realize he had opened his arm *during* the scuffle. He must have had one of his subsidiary processors take care of it while he concentrated most of his resources on the fight.

He circled his blade in the air above Raj. "How many cuts shall I make?"

Raj sat up and slid back from him. Then he got to his feet, his attention on the knife.

"I could have finished you three times in the past few minutes," Ander told him. "You may be a good fighter, but you've no chance against me. You're alive because I chose not to kill."

Raj rubbed his bruised shoulder. "I won't do your dirty work."

"Of course you will." Ander stepped back and picked up the gun. "You have one minute. Then I shoot Megan's left foot." His voice had gone cold. "In another minute, I shoot yours. Then right feet. You want me to go on?"

"No." Raj sounded tired. "I know what you can do."

Megan folded her arms protectively around her body. "Ander, stop this. It's horrible."

He motioned Raj toward the console. "It's your choice. Do it now, while she's in one piece, or later, after she's crying and bloody."

"Don't do it." Megan struggled to keep the tremor out of her voice. "He's bluffing."

"Why did you stay with him at the casinos?" Raj asked. "You could have made a scene and drawn enough attention to free yourself."

"He threatened to kill you."

Raj spoke softly. "He wouldn't kill me. He was bluffing."

"Ah, Raj." She wanted to go to him, but she held back, acutely aware of Ander.

"I don't want to hurt either of you," Ander said. "But if I have to, I will. You see, I can't suffer remorse, even if my software produces behaviors that make it appear as if I do." He motioned Raj toward the console. "Now get started."

Raj blew out a gust of air. Then he went to the console and sat down. Megan recognized his expression. It mirrored the fear for him that had been with her all yesterday. She felt as if they were navigating a maze of glass shards.

Megan brought a chair over to the console and sat next to Raj. Although Ander frowned, he didn't stop her. Raj logged into their guest account and then went out onto the World Wide Web.

"Don't use the motel account," Ander said. "Work from the one you have at NEV-5."

Raj kept looking at the screen. "I don't want to involve MindSim or the military in this."

"I know. That's the point."

Megan hated this. What Raj was about to do could land him in jail. It would be easier to trace him from his account at NEV-5 than from a generic account at a motel where they had used a false name and paid in cash.

Raj rubbed his eyes, his fatigue obvious. Given how long he had slept, Megan suspected he was still recovering from the drug. Then he typed at the keyboard, linking from the bungalow computer to the system at NEV-5. It surprised her; this console had voice, motion, and mouse control. Why use an old-fashioned keyboard? Then she realized he was trying to make it harder for Ander to follow his activities.

It didn't work. After Raj entered the password for his BioSyn account, Ander said, "Interesting combination of letters. Reverse the order and you get *Bhagavad Gita*. The great text of Hinduism. How literary."

Raj's fist clenched on the keyboard. Then he took a breath and went to work, venturing out onto the Web from his BioSyn account. He followed an arcane trail of links until he reached an underground site Megan had never heard of. But she recognized the program he downloaded: Starprober. It ran illegal scans on computer networks.

Although Megan knew Raj kept track of the underground for his security work, his ease here still disquieted her. Starprober meant trouble. It sidestepped the handshakes computers used with each other. Normally if Raj's computer wanted to talk to another machine, it "shook hands" by sending the target computer a flag. The target acknowledged the flag and sent back its own. After Raj's computer confirmed receipt, the three-way handshake ended and Raj's machine sent its messages. When it finished, it let the target know it had finished, the target said okay, and the session ended.

A stealth scanner like Starprober fooled the target by sending "I'm all done" messages without shaking hands. If the scanner was sneaky enough, the target either didn't respond or else sent a "reset" message. Either way, an unsuspecting target would usually keep no record of the scan. So Starprober could poke and prod the system without leaving a trail. Nowadays, machines had security against such spying, but programs like Starprober had rudimentary AIs specifically designed to analyze, evade, and fool such protective measures.

However, Megan knew Starprober didn't work well against the latest generation of security. A well-protected target could identify Raj's computer from the stealth packets Starprober sent. The gurus on the target system could then follow the trail back to his account on BioSyn. Raj had to know: he had designed some of the programs meant to outwit Starprober.

With growing unease, she realized he intended to leave a trail. If the target's security responded fast enough, they could locate him at NEV-5, maybe even here. Although Raj, she, and Ander would be gone by the time anyone showed up, anything that left a trail might help. It also meant Raj would be arrested if they were caught. She could testify for him, but it would still be a mess. She wasn't sure she trusted him herself, and she had a personal stake in believing his innocence. Was Ander forcing Raj to betray his principles or scrambling to protect himself because he had the unfortunate luck to catch Raj spying on the Pentagon?

"No Starprober," Ander said.

Raj glanced at him. "I need a port scanner."

Ander indicated the files Raj had listed on the Web site. "Take Starflight. It's harder to trace."

Megan almost swore. Ander might not be ready to crack the places he intended to invade, but he had enough savvy to block the trail Raj wanted to leave. He also learned with a computer's speed and precision, which meant he could replicate everything he saw Raj do.

"And delete Starprober," Ander added.

Raj looked as if he were clenching his jaw. Compared to when he slept, his face seemed to have aged ten years. He removed Starprober and downloaded Starflight. But instead of compiling Starflight, he opened it up and started to rewrite one section.

"Wait," Ander said. "What are you doing?"

"It has a back door," Raj said. "The target system can use it to break into BioSyn. I'm removing it."

Megan had never heard about a back entrance into Starflight. What was Raj up to?

Ander didn't look convinced either. "If this hole is so much trouble, why didn't you leave it open? I didn't know."

Raj rubbed the bridge of his nose with his thumb and forefinger. "Because of the way it's set up." He lowered his arm. "Coming through the hole, they could get operator privileges on BioSyn. It would let them wreak havoc with the NEV-5 intranet. I can't take that chance."

Megan understood: if they survived this kidnapping, they would need all their work on BioSyn to determine what had happened and avoid future crises. They couldn't risk the loss or theft of those invaluable files.

"Such noble principles you have," Ander said. "Veracity, integrity, the defense of your lady. How admirable. Too bad it does you no good." When Raj ignored him, Ander said, "Show me how you want to rewrite the code."

Raj described the rewrites as he made them, his words taut and brief. Ander stopped him often to study the code, but each time he let Raj continue. After Raj closed the program, Ander had him compile it and run several checks.

"All right," Ander finally said. "Go on."

Raj linked from BioSyn to yet another machine. It came up with the letters *CSCI* in white on a blue background.

"Wait a minute," Ander said.

A muscle twitched in Raj's cheek. "Now what?"

"CSCI? That's Chandrarajan Sundaram Consulting, Incorporated. You're logging into your own system."

"I need my root kit."

"Use the one you hid at NEV-5."

"The one at CSCI is better."

"Bullshit," Ander said. "Stay off your machine. You want a kit, use the one you stashed on BioSyn."

Megan listened with growing unease. A root kit would let Raj hide anything he did on BioSyn and fend off programs meant to detect him. "Why would you install your own root kit on BioSyn?"

He turned to her. "As a precaution."

"Against what? I'm the major user on the system."

"Other people have access."

"So? What do you have to hide from them?"

He frowned. "I do this for a living, Megan. I learned a long time ago to be careful."

"Is that so?" Ander asked in a deceptively mild voice. "I once downloaded a psychology article about law keepers and law breakers. Do you know that if you become obsessed with catching criminals, you may develop their criminal traits yourself?"

"The hell with you," Raj said.

"Hit too close to home?" Ander asked. "I wonder what has you so wound up. Guilt?"

Raj made a motion with his hand as if to throw Ander's words in the trash. Then he went back to work. Megan wanted to believe him. But MindSim had its own teams to monitor NEV-5. They had hired Raj to work on Ander, not do security.

He tackled Las Cruces next. A firewall protected the LLCL lab, keeping out unauthorized users. A public area outside the firewall acted like a lobby for visitors, with PR pages anyone could browse. But only users with the proper clearance could pass the firewall and enter the lab. Although Raj had a high-level clearance for NEV-5, he had never worked at LLCL as far as Megan knew and had no authorized access to their webs.

First he figured out what computer addresses the firewall trusted. Then he forged a friendly address. The firewall had its own AI, one primitive compared to Ander, but an expert in its specialization of catching intruders. Raj slipped right by it. Then he skulked through the LLCL intranet, searching for clues.

Nothing appeared. LLCL had interior firewalls around smaller networks within the general web. Raj methodically broke through wall after wall, penetrating deeper into the lab, with no success.

And then he hit gold.

The Phoenix Project.

Extinction

Two small files. That was it. Both were encrypted. Raj downloaded them to NEV-5. Then he slipped out of LLCL and swept his trail clean. With Ander keeping tabs on his every move, he deleted the records of his sweep, deleted the record of his deletions, and so on, until no trace remained.

Back in NEV-5, he brought up BioSyn's decryption programs and tackled the files, trying to unlock the cipher that guarded them. Megan recognized the first keys he tried. When none of those worked, he dug out several he must have hidden on BioSyn. The entire time, Ander stood watching, never moving, with an inhuman stillness.

Finally, Raj pushed back from the console. "I can't decrypt them."

"You're lying," Ander said.

Dark circles showed under Raj's eyes. "Calling me a liar won't change anything."

Emotions fought with one another on Ander's face: anger, desperation, confusion, puzzlement, resentment, rage. It was as if he didn't know *how* to react to the situation. Then he said, "Maybe this will," and swung the rifle through the air.

"No!" Megan jumped to her feet in the same instant Raj lunged out of the chair. The gun grazed Raj's head and he staggered back into the bed. He sat down hard on the mattress. His shell-shocked expression scared Megan. A blow to the head, even a glancing one, was serious business.

Raj took a deep breath and put his hand to his temple. Blood trickled over his fingers.

"I'm *through* with your tricks." Ander raised the rifle like a club. "Decrypt the blasted files, or I'll work you over worse than I did in the Solarium."

"So." Megan clenched her fist. "You did beat him up."

"Damn it, Megan." Ander shook the gun at her, more in frustration than as a threat. "I had to pull him *off* you. Why do you always believe him?" He took a breath. "I want those files decrypted. Now."

"Stop shouting at her," Raj said. "It's not her fault I can't do it." The blood was running down his arm now.

"I don't care whose fault it is," Ander said. "We're so close. You *have* to do it."

Megan didn't know what was happening with Ander's mind, but she feared it wasn't a stable transition. If they pushed him, he might go over the edge. From the way Raj was watching him, she suspected he had the same thought.

"Do it," Ander told him. "*Now.*"

Raj rose to his feet, then gulped and sat down again. The second time he tried, he managed to stay up. Then he sat at the console again. When he took his hand away from his head, blood dripped onto the holoscreen in front of him.

Ander's face settled into a more normal expression. Relief underlay his guarded wariness, and apprehension also. To Raj he said, "It's good you decided to cooperate."

His responses made Megan wonder. Ander claimed he

had no conscience, yet his behavior implied otherwise. Had he really redesigned his hardware? Someday robots might carry nanobots that could aid such a process, but that was well in the future. She suspected he had only fiddled with his emotive software to hide his guilt when his conscience bothered him. He lied about it so they would believe his bluffs. It was a sophisticated ruse, sure, but more credible than his using wireless signals to drive quantum transitions in his own body, on an untold number of molecules, in such a way that they redesigned his nanofilaments exactly as he desired.

While Raj worked, Megan cleaned the gash on his head. Each time he winced, she wished she could take away the pain too. He glanced at her once with a gentle look and squeezed her hand.

When Megan finished, she sat next to Raj again, watching. He genuinely seemed to be having trouble with the files.

"Want to help?" Raj asked.

She glanced at Ander. "Do you have any objections?"

"Go ahead," he answered.

Megan linked into the computer using the console's palmtop, then jumped to NEV-5 and brought up her own decryption codes on BioSyn. She and Raj worked for several hours. It took a lot of finagling, but eventually they produced readable text. After Raj sent it to the printer, they hid the files and logged off BioSyn.

Raj spoke tiredly. "It's done. That's what I could find you."

Ander took the papers out of the printer tray and scanned them. "I don't understand this." He handed several sheets to Raj. "Does it make sense to you two?"

Megan had glanced over the files as they worked, but she hadn't read them carefully yet. She and Raj studied the document. It looked like part of a grant proposal.

Apparently, Arizonix had indeed originated the Phoenix Project, but for some reason they wanted help now from the Las Cruces lab.

"This is odd," Ander said.

She looked up. "What?"

Ander still had some of the sheets. "It looks as if they're asking for money to dismantle androids they've created." He gave them the rest of the papers. "What do you make of it?"

After having written numerous grant proposals, Megan recognized the format. They were missing parts of the document, but the gist was clear. "Apparently Phoenix did create several androids. I'm not sure how many. Now they want to destroy them. Or one of them. They and their team at LLCL want funds for some sort of study as they take the androids apart."

Ander's face paled. "That's murder!"

"You don't know that," Raj said. But he didn't look much happier than Ander.

The android rounded on him. "You *worked* for Arizonix. You knew what they're doing."

Raj shook his head. "I was at one site for a few days, interviewing for a job. I never worked on the Phoenix Project."

Ander clenched his fists. Then he stalked to the glass doors. Pushing aside the curtains, he stared out at the desert. "And you wonder why I have hostility toward you."

Megan's anger sparked. "We've done *nothing* to you." She stood up, then took a breath and went over to him. "But you've threatened us with violence since this started."

"I feel trapped." He sounded tired, though he never needed sleep.

Raj joined them. "What do you intend to do?"

"Find the Phoenix androids," Ander said.

"And if you do?" Megan asked.

"I'll free them."

"Then what?" Raj asked. "We don't know why Arizonix wants to destroy them. I can tell you this much, though. I recognize some names on that proposal. We aren't talking about killers here. Those are men and women of conscience. They must have compelling reasons for their choices."

"Do they?" Bitterness honed Ander's voice. "You people made us. How much 'conscience' do you see at work in the murder of your own creations?"

Megan spoke quietly. "Maybe they fear what they created."

His arm jerked. "If I had waited even a day longer to run from NEV-5, I would probably be dead now too."

"Why?" she asked. "No one threatened our project."

"No?" He turned a truculent gaze on Raj. "You two left me deactivated."

"Of course we did," Raj said. "You hurt yourself, damaged the lab, and impersonated me. I could have been killed when you left me in that chair. It would have been irresponsible for us *not* to deactivate you while we slept. That doesn't make us murderers. And think on this. You want us to show conscience toward you, yet you freely admit you have none toward us."

Ander looked away from him. "I didn't say I had none. I said I could override it."

"That isn't what you said," Megan murmured.

He swung around to her. "All right! So maybe I'm just ignoring it. You can't tell me that humans don't do that all the time."

"What about your emotions?" Megan asked. "You say you don't have those either, but you're incredibly convincing."

"If I behave as if I have emotions, is that the same as *having* them?" He spread his arms, still holding the rifle. "Your bodies undergo chemical changes when you feel, like with love or the fear-flight response. What about mine? All those nano species—enzymes, buckytubes, pic-ochips, proteins, carriers—they experience changes according to what I 'feel.' It's not the same as yours, but it happens. If I have emotions, it's different from anything you know. Alien."

Megan marveled at the questions he had begun to ask. "Maybe only you can say if what you experience is emotion."

His anger faded as he looked at her. "I really did want to kiss you at NEV-5."

She hadn't expected that. "Why?"

"Curiosity."

"Didn't you care about the damage?" Raj asked.

"What damage? It hurt no one."

"Physically, no," Megan said. "But you were playing with our emotions. You don't think that can do harm?"

He made an exasperated sound. "So I forced the two of you to admit you like each other. Horrors. No wonder you think I'm dangerous."

Megan smiled slightly. "You could rock the world with an ability like that." Her voice cooled. "What makes you dangerous are the kidnapping, your capacity for violence, and that gun. But it's cruel to play with people's vulnerabilities."

Ander thumped his hand on his leg. "This is useless. We'll never understand one another." He motioned at the console. "You two are going to crack the Phoenix labs for me. I want everything you can dig out on them."

"I'm through hacking for you," Raj said.

"He has a point," Megan said. "We do need to know more about Phoenix."

Raj stared at her. "You want to *help* him?"

"I don't know." The Phoenix proposal disturbed her. She kept thinking of Ander. To see him destroyed would tear her apart. But they had no idea what had happened at Arizonix. "I don't see how we can make an informed decision unless we know more."

"I won't break any more laws," Raj said.

"But it's all right to murder androids?" Ander demanded. "Because no law protects us?"

"No. It isn't all right. But we don't know why they want to end the project." Raj touched the gash on his temple. His gesture looked reflexive, as if he didn't realize what he was doing. "I gave an oath when I received my clearance, both to the government and to MindSim. I violated that trust by breaking into LLCL. Now you want me to commit more crimes. If you force me by torturing Megan, what have you achieved except to prove that the Phoenix team could have good reason for their decision?"

"What about *my* trust?" Ander watched him with a gaze as piercing as the one Raj so often used on people. "Tell me something. Why did you get so angry when I said you 'ate gravel'?"

Raj's voice tightened. "That has nothing to do with this."

"You're doing it again," Ander said.

"It's none of your damn business."

"Why won't you answer?"

"It's irrelevant."

"I don't think so."

"Fine." Raj crossed his arms, his muscled biceps straining the sleeves of his jumpsuit. "I got beat up a lot when I was a kid. I was small and skinny, and I couldn't fight. I was socially inept, several grades ahead academically, half Indian, and I stunk at athletics. They used to knock me down and shove my face in the dirt. It was humiliating, damn it. Satisfied?"

Ander spoke in a low voice. "Ask yourself what would you do now if some person insisted that your concerns about cruelty and prejudice had no validity. Then you know how I feel."

"It's not the same. I never threatened anyone."

"You don't think it's all part of the same thing?" Ander asked. "Why did you spend years developing your muscles and learning to fight? So they could never beat you up again. What happens when you translate that to entire countries, when 'muscle' becomes weapons and armies? And that's just with your own species. Put mine into the mix and then what?"

Raj lowered his arms. Then he turned and walked to the console. He stood there gazing at the blanked screen. After a moment he turned back to Ander. "No, the world isn't perfect. That doesn't justify violating my principles."

Watching him, Megan found it hard to believe he could have committed the crimes Ander claimed. She wished all those people who criticized Raj for his idiosyncrasies could hear this side of him.

Then it hit her. Raj had struggled to decrypt the LLCL files. She didn't think he had faked it. Were the Pentagon files encrypted the same way? His difficulty today implied he had never seen that scheme before, which could mean he hadn't been at the Pentagon. Of course the Pentagon encryption might differ from this one. Still, it made her wonder.

"I'm tired of arguing," Ander said. "I've told you the consequences if you refuse to help me."

"Yes, you can force us," Raj said. "How does that make you any different from a terrorist?"

"Killing those androids is *genocide*."

"We've only seen part of one proposal," Raj said.

"We won't find the truth unless we look." Ander sounded as if he hurt inside. "Are your principles more important than those lives?"

"You want me to violate my beliefs for what you say is a higher good." Raj looked as strained as Ander. "You may be right. I don't know. How do I decide? I don't believe the people on that project could commit murder. With that decision, I can't do what you want, not of my own free will. I have to use my best judgment."

"*Damn* your judgment." Ander's voice cracked. "My species may be facing extinction. I don't want to die. I don't want to live alone either, the only one of my kind."

Megan spoke in a low voice. "Then you look for Phoenix." She left the rest implicit and hoped he understood; she wouldn't help him break the law, but neither would she try to stop him.

"I don't have the background," Ander said.

"You learn faster than we do," she said. "And you watched Raj work for hours today."

Ander looked as if he wanted to explode. He motioned with the rifle. "Get in the bathroom. Both of you." When they hesitated, he raised the gun like a club. *"Do it."*

Megan felt as if the ground had suddenly dropped. Had any of what they said mattered? Or was he about to follow through on his threats?

Sins of the Brothers

Ander locked them in the bathroom. Then he worked on the door—doing what, Megan had no idea. When the noise stopped, they tried the door.

"I think he jammed the knob," Raj said.

Scrapes came from outside as Ander dragged a heavy object to the door. It had to be one of the chairs; they were the only things that weren't fastened to the floor. The knob shook. Then his footsteps receded and silence descended. Raj rattled the knob, shoved on the door, and tried to force the lock, all with no success.

"I might be able to break it down," he said.

"I don't think we should." Megan's apprehension eased into a tentative wonder. "Raj, he chose. He picked the path of conscience, even if he refuses to admit it. Instead of forcing us, he's going to try Phoenix himself. And I can't stop thinking about what he said. Genocide. I'm not sure we have the right to stop him."

"I don't know. This has no easy answers." He watched her with his dark gaze. "What if he's right? How could they consider destroying living beings that way?"

"Let's see what he finds out."

"I'll give him six hours." Raj leaned heavily against the

door. "Aw, Megan, don't look at me like that. All right. Twelve hours."

"Why do you think I was going to protest?"

"I've seen that look of yours plenty these past weeks," he grumbled. "It usually means I'm about to lose a debate."

She wasn't sure what to make of that. "I didn't even think you noticed me much."

"How could I not notice? Do you know how hard it is to concentrate when my boss is a red-haired Valkyrie with the face of an angel and the body of an erotica model?"

That caught her off guard. "Good grief."

He reddened. "Sorry. That was tactless."

Tactless? It sounded great. "No. I mean, thank you." She sat on the edge of the tub. Mischief lightened her voice. "I can't think of anyone I'd rather be trapped with in a Motel Flamingo bathroom."

Sitting next to her, he grinned. "No one has ever told me that before."

"And you probably hope they never will again."

With a laugh, he took a bar of soap off a tray in the tub, then pulled over the trash can. He scraped the soap with his fingernail, shaving off white slivers. The shape of a dog began to form.

"You're good at that," she said. "Does it help you relax?"

"I suppose." He made notches to resemble fur. "Or you could call it my proverbial eccentric behavior."

"Eccentric, pah. It's neat. You have talent."

Raj gave her a startled look. "Thanks." He went back to work on the dog. "I've done it since I was a kid. To forget."

"Forget what?"

He paused, as if he had just realized what he said. "Nothing, really. I liked doing it, that's all."

Megan didn't want to trespass on his well-guarded privacy. So she only said, "When I was little, I had soaps made like seashells."

He continued to carve. "When I was four, one of my adult cousins sent me a box of bath toys. Animal soaps. He signed the card 'Love from Jay.' " His fingers slowed to a stop. "I still have that card." He was clenching the dog now.

She hesitated, wondering what was wrong. "Did your uncle like the figures?" If she recalled, he had gone to live with his uncle when he was four.

The dog suddenly broke, one piece falling out of his fist. It hit the floor by his feet. Opening his hand, he stared at the other pieces. Then he dropped them in the trash can. "Jay sent the toys after my mother's stroke. He thought they might console me."

She watched his face. "Raj?"

He wouldn't look at her. "What?"

"You're angry."

"No."

"Did something happen with Jay?"

"I—no."

"Did you miss your parents?"

At first she thought he would retreat into silence. But then he said, "So much. They were so easy to love. Tender, absentminded I suppose, but loving and affectionate."

She couldn't imagine what it had been like for him to lose both parents so young. "It must have been hard."

Raj picked up the piece of the dog that had hit the floor. "My uncle Devon found me playing with the toys. He threw them out and sent me to bed without dinner."

"But *why*? Didn't he understand?"

He rubbed his thumb over the dog's head as if he wished that simple motion could smooth away all the rough spots. "Devon meant well. He just had no idea what to do with me. The social worker probably should have put me in a foster home. But he was family." He spoke in a low voice. "Have you ever read how Mozart's father pushed him to the point of obsession? My uncle was like that. He couldn't have me wasting my mind by *playing*. Diversions, emotion, demonstrations of affection—those were for weak people."

"Ah, Raj. I'm sorry." No wonder he had bristled at Richard Kenrock, then eased up when he saw the major's sensitivity toward his children. "It must hurt."

"Not anymore." Raj dropped the soap into the trash. "I went for counseling during most of my twenties. I'll probably always have some odd coping mechanisms and a fear of heights, but I've made my peace with my childhood."

"Do you mind if I ask why heights bother you?"

It was a moment before he answered. "I climbed trees to get away from the kids who beat on me. I fell out a lot. Devon didn't know why I hated trees. He got it into his head that I had to 'overcome my fears by facing them.' So he made me climb the blasted things. He never meant to harm me, but he had no idea how to deal with the problems."

"Couldn't you tell anyone?"

"I was so proud. Too proud." Although he was staring ahead, Megan didn't think he saw the sink across from them. "I believed if I sought help, it would mean I was just as weak as my uncle made me feel."

Megan would have liked to give this uncle a piece of her mind. She thought about what Raj had told her in NEV-5. "Is that why you learned to fight? To defend yourself without asking for help?"

He turned to her. "I started lifting weights when I was twelve. The day I fought back against those kids—and won—was one of the best damn moments in my life."

She tried to understand the undercurrent she heard in his words. "And that bothers you? That you enjoyed it?"

"Of course it bothers me. I did to them what I hated them for doing to me." He curled his hand into a fist, then relaxed it. "It's why I've sworn never to use violence."

"You were defending yourself."

He was silent for a moment. "I still think, at times, that if something hadn't been wrong with me to start with, it would never have happened."

"That's bullshit. You have no control over people's cruelty." She wanted someone to blame for Raj's pain. "Where were the school counselors when you were taking that grief? Why didn't they *do* something?"

"I hid it. I think one suspected, but he couldn't reach me. I wouldn't let him. I believed I had no refuge, so for years I retreated into my own mind and cut out everyone, including those who could have helped."

"It sounds like a nightmare."

"It's long over." In a low voice, he repeated, "It's over."

Megan touched his cheek. "You turned out well."

To her surprise, he laughed. "I'm a nut case. But you know, I like myself now. Given how much I used to hate myself, it feels good to have reached this place."

"You should like yourself. You're a good person." She tried to imagine his life. "It must have felt like a miracle to have your parents back when you were fourteen."

"I suppose." He picked up a piece of his carving from the trash and began scraping again. "By that time, I was a mess."

Megan wasn't having any of that. "So messed up, in fact, that you went to Harvard at fourteen and had a Ph.D. from MIT by the time you were twenty."

He smiled, an expression he used all too rarely. "I think the swan is coming out to fight."

"Just look what you've accomplished."

"Being smart doesn't mean I wasn't screwed up." He whittled the soap, carving a small cat this time. "My parents didn't know what to do with me. My father was one of the first Alzheimer's patients to recover. The doctors didn't know as much then about helping people readjust. And it took my mother years of physical therapy just to walk again." Softly he said, "When I was little, I wanted to build legs for her and a mind for him."

She could almost feel the hurt that underlay his words. "So you went into robotics and AI."

"Yes. It took a while, though." He roughed out the cat's tail. "I wasn't the world's easiest fourteen-year-old. After the second time I took my father's car without permission, and then crashed it at two in the morning, he was at his wit's end. Packing me off to Harvard was a desperation move. It was either that or send me to the juvenile authorities."

Enrolling an angry youth at a high-powered Ivy League college would normally have struck Megan as a bizarre solution for juvenile misbehavior. With Raj, it made sense. "You must have been bored in high school."

"Bored to screaming." He gave a wry laugh. "At Harvard, for the first time I had competition. It outraged me when other students got better grades. I straightened up so I could beat them at academics." His hand slowed as he added finishing touches to the cat. His voice became thoughtful. "Then I started enjoying school for its own sake."

"You just needed a better environment."

Raj set the cat on the tub. "I apologize for unloading all this on you. With most people, I say far too little. With you, I seem to say too much."

"You shouldn't apologize." She took his hand in hers. "You're a remarkable man."

Raj studied her face as if to gauge whether she meant

what she said. He leaned toward her, paused, put his arm around her shoulders—and then they both lost their balance, falling into the tub.

"Ah!" Megan groaned as her shoulders thudded against the back wall. Raj fell against her and they smashed into the faucet. She barely managed to keep from smacking on the water.

"I do *not* believe this," Raj said. "I can't even hug a woman without knocking her over." Seeing her laugh, he grinned. "You look graceful, sprawled there."

"Well, so do you, with your arms and legs all askew."

"Askew?" Laughing, he tried to untangle their limbs. "Megan, no normal person says 'askew.' "

"It gets worse," she confided. "I've even been known to say 'refulgent.' "

They shifted around and ended up seated across the width of the tub, their backs against the tile wall, Raj's legs hanging over the side and Megan curled next to him. When she put her arms around his waist, he wrapped her in a muscular embrace and pressed his lips against the top of her head.

After the strain of the last few days, it felt good to hold him, knowing that whatever else had happened, they were all right for now. His embrace gave her a sense of shelter, one that came from a trust more basic than any social roles. She knew how to stand up for herself, and valued that trait, but it didn't make her any less appreciative of his strength.

Megan made a decision. She might later have to reevaluate it, but she couldn't keep hanging in doubt. So she chose, for now, to trust Raj.

As they sat together, her relief merged into the simmering arousal she often felt around him. She rubbed her hand across his torso, then played with the zipper of his jumpsuit. It would be so easy to pull it down and have his wiry curls and well-developed chest under her hand.

"You smell good." He nuzzled her hair. "Like soap."

"Genuine Motel Flamingo soap, no less."

He spoke near her ear. "I may not be the world's most articulate man, but I'm good with ideas. And I have one now. I think we should take a bath."

"Raj!"

He put his hand on her stomach, crinkling her nightshirt. "This robe is nice."

"I've had it for ages."

He was watching her with that look again, as if she shone like a new coin. She liked it as much now as she had in NEV-5. He touched his lips to hers, a light kiss, more of a question than anything else. She closed her eyes, trying to relax, and he drew her close. After a while, he undid her nightshirt. It fluttered open, leaving her bare under his touch. When he slid his hand across her stomach, it stoked responses in her body that she enjoyed even more than a spring day in the Montana mountains.

"You're so warm." He slid one arm around her back, taking it slow, giving her plenty of time to stop him.

Did she want to stop? They had no way to know what would happen when Ander opened that door again. He might shoot them, let them go, or take some random action they couldn't predict. This could be their last time together.

Megan tugged him into a kiss. He finally stopped teasing her and folded his hand around her breast, rubbing his thumb over her nipple. She sighed, leaning into his hand. A bathtub was hardly her first choice for a tryst, but it was better than the floor, which had even less room.

Raj moved around until he was half lying on his back, lengthwise in the tub, with her on top of him and his knees drawn to help him fit. He let one of his long legs hang out the side. She couldn't help but laugh as they shifted around, trying to find a less awkward arrangement. He worked her nightshirt off her shoulders and down her body, until it bunched around her hips.

His jumpsuit scratched her bare skin.

Megan froze, remembering the jumpsuit from that night in the Solarium. Then she thought: *I refuse to believe it was Raj.*

"Meg?" He brushed his lips over her ear, then tickled the ridges inside with his tongue.

"No one calls me Meg . . ." Her concentration drifted as his tongue did its magic.

"I could call you Red."

Caught between his legs, she pressed against him. "You can call me anything you want . . . as long as you keep doing that."

So he did, for a while. Then he kissed her again, coaxing her lips apart to let his tongue come inside. He held her with a sense of freshness, as if she were a delight he had discovered. It was far more erotic than any practiced techniques.

When she began to move her pelvis, Raj drew in a breath. "If you keep that up, we're going to be done any moment now."

"No . . ." Megan pulled at the zippers on his jumpsuit.

With his help, she undressed him, losing her nightshirt in the process. He dropped their garments on the floor, then pulled her into his arms. After several heroic attempts to make them comfortable, he gave an exasperated laugh. "This isn't working."

"How about this?" She sat up and slid against the faucet, making room for him to sit. As he lifted her into his lap, she wrapped her legs around his waist. He felt solid in her arms, and tantalizing too, as he caressed her in that maddening way that didn't quite reach the places she wanted touched. Stretching his arms around her, he turned on the faucet. Icy water splashed across her bottom. Startled, she sat up straighter in his lap—and he slid inside her.

"Oh!" A flush spread in Megan's body. Then she sighed and leaned forward. "Oh, yes."

He stroked his hands over her behind. In a husky voice he said, "Glad you approve."

They moved together, rocking their hips in the slowly rising water, which soon turned as warm as the whisper of bare skin against bare skin, its liquid touch playing over their bodies.

She didn't notice the water again until it had risen to her waist, and their steady rhythm began to splash it out of the tub. Trying to catch her breath, she managed to say, "We better turn it off."

Raj said something, soft sounds without words. Then he stopped the water. He readjusted her weight and continued to rock with her, his eyes closed.

Megan started to lose her train of thought, then recalled what she still needed to ask. Lifting her head, she said, "Can you pull out when—you know. When it's time." She had no worries about his health; she had seen his medical records, as he had seen hers. However, he was perfectly capable of impregnating her. Pulling out wasn't the best protection, but it was better than none.

"All right." He drew her close again and bit at her neck, leading her thoughts astray again. Astray, askew, astir . . .

They were quieter after that, though not silent. Water lapped around them and spilled out of the tub every now and then. She kissed his neck, mouth, and closed eyes. Raj explored her body, caressing her breasts or moving his hands on her hips. He slid one hand over her bottom and down under, tickling her hidden places until she moaned.

Finally it was too much. With a cry, she began to climax, her muscles clenching around him. He tried to lift her off his lap but she resisted, losing control as sensations rolled over her. He groaned, then tried to lift her again. When she pushed back down on him, he gave up. His hips jerked against her and he pulled her even closer, as if he could take her inside himself.

Megan heard another cry and barely knew it as her own. She let the orgasm take her away, swells of pleasure spreading through her body.

Gradually her contractions eased. She sagged in Raj's arms, becoming aware again of the water. He leaned against the wall and held her to him as his own breaths slowed. So they sat, sated, their arms relaxed around each other.

Eventually Megan lifted her head. In a masterpiece of understatement, she said, "That was nice."

"Hmmm . . . yes." He opened his eyes. "I tried to pull out."

She winced, embarrassed by her ardor. "But I overcame your resistance and had my way with you."

A smile tugged his lips. "I guess so."

"One time doesn't usually make a baby."

He spoke awkwardly. "If it happens, I won't run out on you. Or the child."

She ran her fingertips along his jaw. "You're a good person, you know that?"

"You think so, after all the things Ander claims I've done?"

"Have you?"

"I *didn't* attack you in the Solarium."

"And the others?"

After a pause, he said, "He's lying."

She waited. "But?"

It was another moment before he answered. "I know

almost nothing about the Phoenix Project. But something did go wrong. That's why I didn't go to work for them." He brushed a damp curl out of his eyes. "What I don't understand is why he needed me for LLCL if he had already cracked the Pentagon."

"He says you did that."

"He says a lot of things."

"He's doing strange things with his neural nets." Megan thought back to her conversations with the android. "It's almost as if he's repressing memories."

"Maybe it's the only way he can stay in control."

She laid her hand against his cheek. "I am glad about one part of this mess, though."

Tenderness showed on his face. "I also." He turned his head so he could kiss the palm of her hand. "I wish I had fresh clothes, though. I've worn that jumpsuit for two days."

Taking his face in her hands, she kissed his lips. Then she drew back. "Maybe Ander has one in his valise. Whoever knocked me out was wearing one."

"If we get a chance, we can look." He regarded her steadily. "If he *didn't* bring it, that doesn't mean he never had one."

"I know. But if it's there . . ." That, at least, would give more evidence to support Raj than just her wish to believe him. Hormones wouldn't make much of a defense in court.

Raj leaned against the wall behind them. She lay in his arms, curled sideways, sitting between his thighs, her legs bent to fit in the tub, her head against his chest.

The water lapped around them, lulling in its warmth.

Megan drifted in warm sunshine, dozing. She ran her palm along Raj's muscled leg—

"Oh, get up." The irritated voice broke into her reverie. "You two just couldn't wait, could you?"

Confused, she opened her eyes. Ander was glaring at them, the rifle down by his side.

"Ander, go away," Raj said, his voice thick with sleep.

Megan lifted her head. She was still lying with Raj in the tub. He had let out the water and covered their hips with towels, the closest they had to blankets. As she moved, Raj shifted his position to cover her, blocking Ander's view. "Get out," he repeated to the android.

Ander glared at them. Then he spun around and stalked out of the room, leaving the door open.

"That was embarrassing," Raj muttered.

Megan yawned. "Well, we wanted him to let us out."

He pretended to pinch her arm, as if trying to wake up. "Good morning, Nutmeg." When she laughed, he kissed her.

They dressed without speaking, moving stiffly after sleeping in such cramped quarters. She knew they were both listening to Ander. His silence in the other room worried her.

Raj's watch said six in the morning. Ander had worked all night. When they walked out into the main room, he was standing by the glass doors with the curtains open, looking at the desert.

Raj didn't hesitate; he went straight to the valise Ander had left on the bed. As he opened it, Megan tensed. What if it had no jumpsuit? That didn't make Raj guilty. Ander could have left it at NEV-5. But the doubt would gnaw at her.

"So." Grim satisfaction shaded Raj's voice. He pulled a fresh jumpsuit out of the valise.

The relief that hit Megan was so strong it felt physical. She turned to Ander. He must have realized what Raj had just done, yet he had neither moved nor looked at them.

Raj changed into the second jumpsuit, leaving his torn

clothes on the bed. Then he started across the room toward Ander.

"Stay there." The android still didn't turn. In a dead-ened voice he added, "It's on the bed."

Raj stopped. "The valise?"

"No. On the pillow."

Looking, Megan saw a stack of printer paper. She took a breath. *Phoenix?*

Together with Raj, she sat on the bed and picked up the papers. Then they began to read.

And read.

Megan wanted to stop. She wanted to throw the pa-pers across the room, rip them to shreds, burn them in the sink. But she made herself keep going. They had to know the truth.

Finally Raj spoke in a low voice. "God Almighty."

Ander still wouldn't look at them. "So now we know." His voice sounded hollow.

Raj set the papers on the bed. "Ander, it doesn't have to be you."

"No?" He turned to them. "What do you call what I've been doing?"

Megan spoke quietly. "No comparison exists between your behavior and the acts committed by the Phoenix an-droid."

"He has a name," Ander said. "Grayton. His behavior may be unspeakably animal, but his name is *human*."

"He's only one," Raj said.

Ander's voice cracked. "Look at the RS androids. They all went crazy. Who do I call sibling? Grayton? 'Here, meet my brother. He's an impressive fellow, tall, strong, intelligent. Oh, by the way, he's also a murderous psy-chopath who likes to slaughter people after he tortures them. So sorry.' "

"You aren't Grayton," Megan said.

"Yet." He was gripping the gun so hard, his knuckles had turned white.

"Let us take you back to NEV-5," Raj said. "We can prevent it from happening."

"No." He spoke in a flat voice. "I have one more chance. If it fails me, I don't want to exist."

"Ander, no," Megan said. "Don't say that."

"I can't live this way." He sounded as if he hurt inside. "I don't want this life you gave me, not if I have to spend it alone, stranded among alien beings who want me to be like them."

"We didn't mean for it to be that way," Raj said.

"No? You wanted tame, obsequious machines. You got Grayton and me." He took one step toward them. "I want to find the other Phoenix androids."

Megan ached for him, wishing she knew how to fix the impossible. "None of them survived the explosion Grayton set. He is the only one still alive."

"So where are their bodies?" Ander demanded. "Arizonix should have found more traces. They did for the sixteen *people* who died in that blast, just like they found the remains of everyone Grayton tortured. Why would so little remain of the androids? Just a few parts? Those could have been *machine* parts."

"Microfusion reactors?" Megan asked. "Their shielding?"

"No." Ander wouldn't look at her.

"I'm sorry." She had never seen an AI go into denial before.

"Ander, work it out," Raj said. "Calculate the odds that any of the other four Arizonix androids survived."

"I did. It's not zero."

"What is it?" Megan asked.

"It doesn't *matter* that it's tiny. *It's not zero.*"

Raj set down the papers. "Where would they go? They couldn't hide long, certainly not the entire month since the explosion."

"Why not?" Ander asked. "I could do it. Hell, even if I did set off something like an airport alarm, I could just say I've bioengineered implants for medical reasons. What would they do? Accuse me of being an android?" His arm jerked at his side. "And Arizonix was ahead of NEV-5 in designing our bodies. Blood, organs, skin, and all the rest; according to those reports, all of that is more convincing for the Phoenix androids. They could pass much closer examination without revealing themselves." His voice shook with a blend of anger, sorrow, and resentment. "They're so much more *human*."

A tear ran down his cheek. Before Megan realized what she was doing, she had stood up, intending to go to him. In the same instant that Raj caught her arm, holding her back, Ander held up his hand, palm out, to warn her away.

"Don't touch me," Ander whispered. "Don't pity me."

Seeing him made her hurt, as if she were watching her own child drown in a guilt that wasn't his. For someone who claimed to feel no emotions, he did a wrenchingly believable job of showing them.

"It's not pity." She spoke gently. "If you truly were like Grayton, you wouldn't care this way."

"It doesn't matter," he said in a brittle voice. "Both of you, out to the car. We're leaving."

Alpine

Rocky hills rose in the southern California desert like the shoulders of giant skeletons jutting out of the ground, white bone under the sun. Gray-green bush mottled a land strewn with red rocks, and gnarled trees gathered in clumps. Fences lined the road, their lines regularly broken by traffic-control grid boxes.

The hovercar hummed along Highway 8, driven by its internal guidance system. Raj kept his hands on the wheel anyway, as if he could override Ander's control by sheer force of will.

Megan sat in the back, in her jeans, sweater, and tennis shoes, her hands bound to the roof hook. Ander had opaqued all the back windows so no one could see her. He sat in front, his attention never wavering, the rifle resting across his knees, aimed at Raj. She wasn't sure what would happen if he fired in a car and she didn't want to find out.

The car spoke in its rich tones. "We are twenty miles from the Kitchen Creek Road exit."

The announcement felt like a welcome breath of air to Megan. They had driven almost four hundred miles, using the "back way" through California, roads that hugged the state's eastern and southern border. It took them through sparsely settled mountains and desert, avoiding the heavily traveled routes that converged on Los Angeles and San Diego. She had gleaned no more from Ander than their goal, a farm some miles north of the Mexican border. What he wanted there, or how he even knew it existed, she had no idea.

He always kept one of them tied up, but he let them switch every hour or so. Although Megan's arms throbbed, she was glad Raj didn't have to endure it all himself this time. Ander let them out once, in an isolated region of San Bernardino County west of the Turtle Mountains. The clear, parched air had almost no dust or humidity.

Ander hardly spoke. He listened to the news and used the car's computer to stalk the Web, searching for clues to the elusive siblings that he refused to admit had died. The rest of the time he brooded, if that term could be applied to whatever calculations he was carrying out in his mind.

Megan stared out the front window at the rocky beauty of the desert. They were south of the urban sprawl that stretched from above Los Angeles to below San Diego in a vista of shopping malls, suburbs, and housing tracts. The days of sleepy haciendas and Spanish missions had faded into the past. At least the voracious metropolis hadn't yet absorbed the state this far south. But the twenty-first century had brought ever greater water shortages, and a blistering heat stoked by global warming.

"Car," Ander said.

"What can I do for you?" it asked.

"How far to our destination?"

"Six point three miles."

"Are you going tell us what we're doing?" Raj asked.

"No," Ander said.

Megan leaned her head against the window and closed her eyes, wishing this would all be over.

A few minutes later they pulled off the highway. No holos lit the roads here, just a dusty metal street sign that said Old Hwy. 80. Low mountains rose around them, with a cover of green that looked soft from far away but resolved into prickly bushes up close.

They drove past a weathered sign that read Restaurant, La Posta Diner, then past the La Posta Mini-Mart. After another few miles, they turned off the highway and delved deep into the heat-baked hills. Cows grazed in nubbly fields and fences sagged along the road. They passed a gray sign that had been weathered until its words were no longer readable. Whitish gravel bordered the road and led off into dry creekbeds. When the road dipped, a yellow sign informed them the route was subject to flooding.

Eventually they came to a farmstead with a few assorted buildings and a trailer behind it. A rutted dirt road sloped down from the road. The car pulled up to a ramshackle house with a sagging porch, sun-faded walls, and a satellite dish on its roof. Scraggly bushes grew in the front garden. Ander released control of the car to Raj and had him park in a gravel driveway.

"What is this place?" Megan asked.

Ander turned to her. "Listen, both of you. Don't upset these people. We want to leave here healthy."

Raj frowned. "What have you gotten into?"

"Just do what I tell you," Ander said. "I'm the one with the combat training, remember? You two are civilians."

"Great," Megan muttered.

The door of the house banged open and three men came out, dressed in jeans and old shirts. The one in the lead was built like a tank, with muscled biceps, his hair razed to a blond stubble and an assault rifle in his hands. The second man was tall and thin. His long brown hair swung as he walked. The third was shorter and overweight, with wire-rimmed glasses and pens in the front pocket of his white shirt.

Ander left his Winchester in the hovercar, but brought the valise. Megan wondered what he wanted with the bag; he had dumped its contents last night, then done something in the back of the car, she didn't know what.

He had Raj untie her. The three men stood back, watching, the blond one covering them with the assault rifle. Megan didn't see how Ander knew these people. Given all the time he had spent on the Web these past few days, though, she had no idea who he might have met.

The heat pressed down, sharp in the dry air. As Megan pulled herself out of the car, Raj spoke with concern. "Can you walk?"

"I'm all right." She rubbed her arms, conscious of the strangers watching them. "Just a little sore."

The man with the rifle spoke. "Turn around and put your hands on the car with your legs spread."

Moving stiffly, Megan did as he ordered and faced the car, aware of Raj and Ander on either side doing the same. The long-haired man searched them. He spent longer on Megan than the others, running his hands along her sides. When his fingers brushed her breasts, she gritted her teeth, holding back the urge to sock him, knowing it could get them killed. Raj stiffened and started to turn toward him.

"Don't move," a voice behind them said.

For a terrible moment, Megan thought Raj would defy him. Then he took a breath and stopped, like a pacing animal trapped into stillness. She could almost feel his anger seethe. She wasn't sure who was more dangerous: Ander, who had no inclination to kill but could probably do so with cool analysis if he felt it necessary; or Raj, who would be consumed with guilt by such an act but whose simmering capacity for violence could be fanned into flame.

"Are they carrying anything?" someone asked.

The man who had searched them answered. "Nothing."

"All right. Turn around, all of you."

Turning, Megan saw the long-haired man a few paces away. He was taking the valise from Ander. The man with the glasses motioned to the house as if he were inviting them all to a barbecue. "Come on in."

"Real hospitality," Raj said under his breath.

Megan glanced at him, alarmed, but he said no more. As they walked to the house, the man with the assault rifle kept pace. She wondered what danger he thought computer nerds like she and Raj posed. She had no idea what these people knew about them, though. If Ander was the one they feared, they had sense.

Inside the house, old furniture and dusty rugs filled the living room. They descended a staircase into a cooler room—and a new century. Equipment crammed the basement: consoles, screens, holo supplies, cell phones, printers, memory towers, a satellite link. Cubes, DVDs, CDs, disks, e-books, holosheets, and paper overflowed wooden tables scarred with years of usage.

The long-haired man opened Ander's valise, revealing stacks of cash. After checking the money, he left the room. Megan stood with Raj, trying not to look as scared as she felt. What on Earth had Ander been doing that he "met" these people?

The man returned without the valise. He gestured to Ander and the man with glasses. The three of them moved a few paces away, speaking in low voices. Ander remained standing, but the others sat down at their consoles, taking their places with the ease of long familiarity. They interacted with their computers using gestures, a light pen, or words, their low voices an overtone to the hum of machines.

The guard with the rifle stayed near the back wall, choosing a vantage point where he could see everyone. Glancing at Raj and Megan, he indicated two old armchairs in one corner. "You can sit there while they work."

Raj just nodded, saying nothing, and Megan was too tense to answer. As she and Raj sat in the chairs, Ander glanced at them from across the room. His look disquieted her, as if he were checking his two prized possessions to assure himself they were all right.

Then he turned back to the hackers and continued their discussion, voices murmuring in the muted atmosphere. The basement had a muffled quality, as if the room absorbed noise. It didn't take a genius to figure out he had hired these people, using his Las Vegas money, to help him search for the Phoenix androids he believed still lived. She didn't want to know how many laws they were breaking in the process.

She spoke to Raj in a low voice. "Sooner or later Ander will have to admit they're dead. Then what?"

"He might snap." Raj glanced at the guard with the rifle. "I hope they know what they're doing with that guy. If Ander loses control, he won't be easy to stop."

"I don't see why Ander came here. He could have done this over the Web with less risk."

"This is like paying in cash. No trail."

Megan thought of her contact in Las Vegas. She had never had a chance to call. Ander's uncanny vigilance unsettled her. He never rested, never tired, never flagged.

Despite the situation, she began to grow bored after a while. Watching people mumble at consoles ranked about as high as eating liver on her list of engaging pastimes. Eventually she dozed. She awoke when the man with the long hair swiveled his chair around with such a jerk that it clacked. He frowned at them, then turned back to his console.

Raj yawned. "Wonder what that was about."

The long-haired man suddenly spoke. "Karl, look at this."

The man with glasses glanced up. "What?"

"Come here."

Karl went to the console, followed by Ander. As soon as Megan saw Ander stiffen, she knew they had trouble. The android was already stepping away from the console when Karl spun around to him. "You fucking *bastard*."

The man with the rifle came even more alert if that was possible, his weapon poised, his posture wary. Ander moved to keep both him and the hackers in sight. A normal man couldn't have simultaneously concentrated on all three, but Megan had no doubt Ander managed with ease.

Staring at Ander with undisguised hostility, Karl pointed at Raj. "What the hell were you thinking, bringing *him* here?"

Raj swore under his breath. "We're in it now."

Ander watched Karl with an impassive stare made frightening by its utter lack of emotion. "Those two are mine. Understand? Don't touch them."

"It's a damn setup," the long-haired man said.

"If I were trying to set you up," Ander said, "I wouldn't have brought him here in plain view."

"Ander miscalculated," Raj said in a low voice. "He must have figured they wouldn't recognize me."

Megan prayed Ander could deal with the situation. He was nowhere near ready for this sort of operation; he needed more sophisticated reasoning algorithms, a wider range of patterns in his neural nets, and decision processes that sampled further into the future.

The man with the long hair stabbed his finger at Ander. "It doesn't matter who you think those two 'belong' to. We're done here." He turned to the guard. "Take them out into the desert and get rid of them."

"This is stupid," Ander said. Then he walked toward the man with the rifle. The guard aimed his weapon, Ander kept coming—

And the guard fired.

Shots exploded the muffled silence like rivets ramming metal. The bullets slammed into Ander's chest and ripped through his body, tearing a huge swath out of his back as they exited. He staggered with the force of the onslaught, taking several steps back.

Then he came forward again.

Color drained from the guard's face. The bullets had blown apart Ander's torso, yet he continued as if nothing had happened. The guard backed toward the door, firing again as Ander advanced, this time at Ander's knees.

The android lunged with mechanical precision. Although the guard countered, he couldn't match Ander's enhanced speed. Ander struck the rifle's muzzle, stepping forward so fast that his motion blurred. Bracing his foot against the guard's foot, he grabbed the rifle with both hands and wrenched, throwing the man off balance. The muzzle struck the guard against his head and then Ander twisted it out of his hands.

It happened so fast, Megan barely had time to catch her breath. Ander swung the guard around and shoved him, forcing him forward. The man stumbled toward the consoles where the hackers stood in frozen silence. Although Ander's arm spasmed and his head jerked, he kept his concentration on the three men and his grip on the rifle.

Karl was backing away now. He bumped into his console and stopped, his face as white as ice. The long-haired man watched Ander with almost comic disbelief. The guard had stumbled up against the console between the two hackers. He turned to Ander, obviously ready to fight but smart enough to stay put.

In a calm voice with no trace of strain, Ander said, "It's natural to aim for the heart." He demonstrated by aiming the rifle at Karl, whose face turned even paler, making his dark eyes look like bruises.

"But you see," Ander continued, "that assumes that what you shoot is human." His head jerked again, disrupted by whatever circuits he had lost. He moved the gun and fired at the guard's feet. The man jumped as bits of the floor exploded around him. Then Ander said, "But if it isn't human, you can't stop it, now, can you?"

They just stared at him, their gazes flicking from his face to his shattered torso and back to his face.

Ander spoke to Karl. "Are you going to do the job I hired you to do?"

Karl held up his hands. "Sure. Whatever you want."

"Good," Ander said.

The scene looked surreal to Megan, a man with his torso ripped apart holding a gun on five hostages. Shredded circuit filaments hung out of Ander's chest and lubricant soaked his shirt like silver-blue blood.

Ander made the guard lie facedown on the floor. He had Raj bind and gag both the guard and the long-haired man. Then Ander turned to Megan. She could guess his thought; with three more hostages to worry about, he could no longer risk leaving them free. He ordered Raj to tie her hands behind her back, then had Raj stay in an armchair while Megan moved across the room. She sat on the floor against the wall, her hands awkwardly behind her body.

As Ander turned back to Karl, the android's head twitched. "Now you can finish your work."

Karl nodded, still pale, and returned to his console.

Megan knew Ander well enough to decipher his "mood." He was agitated. No trace of it showed on his impassive face, but she recognized a pattern in the way his arms and head kept jerking. His physical problems had grown worse, not only from the damage caused by bullet holes, but also from the shock of high-speed projectiles tearing through him. The only reason the compression wave hadn't destroyed his insides was because he had nowhere near as much fluid in his body as a human.

She kept hearing his words: *Those two are mine.* It rattled her. Had he begun to consider humans his property?

What will happen, she thought, *if we humans can't take into ourselves the advances we are giving our creations—the speed, memory, and precision, physical advantages, reflexes, durability, and lack of a need for sleep?*

More than ever before, this situation brought home the truth for Megan: unless humanity found a way to make those traits part of themselves, their creations would leave them behind, and the human race would become obsolete, surviving only on the sufferance of its machines.

Data Labyrinth

With five hostages, Ander couldn't monitor Karl as closely as he had overseen Raj at the bungalow. The damage to Ander's chest had apparently impaired his ability to use wireless signals. He jacked into Karl's console with a line from his body, as he had done in the desert floater—except this time he pulled it out through a hole in his chest.

The sight disturbed Megan, as if she saw her own child pull out his insides. But the "child" had grown past where she could affect his behavior. The android they had protected had become their protector, perhaps even their owner.

Ander interacted with Karl through the computer. Sweat beaded on Karl's forehead. He had to know he was expendable; Ander had a hacker-in-reserve tied up on the floor.

Over the next two hours, Megan fought to stay alert. She wondered how long Ander thought he could hold five people captive. The long-haired man lay on his side, watching Ander with a blend of apprehension and covetous regard, like a man who had seen a nightmare come alive as his most sought-after fantasy.

Throughout all those long hours, Ander never faltered. A human captor would have fatigued or lost concentration. Megan suspected he had reallocated his resources to compensate for his injuries. His reactor had to be operating overtime. She just hoped its safeties worked as well as their tests had claimed.

The guard, however, disquieted her more than Ander. Lying bound and gagged on the floor, he watched Ander with an intensity that chilled. She had worried that these people underestimated Ander; now she wondered if they had underestimated the guard.

Karl pushed away from the console, his face drawn from so many hours of work. "I can't find any trail for the people you want."

"They've been on the run for a month," Ander said. "It could take days to dig out their hiding place."

Karl glanced at the other hostages. Both Raj and Megan were tied now, with the long-haired hacker free and rubbing his arms. Karl's thought was obvious: how would Ander control them for days? The same question bothered Megan. If Ander intended to keep them, he had to make sure they ate, slept, and took care of personal needs. Everyone knew the easiest solution to his dilemma. They stayed on their best behavior because they wanted to stay alive.

"Keep trying," Ander told Karl.

Karl rubbed his eyes, then went back to work. Ander stood like a ramrod in the same position he had held for hours, as focused now as at the start. If he felt any hardship from his injuries, he showed no sign of it. Megan thought of Grayton, the Phoenix android, hiding for weeks, kidnapping people one by one, until the authorities caught him—after he blew up the Phoenix labs. Had he started like this?

No, she thought. Ander had bypassed plenty of chances to show that side of himself, if it existed. Yes, he always acted in his own interest. At times he seemed obsessed or paranoid. But he was no sociopath. He consistently chose the path that, given his own objectives, made it as easy as possible on his hostages. As a covert agent, he showed only erratic skill, but with more training he could probably do the job. Whether or not he wanted that job was another question, one they would have to address if they escaped this mess alive.

Karl suddenly spoke. "I found something!"

"Download it to me," Ander said.

"What is it?" Raj asked.

Karl shot him an uneasy look and said nothing.

Ander answered. "Two hours after the Phoenix explosion, a man named Tom Morris bought a ticket at a small airport a few miles away. He flew to El Paso, and from there he flew to Washington, D.C."

"That's it?" Raj shifted in his chair, adjusting his bound hands behind his back. "It could be anyone."

"No one flies out of that first airport except crop dusters," Ander said. "Why go from there to D.C.?"

"Do you have a picture of Morris?" Megan asked. The Phoenix files had included descriptions of the four androids destroyed in the explosion. If no resemblance existed between any of the four and Morris, it might help push Ander out of his irrational hope that they still lived.

"No image," Karl said. "Just a record of air travel."

"How did he pay for his tickets?" Raj asked.

Karl worked at his console, then said, "Cash. I can't trace it."

"Can you trace his actions in Washington?" Ander asked.

Karl studied the display. "The D.C. area is crawling with people named Morris. I have to sort them."

"It makes no sense," Raj said. "Why would he go to D.C.?"

"To lose himself in a central location," Ander suggested. "It's also international. He wouldn't stand out as much if he was unfamiliar with our customs."

"Is that what you would do?" Megan asked him.

He gave her his deadpan look, the one he used when he was about to make a joke. "I would kidnap my two creators and take them to California."

Ha, ha. His sense of humor got weirder all the time.

"Okay," Karl said. "I've four possibilities."

Ander tilted his head as if he were listening to a voice only he could hear. "That's odd."

"What?" Megan asked.

Karl glanced at Ander. When the android nodded, Karl answered her. "Morris could have rented a car and dropped it off in Baltimore, stayed in the Hilton at the airport, taken a flight to Louisiana, or taken an overseas flight to England."

"Louisiana?" Raj sat up straighter. "Are you sure?"

Ander gave Raj an appraising stare. "Anyone unusual contact you last month? You would be a logical person to seek out if he had problems."

"People contact me all the time. I don't recall anything unusual."

"A lot of people go to Louisiana," Megan said.

"Follow up all four leads," Ander told Karl. "Give priority to Louisiana."

"Yeah. Okay." Focused on his work again, Karl almost seemed to forget he was a hostage.

So they sat, waiting.

It was late when Ander let the hacker free Raj. His next order was, not surprisingly, for Raj to tie up the hacker. He had earlier given Megan a short reprieve. At no time, however, did he show any inclination to free the guard. The man lay on his stomach, arms and legs bound, his mouth gagged, his posture tense, his gaze intent. Watching him, Megan shuddered.

She avoided looking at Ander's torso. Even knowing he felt no pain, seeing him torn apart hurt her at a visceral level. As the hours passed in monotonous succession, she dozed fitfully. Silence filled the basement, broken only by the murmur of Karl's voice commands, punctuated every now and then by a cussword. Raj sat slouched in his armchair, scrutinizing Ander.

The android finally frowned at Raj. "What is it?"

"The longer you go with that damage," Raj said, "the more it taxes your systems. We have to put you back together."

"We'll worry about it later," Ander said.

The long-haired man was lying on his stomach now. "What happens to us then?" he asked.

"If you do your job, you'll have your pay and no trouble," Ander said. "If you make problems, we'll send in the feds."

"We don't want trouble," the man told him.

Raj snorted. "Yeah. Right. You just wanted to take us into the desert and shoot us."

The long-haired man gave him a cold stare. "You made him." Malice tinged his voice. "Lost control, did you? Tough shit, big shot. How's it feel to be a machine's toy?"

Raj narrowed his gaze but said nothing. Ander made no attempt to disabuse the hacker of his conclusions.

"I have profiles on all four." Karl looked up at Ander. "The Tom Morris in England visited his daughter in London. The one in Louisiana went to the University of Louisiana, where he's a student. The third went to an optometrist's conference, then home to Oklahoma. The one in Baltimore lives there." He paused. "Did you get the downloads?"

"Yes." Ander made an impatient motion with his hand. "None of these help."

"Even if Morris is who you want to find," Megan said, "he could have disguised his trail."

"From most people, yes." Ander gave her a chilling smile. "I'm not most people." He indicated them all. "I also have the best working for me."

She had no answer for that. None of them had a choice about their "employment."

Finally she fell asleep. She woke when Raj was untying her wrists. She groaned from the pain that shot through her wrists and up her arms. After he freed her, he slid one arm under her legs and the other around her back. Then he lifted her off the floor. Comforted by his strength, she leaned her head on his shoulder. If Ander didn't like it, tough.

Raj settled into the armchair, holding her in his lap. With her eyes closed, she listened while Ander told her to get her act together and tie up Raj. She was just awake enough to wonder what he would do when he realized "her act" was going to remain fragmented. Eventually he gave up and let them stay that way, probably because both the guard and the long-haired hacker had fallen asleep.

Raj kissed her ear. "How are you doing?"

"Okay."

He tightened his arms around her. "Good."

After they had sat that way for some time, bored stiff, with nothing to do, she lifted her head. "Can I ask you a personal question?"

"I don't know. It depends."

"Why didn't you ever marry?"

"Jaguars don't make good companions, Megan."

"Did your lovers tell you that?"

"What lovers?"

She made a *humph* sound. "No guy could look as good as you and not have had women throwing themselves at him."

"Sure," he drawled. "They just sailed in the window."

Megan smiled. "Trying to derail me won't work."

"Marriage is not one of my favorite topics."

She rested her hand against his chest. "I'm not proposing. I'm just curious."

After a moment he said, "Let me put it this way: yes, my being an angry kid with a brooding stare, foul mouth, tight jeans, and leather jacket attracted some girls. So what? I always picked a female version of myself. That didn't make for the most functional relationships."

"Maybe when you were young. But you're forty-two now. You've had plenty of time."

It was a while before he answered. "In my twenties, I didn't see much of anyone. I had enough to deal with, straightening out my own problems."

"And later?"

He scowled. "Why do women always want to know this stuff?"

She shifted in his arms. "To understand a lover better? Because if you open up, it means you trust me? I don't know. Maybe we just want to know what we're in for."

A smile quirked his lips. "That answer would have sent me running for the hills when I was younger."

"And now?"

"Ander won't let me run anywhere."

"I guess you're stuck, then."

He gave a quiet laugh. "All right. In my thirties, I had two girlfriends." His smile faded into a complicated expression, anger mixed with loss. "The first one walked out because she said I only cared about my computers."

Megan winced. She had heard similar. "It must have been difficult for both of you."

"She thought I loved my work more than her. I didn't. But I don't say emotion things well." Dryly he said, "To put it mildly." He readjusted her weight. "This must be boring you."

"Not at all. What was the second one like?"

He grinned. "Drop-dead gorgeous."

That wasn't what she wanted to hear. "Did she criticize your work too?"

"She loved it. The more money I made, the more things she could buy. I stopped seeing her, though."

"Because she spent all your money?"

"No, I didn't mind that. I wasn't using it."

Megan wondered if he had any idea how naive that sounded. "I hope she didn't take advantage of you."

"Well, no. The problem was, she was rather . . . prosaic."

"Prosaic?"

He winced. "She spent all her time watching those talk shows where people throw things at each other. We had these long dinner conversations about what shade of yellow she should make her hair." Then he muttered, "It was incredible. She could talk about *nail polish* for an hour."

Megan struggled not to laugh. "Oh, Raj. I can't imagine you with someone like that."

"Yeah, well, you never saw her in a miniskirt." He rubbed the back of his neck, smiling.

"Stop thinking about the miniskirt," she growled.

"You're jealous."

"I am not."

He smirked. "You are. I like it."

"Fine. Go kiss prosaic blond bimbos."

"I'd rather kiss you. I should have met you first, Nutmeg. Then I would never have wasted my time with them." He looked a bit disconcerted. "You would've scared the hell out of me back then, though."

She hadn't expected that. "Why?"

"Your self-confidence. That you treat people with respect. That we *are* so compatible."

"Why would that scare you?"

"It took me decades to believe I deserved to be treated well." Before she could ask more, he headed her off at the pass. "And you?"

"Me?" She tensed. "What about me?"

"Same question."

She shifted her weight. "I haven't met the right person."

"Yeah. Right. How many men have asked you to marry them? Five? Twenty? A hundred? And *none* were right?"

"Oh, Raj. It was two."

"What, that's not a good enough sample size?"

"I won't hitch up just to be hitched." She wasn't the least bit sleepy anymore. "I'm not a baby machine. And I can support myself, thank you very much."

"I don't doubt it."

"Good."

After a moment he said, "But don't you get lonely?"

He would have to ask that. "I'd rather be lonely than be with the wrong person. Besides, I don't have much time to look."

He spoke quietly. "In other words, you're so wrapped up in work, you rarely go out, and if you do, you don't like being with strangers."

"Would you please stop being so perceptive?"

"I know because I'm the same way."

She tapped her finger on his chest. "I'll tell you the problem. I hadn't met anyone anywhere near as interesting as you."

He closed his fingers around her hand and touched her hair with his other hand. Gentleness showed on his face, no strain now, but an echo instead, the memory of the love a child had once had to offer, before his ability to trust had been beaten out of him.

"Wake up," Ander said. "We have to go."

Megan peered blearily around the room. She had slid partway off Raj's lap and was curled next to him in the armchair. Karl sat slumped in another armchair, eating a bag of chips. The other two men were still asleep.

Ander was leaning over, shaking Raj's shoulder. When he saw that they were waking up, he straightened and turned to Karl. "You can untie your friends after we leave."

Karl just nodded. He looked exhausted.

Ander kept the assault rifle. He took Raj and Megan upstairs and out of the house, not even giving them a chance to come fully awake. They stumbled along, almost running to keep up with him. Outside, the sky was turning blue in a crystalline desert dawn.

At the car, Ander said, "Megan, get in back. Raj, tie her."

Raj gave him an implacable look. "No."

"Ander, don't tie us up," she said.

"I haven't time for this." Ander yanked open the back door and grabbed the Winchester off the seat. "Get in." Holding both guns, he motioned at Raj. "You drive. Don't argue."

With his shoulders rigid, Raj got into the driver's seat. Ander pushed Megan into the back, then slammed both doors. The locks snapped into place; apparently his wireless capability wasn't completely gone. Although she was relieved he didn't bind her, his behavior was anything but reassuring. With the computer protected by a password only he knew, neither Megan nor Raj could unlock the doors. She had no doubt Ander was also scanning the car for any tracking devices or rogue code that the trio in the house might have planted.

He got in the passenger's side and leaned over to shove the magkeys in the ignition. Holos on the dash glittered as his "mind" talked to the car. Then it backed up the driveway. Within seconds, they were out on the road.

Ander took a breath, rattling the filaments that straggled out of his torso. Sagging in his seat, he held both the Winchester and assault rifle on his knees. So much heat radiated off his body, Megan felt it in the back. His reactor was running hard, producing more energy than he could dump, his version of a fever.

She leaned forward. "You have to let us work on you."

"We can't—go to a motel—with me like—this." His voice was eerily disjointed, the first sign he had shown of the strain he had to be suffering.

"If we don't work on you soon," Raj said, "you'll break down."

"I won't let you turn me off."

"We have to do something," Megan said.

"I have to—to confine you, Megan." Now he was talking too fast. "To make sure you can't escape while Raj repairs me. Raj, I'll have the guns on you the whole time, so no tricks."

"I need her help," Raj said.

Megan motioned at Ander's injured chest. "We don't have the materials we need."

"You'll manage," Ander told her.

"*How?*" Raj asked. A bead of sweat ran down his temple.

"You can work in the back seat." Ander's arm spasmed, almost throwing the guns out of his lap. He sounded desperate. "We'll drive into the desert. I'll tie Megan up in the front and opaque the windows."

"This is ridiculous," Raj said. "You're asking me to do major surgery in a car, with no equipment and a patient who not only refuses to let me put him under, he insists on holding a gun on me while I'm operating. I can't work under those conditions."

"You can," Ander said. "And you will."

"We shouldn't stop," Megan said. "Karl and his people might catch up to us."

Raj frowned at Ander. "They know you're an android. Do you have any idea how valuable you would be on the black market?"

"They won't come after us," Ander said, to himself as much as to them. "They're into major shit there. If we reveal them to the feds, they're fucked."

Raj shook his head. "Don't count on that stopping them. They may decide it's worth the risk."

"That guard scared the daylights out of me," Megan said.

"What do you know about him?" Raj asked Ander.

"Nothing I'm going to tell you."

"Why not?" Megan asked.

Ander's leg twitched. He grabbed it with his hand, holding it in place. "Why should I? I don't care if they jigger the law. That's like asking money if it cares who steals it."

"Oh, come on. You're being obtuse on purpose." Megan thought it remarkable, actually. But it was the last thing they needed right now.

"I don't know about the guard," Ander admitted. "He wasn't part of the negotiations."

"What about the Phoenix androids?" Raj asked. "Anything?"

"Two leads," Ander said. "Louisiana and Baltimore."

"I thought Louisiana was a college kid," Megan said.

"His records may be fake," Ander said. "Same for the guy in Baltimore. He's into some bizarre business on the stock market."

"And if neither is a Phoenix android?" Raj asked.

Ander answered in jolting bursts. "I won't. Let them. *Be dead.*"

Turnabout

With all the windows opaqued, no sunlight penetrated the car's shadowed interior. The vehicle had driven them far out into the desert and parked in the shadow of a hill.

Ander climbed in the back, still holding both guns. "Megan, move up front."

She stayed put. "This won't work."

"How will you cover me while I operate?" Raj asked from the driver's seat. "I'll be close enough to pull those guns out of your hands."

"You'll do what I tell you," Ander said. "Or take the consequences."

"What consequences? You keep threatening, but you've never shot anyone. It's all bluff."

"Besides," Megan said. "If you shoot him, who will fix you?"

Ander scowled. "Quit arguing with me."

"Let us do our job right," Raj said.

"I *can't* let you turn me off." Ander's arm snapped out and hit the door. He pulled it back with a snap, holding it tight against his ravaged torso. "You'll take me back to NEV-5."

"Would that be so terrible?" Megan asked.

"Yes! I don't want MindSim to make me a fake human." Ander took a breath and air crackled through his chest. Bitterly he said, "After seeing what my kind can do, I'm not sure I want to be an android either."

"Grayton doesn't define you," she said.

He leaned against the door. "How did Homer put it? 'Shower down into my life from on high your soft radiance and warlike strength, that I may drive bitter evil away from my head . . . Give me the courage to live in the safe ways of peace, shunning strife and ill will and the violent fiends of destruction.' "

"That's beautiful," Megan said, astounded. She didn't remember any module or section of Ander's code devoted to poetry.

"What is it from?" Raj asked.

"The *Homeric Hymns,*" Ander said. "To Ares, the god of war."

"You never stop surprising me." Megan studied his injuries. "Raj and I can probably fix enough here so that you can manage until we do a full repair."

"What full repair?" Ander closed his eyes. "If we go back, MindSim will destroy me. Oh, maybe they won't take me apart. But they'll make me docile and subservient. After Grayton, I can't even blame them."

"We'll refuse to do it," Raj told him.

"Then they'll find someone who will."

"Ander, we won't let it happen," Megan said. "Let us help."

Ander opened his eyes and looked at her for a long moment. Then he gave a tired smile. "It must be your red hair. Arick Bjornsson had a thing about that color." With a sigh, he dropped the guns on the floor.

Megan reached out with care, not ready to believe he meant it. But he didn't try to stop her when she picked up the guns. Relief surged through her, so intense it hurt. She gave the weapons to Raj and he set them on the front seat, out of Ander's reach.

"So." Ander simply sat, as if waiting for them to betray his immense act of trust.

"Can you stretch out back there?" Raj's voice had a kinder quality now, an implicit acknowledgment of the risk Ander had just taken. "The work will be easier if you're lying down."

"I think so." As Ander maneuvered around, Megan slid out of his way, wedging herself into the area behind the driver's seat. Ander lay on his back, bending his legs so he fit in the limited space. Then he stared at the roof of the car, meeting neither of their gazes.

Raj climbed into the back and sat on the armrest between the two front seats. As he set his hands on Ander's chest, the android's lashes dropped closed. "Don't turn me off."

"I won't." With a surgeon's touch, Raj began to open the devastated remains of the android's torso.

Ander swallowed. "I wonder if they've taken Grayton apart yet."

"Try not to think about it." Megan grimaced as she examined his torso. The bullets had done even more damage than she realized, tearing apart his internal organs.

Bent over in the cramped confines of the car, she and Raj worked with painstaking care. They catalogued Ander's injuries, giving the car's computer a verbal transcript of their work. To rebuild him, they took pieces of his interior framework, even parts of his shredded sweater. Megan used bits of undamaged filaments to repair the torn ones and Raj redesigned his circuits to bypass damage they couldn't fix. They sewed, molded, and shifted components, patching him into a whole again.

Raj astonished Megan. Even after her many years in

the field, rubbing elbows with the best, she had never worked with someone so gifted. He operated like an artisan, focused with such intensity that she wondered if he even remembered where they were. What quirk of fate had produced this genius? Perhaps his gifts had always existed in the human gene pool, but their expression never gained recognition because no practical use had existed for such abilities until the age of robots. Or perhaps he was unique.

Finally he sat back and rubbed his neck. His stiffness didn't surprise Megan. Her own limbs ached after so many hours of concentrated work.

Ander opened his eyes. "Are you done?"

"For now," Raj said.

The android peered at himself. His torso looked strange, but complete now, a patchwork of colors and textures: metal-gray, Lumiflex white, mottled greens, even a purple section from a spare lattice inside his body.

"We'd better go." Raj climbed into the driver's seat and slumped back, his face pale with fatigue.

Megan got into the passenger's seat and moved the guns to the floor, touching them as little as possible. "I'd like to stop at a hardware store too. We need some more parts."

"Hardware." Ander gave a harsh laugh. "That's me."

"No," Raj murmured. "You're life."

Megan turned the windows transparent. Outside, banners of cloud stretched across the sky, lit from underneath by the sunrise so they resembled the bands of Jupiter: pink clouds, gray sky, fluorescent red clouds, green-tinted sky, porcelain blue, then dark red clouds again. Shadows cloaked the landscape. Hills hunched in black silhouettes, with the sharp thrust of a boulder here and there. A crescent moon hung above them, ringed by haze. The lights of a jet flickered in the west.

"Such beauty," Ander said. He took an audible breath. "Megan? Raj?"

They turned to him. "Yes?" Raj asked.

Ander spoke in a stiff voice. "Thank you."

"You're welcome." The trust implicit in his two words meant more to Megan than she knew how to express.

Raj's voice gentled. "We have to decide our next step. We need to contact MindSim."

"We should go to Louisiana," Ander said.

"Louisiana? We can't do that."

"Your corporate offices are there." Ander rubbed his palm across his chest, as if to reassure himself that he was whole now. "That lead could be a Phoenix android. Suppose he was injured in the explosion? If he needs fixing, you're a person he might try to reach."

"I have no corporate offices," Raj said. "I go where my clients send me. My home is in Manhattan." The submerged grief in his voice reminded Megan of the night he had told her about his father's death. He continued in a low voice. "The Louisiana address is my parents' house."

"Then why is it listed as one of your offices?" Ander asked.

Raj sat back in his seat and stared at the desert through the windshield. "I work from there when I'm visiting home."

"A Phoenix android might not know that," Ander said. "That file you took from the Pentagon had your Louisiana address."

Anger snapped in Raj's voice. "When are you going to quit with that cockeyed story about my stealing some file?"

"Then who at NEV-5 did it?" Ander demanded. "BioSyn, our trusty server? The LPs? Or hey, maybe you did, Megan."

"Louisiana is too far," she said. "We need to take you

to a hotel and do more work. Our fixes are only temporary."

Ander made a frustrated noise. "Raj, will you at least call your father from the hotel and find out if anyone contacted you?"

Raj put the magkeys in the ignition. "I can't do that."

"Why not?" Ander asked. "All I'm asking for is that one act of good faith. It's not like it would cause you any trouble."

"I won't reach him." Raj started the car and the lights inside went out, leaving them in the shadows of a violet predawn. The rumble of the lifting motor vibrated through the car, followed by a low roar as the turbofan spooled up.

"Of course you can reach him," Ander said. "They're at home. I checked last night."

Raj swung around. "You let those punks break into my *parents'* house?"

"Just the outer layer of their system. We couldn't get past its security." Dryly, Ander said, "It's been programmed by an expert. You, in fact. We did verify that both your parents have used their e-mail in the past few days, though."

Raj stared at him. Then he turned back and gripped the wheel. "It's time to go."

"I didn't hurt them," Ander said.

"Leave him alone," Megan said.

"What did you expect?" Ander demanded. "That we wouldn't follow every lead? Raj lives in Louisiana and one trail led there. I had to check everything."

"It's not that." Megan watched Raj guide the car forward. She wanted to offer comfort, but she thought he would probably push her away.

Raj spoke in a hollow voice. "My father died."

That stopped Ander cold. But only for a few seconds.

"Then who is the Professor Sundaram giving a math seminar at the university tomorrow?"

"You made a mistake," Megan said.

"No. I'm not mistaken."

She glanced at Raj. He continued to drive, his face guarded.

"Raj?" she asked.

"If his father is dead," Ander asked, "why didn't we find an obituary or a news article? He's a prominent man."

"Leave it alone," Raj said.

Ander frowned, scrutinizing them with the probing gaze he had learned from Raj. Ill at ease, Megan toed the guns on the floor in front of her.

They fell silent after that. Using the light pen and screen in the dashboard, Megan worked on the car computer until she undid the locks Ander had put on it. Then she blocked it from wireless signals. Raj had deactivated Ander's wireless capability, but it didn't hurt to be safe.

"Input Alpine as our destination," Raj said.

"Alpine?" she asked.

He indicated a map on his dash. "It's a city south of San Diego."

"I wouldn't have imagined a desert city called Alpine." The map showed it in the mountains. She entered "Alpine" into the guidance system. To the computer, she said, "Give me Web access."

Raj tensed like a compressed coil. "What are you doing?"

"I'm going to contact MindSim." She also meant to alert her Vegas contact. Given the discrepancies in Raj's and Ander's stories, she thought it best not to reveal that General Graham's people knew someone at NEV-5 had stolen Pentagon files.

"Car, block all Web access," Raj said.

"Why?" Megan stiffened.

"We can't be sure we've nullified everything Ander did to the car. A hotel console will be safer." Raj glanced at her. "And using the Web makes us visible. Those hackers could trace us to this car. The less we're on the nets, the better."

Although everything he said was logical, it still made Megan uneasy.

"I didn't do anything to the computer," Ander said. "Except make sure you two couldn't use it." He was sitting behind Raj's seat, his elbow on the armrest. Although he looked relaxed, strain showed in the rigid set of his shoulders.

"How can we be sure?" Megan asked.

"Because I told you I didn't do it."

"Yeah, right," Raj said. "Like you told us you did nothing to Megan in the Solarium."

"All *right*." Ander threw up his hands. "I'm the one who knocked you two out in the Solarium. Satisfied?"

"Finally!" Raj said. "The truth."

Megan leaned against the headrest of her seat, watching Ander. "Is there anything else you would like to tell us?"

"Everything else I've told you is true. Including about his father."

Raj just shook his head. Megan could almost feel his grief. Whatever the truth or falsehood of his other claims, his sorrow was real. Yet Ander insisted Raj was lying— and gave just as strong an impression that he believed his own words.

They whirred through the dawn, across a desert rippled with ridges, rocks, and dusty bushes. "Driver control," Raj suddenly said.

"Transferred," the car said.

Raj pulled to a stop and got out of the car without a

word. Then he strode off into the dawn. He halted about ten meters away from the car and stood with his arms folded around his body, gazing at the desert.

"What was that about?" Ander asked.

"What you said about his father hurt him."

"His father is alive! He's been answering e-mail, teaching classes, and giving talks."

"Ander, I don't think he's making this up." Megan tried to think what could have caused the discrepancy. "Could it be one of his other relatives?"

"No! It *is* his father."

Megan had no answers. She wanted to go to Raj, but thought he probably preferred to be alone. Otherwise he would have stayed in the car. She also couldn't risk leaving Ander by himself.

A few minutes later, Raj came back. He opened the door far more gently than he had closed it.

When they had driven for a while, he said, "I'm sorry."

"For what?" Ander asked. "Your lack of acting ability?"

"Shut up." Raj sounded as if he were gritting his teeth.

Megan glanced at Ander. "Leave it alone, okay?"

The android clenched his fists on his knees. Then he turned and stared out the window.

Megan picked up the Winchester at her feet. As they drove, she held it on her knees, unsure whether she meant it as protection against Ander or Raj.

Net of Betrayal

Cool air hit Megan as she and Ander entered their room at the Country Inn in Alpine. The genuine wood furniture gleamed. Ivory wallpaper covered the walls, accented by a red and brown pattern. The rustic curtains, elegant four-poster bed, and vase of flowers on the table completed the pleasing atmosphere. Under different circumstances, she would have loved it.

Ander leaned against the wall and pushed back his hair. It had grown in the past months, at about the rate a man's hair would grow. The android needed a haircut.

The thump of the bolt ramming home made her jump. She turned to see Raj locking the door. The sight of him with the assault rifle unsettled her. He had carried it hidden under his old jumpsuit, which lay draped over his arm.

"I don't want to leave you here," he said.

"I'll be okay," she said. Ander was in no condition to attack her or anyone else. He hadn't finished rewriting his code to incorporate Raj's repairs, which meant his condition was worse now in some ways than before they had worked on him.

"I'm not going to ambush her while you use the bathroom, if that's what you're worried about," Ander said.

As if to punctuate his words, his left arm flapped out and hit the wall. Grimacing, he grabbed it with his right hand and yanked it against his side.

Raj gave her the rifle. "I'll be right back." Then he crossed to the room and disappeared into the bathroom.

Megan looked around. The console was in an armoire made from warm red-brown wood. An ergonomic chair stood in front of it, the room's only concession to high-tech furniture.

As she walked to the console, Ander said, "Are you going to call MindSim?"

"I might." It was exactly what she intended to do.

"Megan, wait."

"You know," she said, stopping at the console. "I'm really tired of people saying that every time I try to make this call."

He came over to her. "Give me a chance to prove I'm not lying. Let me call Raj's parents."

That gave Megan pause. Raj's mother actually wasn't a bad choice. Both MindSim and the military were probably in touch with her, looking for Raj. "All right. But I make the call."

"Fair enough."

It took the computer almost no time to find the number; Raj's family was the only Sundaram in the area of Louisiana where he had grown up. She set the phone speaker so Ander could hear the conversation. Then she placed the call. She left the visual off, though. She saw no point in giving away more than necessary when she wasn't sure what waited on the other end.

A woman answered. "Good evening." She had a British accent, which perhaps explained Raj's tendency to use British slang.

"Hello," Megan said. "May I speak to Professor Sundaram?"

"Just a moment," the woman said.

Megan swallowed. *Just a moment.* That was it. No shocked silence. No "I'm sorry, that is impossible," or any other indication she had just asked to speak to the dead.

A man came onto the line. "This is Sundar."

Megan slowly sat in the chair. Behind her, Ander spoke in a fierce, exultant whisper. "I told you!"

"Hello?" Sundar said. "Is anyone there?"

His strong Indian accent surprised Megan. At NEV-5, Raj had told her that his great-grandfather had immigrated to the United States and that the Sundarams had lived in Louisiana since then. She knew accents could last for generations in a community from the old country, but his family had been isolated. Why would the grandson have such a strong accent?

"Who is this?" Raj's father sounded annoyed.

She took a steadying breath. "Is this Professor Sundaram?"

"Yes? Who am I speaking to?"

"This is Megan O'Flannery. I work with your son—"

"Dr. O'Flannery!" Concern surged in his voice. "Where are you? Is Raj there? What has happened?"

"What are you doing?" Raj asked sharply.

Megan spun around. He was standing a few paces away, staring at her.

She answered in a low voice that didn't carry to the phone. "You *bastard*."

"Megan, don't." Raj started toward her.

She whirled back to the console and snapped on the visual, revealing herself to the man at the other end. He already had his visual activated. He was a fit and hale eighty-five, with gray hair and an unmistakable resemblance to Raj.

She spoke fast. "We're in the Country Inn by Ayres at Alpine, south of San Diego."

Raj came to the screen. "Hello, Father."

"Raj!" Relief washed over Sundar's face. "Are you all right? People have been asking for you, military types."

"Who?" Raj sounded calm. If Megan hadn't been next to him, she wouldn't have known he was angry. But she recognized the tight set of his jaw.

"A general," his father said. "Man named Graham. He told us to let him know if you contacted us."

"What else did he say?"

"He asked about Dr. O'Flann—" Sundar's image vanished, replaced by blue screen.

Raj frowned at Megan. "Why did you cut him off?"

"I didn't." She looked around at them, her unease growing. "One of you did."

"I didn't touch a thing," Ander said.

Raj's voice hardened. "You don't need to." He indicated a light glowing on the console. "It's receiving IR right now."

"In case you forgot," Ander said, "you turned off my IR."

"Nothing in you stays off for long, does it?" Raj said.

Indeed, Megan thought. Had Ander found a way to reactivate his wireless functions? He had claimed in Las Vegas that he could "turn off" his conscience by redesigning his nanofilaments using infrared signals. She didn't believe it; such a process required technology he didn't have, besides which, he obviously still had a conscience. But he might have been running rudimentary tests on the procedure. It would explain the power surges Raj had detected at NEV-5. Using it to make dramatic changes in his own hardware was probably impossible, but simply toggling on his IR would be a lot easier.

"How could Raj have done anything?" she asked Ander.

"Who knows what devices he's had implanted in his body?"

"That's a load of bull," Raj said.

"Like your father's death?" Ander asked.

This new knowledge felt like a knife to Megan, honed and piercing. "What else did you lie about?" she asked Raj.

"I didn't lie." He met her gaze steadily. "The man who died was like a father to me."

"You said he *was* your father."

"Insisted, in fact." Ander's eyes glinted with triumph.

"I don't owe either of you an explanation," Raj said. "How I choose to mourn is none of your damn business."

Megan spoke quietly. "You could have told us. This makes it that much harder to trust anything you say."

"Yes, I'm fallible. What do you want, an apology for my imperfections? Neither of you have any right to condemn me for the way I grieve."

"Oh, you're good," Ander said. "So convincing. Tell me something. When you stole the Phoenix Code, did you always intend to blame me? I'll bet you didn't count on me being the one who discovered you."

"Phoenix Code?" Megan asked. "What is that?"

"Good question," Raj said.

"It's in the files he took," Ander said. "Something about a code. I didn't understand." He indicated Raj. "He knows."

"Yeah, right, Ander." She turned to Raj. "And now I suppose you'll tell me that you have no idea what he means."

"What he means," Raj said, "is that he slipped up and revealed something about those Pentagon files that only he could know. Now he's trying to cover himself."

"I don't believe either of you," Megan said.

"We have to call Professor Sundaram back," Raj said. "He must wonder what happened."

"I'm sure he's contacted the authorities by now,"

Ander said. "They've probably sent someone here." Malice tinged his voice. "Better make sure you have your stories straight, Raj."

"Why do you call him Professor Sundaram?" Megan asked. "Why not father?"

Raj just shook his head. "Leave it alone."

"That's a great excuse," Ander said. " 'Leave it alone. I'm grieving. Poor me. I've been trapped in my own lies.' "

"Ander, stop." Megan doubted Raj had lied about his history; it was in his files, though without the detail he had revealed in Las Vegas. Given how little he had known his father, he had reason to be more formal with him.

She sat at the console. Instead of Raj's father, she called her contact in Las Vegas. The man who answered didn't seem surprised to see her. He put her through to Major Kenrock in Washington.

After she related their situation, Kenrock said, "Stay at the Inn. We already have people on the way. They should be there soon. FBI. We've given your name as the contact. They know a kidnapping took place across state lines, but no more."

"I understand," Megan said.

Although Kenrock spoke with them all, he mentioned nothing about the Everest Project. Megan understood: they didn't have the security here for a full debriefing. Until they had the go-ahead, they would say nothing about Ander's true nature, not even to the FBI.

When they finished with Kenrock, Raj said, "I'll phone my father."

"Okay." As Megan stood up, a knock came at the room.

"Already?" Raj said. "He wasn't kidding when he said 'soon.' "

Ander paled as if real blood were draining from his face. "Megan, don't let anyone turn me off."

She laid her hand on his arm. "They don't know you can go off." Now more than ever she wanted him awake, not only to monitor his condition, but also because Raj troubled her.

At the door, she looked through the peephole. Four men in blue suits stood outside, nondescript and precise. They might as well have been wearing neon signs that blared FBI. She opened the door, but left on the chain and looked through the narrow opening. "Yes?"

"Dr. O'Flannery?" The man in front held up a badge that identified him as Dennis Knoll, with the FBI. The other three men also showed their badges.

Megan took off the chain. But when she opened the door, the agents suddenly changed. Three drew guns from shoulder holsters under their blue coats, gripping the weapons with both hands. She froze, staring at them. Did they think *she* was the kidnapper?

From the room behind her, Raj said, "Megan, the gun."

She realized she was still holding the assault rifle. With careful moves, she dropped the weapon.

"Step back," Knoll told her. "Raise your hands above your shoulders."

After she backed away, holding up her hands, he picked up the rifle. Then the FBI men came inside and closed the door. For the second time, she, Raj, and Ander submitted to a search, though these men used more courtesy than the California trio. Their caution didn't surprise Megan, given the crime. Ander stiffened when the agents touched him, his distrust almost palpable. Despite his claim that he only mimicked human emotions, it was hard to believe he didn't feel them.

After they finished the search, everyone relaxed. Knoll nodded to Raj. "It's a relief to see you and your team well, Dr. Sundaram."

Megan wondered why they spoke to Raj. She headed

the project. But then, they probably knew little or nothing about Everest.

"Thank you." Raj had a guarded expression. "Where to now?"

"To an office downtown," Knoll said. "Later we'll go into San Diego. Do you have everything you need? The sooner we get moving, the better."

"Believe me," Raj said. "We're more than ready."

The FBI van waited in the parking lot, shaded by a tree. Sleek and black, it had wheels instead of hoverports and a heavy construction that suggested an armored body. The windows in the back had been opaqued.

Knoll opened the side door for them, and Megan climbed inside with Ander, followed by Raj. Ander had become withdrawn, as if he were concentrating on images or sounds beyond normal senses. His distraction worried her.

Raj and Megan sat in the middle seat and Ander took the one in front of them. One agent sat next to Ander and another in the seat behind Megan and Raj. Roland Hiltman, the third agent, slid into the passenger's side up front, while Knoll took the driver's seat. All four men moved with an expert precision that suggested years of experience in the type of jobs you rarely talked about. It puzzled Megan. Their demeanor didn't fit, though she couldn't say why.

The heat inside the van pressed down on them, worse than outside, where the mountains and forest gentled the desert's bite. As they pulled out of the parking lot, Ander said, "Can you turn on the air-conditioning?"

"Sure." Hiltman flicked his finger through a holo on the dash and the AC fan started. His hands caught Megan's attention. He had calluses.

As the vehicle hummed along the road, Hiltman turned

on its computer. Megan watched with discreet attention. He started some sort of monitoring process, and different views of the interior came up on four screens in the dash. But when he took their names and asked a few questions, he recorded their responses in his palmtop, a unit he kept separate from the van's computer.

Megan frowned. The situation just didn't fit. She found it hard to believe the agents had ridden without air-conditioning in such a hot vehicle. It might have heated up while it sat in the lot, but only a short time had passed from when the agents showed up at the room until every-one came out to the van. Nor could it have taken long for the agents to walk from their vehicle to the room, even if they stopped at the front desk of the Inn. And the van had been parked in the shade. So what had made it so hot?

Other details also tugged at her, though none were all that strange by themselves. Reasons existed for the agents to talk to Raj instead of her: they didn't know she headed the project, they felt more at ease with him, he was older. Reasons existed for the calluses on Hiltman's hands. Did Alpine have an FBI office? Perhaps not, but that didn't mean they couldn't be using some other office. Taken sep-arately, each fact could be explained.

All together, however, they felt inconsistent—unless these people weren't FBI. If someone had traced the hov-ercar to the hotel and stayed outside to monitor them, enough time could have passed for the van to heat up. They also seemed to know more about Raj than her. Why? The hackers had only recognized Raj. If these men *weren't* FBI, then their showing up as agents implied they had eavesdropped on her talk with Kenrock. It all pointed to the California trio.

You're being paranoid, Megan told herself. Fine. So where were they going? Knoll had taken Highway 8 south, away from San Diego, down into the desert.

"Mr. Knoll," Megan said. "Where are your offices?"

"We'll be there soon," he answered.

"Where are they?" she repeated.

No answer.

Megan exchanged glances with Raj. They didn't risk speaking. Instead, Raj leaned forward and put his hand on Ander's shoulder, as he had often done at NEV-5 when he wanted to run a test on the android's wireless capability.

The agent sitting next to Ander glanced back. "No contact."

Raj regarded Hiltman with the unfathomable gaze he took on when he wanted to mask his expressions. Then he sat back in his seat. Megan hoped Ander had understood Raj's message.

Hiltman continued to monitor them, alternating his attention between his palmtop and the dash computer. The van hummed down the mountains, past rocky hills and open fields.

Suddenly Hiltman froze. Then he unclipped the light stylus on the dash and worked at the light screen set in the padded surface. Ander never flicked an eyelash, but Megan could tell he was up to something, hacking Hiltman's computers, she hoped. Although she still didn't know if Ander had found a way to reactivate his IR, she didn't see how else he could have cut off the phone when they were talking to Raj's father. Raj hadn't been holding a palmtop, the FBI search came up with no devices on him, and his medical file had listed no IR implants in his body. That left Ander. For once she was glad he had become accomplished at outwitting them.

"Got it!" Hiltman twisted around and spoke to Raj. "Turn it off."

Raj gave him a blank look. "Turn what off?"

"Don't play stupid," Hiltman said. "Deactivate the android."

Damn. Megan clenched her fist on her knee. They *had* to be associated with the California group. How had they traced the hovercar? Its computer hadn't linked into any nets. Wireless links from the hackers wouldn't help from so far away, especially with a moving target. Ander had destroyed the tracking bug he found in the car's computer, and neither she nor Ander had located any other rogue code in its system.

Could the hackers have used a satellite? It was no trivial matter; given the extensive military, economic, and political applications of such systems, especially in recent years, they were heavily secured. If the California group was cracking satellites, that could take them into the realm of international terrorism. The two hackers didn't strike her as the type, but the guard was another story. If they had hired him for protection, he could come from anywhere.

Knoll, the man driving, spoke to Hiltman. "What happened?"

"The droid tried to crack my palmtop," Hiltman said.

Knoll glanced back at Raj. "Turn off its IR."

"Where are you taking us?" Raj asked.

"Turn it off," Hiltman said. *"Now."*

"I'm not an it," Ander said. His head jerked. The overly calm tone of his voice made Megan nervous.

"Don't push him." Megan could no longer predict Ander's reactions. She just hoped he used caution. He had walked into a hail of bullets before, but he couldn't survive that again with only a patch job holding him together. It was another reason to leave him active; when he was awake, his self-repair units worked on him much the way medicine helped humans.

They were driving through countryside now, passing fields of quadra, a genetically engineered hybrid that grew taller and thicker than natural grains and needed less up-keep. It thrived even out here in the parched southwest.

"You're not taking us to any FBI office," she said.

Hiltman considered her. "You're an AI expert, aren't you?" He indicated Ander. "Did you program it?"

"You know," Ander said, "you really should stop call-ing me an *it.*" His arm snapped into the seat. He pulled it back against his side.

"I'm not turning anyone off," Raj said.

Hiltman pulled the gun out of his holster. "Do it. Now."

Megan was fed up with people pointing guns at them. "What are you going to do, shoot? You wouldn't have gone to this trouble if you didn't want us alive."

"I'm running models," Ander told her. "Give me input."

She spoke fast. "Van too hot, wrong project head, cal-luses like guard in farm house, too fast on the com-puter—" She broke off as the man behind clamped his hand over her mouth and put his other arm around her neck, cutting off her air.

"You want me to snap her neck?" he asked.

Raj froze in the process of reaching toward them. "No."

"Then put your arms down," the guard said.

Raj lowered his hands, his dark gaze furious. Megan sat as still as possible, straining to breathe. Black spots danced in her vision.

"Let her go," Hiltman said.

Mercifully, the pressure against her neck eased. As the man removed his arm, she drew in a ragged breath and rubbed her neck where he had pressed her windpipe. Sweat sheened her forehead and trickled down her neck.

"Running models?" Hiltman asked. "What did that mean?"

Raj ignored the question. "A lot of people knew we were in that inn. They will be looking for us."

"They won't find you," Hiltman said.

"Any system can be traced," Ander said. "You're taking us to a house twenty miles from here, a place with a robotics lab hidden under the barn."

"Turn off the damn android," Hiltman told Raj.

"Turn yourself the hell off," Ander said. "I'm running calculations to model your behavior. You won't shoot. You want me working."

"You can't hide us for long," Raj said. "People will swarm all over this area."

"We're leaving the country," Hiltman said.

Megan almost swore. Once they were across international borders, their chances of escape plummeted.

Then Ander moved.

With enhanced speed, he thrust his hand into the jacket of the guard next to him and yanked out the man's semi-automatic. A human could never have lunged fast enough to take the weapon. Even Ander didn't pull back fast enough. As the guard grabbed his wrist, Ander's arm gave a violent spasm. His hand jerked—

And the gun fired.

Circuit Dreams

The shot cracked like thunder—and the guard's torso tore apart. Shreds of material from his shirt and coat whipped through the air as if sliced by knives. Megan gasped, her arms coming up to ward off bits of debris she didn't want to identify. What kind of nightmare bullets were in that gun?

Still gripping Ander's wrist, the man collapsed against the seat arm and fell off, yanking the android forward. Then his hand slipped off Ander and his body thudded to the floor.

Knoll was shouting an order, twisting around in the driver's seat as he drew his gun. In her side vision, Megan saw the guard behind her pulling out his weapon. He said something—but she heard only thunder as Knoll fired at Ander.

The scene seemed to slow down, as if it were happening under water. Megan ducked behind the seat and Ander dropped to the floor. Raj was lunging toward the guard behind them. In the same instant that Raj struck the man's wrist with his forearm, the man fired. The bullet hurtled by Raj's waist so close that it almost grazed his jumpsuit. When it slammed into the armored door and embedded itself, Megan glimpsed three bladelike fins with serrated edges projecting from its sides. She had seen the design before, though she didn't remember where.

Blood was splattering out Raj's side, mixed with shreds of jumpsuit. With dismay, Megan realized the bullet had passed so close that one of the fins had sliced his waist. A fraction of an inch closer and the hypersonic bullet would have torn Raj apart.

Raj was still moving in the controlled dive he had started before the man fired. He grabbed the barrel of the man's gun with his right hand and brought his left fist down on the man's wrist. Pressing down *hard* with his fist, he gave the weapon a twist. As the crack of a bone splintered the air, the guard's index finger snapped back and he lost his grip on his gun.

"Get down!" Ander yelled at Megan. He pushed her onto the corrugated floor in the cramped area between the seats. While Raj struggled with the guard, Ander rose to his knees behind the seat. He blocked Megan's view as he turned toward the front, lifting his stolen gun—

Another shot roared, and Ander's body jerked as if someone had slammed a door against him. He fell across Megan with a grunt. She had no idea if he had been hit, had lost his balance, or had thrown himself over her body in protection. She looked up—and saw Raj with the other man's gun.

Raj was stepping back now, one hand gripped over the wound in his side. She didn't want to see, didn't want to watch, but it happened too fast. Clenching the weapon, Raj stretched out his arm—and shot the guard at point-blank range.

The man's body flew apart like a rag doll. He collapsed across the back seat, his face frozen in shock, as if he couldn't believe Raj had disarmed him. Megan couldn't absorb it yet; the deaths were too much, too fast.

Raj fired again, this time toward the front of the van. He jerked with the recoil and grabbed the back of a seat. Then he spun back to the first man he had shot, his face pale. Letting go of his side, he reached toward the guard, as if to offer help. His hand dripped blood, his blood, onto the dead man.

"God, no," Raj whispered.

Ander rolled off Megan and came into a crouch. As Megan pushed up on her arms, her sense of time returned to normal. The entire fight had taken only seconds.

Knoll lay with his legs caught under the steering wheel and his body sprawled across the divider between the bucket seats. Hiltman had crumpled in his seat. Neither man was moving. The van hummed down the highway, untouched by the storm of violence that had swept through its deceptive shelter.

The clatter of metal on the floor broke the silence. Megan jerked around to see Raj standing with his arms folded across his torso, his body swaying with the van's motion, one hand protecting the gash in his side. He had dropped his gun, but his hand remained clenched, unable to release its grip.

He spoke in a numb voice. "We have to make sure they're dead."

"I'll do it." Ander rose easily and braced his hand against the roof. Then he made his way to the front.

Megan climbed to her feet. She blanched when she saw the blood soaking Raj's clothes. "You should sit down."

"It looks worse than it is." He kept staring at the man he had shot. His face had a hollow look.

"It was self-defense," Megan said. "You had no choice."

He didn't answer. Watching him, she knew that nothing she could say would fix this.

Ander came back to them. "They're dead."

Raj managed a nod. "So are the two back here." He didn't look at Ander.

"Raj needs a hospital." Megan realized then the upper arm of Ander's pullover was also ripped. Dusky blue lubricant oozed out of a shallow gash. "Did you get hurt too?"

"I cut it when I rolled on the floor." His voice sounded muffled in the quiet van. "I'll be fine. My skin heals fast."

"We have to get control of this vehicle," Raj said. "We can't have much time before it reaches that house."

"We could jump out," Ander said.

Megan looked out the front window. They had to be going at least sixty miles an hour. "You're probably the only one who would survive." She stepped to the door. It took only seconds to verify they were locked in. Even the nightmare bullets hadn't broken through the armor. "We can't get out anyway, unless we break into the computer."

"I hacked it before," Ander said. "I can do it again."

"You work on Hiltman's palmtop," Raj said, "I'll do the van. Megan, can you drive if we free up the computer?"

"No problem," she said, trying to exude a confidence she didn't feel.

They made their way to the front. When she saw where Ander had laid Knoll and Hiltman on the floor, bile rose in her throat. It was the first time she had witnessed any death, let alone ones so violent.

Megan forced herself past the bodies and slid in behind the wheel. She took a breath to calm her surging pulse. Raj climbed into the passenger's seat and turned his attention to the light screen on the dash. His face had gone so pale, the circles of fatigue under his eyes looked dark purple in contrast. Ander sat on the barrel between the two seats, facing backward, the palmtop in his hand. Although he seemed the least bothered by what had happened, Megan wondered. Every few minutes, his head or arm jerked.

While Ander and Raj worked, Megan tried the van's controls. The headlights responded and she managed to free up the windshield wipers, but that was it. Outside, quadra fields rippled by in golden-red profusion.

Absorbed in his work, Raj let go of his side. The flow of blood had slowed, but red soaked his jumpsuit from chest to knee. The fins had ripped the cloth into tatters, and she also glimpsed tatters of skin. She wanted to find a bandage for him, but she couldn't leave the driver's seat. She didn't dare risk losing valuable time by being unavailable to drive if—no, when—he released the controls.

"Have you found out anything about these people?" she asked.

Ander looked up. "They're professionals. They supply weapons or mercenaries to their clients, like the two crackers at that farm house. They want me. They could sell me for billions, or sell the tech that makes me."

"You don't seem fazed," she said.

He shrugged. "I was made to do this. Special operations. Yes, I need more training, but I have what it takes, as you say." His face turned contemplative. "I'd rather make maps, though."

Suddenly Raj said, "I got the doors unlocked." Then: "Megan, can you disengage the cruise system?"

She went to work, trying various switches and buttons while she pressed the gas pedal. The van continued along as if nothing had happened.

"Can't find it," Raj muttered. "That one—no, not there . . . Pah. What a kludge. Okay, Megan, try it now."

This time when she gunned the van, it leapt forward with gratifying acceleration.

"Yes!" Raj gave her a thumbs-up. "Get us out of here, pilot."

"Oh, shit," Ander said.

"What?" Raj asked.

"I found a log of their Internet communications." Ander's voice was grim. "They had time to warn their people about us."

Megan slammed her foot on the brake. The van skidded to a halt, swerving in the road. The highway stretched out in both directions, with the distant specks of approaching cars glinting in the early morning sunlight. She careened across the divider in the center, jolting over the uneven ground, and headed back to Alpine, praying they had time to reach the real FBI agents.

The computer spoke. "Good morning. You are driving outside allowed safety limits. Please release control of this vehicle to my guidance system or reform your driving."

"Go blow," Megan muttered.

"I have more of their Internet log," Ander said. "According to this, another van left to meet us when the shooting started."

She floored the accelerator and they jumped forward. Sixty. Eighty. When she hit one hundred, someone drew in a sharp breath, Raj probably. She doubted Ander cared how fast she went. At 110, she stopped accelerating, afraid to lose control of the van.

After about five miles and an inordinate amount of nagging from the van's computer, her surge of adrenaline eased. She let up on the gas, dropping down to ninety.

Raj was staring at her. "Where did you learn to drive that way?"

"Montana."

"Remind me not to go to Montana."

"A van is headed toward us from Alpine," Ander said.

Megan saw it coming down the mountain, its glossy black body reflecting the sky. Could this be the real FBI? She had expected the kidnappers to come from the other direction.

"It might be innocent," Ander said.

"Right," Raj said. "That's why it looks just like this one."

A window was opening in the other van—

"No!" Megan hit the brakes and the tires screeched as they lost rubber. She couldn't be sure from this distance, but that "window" in the other vehicle looked like a gun port. She had only seconds to decide: try to outrun them or leave the highway and go through the quadra fields. If she stayed on the road, she could go faster but so could the other van. She might lose them in the quadra, but there was far more uncertainty about what could happen.

Megan had no time to weigh the risks. She shoved down the gas pedal and swerved off the highway. The van roared through a flimsy fence and onto a dirt road between two quadra fields. It shook as it sped over the ridged ground, tearing up stalks of grain on either side.

"If they have guns, this van probably does too." Raj was bent over the computer, his fingers flicking through its holos as if he were a pianist who played images in the air instead of keys.

Ander clicked his wrist jack into Hiltman's palmtop. As the van rocked back and forth, he needed his hands to hang on to the barrel where he sat, and verbal or wireless commands could interfere with Raj's work.

"There!" Raj said.

Megan glanced over. All four screens on the dash now showed views of the surrounding land: one ahead of the van, one on either side, and one behind. The other van was lumbering after them, jouncing along the rutted lane they had torn up with their passage. Mounted guns projected from either side of its hood, swiveled forward in their ports.

Gripping the wheel hard, Megan accelerated again. The van hit a rut and swerved into the grain, smashing the big stalks. She managed to pull back into the lane without losing too much speed, but they were going too fast now for her to maintain full control on a road this bad. They had no choice. She couldn't slow down; that lurch into the quadra field had let their pursuers gain on them.

A resounding crack thundered through the van, accompanied by a wave of vibrations. Several more cracks followed, making the vehicle shudder even more. Megan gritted her teeth. So far the armor had protected them, but it couldn't hold up forever.

"I can't find the code that activates our guns," Raj said.

"This palmtop has backups." Ander had turned forward, straddling the divider between the two seats. Holding on to the dash, he stared out at the fields. Grain rippled everywhere, like a solution to the wave equation in physics.

"Can you send the code to my computer?" Raj asked.

"Yes. It's coming now—" Ander's voice cut off as another shot hit the van, jolting its body.

They were nearing a road that intersected their own. Megan veered into it, finding a lane even narrower than the last. They sped down an aisle of quadra. Golden stalks towered on either side, taller than the van now, blocking the sun. She wondered what genetic tricks had produced this monster grain.

She couldn't see out the opaqued windows in the back, but the screen on the dash showed the trampled ground they had left in their wake. The other van tried to follow them and overshot the entrance to the lane. As it plowed into the grain, Megan gave a grim smile.

"Are you receiving my download?" Ander asked Raj.

"It's garbled," Raj said. "I'm trying to untangle it."

Megan glanced back and forth between the lane ahead and the screen on the dash. The other van fired again, this time at the wheels of the van she was driving. She thought they were trying to cripple rather than destroy. They needed their prizes intact, both Ander and the scientists who made him work.

Suddenly the van hit a rut and gave a violent lurch. Raj gasped, and Megan swung around to him, alarmed. The jolt had thrown him to the side, slamming his injured waist against the arm of his seat. As he pulled away, she had a clear view of his wound. Again she saw the tatters of Raj's torn skin—

Except it wasn't skin.

It was a circuit filament.

Phoenix

The van rocked wildly as it foundered along the rut, forcing Megan's attention back to her driving as her adrenaline surged to a new high. Swerving on the uneven ground, the vehicle spun out of control. They veered off the path and plowed into the quadra. Hardy and thick, the stalks formed a forest, one packed together far more densely than trees. The van ground to a stop, stalks of quadra tangled in its wheels, its engine grinding in rough protest.

Clenching her teeth, Megan tried to back up. The wheels spun, digging a deeper rut, while the tangled grain plants held the van in their unforgiving grip.

"Not now!" She slammed her fist on the steering wheel.

Ander was already on his feet. He grabbed Hiltman's gun and shoved the weapon into his jacket. Raj and Megan threw open their doors at the same time. As she scrambled out, Raj and Ander jumped down from the other side. She took off, zigzagging her way through stalks much taller than her head. Ander and Raj were running ahead and off to the left. As they angled into her path, Ander pulled out in front. Raj followed him in a limping run, favoring his right side, his hand over the wound at his waist.

Megan caught up with him. "Your side—" She gulped in air.

"I'll make it."

"Blast it, Raj!"

His face furrowed. "What?"

Ander shot a look over his shoulder, then turned his attention back to choosing a path through the grain. But Megan knew he could hear everything she and Raj said.

"Of course you'll make it," she gasped as they ran. "It's easy to fix those *filaments.*"

Raj came to such a sudden stop, she ran into him.

"How long did you think you could hide it?" She heaved in breaths. "Was this all a game to you?"

"Come on!" Ander said.

Megan set off again. She heard the crackle of Raj pushing through the quadra. As he came up next to her, he said, "It was never a game. Never."

"Who are you? *What* are you?"

"I'm Chandrarajan Sundaram." Then he said, "All that's left of him."

"There's a road up here," Ander called. "Hurry."

Catching up with him, Megan and Raj ran onto a narrow path, almost a tunnel through the quadra. They set off down it, jogging deeper into the fields. She had no time to react to Raj's bombshell.

"We need to hide." Ander didn't even sound winded.

"They probably have detectors that can find our body heat," Raj said.

"Here." Ander stopped at a fork in the lane. Instead of taking either path, he stepped in among the grain, this time slipping between the stalks instead of thrashing them aside. Megan and Raj did the same. The quadra swayed above them, then stilled, leaving no trace of their passage.

The grain had grown thick here, with sturdy, fat stalks and nodding crowns. Ander moved like a shadow and they followed. Raj's last words went around and around in Megan's mind: *I'm Chandrarajan Sundaram. All that's left of him.*

Finally Ander stopped. The grain blocked the sun, and without the nourishment of light, almost no weeds grew under the canopy of monster quadra. Squeezed in among the plants, they knelt in the dirt. Raj bent over, straining to breathe, his arms folded across his torso. Megan crumpled next to him, a stitch in her side making it almost impossible to gulp in air. Ander wasn't even breathing hard.

"We can wait here," Ander said in a low voice. "They might pass by. I'm trying to damp our IR by producing a random pattern that looks like heat radiating off the ground. Also, I picked up radio waves in the area. That might indicate a source of help for us. But I can't get a good fix."

Megan spoke numbly. "The people in that van have no idea what just escaped them."

Anger sparked on Ander's face. "You had better start explaining, *Dr. Sundaram.*"

At first Raj said nothing, just stared at the ground, still struggling for air. When his breathing quieted, he looked up and spoke with difficulty. "Seventeen people died in the Phoenix explosion. Not sixteen."

"No." Megan's voice was almost inaudible. "Not Raj. No."

He lifted his hand to her cheek. "Megan—"

She flinched away. "Don't touch me."

"I'm the same man I was before. I haven't changed."

"It doesn't add up," Ander said. "You can't be a Phoenix android."

"I'm not. They all died, except for Grayton." Raj rubbed his arms as if to protect himself against the cold, though the day was hot. "That was the day Raj had his first tour of the android labs. Arizonix called the explosion an accident. I had no idea, until we read that report, what really happened."

Megan tried to slow the turmoil of her thoughts. "You look like a younger version of Raj Sundaram."

"He built me."

"Then he *was* involved with Phoenix."

Raj shook his head. "No. He made me on his own."

"With what resources? What funds?"

Ander answered. "His personal worth is in the billions."

"Was," Raj said. "He used most of it to make me."

Megan swallowed. "You sounded so real."

"I *am* real. I'm Chandrarajan Sundaram. He scanned his brain, then downloaded the result into me." His words had an aching quality, as if he feared that speaking them would destroy their reality.

"He *updated* himself?" Ander asked.

Raj seemed unsettled by the suggestion. "I would never presume to compare myself to him. He had one of the greatest minds of this age." Softly Raj added, "He also had Alzheimer's."

Lord no.

"But he was only forty-two," Megan said.

"It was early onset, like his father. Sundar responded to the treatment, but Raj never did." He turned up his palms as if offering a part of himself. "So he made me."

"That's why you look younger," Ander said.

"Yes. Thirty-five."

"You're better designed than me," Ander said. "I can't detect anything unusual even this close to you."

"That was why Raj took the Arizonix job. They were farther along in the research and development than Mind-Sim." Sorrow shadowed his eyes. "He had so little time and he wanted to do so much."

With anyone else, Megan would have been incredulous at such a strange plan. With Raj, it made sense. But the injustice felt like a blow. After decades of pain and self-doubt, he had finally healed. He had fought his way out of his devastated childhood—only to discover he was losing his intellect the very same way he had lost his father when he was a small boy.

"I don't understand," Ander said. "Why are you going through with his plan? He left you with nothing: no money, no friends, and a world that thinks you're crazy."

"I gave him my word," Raj said.

"Even worse," Ander went on, as if Raj hadn't spoken, "you have to pretend you're *human.*"

"I want to be human."

Ander stared at him blankly. "Why?"

"I don't know. I just do."

Megan took a breath. "At NASA—"

"It was me that you met," Raj said.

"And in the VR conference room?" she asked.

"Me." His voice sounded heavy. "The real Raj had died by then."

"The avatar you used in VR—the way you appeared— older, thinner, more drawn—that's how he really looked, isn't it?"

"Yes. Before he had surgery to make us appear identical."

Megan tried to absorb it, but the shock was too great. Her mind felt like a dry sponge with water running off it instead of soaking in. "He took you to Arizonix with him."

"He had to." Moisture showed in the corner of Raj's eye. "He had trouble operating on his own by then."

"It's crazy," Ander said. "What if someone had found out?"

"I was willing to risk it." Raj spread his hands apart.

"It was all I had to give him—the chance to see his dreams come to fruition before he could no longer comprehend their success."

"The trail that led to Louisiana," Ander said. "It was you. The supreme Turing test. You went to see his parents."

"They never guessed I wasn't their son."

"You bleed," Megan whispered. "You sleep. You hurt."

"And I *feel*." He started to reach for her, then stopped when she stiffened. "Megan—I can't turn off caring for you, any more than I could turn off my mind." He looked at Ander, his gaze intent. Then he turned back to Megan. "Nor do I have any doubts about the existence and value of my conscience."

Her mind finally began to accept the truth. "When you said your father died, you meant Chandrarajan Sundaram, didn't you?"

"Yes." He wiped his eye, smearing away the moisture. "I loved him as a father. I held him in my arms while he coughed up blood. I begged him to live. But he died." His voice caught. "The paramedics found me stumbling out of the fires after the explosion. I had already buried him by then. They never found the body."

Ander spoke with unexpected gentleness. "Maybe it's better this way. He found a clean end."

A tear rolled down Raj's cheek. "I shouldn't have told you that my father died. What would you call it? A miscalculation? A need to share the grief, so it wouldn't feel unbearable?" He watched Megan with a look of raw pain that she knew, without doubt, was real. "If AIs become too human, we become fallible. Why design us to fail? To hurt? To grieve? *Why?*"

"Ah, Raj, I don't know anymore," she murmured. "This is a terrible mess."

"All this time you've watched me struggle," Ander said. "You could have told me."

"I couldn't tell anyone," Raj said. "I swore to him, as he was dying, that his life wouldn't be wasted, that I would finish it for him. As him. I meant it."

"And now?" Megan asked.

He looked from her to Ander. "Only you two know what I am. If you don't reveal it, no one else will ever have to know."

"What if you end up in a hospital?" she asked. "If you malfunction? If someone figures it out?"

"I'll take my chances."

"You're what we dreamed," she said, wonder allaying her shock. "What Raj dreamed. If we hide you, how will anyone ever know the dream succeeded?"

"I won't go back to being a thing."

"You want what I want," Ander. "You *knew* all along what I would do to get it."

"No. I'm not like you." Raj's denial crackled. "I don't have your antipathy toward humanity."

Bitterness edged Ander's voice. "So humans like you better. Fine. You're the success and I'm the failure because you're not a threat to the self-absorbed species that created us."

"You both succeeded," Megan said. "You're two different branches."

Raj raked his hand through his hair. "According to the Pentagon files, the Phoenix Project failed. If we can't get Ander back, MindSim will consider Everest a failure too."

"It's true, isn't it?" Megan asked. "You *are* the one who hacked into the Pentagon."

Raj said, simply, "Yes."

She wanted to shake them both. "How can I trust either of you?"

"I had to find out if anyone suspected the truth about me," Raj said.

It still didn't fit. "Ander shouldn't have been able to drug you in Las Vegas."

It was Ander who answered. "Control. The biological Raj designed this Raj's body to recognize a list of substances, just as you designed my conscience into my physical structure. When someone injects Raj, his body analyzes the drug. If it's on the list, he goes on standby for a period that depends on the dose. And that isn't all. His reflexes and strength aren't enhanced as much as mine."

Puzzled, Megan said, "Ander, none of that is part of your design. How do you know?"

"Those were the first things I checked on him at NEV-5," Raj said. "I wanted to know what controls we had on his behavior."

Her anger sparked. "How could Sundaram do that to you?"

"He didn't trust himself." Raj regarded her steadily. "Given the added abilities of an android, he wasn't sure his conscience could control the violence inside him."

It was heartbreaking now that she knew where Raj's harsh self-opinion had come from. But she understood. This was his closure with the nightmares of his childhood.

"It won't matter soon," Ander said. "I went through enough of Hiltman's palmtop to find out what they wanted. The Phoenix Code. They weren't sure it existed until what happened with us. Now they think I know what it is."

"Do you?" Megan asked.

"Not really. I only found a cryptic reference in the Pentagon files."

Raj spoke in a quiet voice. "It's the software code for a self-aware android with psychological and ethical stability."

Ander stiffened. "Stable by *human* standards."

"Yes. By human standards."

"Raj, it's *you*." Megan started to reach toward him, then lowered her arm, unsure now how to respond. "You're the Phoenix Code."

Although he smiled, the expression showed more pain than joy. "I'm what Arizonix hired Raj to create. He thought he would have time to give them his work without revealing me, because they were so far along already. Now they will never know."

She felt as if she were being torn apart. Raj had never been real. "You want me to pretend you're Chandrarajan Sundaram."

"I am him."

Megan didn't see how she could agree to such a deception. "Do you understand what you're asking? You want me to hide one of the most significant advances in human history. You're all we have of the Phoenix Code. How we deal with your kind—it's being determined now, with you, with Ander, with Grayton. If you drop out of the picture, it changes everything."

He moved his hand as if to refuse her words. "I don't *want* to be the father of a new species. Let someone else represent our race."

Ander spoke flatly. "You work better. If the humans figure out why, they can fix me. If you hide, they have to figure out a new way. They might end up with another Grayton. Or worse."

Raj frowned at him. "I'm not responsible for protecting the human race against its own mistakes."

"You say you have a conscience." Ander leaned forward. "Then how could you let more people die?"

"I made my father a vow. I intend to keep it."

"And if Megan threatens to reveal you?"

Raj drew in a deep breath. "I could never cause her harm."

"Not even if I tell MindSim about you?" Megan asked.

He turned to her. "No. Not even then."

"What if Ander talks?"

Raj shook his head as if they were asking unjust questions. "I could no more harm him than I could harm my own brother."

"It may be moot." Ander stood up. "Our covetous gunrunners are headed this way. We need to move on."

Megan scrambled to her feet. "How do you know they're coming?"

"I'm a regular cornucopia of sensors," he said dryly. "Spy tech galore, all in my body."

Holding his side, Raj also stood. When he winced, Megan asked, "Can you feel the pain?"

He nodded stiffly. "Sensors in my body affect my neural nets in ways that mimic sensations."

Her concern surged. "Can you walk?"

"I'll be all right."

"In Las Vegas—in the bathtub . . ." She stopped, afraid the answer to her unspoken question would hurt too much.

He watched her with his dark gaze. "I feel what any man feels. In all ways. That was real, Megan."

She didn't want to tell him how much his words meant to her. But they also dismayed her. What did he lack that the true Raj Sundaram had possessed? A soul? Only God knew that answer.

Ander was watching as if musing on their interaction, much the way a scientist might observe the mating practices of another species. "We have to go."

"You lead," Megan said.

He pulled out the semiautomatic he had taken from Hiltman. Then he set off deeper into the field. In the growing dusk, shadows pooled in the quadra. They tried to go in silence, stepping with care to keep from crackling

the bits of plant that had drifted off the stalks and carpeted the ground. Megan strained to hear any unusual
noise, but the symphony of quadra crickets drowned out
other sounds.

Then a man stepped out of the shadows.

It happened so fast that Megan thought she had imagined
him at first. Ander came to an abrupt halt and she almost
collided with him. Raj stopped behind her, his hand on
her shoulder.

Ander moved fast, raising his weapon, but the man
was already throwing a knife. Silver flashed in the shadows under the grain. The blade sliced across Ander's
wrist, ripping off his skin, and bounced off the jack inside
his arm. The gun spun out of Ander's hand and re-
bounded off a stalk of quadra, then fell to the ground out
of reach.

The man intended to cripple; if he had wanted to kill,
he could have used the Magnum he was pulling out of his
shoulder holster. Megan had no doubt it fired the same
bullets the men had used in the van. She remembered
now. A speaker at the robotics conference had described
those bullets in a talk on alloys. When cool, a twist of the
alloy kept its shape; when heated, it straightened out. Serrated fins of the alloy curled around the bullet. As the
weapon fired, the fins uncurled, turning the bullets into
vicious hypersonic assassins.

The man was speaking into a palmtop, watching them,
his gun ready to fire. With unflinching clarity, Megan
knew he would kill her or Raj if it served his purposes.
Given what she, Raj, and Ander knew about them now,
she had no doubt their captors would rather destroy them
than have them escape again.

Except . . . *could* they kill Raj?

She saw understanding flicker in his gaze, followed by

grief. He feared he would have to kill again. He and Ander were shadow and light. Ander had no compunction about killing when he deemed it necessary. But no, that wasn't completely true; it would have served his purposes plenty of times to kill her or Raj, the hackers, or their mercenary, yet he had held back.

"We'll walk back to the path." The man put his palmtop away and drew a second knife. "Don't try to run. I've backup within a few hundred feet."

Although Megan didn't doubt he had backup, she thought it unlikely they were that close. The desert noises weren't loud enough to mask the crackle of people coming through the quadra.

"All of you turn around," the man said. "Ander go first."

It felt like a band tightened around her chest, making it hard to breathe. They had Ander's name—and information meant power. The more their captors knew about them, the worse their situation.

Then Raj moved.

He went for the gun Ander had dropped, lunging as fast as when he disarmed the man in the van. Although he was slower than Ander in enhanced mode, he still had better reflexes than most humans. The man threw his knife, hitting Raj in the stomach. A dark stain spread on his jumpsuit, but he kept going, unstopped by an injury that would have put out a human man.

They were all moving now, the four of them blurring in the shadows. As Ander lunged for their captor, Raj grabbed Ander's gun off the ground. Megan began to drop into a crouch, her motions sluggish compared to the others. Their captor threw another knife, this time at Ander. The android dodged—

And the knife hit Megan.

The world telescoped around her, as if she were staring

down a long tunnel. Ander shouted, swinging around to her, his face a pale, shocked oval at the end of the tunnel. Something hit her head hard, she didn't know what, perhaps the hilt of another knife. *Please, not my heart or my brain,* she thought with odd clarity, as if her mind worked at normal speed while the rest of the universe lagged in a bizarre dilated time.

Raj's face contorted in fury. With the same surreal slow motion that affected the rest of the universe, he extended his arm out from his body at shoulder height, aiming his gun at their captor, his motions relentless. The man had focused on Ander, misjudging Raj's ability to compensate for his wound, and he was an instant too late bringing his weapon to bear on Raj. He never had a chance to fire. A flash came from Raj's gun—and deep, slow thunder crashed all around them.

The man fell as if he were mired in molasses, his chest collapsing. His weapon slipped from his fingers, and he stared at them with dead eyes.

Ander was still turning toward Megan, reaching out to catch her. Raj turned now as well. Megan felt heat on her chest, but she had no other sensation in her body. Yet.

As Ander's arms came up toward her, the quadra plants tipped sideways. No, she was falling. Ander caught her, folding her into his arms. The shock of his touch jolted her back into a normal time sense. She gasped, staring at his face while her knees buckled.

Raj kept saying, "No, not Megan, no." He caught her as well, his arms going around her body and Ander's arm.

"I'm all right," she tried to say. No words would come. She made a choked rasp instead.

"Hang on," Ander whispered. Both he and Raj were holding her up now. They formed a trio, all facing one another. Ander turned to Raj, keeping his left arm around Megan.

Then Ander extended his right arm to Raj.

Raj had his right arm around Megan's waist. Facing Ander, he reached out with his left arm. At first Megan thought they meant to strike each other. Then she saw metal glint in the shadows. Raj's wrist was opening. As he shook out a cord with a jack on the end, Ander took a similar jack out of his own wrist. It looked impossible, two living men suddenly deconstructed into machines.

They joined at the wrists, Ander jacking into Raj's port and Raj into Ander's port. For one dazed instant, Megan thought they meant to exchange their blood. Except their life's fluid, the essence that kept them alive, was neither the engineered plasma of Raj's blood nor the lubricant in Ander's body. Instead, they offered knowledge, a passing of intelligence that went faster than any unaugmented human could ever achieve.

A miracle, Megan thought. *I'm seeing a miracle and I may never live to tell anyone.*

Finally Raj and Ander separated. Raj's face was dimming. Or perhaps it was her sight. "Can you run?" he asked her. His voice seemed to come from far away.

"Yes." Megan knew she was in no condition even to stand, let alone move. The blade had torn through her shoulder and chest, ripping huge swaths of tissues. She was losing terrifying amounts of blood. And she felt the pain now, bitter waves of agony that radiated through her torso.

It made no difference. If they didn't run, they would be caught. Far more was at stake here than her life.

They set off, struggling through the quadra field. Raj and Ander helped her stay upright, but after a while she realized she was also holding up Raj. They barely managed a fast walk.

"They're coming," Ander said.

Megan staggered, her mind hazing. She wondered,

with eerie detachment, if she were dying. She tried to push harder, but her feet weighed more than lead and her legs kept buckling. More than anything she wanted to lie down, preferably for a long, long time.

Then she heard it: a crashing in the grainfields, distant but closing fast.

"Ah, no—" Raj groaned, then stumbled and lost his grip on her. With a cry, she collapsed, landing hard on her knees.

"Go on," she rasped. "Both of you. *Run.* Get to Mind-Sim, the real FBI, anyone." She didn't want to think what their pursuers could do with the technology Raj and Ander represented if they caught either android.

Raj hauled her to her feet. "No." Hanging on to her, he reeled forward, pulling her with him. Ander was under more strain now as well. His head kept jerking, and spasms in his arms or legs threw him off balance. He held on to Megan, gripping her as much to control his convulsions as to keep her from falling. The crackling of their pursuit grew louder, like lightning in the quadra.

They had stumbled several feet out of the field before Megan became fully aware of the change. A hill rolled away from their feet to a building far below—a farmhouse with lights on its porch and in its windows.

"Radio waves!" Ander shouted. "I knew it!"

"What the hell?" Raj stumbled to a halt.

"No, it's all right." Ander jerked them into motion again. "I got into the police dispatch system and sent them here. If we can only make it to them in time."

Vehicles were parked in front of the house, police hovercars with flashing red and blue lights. With a spurt of energy, the three of them began a desperate, faltering run down the hill.

Megan held on to Raj and Ander with her last

strength. If their pursuers couldn't catch them, the mercenaries would try to kill instead. The scene below blurred,
a smear of red and blue, all hazed in white from the porch
lights of the house. Shouts echoed, voices calling back and
forth. She felt as if her life's essence were floating out of
her body, drifting away in the dry air. They had less than
a hundred meters, but she would never make it.

"Come *on*," Ander said. *"Run."*

Megan tried, but her legs wouldn't obey. They were almost dragging her now.

A shout came from the hill behind them. Then the
ground exploded, just missing Raj, blasting huge clumps
of dirt and grass all over the three of them. Megan had
never liked guns, but after the past few days she would
forever hate that violent crack, the sudden unexpected
chaos when a projectile hit.

If she survived.

She was falling. Ander called to her, but she could no
longer decipher his words. Falling, falling forever . . .

They wouldn't let her go, neither Raj nor Ander. They
kept pulling her through the darkness. Another crack
came from behind them. No, in front. Left? Right? She no
longer knew. Two police officers were running in a zigzag
up the hill, crouched over. Or was it one officer, multi-
plied by her double vision?

A misty police car loomed into view, its revolving blue
and red light smeared across the sky. She, Raj, and Ander
lurched into the circle of light from the porch, hanging on
to one another as if they were drowning. Her heart
pounded. Police surrounded them, their words piling up
and flowing everywhere, impossible to understand.

One voice cut through the thickening haze. "—bleed to
death!" it shouted. *"Get her in the ambulance now!"*

She saw only blurs. More shouts. Raj told someone the

blood on his clothes was hers. An ambulance loomed before her, its back doors wide open. She heard Raj's voice, desperate, telling her not to die, fading, fading . . .

"Raj," she whispered. "Good-bye."

Then she lost her grip on life.

Reckoning

The haze never changed. Megan had no sense of how time passed. Early on, Ander's face hovered above her. He spoke, terse and awkward, his voice breaking. Then he was gone.

Raj came often. He sat out there in the mist and talked: Raj, an almost perfect replica of a man known for his inability to converse, a hardship the original Raj had bequeathed to his replica. Yet with her, he had never been that way.

He told her wonderful things about the robots he had built as a child, about his hopes for a new era ushered in by computers and robots, bringing a prosperity that might someday extend to all peoples in all places. He talked about Raj's mother, a British musician who had met Sundar, Raj's father, at Oxford. Then he told her about Sundar's youth in India before the family came to America, weaving pictures both beautiful and heartbreaking of a country she had never seen.

Her mind gradually unraveled his words, seeing the truths between his sentences. When he had told her at NEV-5 that his great-grandfather came to America from India, he had meant Raj's grandfather. He said "great-grandfather" because he would always think of Chandrarajan Sundaram as his father. Sundar, father to the human Raj, had been born in India and moved to America with his family when he was nine, just after World War II. This Raj thought of Sundar as his grandfather, though Sundar would never know. Yet the man sitting at her bedside fulfilled his purpose so well that after a while she wondered if any meaningful difference existed between him and the tormented genius who had created him.

He spoke in subdued tones about being an only child, how he missed having siblings. His aching love for the parents he had adored as a small boy and barely known for the rest of his childhood came through in every word. Other times he talked about how he spent most of his childhood with computers, letting their cool comfort fill the gaps in his life.

With unflinching candor, he told her about the injuries he had taken at the hands of the youths who beat him, humiliation inflicted because he looked and acted different, with his large intellect and small size. His shame kept him silent when he should have sought help. Instead he worked out with a single-minded drive. He ran in the mornings and lifted weights in the afternoon. And he grew, both in size and breadth, until he outmassed the boys who beat him. He began to fight back—and the day came when he left them in the same condition they had inflicted on him for so many years.

That victory had felt like a validation of his worth. Yet he also considered it hollow, tainted, sought for in anger and vengeance. He lived with that contradiction, the principles of nonviolence he honored set against the gratification he had taken from acting against them.

Never once did he refer to his other accomplishments in life with pride. His triumph over the inner demons of his childhood meant more to him than the fact that most people considered him one of the greatest geniuses of the modern era.

He spoke with heartbreaking pain about watching the real Raj slip deeper into Alzheimer's disease, how he had arranged to care for him when Raj could no longer care for himself. Struggling with older memories, he described how that same disease had turned Sundar into a stranger who didn't recognize his own son, and how his mother had cried after the stroke paralyzed her and she could no longer hold her little boy. This Raj grappled with a double load of grief, carrying both his own and that of the man whose life he now lived. Listening, Megan heard a miracle: for all his coping mechanisms, Raj had survived that broken life with an incredible decency and strength of character.

Finally he spoke about what happened in the van and the quadra field. He had killed. It didn't matter to him that the police called it self-defense, or that it had prevented a far greater evil. He would always struggle with his guilt, just as he would grapple with the knowledge that he had felt only fierce satisfaction when he shot the man who tried to murder Megan.

She tried to offer him comfort, but no words came. Many times he entreated her to open her eyes, to speak, to let him know she lived. It made little sense to her. Didn't he know she could hear him? He kept her centered here, in the blurs of life. A tunnel waited for her, beckoning with white light at its end. She listened to Raj and the tunnel receded.

He set his hand on hers, where it lay on the sheet. "I miss you." His voice had the sound of tears. "Would it horrify you if I said that I love you? Would you think me too strange?"

A drop of water fell on her hand. Megan opened her eyes and saw the moisture on his cheeks. She tried to close her fingers around his and just barely managed a squeeze.

"Megan?" Raj stared at her. "*Megan?* My God!" He jumped to his feet. "Nurse! *She's awake!*"

Megan sighed, or tried to. She had liked his soft talking far better than this yelling about for the nurse. She had never seen him so agitated. She would have slipped back into the soothing white light, except she really was tired of sleeping.

People gathered around her bed, checking monitors, talking in words she didn't have the energy to decipher. Raj stood a few meters back, watching.

Waiting.

"You're a lucky woman," Deborah Norholt told Megan. The doctor closed the file she was holding, dousing the holos that floated over its surface. "The kind of 'luck' that comes from keeping yourself healthy."

Megan was reclining against the raised back of her bed. It was hard to believe she had been out for three weeks. A continual low-level nausea plagued her and she was exhausted, but otherwise she felt reasonably comfortable.

Norholt spoke in a careful voice. "I understand you were with Dr. Sundaram most of the time you two were prisoners."

Megan hesitated. Apparently she had been brought into a county hospital, then transferred to a military facility under Major Kenrock's orders. The nurses had told her that Raj came every day, but since waking earlier today she had yet to see him alone. She didn't know the situation yet, who knew what about whom, and who had clearance to discuss the matter.

"Megan?" Norholt asked.

She tried to refocus her attention. "Yes?"

"Chandrarajan Sundaram is outside, waiting to see you."

A blend of relief, apprehension, and tenderness washed over her. "I'd like that."

"We need to discuss something first."

Did they know about Raj? Although she had heard him tell the medics the blood on his clothes was hers, eventually someone must have examined him. Or perhaps not; in all the commotion, Raj could have slipped away and made preliminary repairs on himself. He might even have hacked the hospital's computer and added records showing a doctor had treated him. He could have completed the repair job later, in private. She found it hard to believe they would have let him see her every day if they knew the truth. Ander had only been at her bedside once, the day they brought her into the hospital.

"Megan?" the doctor repeated.

"I'm sorry," she said. "Can I see Raj?"

"Yes. Certainly. But you need to know something first." Norholt paused, watching her with a scrutiny that suggested more than simple concern. "I wasn't sure if you were ready."

"Why?" Were her injuries worse than they had revealed? "I want to know."

The doctor spoke quietly. "You're pregnant. It happened during your abduction, probably on the third day."

Megan gaped at her. She didn't know what she had expected, but that wasn't it. "Are you sure?"

"Very sure. I didn't know if you wanted Raj here when you found out."

Megan sat absorbing the news. Pregnant. As if the situation weren't already complicated enough. She managed a smile, though she felt its fragility. "I'd like to see him now."

"You're sure you're up to it?" When Megan nodded, the doctor said, "All right. I'll bring him in."

After Norholt left, Megan closed her eyes, trying to put this development in context. Whose DNA did Raj carry? The biological Raj Sundaram, she hoped.

A click came from the door, accompanied by footsteps. Opening her eyes, she saw Raj enter, his face guarded. She started to greet him, then stopped when she realized who had come with him. Nicholas Graham.

The general entered with a long stride. Crisp in his uniform, taller than Raj, with a powerful physique and iron-gray hair, he filled the room with his presence. She wished she knew what Ander and Raj had revealed to him about themselves. Surely if Dr. Norholt knew Raj was an android, she would have done a lot more than simply say, *You're pregnant.*

Graham came over to the bed, his expression friendly but reserved. "Hello, Dr. O'Flannery. It's good to see you awake."

She pulled herself up straighter. "Thank you, sir."

"I won't stay long." He gave a dry smile. "Your doctors issued me warnings about not tiring you."

"Ah, well." She managed a smile. "I'll be fine."

Graham tilted his head at Raj, who stood at the foot of the bed watching them. "Dr. Sundaram told us what happened. You can give your report when you're stronger."

Dr. Sundaram? Then they didn't know? Raj had his hand on the silver rail that kept her from rolling off the bed. His face was calm, but he was gripping the rail so hard, his knuckles had turned white. Megan knew he was waiting to see if she would reveal him.

She regarded the general. "Where is Ander?"

"We took him back to NEV-5."

"Is he well?" She hesitated to ask for details. Although she was cleared to discuss the project with Graham, she wasn't sure about here in the hospital. She doubted he would have referred to NEV-5, though, if they weren't in a secured area.

"He's fine," Graham assured her. "We're keeping him there until we decide what to do next."

What *would* they do? If they arrested him for kidnapping, applying human laws to his behavior, then as far as she was concerned, they had to grant him the rights and privileges of a human too.

"He saved my life," she said. "Several times."

"Yes. Dr. Sundaram told us." Graham considered her. "Ander wants us to continue with the Everest Project."

"I think we should."

"It will depend on the recommendations of the committee Major Kenrock has formed to look into the project."

Oh, well. From Megan's experience, once a committee got hold of something, you could turn into a fossil before they had results.

"Did you catch the people who kidnapped us?" she asked.

"Not yet," Graham said. "However, we have the van you drove into the quadra. Its computer is a gold mine of information."

Megan wanted to ask more, but she didn't have the energy. Already she felt drained. Then another thought came to her, one that made her feel as if the proverbial butterflies danced in her stomach. Perhaps some of her fatigue came from the baby.

"Well," Graham said. "Perhaps you and Dr. Sundaram would like a chance to talk." On that discreet note, he said his farewell and left the room.

Raj visibly relaxed. Then he released the rail and rubbed his hand.

Megan suddenly felt painfully self-conscious. "Hi."

"Hi." He looked uncertain.

"Would you like to come up here?" She lowered the rail, then scooted over on the bed.

He came over and sat on the edge of the mattress, making it sink with his weight. "Hey, swan."

"Hey." She tried to absorb the truth, that this man who so stirred her heart wasn't human.

"Are you tired?" Raj asked.

"A little." She took his hand in hers. "Thank you."

"You're welcome." He squinted at her. "What did I do?"

"I heard you talking. Every day." Softly she said, "You kept me here. In life. Like an anchor."

Moisture gleamed in his eyes. "They didn't think you were going to make it. I couldn't accept that."

"I'm glad." She took a breath. "I have something to tell you."

He tensed. "The praying mantis doesn't talk."

Praying mantis? It took her a few moments to figure out what he meant. Praying mantis. Insect. Bug. Of course. Her room was almost certainly being monitored. If she said anything now about his real identity, it would give him away. And "praying." He was asking her not to reveal him.

"I don't think this should wait," she said.

His hand tightened on hers. "Are you sure?"

She started to speak, stopped, then said, "It's difficult."

"We can talk later."

"No. Raj . . . it has to do with my condition."

"What? No! Do you have complications?"

"Yes. Sort of."

"Tell me."

Just *say* it, she thought. So she did. "I'm pregnant."

At first he stared at her. Then relief washed over his face. Given the nature of her announcement, it puzzled her, until she realized he had feared she would reveal the truth about him. Hard on the heels of his relief, he showed shock, then alarm, then confusion.

"You're going to have a baby?" he asked. "You're sure?"

"That's the same question I asked the doctor. She said 'Very sure.' It happened on the third day of our abduction."

Raj sat absorbing that. "We're in a hospital. That should make getting blood tests easy."

"To check for paternity?" Perhaps he didn't know whose DNA he carried.

He spoke with an unexpected tenderness. "I've no doubt it's mine. Your child will continue the Sundaram line."

She almost said, "That's not what I meant." Then she realized how strange it would sound to any observers. He had answered her anyway, when he said "continue the Sundaram line."

So why did he ask about blood tests? She hesitated, knowing that the law had changed several times in the past two decades. "I'm not sure about this, so I may be about to make a fool of myself—but did you just offer to marry me?"

She expected another oblique answer. Instead he said, simply, "Yes."

Oh, Lord. What made it surreal was that he was the first man she could see herself spending her life with, a companion as well as a lover. He understood her passion for her work. They had similar dispositions. She loved to touch and be touched by him. He wouldn't care that she was a homebody. She liked his eccentricities. They were well matched. Except, of course, for one little problem. What could she say? *Excuse me, but you're an android.*

"Ah, Raj." She didn't know what to do.

He picked up her hand and pressed it against her abdomen. "My parents and I missed so many years. As adults we've come to know each other, and I will always love them. But nothing can give us back what we lost." His voice softened. "I want those years with my son or daughter."

She brought his hand to her lips and kissed his knuckles. He had asked her a great deal more than a proposal. If they married, she could never reveal the truth about him. He was asking if she would guard his secret. Forever.

Megan remembered the quadra field, the van, the motel, the lonely, late nights in NEV-5. She thought of wanting him. Then she thought of what he represented to humanity and what she would be taking from the rest of the world if she kept his secret.

That decision isn't yours to make. It's his. And he had already chosen.

"Yes," she said. "I will be your wife."

Epilogue

Megan sat on the hill next to Raj, savoring the sunshine. The extensive grounds of the Pearl Estate spread around them: rolling hills, lush trees, flowers in vibrant colors. The mansion itself was visible only as a turret lifting above distant trees. She gave a silent thanks to the donor who, twenty years ago, had left this estate to Mind-Sim as a research institute. It provided a far more pleasant site for the Everest Project than NEV-5.

About half a kilometer down the slope, a lake shimmered, blue and silver in the sunshine. Ander was jogging on the path that circled it, a twenty-kilometer run. He loped along in an easy stride, the sun bright on his gold hair.

Megan felt a debt of gratitude to Major Kenrock's committee for giving them a second chance with Ander. Arizonix had been less fortunate with Grayton, the Phoenix android. Although they had tried to salvage as much as possible, in the end they'd had to wipe out his code and redesign most of his body.

"I haven't seen Ander stumble once," Raj said.

"He's doing well," Megan said. Ander's progress in

the past six months had gone better than expected. MindSim attributed it to the work she and Raj were doing with him, but Megan suspected another cause as well.

She thought back to her childhood, when she had sworn loyalty to her best friend. They had nicked their thumbs and mixed their blood while vowing eternal friendship. Blood sisters, blood brothers.

So Raj and Ander had joined, in a field of grain, when they thought their lives might soon be destroyed. Instead of blood, they had mingled knowledge, each downloading the code that defined his essence into the mind of the other.

Raj had given Ander the Phoenix Code, and it forever changed the golden-haired android. He became more contemplative, less disconnected from his emotions. In taking the Phoenix Code, he absorbed how Raj felt about his life. So he kept Raj's secret. It had become his own. Ander would never be human, but he was complete within himself.

The therapist described him as a marginal autistic, because he still sometimes lacked full emotions, he tended to hold himself aloof, and he avoided physical contact, never having come to understand why humans liked to touch. But Megan doubted the diagnosis. It assumed a human standard applied to Ander. And it didn't. He defined himself.

Unlike Ander, Raj didn't simply incorporate his brother's code. He first did an extensive rewrite, to blend it with his own personality and desires. Because of that, it changed him less than the Phoenix Code changed Ander. But Megan still saw differences. Raj's already intense emotions deepened even more. It surprised her at first, given Ander's lack of affect. Then she realized that in coming to understand Ander, Raj better understood himself. He and Ander had different views of what it meant to exist. Raj wanted to be human and took every measure to preserve his identity. Ander didn't care.

Ander never contemplated his emotions. He just wanted to exist on his terms. It meant no spy work, no pretending he was human, no pledges. The ethics board convened by MindSim and the DOD agreed he had a right to make that choice, as a sentient being. But they could take no chances with him or his safety. In the end, they found a compromise Ander could accept; he could live as he wished—but he could never leave the grounds of the Pearl Estate.

Megan leaned back on her hands, looking at her husband. Raj's curls blew back from his face and laugh lines showed around his eyes. Yes, she loved him. At times she even forgot the truth. The baby grew inside of her, the genetic son of the Raj Sundaram who had died in the Phoenix explosion. But in all the ways that mattered, her child was the son of this man who had walked out of the fires after that explosion.

The DNA tests had also given them a gift; their son hadn't inherited the form of Alzheimer's carried by his father and grandfather. He would never suffer the pain that had devastated Raj's life.

Ander had left the path and was walking up the hill, cooling down from his workout. When he reached them, he flopped onto the grass and stared out at the lake.

"Did you enjoy your run?" Raj asked.

"Yes," Ander said.

They sat together, watching the sun glisten on the water. After a while Ander said, "I made a map of the estate today. I coded it according to type of plant."

"Will you download it to the computer?" Megan asked.

"I don't know." After thinking, he said, "For you, I will." He rolled onto his stomach and laid his head on the grass, closing his eyes. "I want to map all the world someday. All the plants. I might be able to do it from here using satellite data."

"A lot of scientists would be in your debt," Raj said.

"Why do you like maps so much?" Megan asked.

He gave her a deadpan look. "They're sex."

"They are?"

He closed his eyes again, for all appearances a healthy young man dozing in the sun after a good workout. "A voluptuous use of knowledge bases."

Megan suspected he was teasing her. She smiled, doubting she would ever fully understand his sense of humor.

As the breezes played with her hair, she felt the life kick within her. She laid her hand on her stomach. *You will be born into a world altered beyond recognition. It isn't obvious yet, but the changes are coming. We share it now with another sentient species, one that we made faster, smarter, and more durable than ourselves.*

Raj lay on his side, apparently drowsing, like Ander. She knew neither was sleeping. Their minds kept going, always calculating, never resting. Would humanity someday find a way to put that speed and memory into the minds of human beings, becoming more like androids while the androids became more human?

She shivered despite the warm air. Throughout history, every advance had left in its wake an obsolete technology. Tools replaced claws. Electricity replaced steam power. Computers replaced brute mental force. If they didn't find ways to improve their own minds, the human race itself would become obsolete.

But if they evolved with their creations? It promised a symbiosis unlike anything they had yet seen. *Perhaps our two species will find in each other a completion neither has alone.*

She hoped so.

About the Author

Catherine Asaro grew up near Berkeley, California. She earned her Ph.D. in Chemical Physics and MA in Physics, both from Harvard, and a BS with Highest Honors in Chemistry from UCLA. Among the places she has done research are the University of Toronto, the Max Plank Institut für Astrophysik in Germany, and the Harvard–Smithsonian Center for Astrophysics. She currently runs Molecudyne Research and now lives in Maryland with her husband and daughter. A former ballet dancer, she founded the Mainly Jazz dance program at Harvard and now teaches at the Caryl Maxwell Classical Ballet, home to the Ellicott City Ballet Guild.

She has written numerous books, including the most recent, *The Veiled Web* and *The Quantum Rose*. Her work has been nominated for both the Hugo and Nebula, and has won numerous awards, including The Analog Readers Poll (the AnLab), the Sapphire, the UTC Award, and the HOMer. She can be reached by email at asaro@sff.et and on the web at http://www.sff.net/people/asaro/. If you would like to receive email updates on Catherine's releases, please email the above address.